THRYMSAS AND SCEATTAS

IN THE ASHMOLEAN MUSEUM OXFORD

THRYMSAS AND SCEATTAS

IN THE ASHMOLEAN MUSEUM OXFORD

VOLUME 3

BY

D. M. METCALF

Keeper of the Heberden Coin Room

ROYAL NUMISMATIC SOCIETY AND
ASHMOLEAN MUSEUM OXFORD
LONDON
1994

Royal Numismatic Society
Special Publication No.27c
ISBN   1   85444   067   5

British Library Cataloguing in Publication Data

Metcalf, D. M.
  Thrymsas and Sceattas
  in the Ashmolean Museum
I. Title
737.4

Typeset by Lasercomp at
Oxford University Computing Service
Printed in Great Britain
by the Cambridge University Press

CONTENTS

PART IV

CHEMICAL ANALYSES
by Dr. J. P. Northover

PART IV

SECONDARY SCEATTAS

THE GEOGRAPHICAL pattern of minting in England in the secondary phase repeats that already seen in the primary phase, with a shift of emphasis away from the south-east, and towards the periphery. It coincides with a similar shift in the circulation of sceattas.[1] The number of mints is approximately doubled, but most of the new mints are of very minor importance in terms of their contribution to the total output of coinage.

The primary phase had involved a dozen series of sceattas, from almost as many mint-places. The three dominant types, Series A, B, and C, belong to east Kent and Essex (London?), with a northerly zone of imitation in East Anglia or Middle Anglia. There are nine smaller series, which because of their scarcity cannot yet all be attributed with certainty, but which are from York (Aldfrith); probably from inland ports approached through the Wash (Series F, BZ, Z); and perhaps from Mercia (*Æthiliræd*) and Wessex (W) as well. The regions on the periphery, furthest away from east Kent, namely Northumbria and Wessex, mint relatively very small amounts of coinage. There are two more small series to be mentioned. The SAROALDO type remains problematic, but it is from somewhere towards the east of the country, and probably north of the Thames. The VERNVS sceattas will be from somewhere in the south-east, if they are not continental.

The major changes in the secondary phase are that York greatly expands its minting activity, that Wessex now produces its own large series of sceattas, at Hamwic, from as many as 400 to 500 reverse dies, and that the East Anglian kingdom produces an even larger series (R), apparently at several mints. It is puzzling, in view of the many varieties of Series R, that East Anglia seems not to have had a major series of its

---

[1] The developing pattern of circulation was demonstrated in a series of three maps, in D. M. Metcalf, 'Monetary circulation in southern England in the first half of the eighth century', in *Sceattas in* *England and on the Continent*, edited by D. Hill and D. M. Metcalf, Oxford, 1984, pp.27-69, at pp.31, 33, and 35.

own in the primary phase.

East Kent and London retain their importance. A new development, which remains difficult for us to understand in administrative terms, is the appearance of half-a-dozen little eclectic groups of coins, borrowing a miscellany of types, mostly characteristic of the Kentish and London series, K and L, and pairing them with distinctive reverses. The groups seem each to be from a separate workshop, of which the reverse is the 'badge'. Scarce as they are, they are too plentiful and are struck with too much regularity of design and from too many dies to be dismissed as sporadic imitations. Their distribution patterns tend to follow the rather wide-ranging distribution of Series K and L respectively, and the most that one can hope to say about each of them is whether it belongs north or south of the line of the River Thames. One's over-all impression is that the eclectic groups are each from a minor mint somewhere within the general orbit of Series K and L.

York is an influential mint-place during much of the secondary phase, at first with close Frisian contacts (Series J), and later through a controlled royal coinage circulating throughout Northumbria and as far afield as Whithorn in south-western Scotland (Series Y). A corpus of specimens of Series Y allows us to estimate that, over a period of five decades, about a thousand upper dies were used, to strike a coinage which accounts for about 8 per cent of the stray finds of sceattas in England in the 1980s.

From the east midlands there is gratifyingly clear evidence, in the form of a distribution-pattern focussing on west Norfolk for Series Q. Early varieties in this typologically varied series echo Series Z and may be from the same mint-place. The so-called 'Wodan' head seen on Series Z figures again in another secondary series from the hinterland of the Wash, namely *BMC* Type 30, with Type 51 and various saltire-standard types. Its antecedents may perhaps lie in Series BZ.

There is very good distributional evidence to associate Series S, the 'female centaur' type, with Essex – perhaps eastern Essex rather than London.

All the above series can be attributed to their regions of origin by distributional evidence which varies in quality from good to very good.

Several distinctive types remain unlocated, because clear distribution-patterns have not yet emerged. Series O, Type 40 seems to begin early, as it was imitated by the earliest phase of Series Q – which also copied Series N. Both O/40 and N were thus available presumably in Middle Anglia. Their distribution, however, is wide and, in the case of N, confused by the prevalence of copies. Both these features – the widespread distribution and the prevalence of copying – help to suggest that N was from a well-known commercial centre engaged in long-distance trade. London is the obvious candidate. Series O/40 may share the same attribution as N.

The rest of Series O, namely the three related *BMC* Types 38, 21, and 57, has no connection with Type 40. It shows a different distribution-pattern, and is from a different mint-place, although equally early in its date of origin. It appears to be from east Kent, and is something of an embarrassment, in so far as that region is already provided for, by Series V and K.

Series T, similarly, appears to be an east midlands type which is surplus to requirements, since Q and Type 30 have already been located there. It may be a deliberate echo of the *Æthiliræd* runic type.

Series M is a type in search of a region. There are other, smaller issues, such as Series H, Type 48 (which is from a different mint from the rest of Series H; as with Series O, Type 40, the Rigold label is in error and should be disregarded).

Altogether there are twelve or thirteen substantive series, each recognizable by a distinctive design or a small number of conceptually related designs, and each from its own mint-place. Some of the series (R, U) were struck at more than one mint. The eclectic groups related to Series K and L increase the total of mints, and there are one or two similar little groups from further afield. Since about 1980, as new finds have accumulated, types previously known only as singletons, and depreciated as small-scale, unofficial products, have turned out to be part of small groups of related coins, large enough nevertheless to imply public knowledge and acceptance of identifiable designs. The 'animal mask' series is an example. In all, we are looking at twenty to twenty-five series of coins, from as many or almost as many mints or workshops. Not all of them will necessarily have worked continuously or concurrently.

A rough outline, which does not do full justice to the complexities of the evidence and the caveats expressed in the text, but which may help the reader to find his or her way through the alphabetically-arranged sections, is as follows. The approximate percentage of English secondary sceattas minted in each region is based on proportions of stray finds.

		%
East Kent	V, K; U/23d	14
Also east Kent?	O; one or more eclectic groups	1
London and home counties	L; various eclectic groups	13
Also London?	N; O/40	8
Upper Thames?	U/23b	0·4
Wessex	H (c.500 dies)	9
Essex	S	9
East Anglia	R; Beonna	15
East midlands	Q; Types 30/51; T	5
Northumbria	J; Y (Y = c.1,000 dies)	23
Unlocated	M; H/48	1·4

The relative chronology of the twenty or more mints is difficult to establish in detail. Earlier students relied heavily on typological similarities, using them to construct hypotheses of the borrowing or copying of designs between one series and another.[2] This approach led them into the realms of unsupported conjecture. Unless one can be quite sure that copying was from Type A to Type B, rather than vice versa, there is a risk of drawing diametrically the wrong conclusion. There are, indeed, numerous repetitions of motifs – the standing figure holding two crosses, the pecking bird, the monster biting its tail – but they are drawn from a repertoire of widely familiar designs, found also on artefacts other than coins. Salin has shown us how popular and widespread that repertoire was throughout the Merovingian and Germanic world in the early middle ages. More recently, Morehart has reminded numismatists of the sources of inspiration in classical art of many of the motifs found on sceattas.[3] Proof that one coin-type is copied from another coin-type needs to be more rigorous, and to rely on the art-historian's method of noticing the copying of unconsidered details, which were of no thematic significance to the die-cutter.

The alloy of the secondary sceattas has also been used as an argument for relative chronology. On the hypothesis of progressive debasement, it has been assumed that sceattas of widely different intrinsic value could

---

[2]   Undue reliance on typology is seen in C. H. V. Sutherland, 'Anglo-Saxon sceattas in England: their origin, chronology, and distribution', *NC* [6] 2 (1942), 42-70, and in P. V. Hill, 'Saxon sceattas and their problems', *BNJ* 26 (1949-51), 129-54, and in two further articles in *BNJ*.

[3]   M. J. Morehart, 'Anglo-Saxon art and the "archer" sceat', in *Sceattas in England and on the Continent*, pp.181-92.

not have circulated for long at par, and that there would have been pressures to conform: something like Gresham's Law would have operated. Detailed evidence, based on a large number of exact analyses by EPMA conducted by Northover, reveals some test cases which cast serious doubt on that hypothesis. Obviously it is broadly true that the secondary sceattas, which were originally (but only briefly) better than 90 per cent silver, declined progressively, with halts at, for example, 70-80 per cent, *c.*50 per cent, and 20-30 per cent, until in the end some of them contained only *c.*15 per cent silver or even less. Within the official issues of some series, such as R and L, we may be reasonably confident that the long-term trend is downwards, and that baser means later. Variation of as much as 15 or 20 per cent, however, was tolerated within other issues, the coins of which were not differentiated by any changes of design, and which must have been indistinguishable to their users. Between the standard variety of a type and copies of it, or between one series and another, it would be extremely rash to assume that baser means correspondingly later, or that differences in silver contents are in any sort of linear relationship with chronology. In some series, such as Y and perhaps H, the moneyers seem to have made efforts from time to time to revert to an intended alloy standard from which they repeatedly fell away. Copies were sometimes of much poorer metal than their prototypes, although probably close to them in date. Increasingly, the main regional coinages diverged from each other in their alloys and tended to become self-contained currencies. In East Anglia debasement proceeded much further than in Northumbria or Wessex. The London coinage became severely debased, whereas that of east Kent did not. It is difficult, however, to know whether that proves that sceattas of very different alloy were being struck concurrently in London and east Kent, or whether minting in east Kent was in abeyance in the later stages of Series L. We are not required to space each series out evenly through the whole secondary phase, lasting for half a century. Far from it: we should assume that there were different rhythms of production, varying from one series to another according to the political or commercial circumstances of minting, and that there were times when some mints stood idle while others worked.

In the face of such fickle evidence, much the safest way to proceed is to rely in the first instance on the evidence of hoards and grave-finds in which different series of sceattas occur side by side. Into a chronological framework created from a comparative study of the hoards, one may then venture to add details derived from typology or metal contents. By using the hoards as the framework, one may hope to escape from untested assumptions about copying or about debasement, which could lead to radically false conclusions. Even hoard analysis is not completely free from assumptions. The coins in a hoard will not necessarily all be recent issues at the date of concealment. One type may be older than another. The sharpness of striking of sceattas is usually not such as to allow us to notice the effects of five years' wear, – in coins which did not change hands as frequently as modern coins. A comparative study of a sufficient number of hoards, concealed at intervals of five or ten years, would in principle discount most of the pitfalls one can think of. Relative dating of the various series and types of sceattas, established from the evidence of mixed hoards, will certainly override conclusions which rest only on typology or debasement. That is the theory. In practice, there are not enough hoards to create more than a few fixed points. A judicious blend of different kinds of evidence is, until more hoards come to light, the best option.

In east Kent and London, there is a complete break in typology between the primary and secondary phases. The classicizing Series A, B, and C come to an end, and are replaced by entirely different, pictorial types – Series V and K, and probably O, in east Kent, quickly followed by U, and the beginnings of L. The best specimens of Series V, K, and O are of very good silver, but the alloy standard declines almost immediately. It is as if a brave new start was made, perhaps after an interval.

Elsewhere, by way of contrast, there are threads of continuity between the primary and secondary phases. In East Anglia, Series R (the earliest variety of which is present in the Aston Rowant hoard) is a close copy of Series C. (It is debateable, even, whether the borrowing did not occur a few years earlier, Series C being an East Anglian copy of the Kentish Series A.) At York, Series J begins with a direct copy, although in a quite different style, of Series B. In the east midlands there seems to be some typological continuity between the late primary series Z and BZ, and the secondary series Q and Types 30/51.

I

A sequence of eight hoards gives patchy coverage of the secondary phase. The opening stages are made clear by two Northumbrian hoards (Garton-on-the-Wolds and York, Fishergate), supplemented by two continental hoards which are, perhaps, slightly later in date (Hallum and Cimiez). Three widely scattered hoards from the mid to late secondary phase illustrate the localized character of monetary circulation at that stage (Southampton, London, and Cambridge). Finally, the Middle Harling hoard, concealed after the very last sceattas of Series R had been replaced by Beonna's reformed coinage, gives a retrospective glimpse of the currency of East Anglia.

1. A grave-find from controlled excavations at Garton-on-the-Wolds, in the former East Riding of Yorkshire, consists of just 8 sceattas.[4] As a sample it is much too small to provide negative information. It is nevertheless of lively interest for the types that it brings together. Alongside four of the local Northumbrian coins of Series J, namely two of Type 85 (i.e. the direct copy of B) and two of its parallel issue, Type 37, there are two specimens of the continental Series G, one of Series K, Type 32a, and one problematic coin 'muling' Type R1 (*epa* reading inwards) with a cross-and-annulets reverse which appears to be derived from an experimental type standing at the head of Series O/40. All six coins of Series J and G are good, early specimens within their types. If Series J begins early – which one tends to assume because of its continuity of design with Series B – the Garton find will establish an unexpectedly early date for Type 32a, and will make for a crowded chronology in east Kent, where it seems that room has to be found for Series V before Series K, and for Type 33 at a very early date within Series K. Moreover, if a correct view has been taken of the antecedents of the 'mule', it implies an equally early origin for Series O/40.

It is worth pondering that there is a large group of north-of-the-Thames imitations of Type 32a. The Garton coin, however, is of good Kentish style.

2. The message of the Garton find is reinforced by the even smaller York (Fishergate) hoard of 4 sceattas, which were corroded together when they were excavated. Two are again of the local series J, of Types 85 and 37, and one is (probably) a copy of Type 85, with a cross added in front of the mouth, inspired no doubt by Series G. The fourth coin is of the 'triquetras' eclectic group, *BMC* Type 52, which is closely related to Series K.[5] That, again, provides unexpected information, namely that one at least of the eclectic groups had its origins at an early stage in the secondary phase, in relation to Series J.

[4] The find is described and all the coins are illustrated in S. E. Rigold, 'The two primary series of sceattas', *BNJ* 30 (1960-1), 6-53, and pl.4.

[5] I am indebted to Miss E. J. E. Pirie who kindly sent me photocopies of her photographs of the coins, as found and after separation.

3. The Hallum hoard, from Friesland, is equally important for the English early secondary phase. The great majority of the coins in the hoard are continental, but mixed with them were two specimens of Series J, Type 85, in very acceptable style, 3 specimens of Series G, of which one is a good, early, official coin and the other two are copies, and – especially valuable – one specimen which stands early in Series Q.[6] The examples of Series J and Q were quite possibly carried down the east coast of England by Frisian traders. As Series G is known in Northumbria at an early date from the Garton find, it may well have travelled by the same route. The varieties which seem to stand at the head of Series Q imitate Series N and Series O, Type 40. Their origins will therefore also necessarily antedate the concealment of the Hallum hoard. The 'Wodan/monster' and porcupine sceattas which make up the bulk of the hoard and on which we ought, in principle, to rely for its t.p.q. are dated by the stratigraphy of the Ribe excavations and by dendrochronology. Series X begins in c.720. There are, further, two problem coins from Hallum. One is a (?) continental imitation of the 'two standing figures' design, which may have been copied from Series N, or perhaps from Type 30. Alternatively, since there is no need to allow any great interval of time for copying to occur, it may have been copied from Series Q. In that case one would have to add that there is a touch of X in the boldy pelletted border. The other problem coin is a rare Є LVNDONIA 12/5 'mule', which is surely derivative from Series L rather than *vice versa*. Placing the origins of Type 12 earlier than Hallum would drive a coach and horses through the idea of uniformity of alloy at any particular date. There is reason to think, however, that the 12/5 'mule' is intrusive, and was not in fact part of the hoard.

Garton, York (Fishergate), and Hallum usefully support each other in establishing the priority of Series J, G, and K (32a), with Q not far behind, and N and O/40 equally early in the secondary phase. V presumably antedates rather than interrupts K. Thus there seems to be a flurry of new activity, associated with a miniature renaissance of artistic innovation and ingenuity, at various mint-places, early in the secondary phase.

4. The Cimiez hoard, from the south of France, contained a wide range of sceatta types, which could not possibly all have been in circulation concurrently in England. It is a disappointing source of information for our present purposes, for two reasons. First, it is not certain that all the

---

[6] J. Dirks, *Les Anglo-Saxons et leurs petits deniers dits sceattas*, Brussels, 1870, pp.56f. and pl.C and D. I am indebted to Dr. David Hill for enlarged photos of the Hallum coins.

coins in the Morel-Fatio collection came from the Cimiez hoard, even if the great majority did. Just where it is crucial for chronology, therefore, the evidence is open to doubt. Secondly, many of the secondary sceattas in the hoard are imitative. Of course, they are necessarily later in date than their English prototypes, and their testimony that the origin of the prototypes antedates the hoard's t.p.q. is thus secure, – or would be if the provenances were certain. But the flavour of the evidence is inferior. For what it is worth, the secondary types recorded are Series J, Types 85 and 37, Type BIIIc, N, Type 23e, Series X, and an (insular?) imitation of X.[7] The last three are problematic.

There are three more hoards, from the mid to late secondary phase, which do not overlap usefully with the earlier finds or with each other. That merely reflects the degree to which currencies were becoming increasingly fragmented and regional in character, and it does not amount to negative evidence in drawing the outlines of relative chronology as between series.

5. A fire-damaged hoard from the Kingsland district of modern Southampton, immediately beyond the town ditch westwards of Hamwic, consists of 23 sceattas surviving out of a larger number. Two bear the intaglio impression of another coin, now crumbled to dust; and some fell to pieces after recovery. All the surviving coins are of Series H, the local issue, and are of two successive types, Type 39 (3 specimens) and 49 (20 specimens). The latter are of half-a-dozen varieties.[8] The date of loss is difficult to guess. Unless the varieties of Type 49 were all issued concurrently from the start (which is unlikely), they will imply a t.p.q. quite late in the duration of the type, and therefore probably towards the middle of the eighth century. The Kingsland hoard, as a one-series hoard, can have nothing to contribute to the relative chronology of the secondary phase.

6. Tradition records that a number of sceattas were found as a corroded lump in the River Thames in about 1860, presumably at London. Sixteen coins are now in the British Museum, and four more which are from the Evans bequest ex A. W. Franks, ex Thames are suspected of being from the same source; they are catalogued below. The total of 20 is divided between 3 specimens falling with Series K (of Types 32a, 1, and 33, 2), 15 specimens of Series L (Types 12, 3; 13, 1; 14, 1; 15,

[7] P. le Gentilhomme, 'La circulation des sceattas dans la Gaule mérovingienne', *RN* [5] 2 (1938), 23-49. Again, I am indebted to Dr. Hill for enlarged photographs.

[8] P. Andrews (editor), *The Coins and Pottery from Hamwic* (Southampton Finds, vol.1), Southampton, 1988, pp.29-31, where most of the coins are illustrated.

305

3; 16, 3; 18, 3; 19, 1) and odd specimens of Types 23a and 23e.[9] A few of the better coins in the hoard have silver contents of around half, but most have only a third or a quarter. Six or seven of the total are in a style that has been labelled 'Hwiccian', and for which an origin in Hwiccia was proposed in 1976; it is now clear that they must belong to London. The three coins of Series K, ostensibly Kentish, are not what they seem. A specimen of Type 33 (*BMC* 160, M. and W.30) is a copy in good 'Hwiccian' style, and doubtless belongs with the other Hwiccian coins as a London product. Its date poses a crux, discussed below. A second specimen of Type 33 (*BMC* 159, M. and W. 41) is of inferior style, and is a copy of the Kentish 'C-D' style. Its place of origin is necessarily uncertain. The third specimen, of Type 32a (*BMC* 152, M. and W. 34), belongs with a large group of north-of-Thames copies of Type 32a: there is no reason to think that it was minted in Kent. As regards the singletons of Types 23a and 23e, their region of origin is uncertain.

All in all, the Thames hoard is composed solidly of London coins, and reflects the currency of the city at a fairly late stage of the secondary phase, when the alloy standard had been reduced to about a quarter silver, but while a few older, better coins were still in use.

7. The Cambridge hoard was published by Sir John Evans in 1894.[10] It consists of 9 coins of Series Q and R. A few similar coins which came to attention in the 1890s may possibly be strays from the hoard. The silver contents are comparable with those found in the Thames hoard: at best 50 per cent, and more usually *c.*30 per cent or less. Coins of Series Q are generally scarcer than the correspondingly debased coins of Series R. Although the numbers in the hoard are too small to constitute a good sample, Q seems to be over-represented. Of the three specimens, one is in the modelled style (QIV), and two are of the style for which a west-Norfolk or Fen margins origin is indicated (QIIIB and QIIIc). The coins of Series R are of Types R8 (*ep*, 3 specimens), R9 (*spi*, 1 specimen) and R10 (*wigræd*, 2 specimens). The Cambridge coin of Type R10 catalogued below contains only 13 per cent silver, and sets a late date for the hoard – although not quite at the end of Series R, which sinks even further into debasement. The question arises whether *ep* and *spi*, like *wigræd*, are moneyers' signatures, and whether they are from different mint-places within East Anglia. The hoard is too small to contribute to a solution of that problem, and the absence from it of the (late) coins of Tilbeorht may

---

[9] S. E. Rigold and D. M. Metcalf, 'A revised check-list of English finds of sceattas', in *Sceattas in England and on the Continent*, pp.245-68, at p.254.

[10] J. Evans, 'On a small hoard of Saxon sceattas found near Cambridge', *NC* [3] 14 (1894), 18-28, where all the coins are well illustrated. See also Rigold and Metcalf, loc.cit., at pp.248f.

be merely a matter of chance.

8. Finally, there is a hoard from Middle Harling, near Thetford, from the very end of the sceatta series. It is composed mainly of coins of King Beonna, with a few surviving strays of earlier issues. The hoard was scattered by ploughing, and there are some separate finds of sceattas from the same site. The best reconstruction that can be made assigns 49, or perhaps 51, coins of Beonna to the hoard, plus 6 sceattas, all from late or very late in Series R (Types R8, *epa*, R10, Wigræd, 2, and R11, Tilbeorht, 3).[11]   Fixing the date at which the sceatta series came to an end is difficult. The last of Series R was swept away by Beonna's reform, which restored a respectable alloy standard. Beonna came to power after the death of Ælfwald in 749, but we cannot be certain, of course, of the date at which he turned his attention to the reform of the very debased currency which he inherited. It may not have been for several years after his accession. Nor do we know how long Beonna remained in power. More importantly for the present purpose, we do not know whether there was an interval before his coinage reform when minting was in abeyance. Series R came to an end before, say, *c*.760, but it may have ended in *c*.750 or *c*.745. The presence of strays in the Middle Harling hoard, it has been suggested, tends to narrow the gap, supposing that there were one. All that they show, however, is that some of Series R remained in circulation even after the reform. Their *issue* may have ceased some years before they were replaced. The hoard shows us that the demonetizing of the debased coins was not completely effective. Perhaps that says something about the acceptability of coins of varying intrinsic value – even to an individual who was rich enough to own more than 50 denarii.

The secondary phase began after the concealment of the Aston Rowant hoard, in *c*.705-10, and probably very soon afterwards – although, again, there is the intractable problem of recognizing a blank space in the archaeological evidence. It is less uncertain at the beginning than at the end of the phase, because Aston Rowant already contains Type R1, which marks a new beginning in East Anglia. There could, admittedly, have been a gap between C and R1 (as between R12 and Beonna's coins) – or even a gap between R1 and the later varieties of R. It is, however, implausible.

Type R1 offers tidier and better evidence of continuity than can be derived from the various successors of Series B. Rigold's BIIIB, *alias* J, at

[11] M. M. Archibald, 'The coinage of Beonna in the light of the Middle Harling hoard', *BNJ* 55 (1985), 10-54, with full illustration.

York, will not necessarily have followed hard upon the heels of its geographically distant prototype; BIIIA, present in Aston Rowant, seems to lie on the earlier side of any divide that there may have been between the primary and secondary phases; BIIIc is derivative from BIIIB and Type 37, both of which it must post-date: its resemblance to BIIIA is coincidental. No clear dates emerge.

The secondary phase had come to an end, specifically in East Anglia, by *c*.755-60. The duration of the secondary sceattas *in circulation* thus seems to have been 50 or so years. Minting was not necessarily continuous, and the major regions of England – the south-east, Wessex, East Anglia, the east midlands, Northumbria – need not have pursued identical courses. The later hoards, which reflect an increased compartmentalizing of the currency, tell us disappointingly little about the relative chronology, even, of most of the secondary series.

II

The evidence now seems reasonably secure that the secondary sceattas were minted within the period *c*.710/15-*c*.755/60. It would be rash to claim, however, that the hoards enable us to say when most types or varieties were struck, to within better than about ten years. Attempts have been made to anchor the relative chronology to an absolute chronology, by placing a political interpretation on certain types. It is an open question whether the coinage was much influenced by the political circumstances in which it was produced. In general, the commerce which sustained the activity of the mints had its own rhythms. The idea that rulers would intervene in the choice of coin types for propaganda purposes is largely inappropriate to the early middle ages.

In one case, nevertheless, it is demonstrable that there was a deliberate emphasis on designs depicting wolves. In Series K, both Type 33 and Type 32a are closly copied from unexpected sources, namely continental Celtic coins, which must have been chosen because of their wolf-like designs. Series V, from the same mint, depicts the she-wolf and twins. The canine creature on Series K, Type 42, however, wears a collar. If it is a wolf, it can only be because the king kept a menagerie.

Even where there is no conscious intention on the part of the issuing authorities, we may succeed in detecting some influence of political history in the minting arrangements for the sceattas. We start from the understanding that several of the main series coincide in their distribution-patterns with the extent of particular kingdoms. Series Y belongs to Northumbria, H to Wessex. Series S belongs to the kingdom of the East Saxons. The virtual absence of Series R at the major sites of Tilbury (Essex) and near Royston (Middle Anglia) is important evidence that political boundaries could be frontiers to the circulation of coinage.

There is good evidence, too, that the archbishop of Canterbury enjoyed minting rights. A coin of Series K, Type 33, showing a hand raised in benediction, has been attributed to Archbishop Berhtwald. *A fortiori*, kings will have exercised similar rights.

The political context of the secondary sceattas lies in the later years of two senior figures, namely King Wihtred of Kent (690-725) and Ine of Wessex (688-726 x 728); in the long reign in East Anglia of Ælfwald (713-49), the last of the Wuffingas; and in the rule of Eadberht (738-57) in Northumbria.

Of these powerful kings, only Eadberht placed his name on his sceattas. Elsewhere, however, (except in Wessex and Essex) we see a diademed bust on the obverse of the coins, which set the image of the king before his mostly illiterate subjects more effectively than a legend would have done.

None was mightier than Æthelbald. By 731 he had achieved overlordship of the English everywhere south of the Humber, including both Wessex and East Anglia, as Bede tells us at the conclusion of his *History*. He itemizes the provinces of Kent, Essex, East Anglia, Wessex, Mercia, the territory west of Severn, Hwiccia, Lindsey, the Isle of Wight, and Sussex, and then states, 'All these provinces, and the other southern provinces as far as the boundary formed by the River Humber, with their kings are subject to Æthelbald, king of the Mercians.' That was in 731. Can we see any signs of it in the secondary sceattas? Two attempts have been made to suggest that we can.

The first, if it is justifiable, will provide us with an invaluable fixed date in the middle of the secondary phase. It concerns the DE LVNDONIA coinage of Series L, Type 12. The second concerns the 'pecking bird' of Series U, Type 23b and d. The dating of each of these types, alas, has a history of revision. Each (and particularly the second) has wide ramifications, cutting across a number of secondary series. To put the problems into context calls for an awareness of many separate strands of argument. Most of the arguments, unfortunately, involve a degree of conjecture. Weighing them all against each other is so complex a task that the final judgement may appear to be subjective. Reaching a judgement on only half the relevant considerations, would, nevertheless, be a poor way to proceed.

Rigold found the DE LVNDONIA type so explicit, and so unusual in having a clear, meaningful legend, that he proposed to interpret it as advertizing Æthelbald's taking absolute lordship over London as Mercia's outlet to the world, shortly before 732.[12] In that year, Æthelbald is seen confirming particular liberties in the port of London, without reference to any other ruler. The political history of London in the seventh and early eighth centuries is only sketchily documented, but seems to have been complicated. The context into which Æthelbald's action fits cannot be said to be well understood. No-one will wish to dispute the London attribution of Type 12, but can it be dated to 732? Rigold saw the years c.725-30 as the 'watershed' between the primary and secondary phases, and on the basis of that chronology, and of the fineness of the DE LVNDONIA sceattas (around 50 per cent silver), Metcalf pointed out that, if debasement was any guide to chronology, Type 12 could not belong so near the beginning of the secondary phase. An assumption of uniformity of alloy between series underlay that criticism – an assumption on which, as we have seen, Northover's EPMA analyses have since cast doubt. One could have approached the point in another way by asking whether there were any types or series of better alloy which could be attributed to London and which would presumably antedate Series L, Type 12. The answer seems to be that there are no serious candidates other than Series O/40 and N, the attribution of which to London remains conjectural. Unless minting at London was in abeyance in the early secondary phase, therefore, Type 12 might indeed be quite early, its alloy notwithstanding. To say that much is to reveal that one is assessing rival interpretations against each other, rather than drawing on any stock of hard facts. The whole question, however, was rendered academic by Blackburn's new chronology,[13] which followed from the re-dating of the Cimiez hoard. The 'watershed' was thereby moved back to c.710-15, cancelling any problem in dating Type 12 to c.732.

There would be ample room at London, on the new chronological scheme, for Series U, Type 23 to precede Type 12 there. There are two distinct styles, with different distribution patterns, and also a good number of copies. One of the substantive styles was attributed, in 1972, to the upper Thames region (which was rash), while the other was seen as either from London or Kentish. The type as a whole was interpreted as a coinage for King Æthelbald of Mercia. A date close to 732 seemed

[12] Rigold, loc.cit. (note 4 above), at p.24.
[13] M. Blackburn, 'A chronology for the sceattas', in *Sceattas in England and on the Continent*, pp.165-74.

possible.[14] Minting the same type in two regions in itself strongly suggests a political interest in and control over the production of sceattas, and it is not an elaborate hypothesis: it seems to depend only on proving that the two styles definitely were struck in two well-separated mint-places, – under the same authority, and within the same span of years. Nor is it an outlandish hypothesis: the historical implication of assigning *epa* and *spi* to different mint-places, in Series R, are similar.

Typology adds its own persuasion. The full-length figure holding two long crosses and standing in a boat-shaped curve seems, on some specimens, to be wearing a *cynehelm*, or royal helmet. Is this not Æthelbald himself? The standing figure is repeated on numerous later types in Series K and L. The pecking bird of the reverse is also an influential, much-copied design.

We need to be very careful, however. The two groups of Series K, Type 32a, which are clearly evidenced by their different distribution-patterns, do not support a similar conclusion: the northerly group, to judge by its varied and undisciplined style, was produced by a die-cutter or die-cutters who were not under much constraint of authority. We should not assume, improbably, that the Kentish king gave his consent to copies produced north of the Thames, much less that they were minted under his authority. Type 32a cannot, in a word, be described as comprising two substantive varieties (plus some irregular coins), in the way that Type 23b/d can. Thus, between the idea and the evidence that the latter is a royal coinage of Æthelbald, there are more steps and more considerations than appear at first glance.

Observe, now, how Blackburn's new chronology demolishes a fine, brash hypothesis, and creates twice as many uncertainties as there were before. Series U, with its consistently high silver contents of 70-80 per cent, belongs relatively early in the secondary phase – surely earlier than anything in Series L, in spite of what has been said about the pitfalls of arguing from the alloy of the sceattas. If that phase began in *c.*710-15, Type 23d will have been introduced well before Æthelbald took control of London. Morehart was quick to notice that if Blackburn's earlier dating for Series U was accepted, the figure holding two crosses was unlikely to be an image of King Æthelbald of Mercia.[15] The point was well taken. Series U seems to represent an important initiative, and Æthelbald's standing is unlikely to have been sufficient for it while Wihtred and Ine held power. Nevertheless, Æthelbald became king in

[14] D. M. Metcalf, 'The "bird and branch" sceattas in the light of a find from Abingdon', *Oxoniensia* 37 (1972), 51-65.

[15] M. J. Morehart, 'Female centaur or sphinx? On naming sceat types: the case of *BMC* Type 47', *BNJ* 55 (1985), 1-9.

716, and it certainly is not demonstrable that the issue of Series U began earlier than 716, even if its origin lay close to that date. What one can reasonably say is that Æthelbald is very unlikely to have minted *at London,* as one of two mints, in 716-*c.*726.

Observe, next, that the accumulation of new single finds since 1972 (when the attribution to Æthelbald was proposed) has made a London attribution more or less untenable. From London and district, there are just two finds of Type 23b/d, both imitative and both from Barking Abbey,[16] among what is now a substantial assemblage of fifty sceattas. The provenances for Type 23d are still few in number but, such as they are, they are concentrated quite heavily in east Kent. Moreover, there are close stylistic similarities between Type 23d and the undoubtedly Kentish Series K, Type 42. If the standing figure is a powerful king, the detailed evidence of 'when' and 'where' converges to point us towards King Wihtred, Rigold's *gloriosus rex Cantiae,* who died in 725.

But the other substantive variety in Series U, namely Type 23b (on which the standing figure seems to have shoulder-length hair, curling outwards at the ends, rather than a helmet) cannot be Kentish. Its westerly distribution, in the upper Thames valley, and at Hamwic, with supplementary evidence from Type 23c in the same regions, is problematic but clearly not Kentish. Whether it is Mercian or West Saxon, it seems that Type 23 was struck concertedly in two kingdoms. The only ways to escape that conclusion would be to argue that 1) the type was struck in Kent under license, as it were, as happened with ninth-century pennies (in different political circumstances) or that 2) the westerly provenances of Type 23b were thoroughly deceptive – as the 'Hwiccian' provenances in Series L turned out to be. Wide-ranging conclusions turn upon a tiny handful of stray finds.

Type 23b/d is not particularly plentiful (less than 0.7 per cent of English sceatta finds), but its designs were copied far and wide. The 'pecking bird' is ubiquitous. It seems to have been influential far beyond what one would expect from the scale of its issue.

Anything other than hoard-evidence is second-best for dating the type. The fact that it is consistently of good silver is ambivalent. That is worth insisting upon, because the idea was once canvassed that Series U was a very late type on a restored alloy-standard – something analogous to

[16] All the London finds of sceattas are gathered up in P. Stott, 'Saxon and Norman coins from London', in A. G. Vince (editor), *Aspects of Saxon and Norman London, 2, Finds and Environmental Evidence* (London and Middlesex Archaeological Society Special Paper, 12), 1991 at pp.279-325. The Barking Abbey finds are published and illustrated by M. M. Archibald, in *The Making of England. Anglo-Saxon Art and Culture, AD 600-900,* edited by L. Webster and J. Backhouse, 1991, pp.93f.

Beonna's reformed coinage. The idea is mistaken, as can now be seen from very close copies of the pecking bird such as that in the C ARIP eclectic group – so deceptively close that the coin in question was assigned to Series U. It has now been tied in firmly with coins sharing the same obverse design, but with quite other reverses. Also, it has been analysed, and found to contain only 31 per cent silver. Thus it illustrates the very wide differences in fineness that could exist between coins that are (in all probability) close to each other in date.

In order to discuss the political significance of the 'pecking bird' design, it is probably enough to be able to say that Type 23b/d is fairly early. The implications spread very widely through the secondary phase. The pecking bird appears also, at much the same date, on the Hamwic coinage of Type 39. A similar bird, surrounded by a torc, is the badge of Series O, for which high silver contents suggest an origin very early in the secondary phase. Series V, which is equally early, has a pecking bird disposed vertically, in an aesthetically accomplished design quite different from the walking bird of Series U and H. If similar instructions were given to all three die-cutters, they could only have been verbal, and in general terms. Yet another independent design has the bird with head raised, and turned back to peck at berries above and behind it. Thus, four or five designs each interpret exactly the same theme independently. Yet another version is found in the 'modelled' style of Series QIV, on what seems to be an early coin. It is not possible to say whether the die-cutter had another sceat as a model in front of him: probably not. Again in Series Q (another two-mint series?), and less closely copied, although still undoubtedly related in some way, is the standing bird (looking like a seagull) with its wing raised over its back as in Series U – but with no vine or berries. It occurs in the 'linear' style, at a relatively early date in Series Q, as QIE and F. In QIF it is paired with a standing figure holding two crosses, which is evidently the attempt of a not very skilled artist to copy the standing figure of Series U.

Why was the 'pecking bird' design taken up at so many mints? It was derived presumably from an inhabited vine scroll decorating some imported artefact of metal, ivory, or wood. It seems improbable, however, that it was selected in that way quite independently as a model for sceatta types in several kingdoms within a short space of time, and treated in a different way in Types 23b, 23d, Series H, V, QIV, and QI. Nor is it easy to believe that die-cutters in distant places were inspired to create their own version of the bird design because a sceat of Type 23 had chanced to come into their hands, and caught their fancy. In any case, what meaning did they attach to a pictorial design which is attractive enough but which, for us at least, has no hidden political message? Was some reference to Type 23, as an esteemed coinage, intended? Was there, even, concerted political action? The pecking bird is so prevalent in the early part of the secondary phase that any less ambitious hypothesis seems inadequate.

We should be at pains to distinguish between the treatment of a common theme or subject, and what constitutes evidence for the direct copying of another sceat. Series V, and the bird looking over its shoulder, are obviously independent versions. Not quite so obviously, the pecking bird of Series J, Type 39, with chains of pellets replacing the stalks of the vine, treats exactly the same motif as Series U, Type 23 but with artistic independence. Indeed, the same is true as between Types 23b and 23d. There are, on the other hand, imitative coins, generally of a low quality of workmanship, where one can see without any doubt that the die-cutter has had an example of either 23b or 23d in front of him, and has copied various details of the design.

That is sometimes the case with coins which form part of the eclectic groups associated with Series K or L. A coin in the C ARIP group has already been mentioned. Another 'pecking bird' copy stands at the beginning of the sequence of the 'triquetras' eclectic group, paired with a particularly careful reverse. The bird's body is in the 'Kentish' style of Type 23d, but the hatched treatment of the wing is reminiscent of the 'westerly' style of Type 23b, suggesting that both varieties were familiar to the die-cutter.

Yet another 'pecking bird' is seen in Type 23c. It is laterally reversed – symptomatic of copying – and is very clearly derived from a coin of Type 23b (the 'westerly' style), as may be seen in the catalogue below.

A 'pecking bird' among the 'celtic cross with rosettes' group of types is also laterally reversed. Again, it seems to be inspired by Type 23b rather than 23d. It was listed by Hill as a 23c/34 mule (merely because of the lateral reversal, and without due consideration of style), and has been renumbered as Type 93 by Stewart.[17]

The bird looking back over its shoulder is paired with the rare 'archer' type, and also with a version of *BMC* Type 20 and with a dog-like monster. It is copied on what seems to be the earliest specimen of the 'animal mask' eclectic group.

The repertoire of styles in which the 'pecking bird' is depicted is shown by enlarged drawings at pp.560-1 below.

III

The secondary phase witnessed the progressive debasement of the sceattas, from a high standard initially, to a final stage in which they varied from region to region, but at worst contained hardly any silver. They were eventually replaced by thinner pennies of very pure silver, with which Offa's name is particularly associated. Apart from the deterioration in their alloy, the main difference which the secondary sceattas show from those of the primary phase is in their choice of designs: the minting arrangements have more in common, in the two phases, than might appear at first glance.

The secondary phase lasted for some fifty years, during which time a total of the approximate order of five thousand dies was used, in England, to strike sceattas at upwards of twenty mints. Wessex and Northumbria were each relatively isolated, and seem to have had only one mint each – although that at York was surprisingly active. The East Anglian coinage was also quite self-contained, preserving a single, old-fashioned coin design inherited from the primary phase. It was struck at two or three mints. A good half of the English coinage was minted along the south-eastern corridor, which ran from east Kent through London and into the Thames valley, the south midlands, and the east midlands. Within that broad zone there seem to have been many mints, some of which were large and some small. The geographical pattern of the English mints is, in short, not dissimilar from what we begin to see more clearly in the reign of Athelstan, when mint-signature became more widespread. There were typological links between the sceatta mints of the south-eastern corridor, which set the student difficult problems. Copying occurred for a variety of reasons. Certain reverse types became widespread, in particular 'wolf' types and 'pecking bird' types. The latter extended their influence outside the south-eastern zone, to include Wessex, and through Series Q they touched East Anglia.

Within the south-eastern zone, the archbishop of Canterbury minted sceattas (e.g. Series K, Type 33). *A fortiori*, kings did so too. It seems, however, that the pervasive 'pecking bird' type originated at too early a date to be connected with the overlordship of King Æthelbald of Mercia, everywhere south of Humber.

Exact dates within the secondary phase are hard to find. It is not impossible that Series L, Type 12 marks Æthelbald's taking power in

315

London in *c.*732. Even if that dating is accepted, we cannot, unfortunately, relate other series to it, because the hoards do not allow us to construct a relative chronology for the second half of the secondary phase. In the first half, numerous mint-places seem to have made a new beginning at much the same date.

THE MEANING OF STYLE AND CONTENT.
BORROWING, COPYING, AND COUNTERFEITING

TO ANYONE who has never pored over a sceat and struggled to make up his or her mind how it should be classified, it may seem that the process is impenetrable and perhaps to some extent arbitrary. Historians will rightly be concerned that in drawing general conclusions from sceattas, good judgement should prevail, and should be seen to prevail. There should be no mystique of interpretation. The logic of the argument should be laid out. Expertise, however, is legitimate and necessary. When the informed eye falls upon a newly-discovered sceat, it automatically assesses the style of die-engraving, and the quality of the flan and the striking, against a remembered canon of other specimens of the same or related types. The eye also checks over, item by item, the content of the images, – the hair, the nose, the ear, the drapery, the bird's or animal's feet – to see whether the die-cutter has correctly understood and executed all the approved elements that went to make up a design. Style and content merge into each other. Substantive types commonly reflect the work of a die-cutter who over a period of time produced perhaps twenty or fifty dies of the same design. Through repetition of his task he fell into settled habits, and his 'hand' is recognizable. The corpus of a type is an aide-memoire for the expert, when he seeks to place a new coin. He compares it, mentally or against a set of photographs, with all the examples previously known. The question which has to be asked, particularly in the secondary phase, is whether the new coin falls within the range of stylistic variation of the main series (and where exactly it fits into the sequence), or whether it is some sort of copy or counterfeit. A run of coins of coherent style and content will presumably be an 'official' or public issue, but the converse is not necessarily true. The status of coins in irregular styles is much more problematic. They may be just as official, but the work of a stop-gap or assistant die-cutter. Occasionally a die-link between two coins of very different style will give us a salutary reminder that the outward appearance of a coin can be a deceptive guide to its classification.

317

There are certainly many sceattas of irregular appearance, however, which are copies made elsewhere than in the workshop of the type copied. They were intended to gain acceptance by their resemblance to a known and trusted design. The quality of such copies varies very widely. The best of them capture the style of the original amazingly well, and are of a respectable weight and alloy. Their downfall is often through combining elements from two minor variants of the same type – which the numismatist knows were not used in combination on official coins. At the time, it would not have detracted from the copy. Less careful workmen tended to over-egg the cake, inserting elements borrowed from another type altogether.

When one considers the artistic talent and craftsmanship involved in cutting a tiny design into wrought iron in intaglio, and the metallurgical skills needed to case-harden the die – and all the trouble and expense – one marvels that it seemed worth-while. Obtaining and casting the silver (silver melts at 960°C.) and alloying it with appropriate amounts of copper and tin, and cutting and shaping flans of the correct size and weight were child's play in comparison with making the die. The men who did all this were on the same level of competence as the official moneyers, and were in a position to make the necessary investment. They may well have been silversmiths. Given the difficulty of understanding why such excellent copies were made, one hesitates to condemn a specimen as unofficial, unless there is clear supporting evidence. That can only come from a correlation between some faults of style and content, and a different distribution-pattern. For some varieties that is clear, and the general case rests of them. Elsewhere, the evidence becomes stronger if one can recognize more than one copy by the same hand.

Other categories of imitation are less deceptive to the student, and the context in which they were made seems fairly obvious, even if it is difficult to guess at the blend of motives as they would have been perceived at the time. When a new mint was opened, early in the secondary phase, or when work resumed at a mint-place after an interval, the die-cutter sometimes borrowed one or both designs of the established currency of a neighbouring region or of a region that was linked by trade. Imitation was the sincerest form of flattery; or perhaps it was just a lack of inventiveness. In York, when Series J was launched by copying Series B there was no intention to deceive. The content of the designs was the same, but the style was entirely different. Other types were then added to Series J, only loosely related in content, yet manifestly in the same distinctive style. Their common origin is confirmed by their distribution-patterns. But when these same types, of Series J, were very deceptively copied, probably in the Rhine mouths area, the motives were different, as the frequency of plated specimens shows. The Frisian die-cutter sometimes made tiny mistakes, for example in the alignment of the lips in the portrait. It is difficult to distinguish such copies, and one needs to be bold to back one's judgement that there are faults in their style, until distributional evidence helps to build up the case.

In the east midlands the die-cutter or die-cutters of Series Q similarly began by borrowing ideas from their neighbours. One of their earliest productions was a Type 41/40 'mule' which minutely reproduces the designs of Series N and Series O respectively. The high silver contents of this coin confirm its relatively early place in Series Q, which rapidly branched out into a repertoire of other designs, demonstrably very close in date to each other, as shown by die-links. From such linked coins the student can learn empirically how much similarity of style to expect, when there is little or no overlap of content.

The great variety of designs in the early part of Series Q makes it not very different in character from the so-called 'eclectic groups', mostly associated with Series K and L. They are undoubtedly the most curious case of copying in the secondary phase. Each group is small, and seems to be from its own mint-place. Each of these small mints, instead of using its own design in a regular way, as the large mints normally did, borrowed a medley of designs from other series, pairing them with a distinctive reverse, which seems to have served as the 'badge' of the mint-place. The C ARIP group, the 'triquetras' group, and the 'animal mask' group are examples. It is puzzling to know why the moneyers at these mint-places behaved so differently, and in a way that suggests that they were flouting authority. The quality of their workmanship is often very high.

What context can one imagine for the copying of Series X, the 'Wodan/monster' sceattas? The main series is the official coinage of Ribe, in Jutland. A few of these sceattas reached England, but they were in no sense plentiful here, except at Hamwic. There is a substantial series of imitations, using the same obverse and reverse types, but in a style almost as different from that of the Danish prototype as Series J is from B. The distributional evidence is that these imitations are English. It is difficult to identify the English region where they were minted: it seems to have been somewhere in the midlands. Regularity of style and a die-ratio of at least 1:3 point to a sustained output. The 'insular' varieties of Series X fit awkwardly into the broad regional patterns of English minting in the

319

secondary phase. And why was a foreign sceatta type copied?

Earlier scholars were inclined to use shared types, without paying much attention to style, as evidence for the derivation, and therefore the chronology, of the many secondary types and varieties. Where two or more issues employ the same design, however, one coin was not necessarily copied from another coin. There was a stock of images, drawn from mythology and from classical art, which was in common use to decorate artefacts of many kinds, as well as coins. Better evidence is needed, to prove that another coin was the prototype. If inessential or trivial details are copied, one may feel confident of the source.

Some imitations are clumsy and technically inferior. It is tempting to think of them as the work of a small-time forger. Such imitations have a way of gradually acquiring a higher status, as new specimens by the same hand turn up – often in another region altogether.

Plating on a base metal core – sometimes with traces of the mercury amalgam that was used to cement the layers together – seems to offer the clearest evidence of fraudulent intention. In isolated instances, no doubt it does. In Series J, the counterfeits may well be continental. In Series N, where plated coins are particularly common, the explanation is not obvious, and one should reserve judgement.

In attempting to interpret style and copying, it is prudent to look for all the help that is to be had from other aspects of the coins in question. Content and style are the clothes a coin wears, and the way it wears them. We can recognize a uniform, or a fashion in dress. With practice, we may read the subtler social signals, – and, unless we are careful, we may sometimes misread them.

SERIES H

AT HAMWIC (the modern Southampton), where over 150 sceattas have been found, Types 39 and 49 are plentiful. They have turned up occasionally elsewhere in Wessex, but very rarely outside that kingdom.[1] There is not the slightest doubt that they were minted there. Their mint-place will have been Hamwic itself rather than Winchester, where extensive excavations have yielded only one sceat, of a different type.[2] Rigold recognized the attribution by assigning Types 39 and 49 the letter H, as a mnemonic for Hamwic. He included Type 48 in Series H, and it too has been recorded at Hamwic; but recent finds have shown that it has a significantly different distribution pattern.[3]

A corpus of over a hundred specimens of Series H has been checked for die-duplication, and numerous specimens have been chemically analysed. There is a hoard from the Kingsland district of Southampton, from which 23 specimens of the two types survive. The evidence of the hoard, and of style, weights, dies, and silver contents have been taken into account in a classification of the series.[4] It is clear that Type 39 is the earlier issue. It was struck from something of the order of a hundred reverse dies, and is quite uniform in style and detail. Type 49 is a larger and much more complicated issue of roughly 350 to 400 reverse dies, within which it is possible to distinguish a dozen varieties. To some extent they can be arranged chronologically, but the one known hoard is in principle an insufficient basis for a classification. Varieties 1 to 6 and their subdivisions, as described below, can therefore represent only a tentative ordering.

Differences in the silver contents within as well as between the varieties show that the alloy certainly fluctuated over short periods. Attempts were made to control it precisely at certain moments in the

---

[1] This pattern was first recognized in C. E. Blunt, 'Saxon coins from Southampton and Bangor', *BNJ* 27 (1952-4), pp.256-62.

[2] M. Dolley and C. E. Blunt, 'Coins from the Winchester excavations, 1961-1973', *BNJ* 47 (1977), pp.135-8.

[3] See the separate section below.

[4] D. M. Metcalf, 'The coins', in *Southampton Finds*, vol.1, *The Coins and Pottery from Hamwic*, edited by P. Andrews, Southampton, 1988, pp.17-59. A few single-finds from Dorset have come to light since the corpus was prepared.

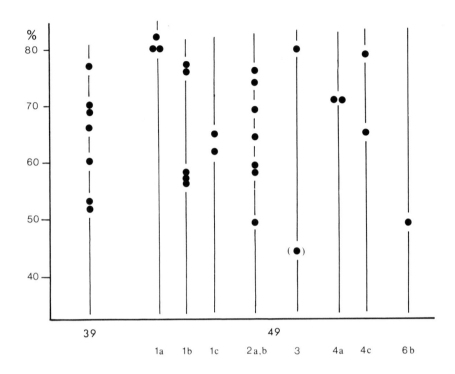

FIG. 'Silver' contents of Series H, Types 39 and 49. Type 49 is classified into varieties 1-6, with sub-varieties, but there may be some chronological overlap between them.

issue of Series H, in particular when Type 49 was first introduced, but either they quickly became unsustainable, or else very inexact standards were tolerated. Type 39 was at best about 70 per cent silver. Type 49 was initially better than that, at 80 per cent silver. Both types tended towards an alloy of little better than half silver.

The date of introduction of Series H cannot be demonstrated by any standard numismatic technique: there are no hoards in which it is associated with other series, nor can the varieties be located on anything resembling a straight-line graph of declining weight or silver contents. The use of the pecking bird motif (which is common to Types 39 and 49) is probably some sort of parallel to, and may be borrowed from Series U, Type 23b/d. One would guess that Type 39 was first struck in the early 720s or the 710s, and therefore within the reign of King Ine (688-726).

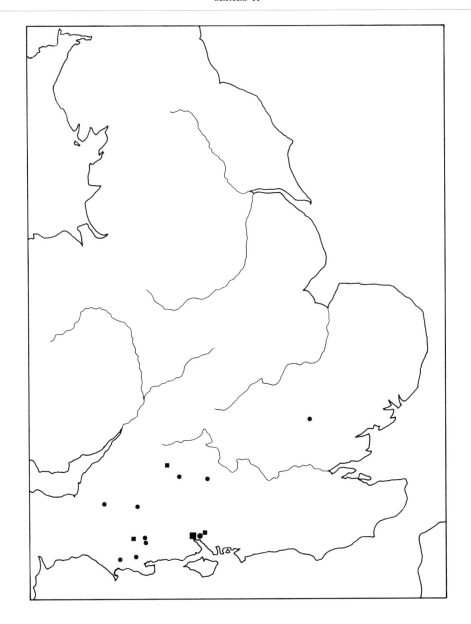

MAP. Finds of Types 39 (square symbols) and 49 (round symbols).

I

In Type 39 the walking bird, with its wing raised over its back, and with a fish-like tail, pecks at a chain of dots, which corresponds with the vine-scroll foliage of Type 23b. Another chain curves above and behind the bird, to end near its rear foot. The intended design, where it is clearest, seems to be that these two chains take their origin from a point or a row of dots towards the upper right.

Single ornamental dots may be added in the angles between the wing, tail, and legs. On one die a group of three or four dots is added beneath one of the bird's feet, and on another a group of four dots is added between the legs.

There is little stylistic development within the type, and such clues as there are come mostly from the obverse, which has been variously described as a 'celtic cross' (although Hamwic is hardly celtic territory) or a 'round shield with bosses'. It is, in any case, a cleverly balanced design, in which one can focus either on the four rosettes, or on the curved outline of the cross. A specimen with a neat, circular central rosette (Hamwic 22) is probably from a carefully made die standing early in the sequence. The central rosette is otherwise often squarish and with smaller dots on one side.

The bird is given a prominent eye on reverses associated with less careful obverses. One specimen (H.31.1) differs from the rest in having rosettes made up of bolder dots.

There are 18 coins in the corpus, against 15 (of which some are no longer traceable) from Hamwic. The 15 include 3 from the Kingsland hoard – where they can be interpreted as the older type, in the minority. The only other recorded provenances in England are from nearby

Bitterne (thought to be the Roman Clausentum: this is the only sceat from the site), two separate finds from Hanford, Dorset (near Hod Hill), and an imitation from Winterbourne Bassett, Wilts. On the imitation, the wire outline of the celtic cross and the pelletted circles of the rosettes are switched. It is an exceptionally compact distribution, even compared with Type 49. One specimen is reported from Domburg among over nine hundred sceattas.

The average weight of Type 39 is not much more than 0.9g.

The alloy, which is often difficult to reconstruct because of the effects of corrosion and leaching, seems to have been generally about 60 to 70 per cent silver. Significant amounts of tin and (usually) also zinc are present in the copper-based component of the alloy – in contrast with the primary sceattas and the early porcupines.

II

The obverse of Type 49 shows a facing, moustached head (the same motif as Series X?), surrounded by roundels each composed of an annulet and pellet, and sometimes with a small cross or other symbol inserted into the circle of roundels at the 6 o'clock position, below the head. The

outline of the face varies from almost circular to egg-shaped to an elongated kite shape, and the number of roundels varies from 10 to 6 or even 5.

The bird is always crested, with three or four pelletted spikes. Although its head is lowered, its beak is closed, and it is not pecking at anything. There is no vine-scroll, and no chain of dots. In what is certainly the earliest variety, the bird's wing and stumpy tail are outlined

325

with small pellets. In all later varieties, the tail is omitted, but the outline of pellets remains, with a second, linear outline added around it. Perhaps the die-cutter's understanding of his model changed, and the raised wing was seen as the bird's tail, while the bag-shaped element was seen as the wing. The peacock is one of the few indigenous large birds that is crested, and of course it raises its tail-feathers in display.

Symbols are added in the field above and below the bird's neck. There is clearly a general correlation between the choice of symbols, and the style of the dies, in particular the outer circle of roundels on the obverse. We are probably justified, therefore, in thinking of the symbols as the identifying marks of separate issues of sceattas – varieties that either were chronologically distinct, or were the work of different moneyers. Certainly there are plenty of little groups of dies, each of the same variety, that belong together. The evidence is not, however, as tidy as the theory, and one is left with problems of interpretation of particular coins, on which only a provisional judgement is possible.

The following scheme of classification into six varieties is based on the number of roundels, and the field-marks on the reverse, in combination with as many other stylistic details as possible. One might guess that there were four successive phases of production, of varying intensity, represented by varieties 1, 2, 3-5, and 6. The evidence of at least two more substantial hoards would be needed to prove the case.

The varieties are defined as follows:[5]

Variety 1a. Ten roundels. Bird with stumpy tail. Pellet above and rosette below the neck. This undoubtedly early variety, of 80 per cent silver, is known from three specimens from a single pair of dies. Note the ornamental groups of dots below the bird's feet and tail. Hamwic 35-7.

Variety 1b. Ten, nine, or eight roundels. Rosette below neck, and sometimes a pellet above neck. This group is by no means uniform in style, and one cannot be sure that all the coins listed as part of it are of the same issue. Hamwic 37.5-47.

Variety 1c. As 1b, but there is a pellet between each pair of roundels. There is a reverse die-link with 1b: 48 = 37.5. Hamwic 48-56.

---

[5] The scheme follows Metcalf, loc.cit.

Variety 2a. Eight or seven roundels, exceptionally nine, always with pellets between. Annulet with central pellet above and below neck. There is normally a cross pommee or a group of pellets at 6 o'clock on the obverse. H.57-8, with uptilted tail, looks early, and might be concurrent with Variety 1. H.59 is possibly imitative (from the workshop of Series U, Type 23b?). H.60 onwards have a crest of only 3 spikes. H.66.7 has a rather bare and simplifed reverse, and looks late, but official. Hamwic 57-68.

Variety 2b. One specimen only, matching 2a except that the field-marks are a roundel above and a roundel/rosette below the neck. The bird's thin body and the treatment of the crest, eye, and feet betray another die-cutter's hand. Probably imitative; only 50 per cent silver. H.65 could belong with this specimen: note the treatment of the 'wing', with inner and outer curve of pellets. Hamwic 70.

Variety 3. Seven or eight roundels, usually with pellets between. Roundel above the neck, cross pommee below, usually with pellets in its angles. Note the treatment of the 'wing', with one pellet inside the linear outline, and a curve of pellets outside. A fairly compact stylistic group. H.74 may be imitative. Hamwic 70.5-74.

Variety 4. Seven or eight roundels, with pellets between. Roundel above the neck, roundel flanked by four pellets crosswise below the neck. There is a cross pommee at 6 o'clock on the obverse. The treatment of the 'wing' varies, suggesting a subdivision into 4a (pellets inside linear outline), 4b (wing as in variety 3), and 4c (central pellet and outline of pellets, linear outline omitted). Hamwic 75-8.

Variety 5. Number of roundels variable, but usually seven or eight. Roundel above neck, cross of five pellets below. There is usually a vertical row or group of pellets at 6 o'clock on the obverse, and sometimes also rows of pellets at 12, 4, and 8 o'clock, co-ordinated with the pellets outlining the head. The variety is stylistically diverse, e.g. in the shape of the head, and the treatment of the bird's tail. The rows of pellets, which do not occur elsewhere, are a good reason for identifying it as a separate variety. H.80 (variety 5b) fits poorly with the rest of the group. Hamwic 78.2-79.5

Variety 6a. Bird laterally reversed. The position of this coin in the series is problematic, if indeed it is an official issue. The obverse, however, seems to be close in style to variety 6b, which doubtless represents a separate phase. The reverse of 6a might, therefore, be experimental. Hamwic 80.7

Variety 6b. Seven roundels, with pellets between, and diamond of 4 pellets at 6 o'clock. The head lacks a linear outline, making the style quite distinctive. Reverse similar to variety 5. One specimen has very high tin contents (exaggerated, no doubt, by differential leaching). Hamwic 81-83.5.

III

The Kingsland hoard coins are severely damaged by burning, and have lost more than half their weight by corrosion and leaching. The 23 surviving coins were found in a pile, with two and a possible third scattered 0.5m away in the same layer of burnt daub. The money may have been wrapped up as a rouleau when lost.[6] Classification is difficult because of the very poor condition of the coins. Of 20 coins of Type 49, only 13 can be assigned to a variety, as follows: variety 1b (1), 1c (1), 2a (8), 3 (2), 6 (1). There are 3 specimens of Type 39 (and none of 48).

The distribution of Type 49 among varieties 1-6 is unsatisfactory, and raises the question whether the classification corresponds to the order of issue. Variety 1 was a large issue, and its relative scarcity in the hoard in contrast with the abundance of variety 2 would suggest a date of concealment late in or soon after the period of issue of variety 2. Varieties 3, 5, and 6 are quite scarce, and their small numbers in the hoard might be by chance. The absence of variety 4 is more puzzling. The seven specimens which could not be assigned to a variety might have changed the picture significantly.

IV

Given such uncertainty over the chronology of the varieties, it is worth noting that silver of two different kinds seems to have been used in minting Type 49, one kind with high gold contents, of about 2 parts to 100 parts of silver, the other with low gold contents, of around 0.5 parts.[7]

[6] M. R. Maitland Muller, 'The Southampton excavations: second interim report, 1947', *Proc. Hampshire Field Club Archaeol. Soc.* 17 (1950), pp.125-9; Metcalf, loc.cit., pp.29f.

[7] Noted by J. P. Northover in Andrews, op.cit., at pp.34f.

Varieties 1 and 2 are of high-gold silver, 3 and 4 are of low-gold silver. Variety 6 has high gold contents – which is perhaps another argument for placing it earlier in the scheme. It seems that the measured gold contents of the Hamwic excavation coins are in some cases, perhaps in many cases, exaggerated by the effects of corrosion and leaching. The results tabulated below therefore need to be clear by a good margin if they are to be accepted as evidence for two distinct kinds of silver, especially as the interpretation involves assuming that Variety 6 is misplaced.

The separation of values is quite clear-cut and persuasive, as may be seen from the following tabulation and diagram:

Variety	Au : 100Ag
1a	2.05, 2.00
1b	2.36, 2.35, 1.74, 3.08
1c	1.69, 1.98
2a	2.01, 1.92, 1.53
3	0, 0.67
4a	1.08, 0.63
4c	0.17, 0.24
6b	1.77, (6.89)

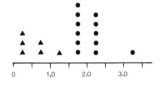

V

Series H was evidently issued over quite a long period of time, as may be judged by the numbers of dies involved and their division into identifiable varieties in Type 49. One may compare Series R and Y. The date-range of H is a topic on which it is difficult to find any unambiguous evidence. It is worth pursuing because it raises two questions of general historical interest, one concerning the origins of Type 39 in relation to the use of the 'pecking bird' motif elsewhere, the other concerning the decline of monetary circulation at Hamwic and the length of time during which sceattas remained in use.

The pecking bird of Type 39 is the same design, although treated independently in a different style, as that used on Series U, Type 23b. Which came first? The alloy of the two types is close enough for it to be probable that they are of similar date. Type 23 occurs in two substantive styles, of which one (23b) is scarce, and has a westerly distribution in the upper Thames valley, and at Hamwic. It is apparently Mercian, but in any case not a Hamwic issue, even though there are five from the Hamwic excavations. The general chronology of the secondary phase, based on the re-dating of the Cimiez hoard, makes it impossible to associate the widespread use of the pecking bird with the ascendancy of King Æthelbald. Yet one is reluctant to think that it is without political significance. The problem has ramifications, e.g. in the east Kentish Series V. All the types in question are obviously secondary and post-date the Aston Rowant hoard. Type 39 can hardly have been introduced until the mid or late 710s.

The characteristic of Type 39 which impresses most is its stylistic uniformity. The sample is none too large: a dozen specimens are well enough preserved to allow their style to be assessed. And the estimate of the original numbers of dies will be subject to wide margins of uncertainty. One wonders, nevertheless, whether the issue of Type 39 may not have involved a recoinage of some of the silver stocks that had accumulated in Hamwic – of porcupines, for example. The relatively high gold contents appear to be compatible with that suggestion.

Type 39 remained in use alongside Type 49, the issue of which could have begun not many years later. Type 49 was introduced on the same weight-standard as 39 (somewhere between 0.9 and 0.95g), but initially on a slightly better standard of fineness. Its introduction is thus set in a context of confidence, and was certainly not a step in the general process of debasement.

Over all, Type 49 creates a very different impression from Type 39. How long did it remain in issue? The many varieties suggest sporadic minting over at least a couple of decades, although the pattern of field-marks might be explained partly as the distinguishing marks of more than one moneyer, working concurrently.

An archaeological assessment of the site of Hamwic is that the peak of the town's prosperity fell approximately within the period c.740 to c.790.[8] This is radically at variance with the traditional interpretation of the coin

[8] P. Andrews and D. M. Metcalf, 'A coinage for King Cynewulf of Wessex?', in *Sceattas in England and on the Continent*, pp.175-9.

finds, which suggest a boom period from *c.*690 to *c.*740 (represented by the losses of sceattas), followed by a virtual blank until *c.*790, and then a modest revival from *c.*790 to *c.*840 (represented by losses of silver pennies). As there is no break in the archaeological record, such as the 'blank' period in the numismatic chronology might have led one to expect, the question arises whether sceattas may not have continued in circulation at Hamwic for much longer than traditionally supposed – and even whether their minting may not have continued for longer, or begun later. The archaeological evidence of context is inconclusive, and the view that Type 49 was still being minted during the reign of King Cynewulf, 757-86, will appear extreme.

Arguments against a 'late' chronology are hard to find, but one may note an imitative Type 49/48 'mule', (H.91.5) which is unlikely to be much later than the closing date of issue of Type 48.

SERIES H, TYPE 48

TYPE 48 shares with Type 39 (and with various other types) the obverse design of a 'celtic cross with rosettes'. Its reverse has a whorl of three animal heads. When Rigold devised his scheme of classification[1] the only provenances on record were Hamwic, where there were two early finds and three more from the modern excavations, plus the rather vague 'south Hampshire'. It was reasonable, therefore, to think that Type 48

belonged to the Hamwic mint, along with Types 39 and 49 – even though there are differences between Types 39 and 48 in the treatment of the 'celtic cross' design.

The year 1986 by chance brought two new single-finds to light, which were enough to arouse misgivings. A third appeared not long afterwards. One was from St. Nicholas-at-Wade, Thanet, another (in very worn condition) was from near Alford, Lincs., and the third came from near Roxton, Beds.[2] Three outlying finds would not normally be sufficient to call the interpretation of a distribution-pattern into question, but Series H (Types 39 and 49) has an exceptionally compact distribution. There seems to have been very little outflow of silver from Hamwic in the period when those types were in use, perhaps because the town's trade generated a surplus of cash.[3] There are no finds of Types 39 or 49 from east Kent or from anywhere north of the Thames. Even three finds of Type 48 from outside Wessex, when set against the three from the Hamwic excavations, imply that the type was being used differently, or was from a different mint: it does not conform to the same commercial or

---

[1] *BNJ* 47 (1977), at pp.27 and 35.

[2] D. M. Metcalf, 'Three sceattas from St. Nicholas at Wade, Thanet', *BNJ* 56 (1986), p.8. (The St. Nicholas at Wade coin is catalogued below.) The Alford coin weighs 0.75g (information kindly supplied by Mr. J. Bispham). 'Coin Register', *BNJ* 57 (1987), no.71 (Roxton).

[3] *Southampton Finds*, vol.1, edited by P. Andrews, Southampton 1988, at pp.18f. for a discussion of the regional balance of payments.

balance-of-payments situation. To match 45 specimens of Types 39 and 49 excavated at Hamwic, there would have needed to be thirty or forty single finds of those types outside Wessex, if the patterns were to be comparable.[4]

At the least, we can say that if Type 48 were from the Hamwic mint, it would have to fit chronologically between Types 39 and 49. One would be reluctant to envisage that it was the earliest type minted there in the secondary phase, because its alloy is only about 50 per cent silver. There would be obvious difficulties in seeing it as the latest type: its weight ranges as high as 1.20g, and its fabric is too good. That only leaves the middle position. It was not present, however, in the Kingsland (Southampton) hoard, which consisted of Type 39 (3) and 49 (20 specimens). If Type 48 were a Hamwic coinage falling between Types 39 and 49, the shift in the pattern of stray losses would represent an abrupt and temporary aberration – which seems completely implausible.

That impression is reinforced by two intriguing finds from Italy – one from Ostia, near Rome,[5] the other from Aosta, on a routeway in the southern Alps.[6] These are the only sceattas to have been found in Italy, other than a Northumbrian coin of Series Y also from Aosta.[7] All three are presumably losses by English pilgrims or travellers to Italy. Each of them might have been carried either from the traveller's home region (e.g. Northumbria) or from the port of embarkation for the Continent. It is remarkable that two of the three coins should be of the same scarce type. They do not in themselves argue against Hamwic, which was a point of departure for travellers. But one would have expected to find the much more plentiful Type 49 in greater numbers.

Three scattered finds from England, then, and two from the Continent are the reason for thinking – in the context of negative evidence from many other sites – that Type 48 was not minted at Hamwic. It is a classic example of a deceptive distribution pattern which was extended over a wider area by the finds of the 1980s, and which now looks radically different.

If Type 48 had never been assigned to Series H, if one were starting afresh, how would one interpret it? Would one not be inclined, on grounds of style, to give it to Series L, along with Types 14 and 34,

[4] D. M. Metcalf, 'How sceattas are attributed to their mints: the case of series H, type 48', *Proceedings of the 10th International Congress of Numismatics, London, September 1986*, edited by I.A. Carradice, (International Association of Professional Numismatists, Publication no.11), London, 1989, pp.333-7.

[5] *Southampton Finds,* at pp.28 and 41 (no.34.7).

[6] M. Orlandoni, 'La via commerciale della Valle d'Aosta nella documentazione numismatica', *Rivista Italiana di Numismatica* 90 (1988), pp.433-48, where the coin is illustrated. It was found during work on the cathedral.

[7] Near a shrine outside the Porta Decumana.

MAP. Finds of Type 48

which have the closest matching version of the 'celtic cross' design – or possibly to see links with Series U, Type 23e, which has a similar whorl of animal heads – or Series U, Types 93 and 106, which 'mule' Series U with the 'celtic cross'? A moment's reflection shows that, although the style of Type 48 is arguably more closely related to this little cluster of types than it is to Type 39, the fact remains that five specimens have been found at Hamwic, whereas none of these other types has been found there.

Five specimens may not seem many, but if the loss-rate at Hamwic for Type 48 was similar to that for Types 39 and 49 (and it is difficult to see how it could have been radically different), then tens of thousands of coins of the type will have been available in the town. If the output of some five hundred reverse dies of Types 39 and 49 remained largely within Hamwic and generated 45 casual losses, then the corresponding 3 losses of Type 48 might imply, with margins of statistical uncertainty, a quantity of coins equivalent to the output of something of the order of 30 dies. Halve the estimate, and halve it again: it still serves to make the point that we are not looking at a mere handful of sceattas spent in Hamwic by pilgrims or travellers to the Continent, and lost in the normal way as they passed from hand to hand in the town thereafter.

The Hamwic finds thus suggest that, if Type 48 was not minted in the town, it is nevertheless from a mint that was closely linked to Hamwic. We should keep open the possibility of an undiscovered mint-place on the south coast, not too far from Hamwic. Could there have been a second mint elsewhere on the Solent? – We are told that Willibald sailed for Rome in c.720 'from the mouth of the Hamble'. But it seems out of keeping with what we think we know about the distribution of mints. Could there, more plausibly, have been another mint just outside West Saxon territory in the Portsmouth area? Perhaps we should even ask ourselves whether Type 48 could be from a north French port. A cross-Channel link might make sense of the quantity of finds from Hamwic.

Although it is no doubt a sound principle not to multiply mints unnecessarily, we should not rule out the idea that Type 48 is the distinctive coinage of a minor mint in a port from where pilgrims and other travellers crossed the Channel. The chance discovery of a productive site at or near the type's place of origin would probably move the argument onto new ground, for a statistical contrast with the Hamwic finds would be relatively easy to establish. Meanwhile we are like astonomers who, predicting an unseen planet, are not at all sure where to look for it.

I

Eighteen or twenty specimens are known, among which only one reverse die-link has been noted.[8] (The survival-rate at Hamwic thus looks rather low, which is another argument against the type's having been minted there, although numerically too imprecise to be conclusive.) Although the elements of the obverse and reverse designs are very consistent, the style of die-cutting shows considerable variation, and it is difficult to arrange the dies into a clear sequence of stylistic development. The general impression is of a coinage for which several small batches of dies were cut, over a period of time; thus unlike Type 39.

One phase of die-cutting is distinctive because of the use of coarse graining, of seed-shaped instead of round pellets, both in the outer borders and in other elements of the designs.[9] The 'celtic cross with rosettes' design differs from that of Type 39 in that it always has a pellet in each arm of the cross, whereas Type 39 never does. Type 48 normally has a quite large pellet or boss in the centre of the design, whereas Type 39 always has a rosette. Type 48 sometimes has four small pellets crosswise around the central boss, and sometimes a rosette.

The whorl of three creatures with gaping jaws, which fills the reverse of Type 48, has in the past been described as being composed of wolf's heads (cf. Series K). Although they have exaggeratedly large teeth in the upper jaw, very like the canine teeth of the animal of Type 33, the creatures of Type 48 have no ears.[10] On some specimens they look like dolphins. The whorl is superficially very similar to the design of Series U, Type 23e, and to the East Saxon Series S (whorl of four creatures). Thus it is not peculiar to one region or kingdom of England. There are systematic differences in the treatment of the design. In each type a chain of pellets emerges from the creature's throat. In Type 48 the chain then curves outwards towards the perimeter of the design, and follows the contour of the brow and head of the next creature in the whorl. In Series

[8] *Southampton Finds,* at pp.40-1.
[9] ibid., nos.32.3 and 33.

[10] The St. Nicholas at Wade specimen is a possible exception.

U and S, by contrast, the chains curve inwards to meet at the central pellet.

We can press the stylistic analysis a little further. The wire outline of the celtic cross on Type 39 goes about three-quarters of the way round each rosette, in a horse-shoe shape (a), and the ends of the arms of the cross follow the curve of the edge of the coin, which thus has an interrupted wire border. The balance of the opposed curves is handled by the die-cutter with outstanding aesthetic skill. Type 48 is another story. Sometimes the wire outline of the cross is as described, although tending

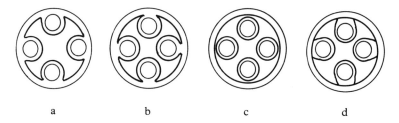

a   b   c   d

to be clumsy. Sometimes there is an uninterrupted wire border forming a complete circle around the edge of the coin, and each rosette is enclosed in a completely circular wire border, not touching the outer border (c). This is no longer strictly a celtic cross. Sometimes the rosettes are almost completely encircled (b). Occasionally we see a garbled mixture (d).

One might have hoped to correlate the various criteria (central pellet/rosette; form of wire border; seed-shaped graining; weights; alloy) in order to put the dies into a sequence. It is, unfortunately, not at all clear what the guiding principles should be. One would prefer to see the heavy coins as early. The seed-shaped graining might be late. But that is little better than guess-work. A hoard concealed part-way through the issue of the type is needed.

II

One remarkable coin stands on its own. The whorl is laterally reversed, and is of exceptionally careful modelling and delicate workmanship. The dies are so fine and smooth as to make one think that they were of superior metal – perhaps even of bronze. The coin (catalogued below) was a chance find from Ostia. Everything about it – the lateral reversal, the quality of workmanship, and the provenance – should lead one to ask whether it could be a contemporary imitation, or even a modern fabrication. The reliability of the story of its finding, in 1982 or 1983, is attested by a respected third party who was present, in his apartment in Rome, when the finder offered it to a British dealer as an ancient coin of Tarentum – an attribution suggested no doubt by the dolphins or dolphin-like creatures on the reverse. Chemical analysis by both XRF and EPMA has shown convincingly that it is not a modern fabrication.[11] The uncleaned surface gave a reading of 76 per cent silver, while EPMA on the cleaned edge showed 51 per cent. The surface patination is acceptable, and the range of minor constituents and trace elements is unlikely in a modern fabrication. The high tin contents, by both methods of analysis, make it appropriate to describe the alloying metal as bronze.

Could the Ostia find be interpreted as an early, experimental issue of a new mint? All the features that have been mentioned could well be read in that way. If the lateral reversal were the result of unskilled counterfeiting, one would not expect to find it in association with such careful and delicate workmanship. The wire border on the obverse is continuous, showing a lack of understanding of the 'celtic cross'.

III

Six specimens of Type 48, including the Ostia find, have been analysed chemically.[12] The 'south Hampshire' find, like that from Ostia, has been analysed both by XRF and EPMA. The XRF result of 68 per cent silver is corrected by EPMA to 47 per cent. Where only XRF results are available, we should be prepared to discount them as being possibly too high. One such is (again) 68 per cent, and another is 45 per cent. Two EPMA results, from seriously corroded coins, are 56 per cent 'silver' (reconstruction: Ag 40 per cent, Pb 16 per cent!), and 'probably more than 37 per cent 'silver' (Ag 30 per cent, Pb 6 per cent, in a total of only 65 per cent).

From the above, there is no positive evidence that the original alloy standard of Type 48 ever exceeded c.50 per cent; and the silver contents of the Ostia find do not, on that basis, preclude its being an early, experimental issue.

IV

The widely scattered finds of Type 48 point to its being used, characteristically, by travellers to Italy. It was present in substantial

[11] *Southampton Finds*, at p.41 (no.34.7).
[12] ibid., at pp.40-1.

quantities in the currency of Hamwic. The best guess one can make, in the absence of definite evidence, is that it is from a small mint on the south coast, perhaps in the Portsmouth area. No doubt it deliberately imitated the 'celtic cross with rosettes' design of Series H, Type 39. That raises the question whether the whorl of animal heads was also in deliberate imitation of a neighbouring regional type – or, alternatively, was the model which was imitated. The critical finds of Type 14 from Cosham (Portsmouth) and Type 34 from the Brighton area are both, for different reasons, of uncertain value as evidence. They are discussed under Series L.

NORTHUMBRIAN SCEATTAS: SERIES J

YORK is the home of Series J, which has had a history of misinterpretation. In 1960 Rigold saw it as a Kentish coinage, in continuation of Series B.[1] Metcalf in 1966 argued that it had a quite different distribution-pattern from B, on the periphery of the zone where sceattas were used, and in short that it began as a Mercian copy of Series B, under the authority of King Æthelbald, at a mint in the upper Thames region.[2] Many more finds have come to light since 1966, and it is now possible to see that the balance of the distribution is much more northerly than, for example, that for Series U, Type 23b, and to argue that the series belongs to Northumbria. The choice between Mercia and Northumbria is, however, far from self-evident, as may be judged by comparing the two distribution-maps, for Series Y and J. The one is quite obviously centred on York, whereas the other sprawls over the whole country. Series J is also particularly plentiful (for an English series) in the Low Countries,[3] and one needs formally to consider whether all or part of it could be continental. The best general explanation seems to be that from York it was carried over long distances, both by inland routes through Lindsey and into Mercia, and also down the east coast by sea. The Frisian trade with Northumbria ensured a strong presence for Series J in the area of the Rhine mouths. It has been found not only at Domburg (23 specimens) and Dorestad, but in the Hallum hoard and at Nijmegen, Utrecht, Ophoven, and in Friesland.[4] It was probably from the Low Countries, rather than direct from Northumbria, that coins were carried back across the North Sea and down the Channel to the south coast of England, e.g. finds from Pyecombe, Sussex, and Hamwic.

The official issues of Series J were very freely copied, both clumsily and skilfully. Deceptive imitations are found in Mercia, in south-eastern

---

[1] S. E. Rigold, 'The two primary series of sceattas', *BNJ* 30 (1960-1), pp.6-53, at p.22 (with the assertion that 'Northumbrian royal sceattas are absent'!)

[2] D. M. Metcalf, 'A coinage for Mercia under Aethelbald', *Cunobelin* 12 (1966), pp.26-39.

[3] W. Op den Velde, W.J. de Boone and A. Pol, 'A survey of sceatta finds from the Low Countries', in *Sceattas in England and on the Continent*, 1984, pp.117-45, recording 23 specimens from Domburg, cf.8 of Series L, or 5 of Series V and K.

[4] ibid.

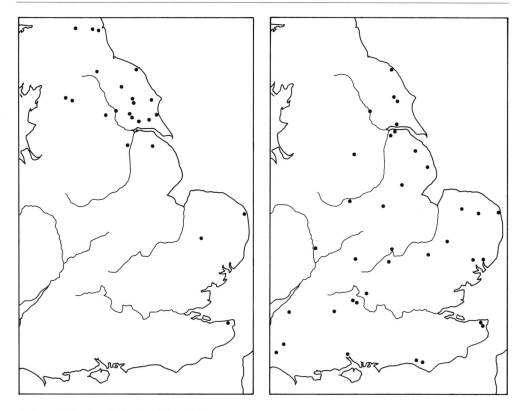

MAPS. Finds of Series Y and J.

England, and on the Continent. Unless the copies are carefully distinguished by a stylistic analysis, interpretations of the distribution pattern for the series as a whole are liable to be more than usually misleading.

Five types are assigned to Series J, namely Types 85 (= Rigold's BIIIB), 37, 60, 72, and 36.[5] A sixth type (84) is untraced, and its existence may be doubted. One should also mention an eye-catching continental copy which mules the two facing heads of Type 37 with a reverse design consisting of the two large letters R M with titulus. The first two types, 85 and 37, are substantive issues that certainly belong together as a pair, as their style and the find-evidence show us. The next two are, respectively, excessively scarce and scarce types that look as if they should be a second pair of types from the same mint as the first, but which turn out on detailed inspection to be problematic. The fifth type

[5] Type numbers from 77 onwards are assigned in I. Stewart, 'The early English denarial coinage, *c.680-c.750', Sceattas in England and on the Continent*, pp.5-26, at pp.22ff.

FIG. Series J, Types 85, 37, 60, 72, and 36.

assigned to Series J, namely Type 36, is a substantive English type which is very closely connected by its general style with Types 85 and 37, and which probably also comes from York.

Type 85 is a free copy, in no way deceptive, of the designs of Series B. It omits the legends, substituting a double border of pellets. The reverse is treated in a thin, linear style, the spiral-winged bird being drawn with artistic confidence and flair in a single, continuous line.

Type 37, by the same hand, has conceptually related designs, namely two facing diademed heads, separated by a cross on stand, and on the reverse a whorl of four birds, around a small cross pommee. Again, there is a double border of pellets.

Type 60 has the same obverse design as Type 85, while Type 72 has the two facing heads of Type 37. In that sense they look as if they should be a second pair, replacing Types 85 and 37 as the official issues at York. The new reverse types are more in fashion with the secondary than the primary phase. That of Type 60 has two interlocking bird-headed torcs (reminiscent of Series K, Type 32a) while Type 72 has a walking bird, with head turned back (reminiscent of the 'archer' type, and perhaps contemporary with the birds of Series U, Type 23 and Series V). The bird is encircled by a serpent-headed torc with gaping jaws.

Type 36 replaces the head of Type 85 by a bust, with a cross in front of the face. Its reverse design is another walking bird, with a cross in front, and a second, smaller bird above and to the left.

For various reasons, discussed below, it seems likely that Types 85 and 37 were issued in parallel rather than successively. Their designs suggest that in that case they were the coinage of the king, and of the king with the bishop of York, respectively.

This reading of the numismatic evidence strains historical credulity, even though there were parallel coinages from c.737 onwards for Eadberht, and Eadberht with Ecgberht.[6] Series J is not represented in

[6] See Series Y below.

the Aston Rowant hoard, from *c.*710, but one would wish to set its origin at as early a date thereafter as conveniently possible, if only because it is imitated by Type BIII c. (It could even antedate the hoard by a year or two, being absent from it because of distance.) It must fall well before 735, when Ecgberht received the pallium. St. Wilfred died in 709; and King Osred, who succeeded in 705 at the age of eight, acquired the reputation of a worthless youth, who damaged rather than added to the privileges of the church. The only political context for such an initiative of cooperation between church and state that seems remotely plausible, within the probable date-range for the origin of Series J, is the reign of King Coenred (from 716), when John of Beverley was bishop.[7] One can easily enough understand the political considerations leading to a joint coinage by Eadberht and Ecgberht, with a Canterbury precedent to encourage them.[8] John of Beverley, however, was not the king's brother, and he was not a metropolitan. Perhaps, if Coenred spent more of his time at Bamburgh than at York, he laid secular tasks on the bishop in York, to oversee the king's peace and justice in his wic, and rewarded him with the right of coinage.

Moreover, Type 37 is just as plentiful as Type 85, whereas Archbishop Ecgberht's coins were struck in smaller numbers than the total for King Eadberht's varieties A-G. It would have been surprisingly generous on the king's part to give his bishop an equal share in the profits of the coinage – even though they were a minor element in the royal income.

Historically the case is so unexpected that the attribution and dating of the coins demand to be studied with special care.

Sub-sections I to X set out the detailed numismatic evidence for the various types that make up Series J, and address the difficult problem of identifying imitations. That prepares the way for a more concise statement, in sub-section XI, of the crux of the argument for an attribution to York rather than the midlands, by assessing and comparing the relative plentifulness of Series J in various regions, in the context of other primary and secondary types. The detailed discussion of Type 36 is deferred to sub-section XII, in order to make use of the results of the regional analysis in XI to argue that, in spite of superficial appearances to the contrary, the type should be assigned to the York mint. The evidence for parallel minting by the king and the bishop is then reviewed in sub-section XIII.

[7] F. M. Stenton, *Anglo-Saxon England*[3], Oxford, 1971, pp.145f.
[8] See under Series K.

I

Rigold's corpus of Type BIIIB (now Type 85) listed a dozen obverse dies, in a total of 16 specimens.[9] The total has now risen to at least two dozen specimens. They include such a high proportion of coins which one would be disposed to dismiss as deceptive copies, that the tail appears to be wagging the dog, and a prudent critic will ask whether many of them, in spite of their appearance, may not be officially sanctioned issues. It becomes debateable, in other words, where one should draw the line between official and unofficial issues.

Type BIIIc (discussed in an earlier section) is a copy, which might have deceived. a casual user, although it would not now confuse a numismatist. There are outright forgeries of BIIIB, such as the plated copy found at Winteringham, on the south bank of the Humber. And there are careful but amateurish copies in passably good silver, such as one recently found in the Sheffield area, the unoffical status of which is obvious. From the Continent, too, there are coins which are so obviously imitative that they need not delay us: Belfort 6218 (found at Domburg)

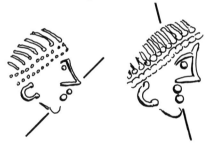

will serve as an example. But then there is a large proportion of coins which do not quite conform to the prototype, and which could in principle be either imitations struck elsewhere than York, or a later phase of the York coinage. Poor weight or alloy are not necessarily evidence of imitation: a later phase might have gone downhill. Distribution-patterns are really the only sure guide.

The best specimens, which form the stylistic nucleus of the type, have a group of four pellets in front of the bird, and groups of three to left and right of the cross. The annulets often have a pellet lightly engraved in the centre, and this is a good art-historical criterion because it is such a trivial

[9] Rigold, loc.cit. *BNJ* 1966, p.6 adds BIIIB, 13 and 14.

FIG. Coins which conform to the criteria: two from the Garton-on-the-Wolds grave-find; York (Fishergate); Hallum; Whithorn; Alford.

detail. Another important criterion, which betrays the workman's hand, is the angle of the lips. If the coins are placed so that the straight line defining the bottom of the nose is horizontal, a line drawn through the two pellets which represent the lips slopes down towards the left.[10]

Coins which conform to the criteria and details just described include the two in the Garton-on-the-Wolds grave-find, from north of Humber, the two in the York (Fishergate) hoard of 1985, the two in the Hallum hoard, and finds from Whithorn,[11] Alford, Lincs (from the same dies as BIIIB, 1)[12], Hamwic (92), Reculver (*MEC* 695), and its die-duplicate in the Dutch national collection, ex Man and presumed to be from Domburg.[13]

A find from Reculver (BIIIB, 2 = *BMC* 141, pl.3, 12) conforms in all particulars to the model but is somehow unconvincing. The pellets are all

a little too large, and in particular the triple row of pellets representing the diadem and the 'roots' of the hair is too equal in size and too regimented. It is inevitably a matter of subjective judgement, however, whether such a coin is imitative, unless others that are from the same dies or manifestly by the same hand serve to create a distribution pattern at variance with the standard one.

A question-mark must stand against two further coins, very similar to each other, in the Fries Museum, Leeuwarden [14] and in Brussels.[15] Their

[10] Metcalf, loc.cit.

[11] I am indebted to Miss Pirie who kindly sent me photographs of both the Fishergate and Whithorn finds.

[12] J. Bispham, 'Recent metal detector finds from Essex and Lincolnshire', *BNJ* 56 (1986), pp.183-5, item L2.

[13] Hill photo 395, 1.03g.

[14] Hill photo 266.

[15] Hill photo 28.

FIG. Coins in the Fries Museum, Leeuwarden and in Brussels.

style is again very persuasive, and the only faults one could hold against them are that the bird's three drooping feathers are too nearly vertical, the base of the bird too nearly horizontal, the man's cheek not quite chubby enough, the nose vaguely defined, and that there is more empty space than usual in front of the face. All one's instincts urge that Type 60 (below) is by the same hand as these two handsome coins.

If we admit them to the canon, then we have to say that the distribution pattern is a dual one, divided between Northumbria and the Low Countries. If we hesitate over two such similar coins from the Low Countries not being matched elsewhere, we are talking about imitations which are extremely deceptive.

The group of specimens in the best style includes a unique variant with a small cross pommee in front of the mouth (York, Fishergate hoard).[16] It would be natural to think of it as an early, experimental coin, the nose being shortened to accommodate the cross, but one ought perhaps to reserve judgement on its dating. The cross could be copied from Series G (which was represented in the Garton-on-the-Wolds grave-find).

On the Alford and Reculver coins the pellets in the annulets are invisible or missing, but their general style makes their attribution to the group persuasive. Unprovenanced coins which also belong to the group include BIIIB, 1 (catalogued below: no pellets in the annulets), and BIIIB, 4.

We return now to the area where judgement is very difficult. Under BIIIB, 3 Rigold recorded three specimens from three different reverse dies as being (very unusually) from the same obverse. In fact BIIIB, 3i and ii are not from the same obverse, although closely similar. On these dies, the angle of the lips slopes the other way. Further, the base-line of the schematized bird, which is tilted on most specimens, is here horizontal. The two provenanced specimens of BIIIB, 3 are from Cimiez

[16] Again, I am indebted to Miss Pirie for a photograph.

FIG.   Cimiez   hoard. BIIIB, 3.

and Southampton. Putting style and provenance together, it seems highly likely that they are clever copies of the York type, correct in all details except the lips, and made perhaps on the Continent, from where one of the finds reached Hamwic.

BIIIB, 8 lacks the groups of three pellets on the reverse, and the bird is a clumsy imitation. Although the angle of nose-to-lips is acceptable,

FIG.   BIIIB, 8   and   Sheffield area.

there are two fine lines running back from the pellets to define the lips more fully; and the line of the nose is continued in front of part of the diadem. Rigold records two reverse dies, with specimens from the Dutch national collection and from Utrecht. Again, a continental origin seems a distinct possibility.

There are finds from the English midlands, too, which are generally similar. A coin from Sharnbrook, Bedfordshire,[17] has lips sloping the wrong way, and omits the groups of three pellets on the reverse and also the pellet at the top of the cross. The bird is a good if saucy copy, but the line is broken near the tail. A find from Shenley, Milton Keynes, is obviously imitative.

FIG.   Shenley

Other problematic specimens lack the groups of three pellets on the reverse. The finds from Whitby[18] and Repton[19] fall into this category.

[17] M. A. S. Blackburn and M. J. Bonser, 'Single finds of Anglo-Saxon and Norman coins – 3', *BNJ* 56 (1986), pp.64-101, no.125.

[18] Illustrated in *BNJ* 47 (1977), pl.2, 19.
[19] ibid., pl.2, 21.

The Whitby coin is from a characteristically soft or blurred obverse die, reminiscent of the very best class of (presumably) continental imitations described above.

The Norwich (Fishergate) find is certainly imitative, and is apparently plated. No dotted border is visible on the obverse.

The evidence of style and provenance in combination is that Type 85 was extensively copied, no doubt in more than one locality. There is a Northumbrian nucleus of finds which are consistent in style and detail. The residue of the type does not seem sufficiently uniform in style to represent a later phase of work at the York mint; and its distribution is very different, being heavily continental and southern. One would guess, therefore, that in the context of the Frisian trade with Northumbria, Type 85 was carried down the east coast (e.g. to Reculver) and to the Rhine mouths area, where it was of course counterfeited. From there, coins both genuine and false may have been carried back to England (e.g. to Hamwic).

The scatter of finds in the midlands, which prompted the 1966 attribution to Mercia, is now balanced by the more northerly finds. Even if one lumps together coins in all styles, a regional matrix analysis (below) points decisively towards Northumbria rather than Mercia as the home of Series J. Coins could have reached the midlands either overland from Humberside, or from the south-east, or from Hamwic. The small numbers of finds available, and the uncertainties of the stylistic analysis, make it difficult for the time being to press the interpretation of Type 85 much further.

II

Few weights are recorded for specimens of Type 85 in the best northern style. The average seems to be roughly 1.0g, but the two (early? – or well preserved?) coins from Garton-on-the-Wolds weigh 1.10 and 1.13g.[20]

Interpretation of the type's metal contents depends upon comparisons with Type 37 (of which more specimens have been analysed). BIIIB, 1 has been shown by EPMA[21] to be 89 per cent 'silver', with 1.6 per cent

[20] Rigold, loc.cit., at p.49.
[21] Analyses by Dr. J. P. Northover.

tin and 0.5 per cent zinc. A coin in the National Museum of Wales (E.030) is 81 per cent 'silver', with 2.5 per cent tin and 2.0 per cent zinc. Hamwic 92, which is from the same obverse die as BIIIB, 4, is only 49 per cent 'silver'. There is no good reason to believe that the coin is plated, [22] nor to doubt the substantially higher tin and zinc contents (2.3 and 2.5 per cent respectively, which should be discounted against the higher copper contents). Hamwic 94 was found to be plated; and so is an imitation catalogued below (cf.BIIIB, 8) which gave EPMA measurements of 43 per cent on the surface, and 0 per cent 'silver' in the core.[23] The Winteringham coin was found by XRF to be plated (Sc.1).[24] The Repton find appeared from inspection to be base.[25]

There is thus only limited evidence (i.e. two analyses) to establish that the official series was of good silver. One need not doubt, however, that if the appropriate specimens could be analysed, many of them would prove to be 90 per cent 'silver' or better. Type 37 was of silver of that quality (and it also used a 50/50 alloy).

Whether Types 85 and 37 were successive or concurrent issues, and whether there were debasements and restorations of the alloy standard are arguments which interact. Unfortunately neither is secure enough to provide proof for the other. The most we can say is that it seems that there are official coins of Type 85 (e.g. Hamwic 92) which contain only *c*.50 per cent silver, and that this is likely to have been a deliberately adopted half-and-half alloy. If so (and the analytical evidence is, obviously, slender), the concurrent issue of Type 85 and 37 is a more plausible interpretation than two separate debasements.

III

Theories of the derivation of one sceatta type from another, by degeneration or by the duplication of elements of the design, are out of favour. Too many facile explanations have been offered in the past, and relative chronologies have been built on speculative arguments in isolation from any hoard evidence. Type 37, in particular, has attracted more than its share of uncritical interpretation in the context of a reliance on the apparent affiliation of types, by writers from Keary onwards.

A possible prototype for the two facing heads of the obverse has been

[22] See the note under Hamwic 94.

[23] Earlier XRF analysis of this coin (Ca.2, in Metcalf, Merrick, and Hamblin, 1968) failed to recognize that it was plated, although the surface was noted as being very inhomogenous.

[24] ibid., p.41 (not illustrated).

[25] D. M. Metcalf, in *Anglo-Saxon Monetary History*, ed. M. A. S. Blackburn, Leicester, 1986, pp.124-6.

found in a scarce Celtic coin, perhaps minted in Kent.[26] There is a Merovingian parallel, in an equally scarce coin attributed to Savonnières and showing the facing heads of St. Gervase and St. Protase. It is arguable that the French coin was copied from Type 37, which is earlier in date. Prototypes in Merovingian or Visigothic gold coinage have also been mentioned.

The derivation of the reverse type, a whorl of four birds around a cross, has been discussed at length by Morehart, [27] who has found sources of inspiration for the die-cutter in ornamental metal-work.

IV

Type 37, which is at least as plentiful as Type 85, [28] is less amenable to stylistic analysis. Two specimens in the Garton-on-the-Wolds grave-find and one in the York (Fishergate) hoard provide a starting-point from which to judge such small variations of style and detail as there are. The

lips-to-nose angle conforms with Type 85. One can also look at the angle between the two noses, which may be as much as 75°, but is more often 45° or less. The inclusion of ears raises doubts. The treatment of the diadems and the 'roots' of the hair is diagnostic, and so is the alignment of the central cross in relation to the birds' bodies. *SCBI Hunterian* 82 is from an exceptionally careful obverse die, on which the diadem is made up from two rows of what are almost grains rather than pellets – as on the

[26] L. Sellwood and D. M. Metcalf, 'A Celtic silver coin of previously unpublished type from St. Nicholas at Wade, Thanet: the prototype for Anglo-Saxon sceattas of *BMC* Type 37?', *BNJ* 56 (1986), pp.181f.

[27] M. Morehart, 'Some dangers of dating sceattas by typological sequences', *BNJ* 39 (1970), pp.1-5.

[28] There is a corpus, which could now be considerably extended, in *Cunobelin* 12 (1966), at pp.31f.

most careful examples of Type 85. The experimental character of the die is further suggested by an extra pellet in the base of the obverse cross. There is a die-duplicate of the Glasgow coin in the Dutch national collection, ex Marie de Man and presumed to be from Domburg.[29]

Copies of varying quality are to be found. A coin like Lockett 251d,[30] with lateral reversal of the whorl, is a blatant imitation. Cimiez 329 (Le Gentilhomme 63) is not much better: note the large eyes and rounded modelling of the faces, and the fact that the reverse cross is out of alignment with the birds' bodies. A good many more coins are perhaps deceptive imitations – the equivalents of BIIIB, 3 or 8. One example catalogued below has 'hair' springing from the eyebrows and curving in front of the diadem.

Weights and silver contents, in conjunction with style, form some sort of basis for judgements on authenticity, but a larger corpus is needed. The Garton-on-the-Wolds coins weigh c.1.10 and c.1.07g.[31] Other well-preserved specimens weigh 1.04 to 1.07g, and if a reliable comparison could be made, it seems that the type would prove fully as heavy as Type 85.

Type 37 is obviously from the same mint as Type 85, and has a similar sprawling distribution throughout England and on the Continent. What is of interest is to know how many of the (numerous) finds from England south of the Humber are imitative, as the answer will influence one's judgement on York vs. Mercia as the mint-place. Midlands and southerly provenances include Banbury (plated imitation),[32] Chislehampton, Oxon.,[33] Sharnbrook, Beds.,[34] Shenley, Bucks. (plated), Cambridge district, Woodbridge ('plated'), Barham, Suffolk, Hamwic (plated), and Pyecombe, Sussex. There are relatively few finds from north of Humber

---

[29] Hill photo HPK 389.

[30] British Numismatic Society photographic record (negatives kept at British Museum).

[31] Rigold, loc.cit., at p.49.

[32] See *BNJ* 46 (1976), at p.7.

[33] Shown in Ashmolean Museum, April 1990.

[34] Blackburn and Bonser, 'Single finds – 3', no.126.

against which to assess them. Two from Cottam, near Sledmere, on the Yorkshire Wolds, are in any case quite diverse in style.

V

No fewer than nine specimens of Type 37 have been analysed, mostly by EPMA. The best specimens contain 90-92 per cent silver, with 1-1.5 per cent tin and 0.2-0.5 per cent zinc. One of the coins catalogued below contains only 78.5 per cent silver, with 2 per cent tin. The Caister-by-Yarmouth find (on which the lips are almost horizontal) contained 60 per cent silver, again with 2 per cent tin. It would be speculative to speak of declining silver contents, when stylistic analysis makes such a limited contribution towards establishing a sequence of dies.

The Winteringham find was analysed only semi-quantitatively by XRF, but apparently contained c.10 per cent zinc, with c.70 per cent silver.[35] The figure for zinc is almost certainly somewhat too high, as it implies an impossibly high-zinc brass as the alloying material. The coin may have suffered severe leaching. The use of brass in the sceatta series is extremely unusual.

Hamwic 94 (in a rather fat style of die-cutting) turned out to be plated on a copper core. The cladding gave a reading of 44 per cent silver, with 3.4 per cent tin. The Banbury find, too, is plated, with very variable surface silver readings of between 10 and 80 per cent. Substantial amounts of mercury were detected, showing that the plating was achieved by the amalgam process.

A coin in Cardiff (E 012) was found to be only 13.5 per cent silver, with the unusually large amounts of 7.6 per cent tin, and 1.8 per cent zinc.[36]

Plated coins in Series J should probably be deemed to be counterfeits until proved genuine. It is curious, however, that there should have been such a spate of them – a higher proportion, it would seem, than in any other sceatta series.

[35] Metcalf, Merrick and Hamblin, 1968, Sc.2, at p.42.

[36] EPMA by Dr. Northover.

VI

Type 60 seems to be known from only two specimens.[37] It is accordingly difficult to think of it as a substantive type. On the other hand its originality of design and its artistic talent are hardly what one would have expected from an opportunist counterfeiter: why produce a novel design, on which suspicion is bound to fall? Perhaps it was an abortive official issue – a new type that was launched to replace Type 85, but which failed for lack of demand for the moneyers' services. Alternatively, could it have been an experimental reverse design preceding Type 85, that was quickly replaced by the bird on cross? That, at least, sounds unlikely, both because Type 85 was based on Series B, and because the inspiration for Type 60 would seem to have been the wolf-headed torc of Series K, Type 32a (which was present alongside Types 85 and 37 in the Garton-on-the-Wolds find).

The two specimens of Type 60 are from very similar but different dies. *SCBI Hunterian* 100 weighs 0.74g, and BM, Barnett 259 weighs 0.97g. Neither is provenanced.

The obverse is exactly as Type 85. The lips-to-nose angle is appropriate, and the style is very acceptable. But as Type 85 includes such deceptive imitations, one ought to look into any die-similarities with Type 85 as carefully as possible. Rigold comments that both obverses are similar to his BIIIc, 2. There are even closer comparanda, e.g. two coins in Leeuwarden and Brussels discussed above, which seem to be by the same hand.

One should reserve judgement, and perhaps hope that a die-link between Types 60 and 85 will turn up. Provisionally, its status seems doubtful, in spite of the quality of its workmanship.

The reverse of Type 60 is imitated on a double-reverse 'mule', *TMP* 1895, pl.2, 26.

---

[37] *SCBI Hunterian* 100 and BM, Barnett bequest (illustrated by Rigold, 1960-1, pl.4).

FIG. *TMP* 1895, pl.2, 26.

VII

Type 72 is known from a dozen specimens, with few if any die-links. They include four finds from Domburg, two in the Brussels cabinet, one in Paris,[38] one from Richborough,[39] one from the Swindon area, and one from Lakenheath, Suffolk.[40] No finds have been recorded from the midlands or the north of England. The four finds from Domburg should be compared with seven of Type 37. The question obviously arises whether Type 72 has anything to do with York, or whether it is not merely a Low Countries imitative type which borrows the obverse of Type 37. The artistic quality of the dies is certainly not impressive in comparison with the rest of Series J.

FIG. Brussels cabinet.

The reverse type, of the walking bird looking over its shoulder, is distinctive and is parallelled in the rare 'archer' type, which is almost certainly English,[41] and which was presumably intended to be seen in relation to other 'pecking bird' types. Its region of origin is uncertain, and it is in any case so scarce that it was not an obvious design to imitate.

FIG. The reverse type in the rare 'archer' style.

[38] Hill photographs.
[39] P. V. Hill, in *NC* 1953, pl.7, 25.
[40] Coin Register 1990, no.187 (Swindon). No photograph of the Lakenheath find was available.
[41] See under Series L.

FIG. Richborough, Cardiff E 013.

The inferior modelling of the two facing heads may best be studied by comparing two well-struck and well-preserved specimens, namely the Richborough find and Lockett 252 (now Cardiff E 013). There is no convincing continuity of style with Type 37. Indeed, one would be more inclined to interpret any stylistically similar specimens of Type 37 (e.g. Lockett 251e) as being imitations probably from the same stable as Type 72.

The bird's feet and tail are its most distinctive features. The three drooping tail feathers are derived ultimately from Type 85, of course, but proximately they are more likely to have been copied from Series J, Type 36, as are the bird's feet. On purely art-historical grounds one would hesitate to say in which direction the borrowing went. Type 36, however, is certainly a substantive English type, which is unlikely to have imitated a Low Countries imitation. If, as argued below, Type 36 belongs to York, it may be that Type 72 used the two facing heads motif at a date when the issue of Type 37 had already ceased.

FIG. Paris.

On one of the Brussels specimens of Type 72 the bird appears to be crested, although the coin's poor condition makes it difficult to be certain.[42]

Weights are variable: the Richborough coin weighs 1.17g. Others, probably after some loss of weight by leaching, are only 0.7-0.9g.

The Cardiff coin, weighing 0.69g, is plated. EPMA shows a base metal core, with surface readings of 58 per cent Ag + Au, and 8 per cent lead. Other specimens look base.

VIII

Type 84 is described as having *obv.*, two facing heads and *rev.*, animal-headed torc. It is known only from one specimen, unillustrated, which

[42] Hill photo 35.

cannot now be traced.[43] The coin may be an imitation 'muling' Types 37 and 32a, but it is also very possible that it is a misread specimen, in poor condition, of Type 72.

IX

A coin found at Domburg[44] with *obv.*, two facing heads and *rev.*, RM ligate with a titulus above the M, and pellets scattered in the field is related to other coins reading RM, which have been provisionally

attributed to Rheims.[45] Whether it was from the same mint as the other RM coins, or from the Low Countries, is difficult to judge. There is no reason to suppose that it is English. The angle of lips to nose, and the quality of the obverse generally, show that so far as Series J is concerned it is imitative.

X

From Dankirke near Ribe in Jutland there are two separate finds, among a dozen coins of the seventh and eighth centuries, which have been published as being of Types 85 and 37.[46] The former is in fact a Type 36/85 mule like that from Repton, and is discussed in another section. The latter is of poor quality and is perhaps a Low Countries imitation, reminiscent of Type 72.

SCBI Copenhagen 49 and 50 are described as 'Frisian versions of Type 37'. The coins are from the Thomsen collection, but are otherwise unprovenanced. Their affiliation to Type 37 is tenuous.

XI

A survey of Series J type by type shows that Types 85 and 37 are substantive English types (as is Type 36 – see below). All the other

[43] Carlyon-Britton sale catalogue, lot 169c.

[44] P. O. Van der Chijs, *De munten der frankische- en duitsch-nederlandsche Vorsten*, vol.9, 1866, pl.6, 83.

[45] *MEC* vol.1, 604-5, with a note at p.633.

[46] K. Bendixen, 'The first Merovingian coin-treasure from Denmark', *Mediaeval Scandinavia* 7 (1974), pp.85-101 (where the coins are illustrated).

TABLE 3. *Proportions of various categories of sceattas in selected regions (Sources: for Domburg, Op den Velde, de Boone, and Pol, 1984; for Hamwic, Andrews, 1988; for other regions, an up-dating of Rigold and Metcalf's check-list, 1984.)*

All figures are %

	Domburg	Hamwic	Kent + London	East/Middle Anglia	Midlands/upper Thames	Northern England	York/E.Riding
Primary	3	2	24	11	16	5	6
Intermediate (D, E)	73	17	22	23	25	22	16
Other continental	18	9	1	0	5	1	1
J	2	4	4	4	7	5	5
Other secondary	2	67	49	61	47	14	5
Y	0	1	0	0	0	53	67
	100	100	100	100	100	100	100
Sample size	935	125	152	256	81	199	119

Ratios derived from the percentages above.

J (Other secondary = 100)	100	6	8	7	15	36	100
J (D, E = 100)	3	24	18	17	28	23	40

related types are continental, or extremely scarce, or of questionable status. An attribution of Types 85 and 37 to York rather than to a mint in the midlands or elsewhere seems to depend rather heavily on the results of stylistic analysis, and on the rejection of a surprisingly high proportion of the known specimens of Type 85 as imitative. If however we compare the relative plentifulness of Series J in selected regions, against other secondary types, a better assessment becomes possible.

The table below is based on all coins of Series J, including imitations. The Fishergate hoard and the Garton-on-the-Wolds grave-find are each scored as one find only. The numerical results will therefore understate the case for York. If it seems nevertheless that they prove it, we can say that if we were in a position to exclude imitations, the case would be proved by an even wider margin.

The selected regions include northern England, and, counting the same finds over again, a smaller part of it, namely York and the (former) East Riding.

The table shows that Series J as a whole accounts for a slightly larger proportion of all sceatta finds in the midlands/upper Thames region and in the north (5-7 per cent) than in eastern or southern England (4 per cent). It is actually more plentiful in the midlands (7 per cent) than in the north (5 per cent) or even (within the northern region) in York itself and the East Riding (6 per cent). Thus far, a numerical analysis is inconclusive as regards a choice between York and the midlands, although favouring the midlands, and does not help us to escape from the difficulties of deciding where to draw the line between official coins and copies.

When we look, however, at the ratio of Series J to all other English types of the secondary phase (other than Y), a much stronger contrast emerges: 6-8 per cent in southern England, 15 per cent in the midlands, 36 per cent in the north, 100 per cent in York itself and the East Riding. The point about that set of figures is that if Series J had been minted somewhere south of the Humber and had been carried to Northumbria, along with other southern secondary types, one would not have expected it to exceed, in the north, the ratio that it achieved in its region of origin – and certainly not to exceed it as spectacularly as it does.

The dating of the various secondary series could provide a partial explanation. As Series Y was a controlled currency which entailed the reminting of all other types that arrived in York, then any sceattas minted after $c.740$ or arriving after $c.740$ will be excluded, and J (which is from the 720s or thereabouts) will enjoy an advantage in the statistics. So many other series were being minted well before $c.740$, however, that differences of date alone cannot plausibly account for the whole of the contrast in the ratios.

If J were from the midlands it might have reached the north in greater quantities than other secondary types simply because its region of origin was closer to the Humber. That assumes that inflows into the currency of the north were mainly by land routes from the midlands rather than by sea up the east coast. It is logically a possibility, but common sense says that it has little to recommend it as a hypothesis.

Thus, the occurrence of Series J in comparison with other secondary types strongly suggests that it belongs in Northumbria. Its mint-place is likely to have been a major wic, and York is the obvious candidate.

Finally, one ought just to add that a second set of ratios can be calculated (J measured against D and E), which serves to rule out a

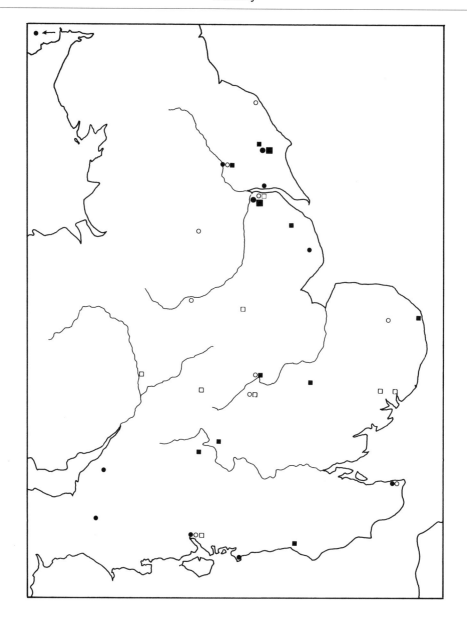

MAP. Single finds of Types 85 and 37 (round and square symbols respectively). Coins that are certainly or probably imitative are shown by open symbols. (But note that the canon of coins in acceptable style is decided partly on the basis of northerly provenances — p.346 above.)

Frisian origin for J. The ratio, which is anything from 17 to 28 in the English regions, and 40 in York and the East Riding, is only 3 per cent at Domburg – where several of the specimens of J counted in the total are undoubtedly imitative. Had J been imported from the Low Countries to England, one cannot imagine any circumstances in which it could have been from five to ten times as plentiful as in its region of origin, compared with the porcupines and Frisian runic sceattas (of slightly earlier date) which were the dominant types in the area of the Rhine mouths.

XII

Type 36 is known from nine or ten specimens. No die-duplication has been found. On the obverse the head of Type 85 is modified to a bust. Three additions are made to the earlier design, with great regularity: a cross is added in front of the face; there are two straight wreath ties; and the drapery of the bust is indicated by eight or nine lines in a regular pattern. The reverse is an untidy composition of a walking bird, with a cross in front of it, and another smaller bird above and to the left. There are half-a-dozen English finds, including one from the Fishergate excavations at York, but none from Domburg or elsewhere on the Continent. As it is a sensible adage that mints should not be multiplied unnecessarily, need we hesitate in attributing Type 36 to York?

FIG. York (Fishergate) and Hamwic finds.

The list of provenances may seem a strange basis for such an attribution: York (Fishergate),[47] Scunthorpe and also Sleaford, Lincs,[48] North Elmham, Norfolk,[49] Barham, Suffolk,[50] and two separate finds from Hamwic.[51] If we calculate ratios, however, as in the preceding table, for Type 36 as a percentage of secondary sceattas other than Series J, the northern region and especially York have the highest figures. This does

[47] I am indebted to Miss Pirie for a photograph of the find.

[48] Both catalogued below.

[49] Misidentified as Type 85 var in both editions of the check-list, but illustrated in *BNJ* 47 (1977), pl.2,

20, and obviously Type 36!

[50] Not seen by the writer.

[51] Hamwic 95, and a new find from the Six Dials site, 1986, SOU 258. Weight, 1.02g.

not amount to any more than saying that, although there is only one find of the type from York, even one of a scarce type, among a very small total of secondary sceattas, is more than one would have expected had it been imported into Northumbria from south of the Humber. The argument from regional ratios rests entirely on that one coin; before the Fishergate excavations brought it to light in 1986 – indeed, before the Sleaford find of 1988 – how could one have ventured to argue that the type was Northumbrian? Until the mid-1970s, North Elmham was the only provenance.

FIG. North Elmham find (plated, ?imitative).

An alternative hypothesis might be that the type is from another mint, presumably somewhere in the north-east. The Sleaford and Scunthorpe finds and the Repton imitation are the only basis for such an idea. When a few more finds have accumulated, the uncertainty should be resolved.

Several of the coins are from very similar but not identical dies: the issue is stylistically compact. On the more careful dies the bird's legs are jointed. Each foot is shown by two concentric curves, making a clumsy effect. The Fishergate coin has more naturalistic feet, reminiscent of the 'plumed bird' porcupines. Perhaps it is an early variant. The North Elmham coin appears to have a hand holding the cross.[52]

FIG. *SCBI Hunterian* 78

SCBI Hunterian 78 is very probably an imitation, and 79 may also be, as it is small and light. Neither of these is provenanced.

BMC 164, catalogued there as Type 36, is certainly imitative, being

part of an eclectic group which 'mules' Type 36/85 (e.g. a find from Repton) and copies Type 36 before settling down to imitate Series G. It is discussed elsewhere.

[52] See below: its alloy helps to dismiss it as imitative.

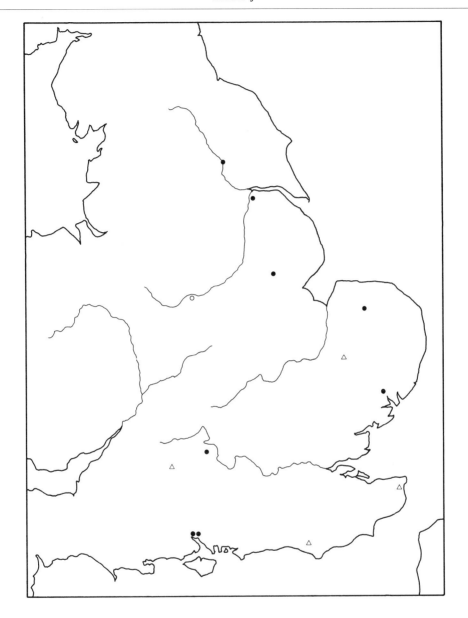

MAP. Single finds of Type 36 (round symbols) and of Type 72 (triangles).

We are fortunate in having three EPMA analyses of Type 36.[53] Hamwic 95 is 67 per cent 'silver', with 4 per cent tin and 1 per cent zinc. The Sleaford find is 59 per cent 'silver', with 3 per cent tin and 0.4 per cent zinc. The North Elmham find is plated, on a copper core. Two separate readings on the surface showed 21 and 38 per cent 'silver' respectively. Armed with that knowledge, one may venture to find fault with the style of the coin: its small dies; the angle of the cross, the skewed position of the drapery; the absence or sketchy treatment of the smaller bird.

The official coins may have been aiming at a standard of about two-thirds silver.

There is no sign that Type 36 is one of a pair of types. Perhaps Type 37 could have continued alongside it. The Caister find, for example, is of similar alloy.

XIII

If Types 85 and 37 were successive, there need be very little doubt that Type 85 came first, because it is a straightforward copy of Type B. The Hallum hoard contained two specimens of Type 85 and none of 37, but that is poor evidence that its concealment antedates Type 37: it might be by chance when only two coins are in question.

The arguments which suggest that Types 85 and 37 were concurrent rather than successive are as follows:

1. Type BIIIc apparently borrows elements from each, namely the long cross pommee from Type 85 (not otherwise used in Series B) and the stylized bird from Type 37. It is artistically unlikely that the borrowing of the bird motif is in the other direction. If this observation is correct, the introduction of BIIIc must be dated after the introduction of Type 37. That is a reason for dating Type 37 as soon as possible after the introduction of Type 85.

BIIIA is present in the Aston Rowant hoard, and one would prefer to keep BIIIc as close to it, and as early in date, as possible.

2. Types 85 and 37 occur together in the York (Fishergate) hoard and the Garton-on-the-Wolds grave-find, and reportedly also in the Föhr hoard from the coasts of Jutland. All three finds could of course have been concealed during the currency of Type 37 if it were successive: the odds are not very long against three hoards clustering in date by chance.

All four Garton coins, more interestingly, are of good weight and

---

[53] By Dr. J. P. Northover.

careful style, and those of Type 85 are in fresh condition. Of these three points, only the style is of consequence. Individual weights varied, and they can be seriously affected by leaching and corrosion. And coins are sometimes found in fresh condition even if they were old when they were hoarded.

3. The evidence of metal contents is inconclusive. If there are good silver and debased specimens of both types, that might be because the introduction of Type 37 was accompanied by the restoration of a good silver standard. It would be a natural reading of the evidence, however, to see the types declining in parallel, especially as there is (some) evidence for a half-silver standard in both types. Hamwic 92, with 49 per cent 'silver', is the crucial specimen in Type 85. There is ample evidence that Type 37 was initially *c*.90 per cent silver, and the restoration hypothesis is rather strained.

Tin and zinc contents seem to be much the same for both types.

4. Fine graining of the diadem occurs in Type 37 as well as 85. Here, *SCBI Hunterian* 82 is the crucial specimen. Again, such evidence is logically inconclusive, as the detail could very easily have been copied at a later date. Nevertheless, the natural reading of the evidence is that the graining is from a single phase of careful workmanship early in the issue of Series J.

5. Given that Series J belongs to York, and that Type 37 is in any case very close in date to Type 85, the typological argument may be judged to be at least as persuasive as 2, 3, or 4. If the single head of Type 85 was meant to represent the king (and Aldfrith had minted in Northumbria), the two heads would surely have been taken to refer to two persons. The design may have been suggested by a Celtic coin or some other model, but that does not preclude its having a contemporary relevance. The two

heads are unlikely to have been merely a die-cutter's *jeu d'esprit,* isolated from any political context. Coinage was not apolitical.

Twenty years later there was a dual series of coins which without any doubt were struck respectively for the king and jointly for the king and the archbishop. What could be more obvious than the possibility that Series J reflects an earlier but similar sharing?

None of the five arguments is certain. To remove all doubt about the concurrent issue of the coins, one would need a sizeable hoard of the two types, from part-way through their issue, in which less than the full range of dies was represented, for both types. Archaeological excavation of superbly stratified contexts, rich in coins, could in principle yield the same certainty, but it is a pipe dream.

Even if the concurrent issue of the coins were proved, the significance of the designs would remain a matter for historical judgement.

XIV

It always was a weakness of the hypothesis of an upper Thames origin for Series J that a plentiful coinage should have been minted other than at a coastal wic. Also, although one could envisage coinage being carried northwards through Mercia and across the Humber, and southwards from the upper Thames to Hamwic, the strong representation of J at Domburg was more difficult to account for if it originated at an inland mint. An attribution to York escapes those difficulties. Like Lincoln, York was accessible to east-coast shipping. The Fishergate site, in the southern suburbium, has yielded porcupines, Frisian runics, the odd East Anglian coin, and a specimen of Series G, as well as Series J – an assemblage beginning, apparently, in the 710s.

The stylistic link with Series U, Type 23b must now be seen as illusory. As new finds have accumulated, the distribution patterns for Series J and Type 23b have diverged, and are now clearly very different from each other.

Series J unexpectedly fills the gap between the Northumbrian coinages of Aldfrith and Eadberht. In fabric it is very unlike Aldfrith's coins. Of more historical interest than the difference in fabric is that Series J was diffused so much more widely. One of Aldfrith's coins, it is true, reached Hamwic (via Frisia?), and two others have recently been reported from Middle Anglia, but the earlier issue had an essentially very compact area of use in Yorkshire and Lincolnshire. It seems, therefore, that trading contacts between Northumbria and the Frisians developed with dramatic speed in the 710s and 720s. Series Y thereafter reverts to a compact distribution. Although there are technical reasons for the virtual absence of other types in Northumbria during the currency of Series Y, the argument does not apply in reverse: there is no reason to think, for example, that such coins are absent at Domburg because of a policy of reminting foreign sceattas there.

Outflows of money from Northumbria during the currency of Series J might be construed either as suggesting a balance-of-payments deficit, or three-cornered trade with deficits in one direction and surpluses in another. This is not the place to attempt a detailed evaluation of Series J in terms of its evidence for monetary history. The point that should be made here is that in terms of the classification of the coins, and in particular in distinguishing imitations, we really have no way of knowing what sort of regional trading patterns and balance-of-payments patterns Northumbria sustained, and therefore no way of knowing what sort of distribution for Series J is to be expected. All we can be sure about is that it was worth-while to the Frisian merchants and navigators to visit York – and that the diffusion of coinage from York allows us to recover information of a more comprehensive and balanced character, as regards regional patterns, than that derived from written sources.

DISTINGUISHING THE COINS OF THE KENTISH AND LONDON MINTS

In the ninth century Canterbury and London were leading mint-towns, accounting for an estimated 41 and 16 per cent respectively of the coinage minted south of the Humber (East Anglia taking 18 per cent).[1] Their coins were used throughout southern England, both north and south of the Thames, and were carried over long distances, to be lost as far afield as the Cotswolds and beyond. The extent of their respective circulation-areas was more or less the same. If the coins were not readily attributable to their mints, it would not be obvious from a glance at the map of single finds that their distribution patterns were significantly different. If we tabulate the proportions of coins of the two mint-places found north and south of the Thames, however, a contrast becomes clear. The question then arises whether the patterns of monetary circulation in the first half of the eighth century were analogous. Rigold suspected that there were major mints producing sceattas of the secondary phase in east Kent and London, and he identified two series by the mnemonics K and L. Sceattas attributed to these two series made up 5.8 and 6.2 per cent respectively of all the finds from the 1980s.[2] As a proportion of southumbrian secondary sceattas the figures would be closer to 15 and 16 per cent: the Kentish mint was less prominent than it became in the ninth century.

Although it might seem obvious that Canterbury was the mint-place in eighth-century east Kent, as it was in the ninth and later centuries, one ought to keep an open mind. It is virtually certain that in eighth-century Wessex the mint of Series H was at Hamwic, rather than at Winchester, only a few miles away. Arrangements may have been similar in east Kent, where there is some reason to suspect that the mint of Series K was on

---

[1] D. M. Metcalf, 'The economy of ninth-century England south of the Humber: monetary evidence', forthcoming (paper read at a seminar in Cambridge, 11-13 April 1988).

[2] Figures from Table 1 above.

368

MAPS. Finds of ninth-century pennies of the Canterbury and London mints (left and right respectively).

the Wantsum Channel. The channel is now silted up, and Thanet is no longer by any stretch an island; but in early medieval times ships could sail from the River Stour to the River Wantsum (at least at high tide), and thus avoid a detour around the North Foreland. The obvious guess is that the minting of coins was carried on at Sarre, or Sandwich – or both. There is reason to think that Sandwich was of commercial importance in the time of Offa, and perhaps earlier. Finds from Sarre go back to the seventh century. From Richborough, too, there are early finds. The greatest number of sceattas come from Reculver and its vicinity on the north coast of Kent, but that may reflect coastal erosion (cf. Domburg) rather than being a true measure of Reculver's commercial importance. The shore-fort had, in any case, become the site of a minster church in 669, and it seems an unlikely choice for a mint-place.

It may be that there were two mints in east Kent. The early issues of Series K seem to be heavily concentrated among the finds at Reculver, but there are small hints that other types, specifically Series O, were similarly prominent in places towards the southern end of the Wantsum Channel. The geographical pattern of finds from further afield in southern England cannot be expected, of course, to contribute to a choice between Canterbury, Sarre, Sandwich, and Reculver as the chief Kentish mint-place.

If we make a general map of finds of Series K and L in the context of all finds from southern England, it is apparent that, like the ninth-century pennies, both series have a very widespread and overlapping distribution. Series K, however, is relatively more plentiful south of the Thames, and Series L north of the Thames. Unfortunately, the problem of attribution is not quite as simple as that. The argument that has just been set out assumes that we can identify (by legends, types, style, etc.) two coherent groups of coins, which we can then proceed to map and compare. In fact we have a medley of at least three dozen types of sceattas which are conventionally assigned to either Series K or L. For each series there is a nucleus of types which can very plausibly be attributed to east Kent or London respectively. But in addition there is a wide variety of scarce types which may show general affinities with Series K or L but which are, truth to tell, unattributable. They could belong to London or east Kent or, perhaps, Rochester, or, for all we can say, somewhere else. We do not know for a fact that minting in the south-east in the eighth century was concentrated in two or three mints, in east Kent and London. If a comparison of proportions north and south of the Thames produces evidence of a clear difference, in spite of the uncertainty of attribution of the scarce types, then we may be disposed to accept the broad conclusion. But that certainly does not validate individually the attribution of all the scarce types that are conventionally assigned to Series K or L. Within the framework of the general argument, we need to look critically at the details, to see whether any of them carry weight independently as evidence.

I

If sceattas minted in both east Kent and London were carried westwards to supply the currency in northern Wessex, the Thames valley, and the south midlands, we might expect the stray finds from the London area to include specimens from both mints. Although London coins will occasionally have been carried eastwards too, to be lost in east Kent, the

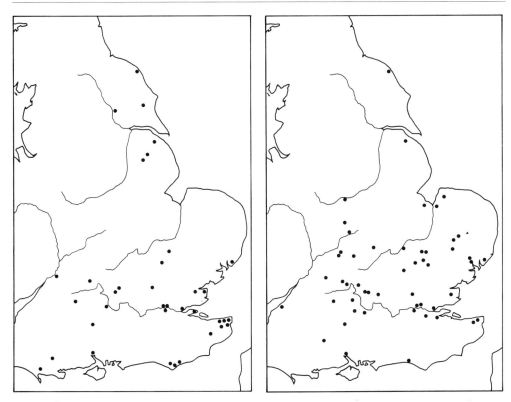

MAPS. Finds of sceattas of Series K and L (left and right respectively). The eclectic groups have been included as follows: with Series K, the 'triquetras' group; with Series L, the **C ARIP** , 'celtic cross', and 'Victory' groups.

general drift was necessarily westwards, into regions which lacked their own mint-places. The proportions among the stray finds from east Kent should therefore be of particular interest in revealing the influence of the local mint. The statistics from east Kent are encouraging: 13 finds of Series K, against only 3 of Series L. In percentage terms, that is 81 per cent K, 19 per cent L. From London there are not many relevant single finds: one of K to 3 of L. Percentages derived from such a tiny sample will be liable to change appreciably as the sample size increases. For what they are worth, the figures are 25 per cent K, 75 per cent L. We can also take into consideration the London (Thames) hoard of 1860 (with something like 3 specimens of Series K to 17 of L, counting Types 23a and 23e as L). We can look at the major sites of Tilbury (14 of K to 9 of L) and Royston (8 of K to 10 of L). For all other sites grouped together, north and south of the Thames respectively, the totals are 7 of K to 26 of

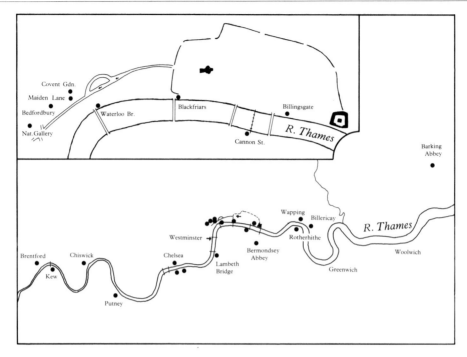

MAP. Finds from London and the Lower Thames.

L, and 15 of K to 9 of L. Altogether, the range of proportions makes sense topographically:

	%K	%L
East Kent	81	19
South of Thames, other	62	38
Tilbury	61	39
Royston	44	56
North of Thames, other	33	67
London	25	75
London hoard	15	85

These figures are more clear-cut than the corresponding figures for the London and Canterbury mints in the ninth century. In broad terms they prove satisfactorily that Series L belongs to London, and Series K to east Kent. (And they raise the interesting question whether the intervening coins of Offa, which have been divided between London and Canterbury, might not also be expected to show a contrast among finds from north and south of the Thames).

The over-all numbers of single finds, which should be a rough guide to mint-output, are sufficiently equal (61 of K, 77 of L) not to distort comparisons betwen the proportions in different places. In comparison with the ninth century, London – or, more precisely, Series L – is much more prominent. We can see from the ninth century, however, that the balance between London and Canterbury could fluctuate considerably in the short term. The London mint was especially active, for example, towards the end of the reign of Burgred.

II

A few specimens of Series K are known to be as much as c.85 per cent fine, but in general coins of Series K and L are rarely better than about 50 per cent silver, and are often only about one-third fine. Series L eventually falls to still lower levels.

The numerous varieties which seem, from their designs, style, and alloy to belong with Series K or L can be grouped into half-a-dozen clusters of types, all of which are much more variable in their motifs than the primary sceattas. There are three clusters of substantive types, and six or seven groups of scarce types.

There are, first, the 'wolf' sceattas (Type 33, Types 42var and 42, and Type 32a, which in fact conflates three distinct reverse varieties - see Fig.), and secondly the 'London' coins, some of which are actually inscribed LVNDONIA+ (Types 12-13, 15-17 – see Fig.). These two clusters of types each give the general impression of being the output of an active mint. Thirdly, the 'chalice/hawk' sceattas (Types 18, 18/20, 20, and 19 – see Fig.) link the first two clusters typologically. There are stylistic and other arguments for dividing them between London and east Kent (thus keeping the number of major mints down to two).[3] If that scheme of attribution is accepted, however, it has surprising implications of common or concerted action in mint-places belonging to different kingdoms.

These three groupings are the core of Series K and L, and they account for the bulk of the surviving specimens.

We are left with ten or more distinctive groups of well-engraved coins, each of which belong together in terms of their style and motifs, and

[3] See below.

FIG. Substantive types in Series K: Types 33, 42, and 32a.

cannot be considered as contemporary forgeries, but which are known today in very few specimens. We may be looking at only a tiny handful of coins – as few, even, as three or four, but more usually six or eight – instead of perhaps thirty to fifty as in the main groups; and several of the coins in that tiny group may well be unique examples of their 'type'. Statistical methods of die-estimation cannot usefully be applied to six or eight coins among which there are few or no duplicates. But the loss-rate of these scarce types will, so far as one can see, have been much the same as that of the main groups: they are scattered as widely, and their silver contents are similar. Their original total numbers can therefore be assessed on a *pro rata* basis from the numbers of single finds compared with those of the main groups. This argument even avoids the uncertainties of average output per die – the finds should be roughly proportional to numbers of coins in circulation. In the main groups we are far from having examples from every die that was originally used, and we must therefore accept that each of the little groups of scarce types

FIG. Substantive types in Series L: Types 12-13, 15-17.

374

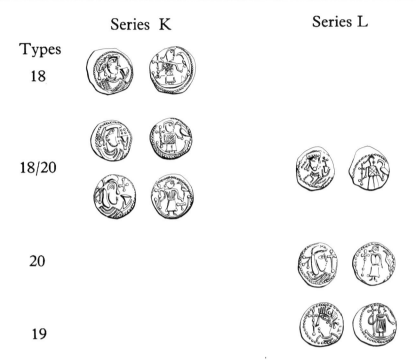

FIG. Substantive types in Series K and L: Types 18, 18/20, 20, and 19.

reflects an issue quite large enough to be interpreted as the work of a regular, if minor, workshop.

The arguments against simply amalgamating them with the issues of one or other of the major mints are, for the most part, arguments about the way die-cutters would behave. We have, in the end, to be ready to say when, as well as where, each variety was minted. In attempting to reconstruct the history of the mints of Series K and L there are considerable problems in putting all the types into a single sequence for each series. We should be reluctant to string types together in such a way as to imply that a moneyer interrupted his settled habits in order to strike quite different designs on a smaller scale.

If those designs are borrowed from other series, they create the impression of an opportunist enterprise, which is difficult to reconcile with the idea of a controlled, royal coinage. The use of two reverse types in combination is a pointer to irregular minting. It is not at all clear what status, if any, was enjoyed by moneyers who behaved in this way; nor why they bothered to produce such a wide repertoire of types. If they were striking, essentially, in the London style, should we think of them as working in London, but independently, in another part of the city? – or in some other trading settlement on the shores of the Thames estuary? The scarce groups were amalgamated with the main body of Series K and L in order to establish the contrast in find-proportions north and south of the Thames. There are too few specimens of each group to carry out the same exercise separately, except for the 'triquetras' group (below) where, by good fortune, we have enough evidence to demonstrate a south-of-Thames origin. That fits with the group's stylistic affinities with Series K. But we should renounce any hope of locating the mint-place any more closely from distributional evidence. If we pose the question whether the 'triquetras' group was struck in the same centre as Series K, or in some nearby place – if, for example, we are wondering about Canterbury, Sarre, Minster, Richborough – then we should recognize that distribution patterns in principle cannot be expected to distinguish between places lying close together, and within the general area of circulation of Series K and L. All that we can do is to describe the coins and their relationships, in a suitably neutral manner. The word 'eclectic' will suggest the combination of otherwise unrelated types.

Of the scarce groups in Series K and L, the one that is most demonstrably coherent, and that can without hesitation be described as eclectic, opens with an obverse bust with the intriguing legend C ARIP. Two (unique) types catalogued below are manifestly by the same hand, but one has a reverse which is a very accomplished imitation of the 'bird and branch' design of Series U, while the other has a distinctive reinterpretation of the curled wolf of Type 32, again certainly by the same hand as the (unique) Type 61. The C ARIP legend was then copied, presumably at the same mint, by an illiterate workman: the letter R falls apart, and the coins eventually read ꬢⱭCb, in combination with more conventional London-style reverses. The C ARIP group is described more fully and illustrated in a separate section below, as each of the scarce groups is.

A similar story is repeated by a group of coins with a distinctive reverse type consisting of a cruciform interlace pattern made up out of four triquetras, with rosettes in the angles. Reverses that are extremely close in style link obverses imitating completely different series (U and L). Again, therefore, it is appropriate to speak of an eclectic group. The 'muling' of two reverse types, and the indiscriminate borrowing, both strengthen the impression that the 'triquetras' group is out of character with, although allied to, Series K. The use of knotted wreath ties is a link, and the interlace of triquetras shows a similar design preoccupation.

Fortunately, nearly all the known specimens are provenanced, and they show a strong southerly bias, including finds from Reculver, Richborough, and Wye (Kent). A mint-place south of the Thames, and probably in Kent, is indicated.

There is one conflicting piece of evidence, namely a coin which combines a 'triquetras' reverse with a MONITASCORVM obverse – which one would have thought belonged with Series L. Its find-spot, however, (just mentioned) is Wye. Another MONITASCORVM coin is said to be from near Canterbury.

We should perhaps discern a third, and maybe a fourth eclectic group, of similar character, among the types which share a reverse type composed of a 'celtic cross' with rosettes in the angles (which is conceptually closely related to the triquetras design). The curvilinear cross has a pellet in each arm, and a pellet or rosette at the centre (unlike the Hamwic type, 39, where the cross is of the same pattern but is always empty). Otherwise, the 'celtic cross' is by its nature a fairly simple linear design which again does not lend itself to secure stylistic analysis in the way that a bust or even a standing figure does. It is the third group of scarce types to include a 'bird and branch' reverse – a prototype that is usually c.80 per cent fine. One begins to suspect a chronological pattern in the origin of a number of eclectic groups.

There is perhaps another clue to chronology in the choice of the wolf-worm of Type 32a as a prototype – for example in a small but varied group of K/R mules.

There is yet another tiny group of distinctive coins, which take up the theme of rosettes again, by adding two or three in the empty spaces of the *obverse* field. This is combined with either a copy of the wolf-worm of Type 32a, or a standing figure with two crosses. There are too few specimens to be sure, but this could well be the beginnings of another eclectic group. Alternatively, it could be part of some larger group, e.g. a continuation, without legend, of the C ARIP group, although the reasons for thinking so could hardly be more slender. One does not want to multiply separate groups of coins more than is necessary. In practice, however, it is better to describe the cognate specimens separately, while recognizing that two pieces of the puzzle may later be seen to fit together.

Five or six intriguing coins are now known with the inscription MONITASCORVM or (in one case) just SCORVM. They are disparate in style, but are presumably from the same mint-place. One of these coins also reads DELVNDONIA.

As has already been mentioned, it is an awkwardness that one of the

377

MONITASCORVM coins should have a 'triquetras' reverse. Pending examination, it seems unlikely that it will link the two groups together as the *œuvre* of a single workshop.

Another group of only four or five coins introduces the distinctive type of a kneeling archer. It uses yet another version of the pecking bird as its 'badge', in association with a variety of obverse types.

Finally, one may mention the rare 'Victory' group, *BMC* Type 22 etc. Three different types are known, in eight or nine specimens, including only one pair of die-duplicates. The coins can be arranged into two stylistic groups, with nothing in common other than the motif of a facing winged figure. In one group, a Roman coin type showing a winged Victory with wreath has been copied, the wing being reinterpreted as a long banner on a standard. The other style has already been included in the 'triquetras' group (above). It seems that two mints produced 'Victory' types, but whether they did so concurrently to mark some particular occasion is unknown.

For the purposes of numerical analysis, the 'triquetras' coins have been treated as belonging with Series K, and the C ARIP, 'celtic cross', and most of the 'Victory' coins as part of Series L. Their mint-places, however, remain extremely conjectural.

III

The evidence of style complicates our understanding of Series K and L. Rigold's definition of the two series as consisting of certain types already took style into account in a general way, along with typology and hoard-evidence: the grouping of Types 33, 42, and 32a into Series K, and 12-13, 15-17 into Series L already involved a judgement that the styles in each group were at least compatible or related. This was a numismatist's working judgement, not formulated in any detail, but natural to an experienced eye. There is, in fact, a very simple criterion to distinguish the styles of Series K and L. In the former, the two ties of the diadem or wreath are wrapped together into a large ornamental knot, whereas in the latter they are straight. (The 'triquetras' coins, just referred to, have knotted wreath-ties).

More laborious studies have identified three styles which run through the various types in Series K. These recognizable portrait styles were originally labelled 'A-B', 'C-D', and 'E-F'.[4] Three main styles have again

---

[4] D. M. Metcalf and D. R. Walker, 'The "wolf" sceattas', *BNJ* 36 (1967), 11-28. See Fig.2. On pl.7 the enlarged photographs are wrongly labelled.

been identified in Series L. In 1976 they were labelled 'London', 'Badsey', and 'Hunterian'.[5] It was again readily demonstrable that a single style ran through a number of different types, allowing one to recognize the die-cutter's hand and to reconstruct the output of a particular workshop.

Thus far there are no conceptual problems: the human reality underlying the styles could be imagined as three separate workshops minting coins in London, and another three in east Kent – a situation which in the ninth century might be more visible in terms of coins signed by moneyers. The evidence of the sceattas, however, appears to be of separate die-cutting, whereas the penny moneyers often shared die-cutters.

The half-dozen styles that have been identified have proved recognizable enough: new specimens can generally be assigned to their stylistic group without difficulty (although there were and are a certain number of coins 'left over' which do not fit into the pattern: contemporary imitations, or moneyers who produced only a few coins?)

The Tilbury site, among others, has produced some extremely debased examples of Series L, which appear to be of almost pure copper. In style, they do not exactly match specimens of the same types, of better alloy. How should one interpret them? – If one thinks of the very great range of styles found in Series R, and of the distinctive style of the latest issues by the moneyers Wigræd and Tilbeorht, with only $c.8$-15 per cent silver, they may suggest that Series L had a long duration too, ending in severe debasement and, perhaps, dwindling mint-output. Few enough specimens of the very last phase of Series R are known, other than those from Middle Harling. In the same way, perhaps, Tilbury may chance to be our main source of the very late coins of Series L.

Differences of style, then, may well be chronological. They might also be regional. Interpretation of the styles on the basis of their geographical distribution has, however, led students into serious errors in the last two or three decades. Regional concentrations of particular styles were made to support the far-reaching suggestion that more than one mint struck the same set of types. Thus, in Series K, separate mints were proposed for the 'A-B', and 'C-D' styles.[6] And in Series L the 'Hwiccian' style was associated with the Severn valley, on the basis that specimens were recorded only from that region or from London itself. If the 'Hwiccian' coins had been minted in London, so the argument ran, they would have been carried afield in all directions, and not just to the territory of the

[5] D.M. Metcalf, 'Sceattas from the territory of the Hwicce', *NC*[7] 16 (1976), 64-74.
[6] Metcalf and Walker, loc.cit.

Hwicce. If on the other hand they were Hwiccian it was understandable that they should be carried to London in connexion with a long-distance trade in wool from the Cotswolds.[7] Since these arguments were advanced, new finds in the 'Hwiccian' style have come to light in Middle Anglia, and near Old Sarum, which have shown that the 'Hwiccian' coins were indeed carried afield in various directions, and that the analysis of 1976 went beyond the evidence in drawing conclusions from too small a distribution pattern.[8] The attribution to Hwiccia has been rendered quite untenable.

It remains true that there is a heavy concentration of finds in Hwiccia in this one style. The analogy of the ninth-century evidence helps to make it understandable: regression analysis of ninth-century coins of the London mint shows that they were characteristically carried over long distances up the Thames valley and westwards, no doubt in the course of inter-regional trade.[9] The 'Hwiccian' sceattas can be interpreted similarly.

The proposal to divide Series K between two or more mints has likewise become less convincing as new finds have accumulated. The suggestion that style 'C-D' belonged to the upper Thames region was influenced by the idea that the coins could be attributed to the same mint as one of the styles found in Series U, Types 23b/d. There was never much distributional evidence to support this hypothesis based on style. On the basis of new finds, it has become clear that the 'C-D' style has a much wider distribution than the 'upper Thames' style of Series U. There was, however, quite a clear contrast in the weights of styles 'A-B' and 'C-D', the latter being heavier, and more carefully adjusted, with hardly any overlap. It was assumed that a single mint would not produce coins of the same type concurrently on two different weight-standards. Style 'A-B' was therefore assigned to a more easterly mint, either at London or in east Kent. Perhaps one should now consider whether the lighter stylistic group could be later in date.

If we try to imagine a situation analogous to that of the ninth century, when Kentish and London coins circulated together over very much the same area, we can see that it is likely to be difficult to argue from distribution-patterns to mint-attribution, and that one needs to look at the finds from the whole of southern England. Too small a sample, or too narrow a perspective, can easily lead one into false conclusions, the more so if it was characteristic of the coins that they were carried over long distances.

[7] Metcalf, loc.cit., p.68.

[8] M. A. S. Blackburn and M. J. Bonser, 'Single finds of Anglo-Saxon and Norman coins – 3', BNJ 56 (1986), 64-101, at p.74, no.29. Old Sarum: 'Coin Register', nos.127-8, in BNJ 58 (1988), 150-1.

[9] Metcalf, loc.cit (note 1 above).

We should be predisposed, then, to attribute Series K and L to the least possible number of mints, and to be sceptical of evidence that styles are localized. If there were three or more styles found concurrently in east Kent, and similarly at London, it may be that a number of moneyers worked independently in each city. We have, after all, clear documentary evidence for similar practice in the late Saxon period, e.g. at Winchester.

Having said all that, there remain some puzzling aspects of the evidence which seem to imply harmonization between the London and Kentish mints. Type 33, for example, is found in two styles appropriate to Series K, which are arguably both Kentish, but also in style 'E-F', which equates with the 'Hwiccian' style,[10] and which there is every reason to interpret as belonging to London. It seems inescapable that Type 33 was minted in both places, but it may be that only a small part of the issue was produced in London. In fact we are talking about only two specimens in 'Hwiccian' style, out of a total of a dozen known specimens of Type 33. One of them was in the London hoard, and the other was found at Stevenage, Herts.[11] Although one should not rely heavily on two provenances, in the case of Type 33 they are certainly in harmony with a London attribution for the 'Hwiccian' style. Slight though the evidence is, it is enough to give one pause before suggesting that the 'Hwiccian' coins were an aberration on the part of the London moneyer, who had no business to be striking Type 33.

Similarly, there is an important specimen of Type 32a, with curled wolf, in the 'Hwiccian' style. It has a prominent and carefully executed legend, including signs that are not readily interpreted as letters of the roman alphabet,[12] with affinities with at least two other obverse dies in 'Hwiccian' style belonging with Type 12.[13] These three or four related dies must be assumed to reflect a larger output than can be dismissed as forgeries or unofficial imitations.

This section of the argument took its start in the proposition that style complicates our understanding of Series K and L. The 'Hwiccian' or London-style coins of Kentish types exemplify the problem very well. Different aspects of their evidence are conflicting: how do we decide which aspects to discount? There are not enough specimens to cast doubt on the perspectives derived from the larger numbers of regular and straightforward coins. On the other hand there are too many for them to

[10] This correspondence was not noticed in the original publication.

[11] Metcalf and Walker 30 (= BMC 160), the examplar for style 'E': from the Thames hoard. The second coin, from different dies, is published in the 'Coin Register' BNJ 57 (1987), no.77: from Stevenage, Herts.

[12] BMC 152, ex Thames hoard, = M. and W. 34. Base silver.

[13] BMC 91 and a find from Badsey, sharing a reverse die: NC 1976, p.72 and pl.12, 9-10.

be dismissed as occasional counterfeits.

The evidence relating to Types 33 and 32a constrains us to consider whether the same arguments do not apply, thirdly, to a larger group of coins: Series K and L converge in Types 20, 18/20, and 18-19. Type 20, with *obv.*, chalice and *rev.*, hawk, has knotted wreath-ties and seems to be mainstream Series K. Type 18, with *obv.*, cross on stand or long cross and *rev.*, hawk, has plain wreath ties, and seems to be mainstream Series L. Again, it occurs in more than one style, including (apparently) the 'Hwiccian'. This last variety, which is catalogued below, may be an imitation by another hand. Type 19 is like Type 18, but laterally reversed.

The standing figure holding a hawk seems to have been used as a reverse type both in east Kent and at London. It presumably represents the king. As Type 33 includes a specimen with a hand raised in blessing, which has been interpeted as an archiepiscopal issue, it may be that the chalice, also, was meant to symbolize the archbishop. Type 20 and 18/20, with knotted wreath-ties, may then be archiepiscopal or joint royal/archiepiscopal issues, while Types 18 (and 19) at London are parallel royal issues.

It is difficult to see how one could add substance to that hypothesis. A stylistic analysis which correlated the obverses and reverses might narrow the options, and a suitable hoard might make the relative chronology of the types more secure. Further find-spots would be unlikely to tell us anything that we do not know already, as regards mint-attribution. The only realistic hope of progress lies in compiling a fuller corpus of dies.

IV

Style is a less powerful tool of analysis when applied to the small eclectic groups, because there are usually too few specimens on which to base comparisons. If any die-links were to be found, however, they would demand careful consideration. There would be a prima-facie case that two coins which shared a die were struck in the same place, although exceptions are known to that rule.

The 'bird and branch' reverses, of which there are now several imitations known in the eclectic groups, present no difficulty. The C ARIP specimen, alone, is of deceptively good style, and was originally assumed to belong with Series U.

The standing figure with two crosses is more difficult to analyse in terms of style. Lateral reversal seems to be a good indication of copying, and the shading or hatching of the torso or of the whole figure may serve to identify the workman's hand. Other details could probably be brought into a stylistic analysis if there were enough specimens from which to recognize the die-cutter's settled habits.

V

The layman might be forgiven for supposing that the legend LVNDONIA+ (or more usually ΓVNOONИ+) offered the most unambiguous evidence for attributing sceattas to a mint at London. In the same way, there should be no doubt about the origin of the thrymsas which read LONDVNIV. There may, however, be exceptions which prove the rule. It would be rash to assert that the scarce Type 12/5 'mule', with its very clear ЄLVNDONIA legend, is from London when the only recorded stray find is from the Low Countries. It has been seen as a prototype, mainly because it was reportedly present in the Hallum hoard. Philip Hill's notes accompanying his Hallum casts, however, state categorically that it is not from the hoard, and suggest that it may be a site-find (on grounds of its different patination?). If some confusion has occurred, we would be free to think of Type 12/5 as a Low Countries derivative of Series L. The specimen catalogued below looks deceptively to be of good silver, but analysis has shown that it is only 25 per cent fine.

SERIES K

EAST KENT, and perhaps a place on the banks of the Wantsum Channel rather than Canterbury, is the mint-place of Series K. It includes four main types, namely Types 33, 32a with either wolf-worm or curled wolf, Type 42 (of which there are three varieties), and Type 20 with its related 'mule', Type 20/18.

It is remarkable that two of the four should originate in precise copies of continental Celtic coins, of types which one would not have expected to find their way to England. The die-cutter, or rather the authority to whom he was answerable, had a compulsive interest in wolves: but how did someone in Kent come to see, as a model for Type 33, a bronze coin which has a well-defined circulation-area in west-central Gaul? Or even, it seems, more than one specimen of the same? – a hoard? That possibility

appears to be envisaged in Dhénin's comment on the type: 'Cette tête de loup ressemble dent pour dent à celle qui figure au droit de bronzes des *Bituriges Cubi* (BN 4220-4285), elle aussi orientée tantôt à droite, tantôt à gauche: gueule ouverte, babines retroussées, crocs apparents, dents figurées par des globules, grande langue pendante sous la tête, souvent enroulée en S, oreilles pointées vers l'avant, chaque détail concorde.'[1] Secondly, Birkhan has drawn attention to the source of Type 32a, in a Celto-German *Schüsselpfennig* with a *Rolltier* or curled animal as its type, from the Rhinelands or beyond. He has illustrated a prototype which, again, is so exactly similar in its design to the sceat, as to impose the conviction that the die-cutter had it in front of him: 'Vor allem die Übereinstimmung in der Rolltierdarstellung geht so sehr ins Detail (gesträubtes Rückenhaar, gepunkteter Leib, Ohren der Schlange, auf

[1] M. Dhénin, 'Homotypies anachroniques', in *Mélanges offerts au docteur J.-B. Colbert de Beaulieu*, 1987, pp.311-14 (illus.).

gekrümmtes Schwanzende), dass man wohl nicht an Zufall denken kann'.[2] That is not the end of the coincidences. Series V, which seems to have been the immediate forerunner of Series K at the same east Kentish mint, takes as its type the she-wolf and twins. And Type 42 has another canine type, variously described as 'hound and tree' or 'wolf and tree'.

Had Series V and K been East Anglian, one would have ventured to assume that their types were making a punning allusion to the name of the dynasty, the Wuffingas. Their distribution-pattern, however, makes it certain that they belong south of the Thames.

Whatever the ideas that governed the choice of types, it is equally certain that whoever was responsible was very selective: someone must have examined numerous other ancient coins, only to pass them over and seize upon the (relatively common) she-wolf and twins, and the (quite unexpected) two with fierce wolf's heads.

I

The relative chronology of the four types that have been grouped as the main body of Series K is very difficult to establish with certainty, in default of an adequate range of hoard evidence. The arguments are of some consequence for the secondary phase as a whole, because an early date has been claimed for Type 32a on the basis of its presence in the Garton find. The type's high average weight – distinctly higher than that of Type 42 – provides strong evidence, but even that is not beyond challenge, because weight-standards could rise as well as fall. And there are conflicting arguments which tend to give Type 42 the priority over 32a, and which hint that Series V and Type 33 are earlier than either of them. Many of the arguments are academic in the sense that we should probably envisage a condensed chronology for the early phase of Series K.

[2] H. Birkhan, 'Pfennig', *Numismatische Zeitschrift* 86 (1971), 59-65, at p.64, and pl.11.

Rigold laid much emphasis upon the Garton-on-the-Wolds grave-find, in which there was a specimen of Type 32a alongside early-looking examples of Series J.[3] He wished to place this coin of Series K very early

in the secondary phase.[4] Even if the coin of Type 32a were the latest in the grave-find, the need to find room for Series V may involve a reconsideration of the date at which Series J was introduced. The ramifications of Rigold's argument involve his type BIIIc, which is demonstrably derivative from J, and its close ally BIIIA, which was already present in Aston Rowant, but which is perhaps, after all, significantly earlier in date than BIIIc.

Metal analyses show very high silver contents for some specimens of three of the four types in Series K. Figures of over 80 per cent 'silver' are recorded for Types 33, 32a, and 42. Much lower figures are also recorded in these same types. For Type 32a in particular we have the following wide range of values: 82%, 37%, 35% (corroded), $c.20\%$ and 1% (plated forgery). The silver contents cannot be judged in isolation from the style of the coins. It so happens that only one of the analyses (82%) refers to the style that is Kentish: the other specimens, as we shall see, are copies from north of the Thames. A small number of analyses, determined by what coins were available rather than chosen in light of a proper stylistic analysis, may thus give an incomplete or even a distorted view of the pattern of silver contents for the Kentish issues.

The analyses deserve to be assessed together with those for Series V and O, both of which also vary over quite a wide range. If V preceded K at the same mint-place, then it is virtually certain that when K was introduced, the coinage reverted (temporarily) to a higher alloy standard.

In this situation, where three types are each known to have included specimens better than 80 per cent fine, but where a temporary return to an intended high standard, quickly followed by decline, cannot be ruled out, the alloy of the coins will offer ambiguous evidence. Similarly the hoards offer totally inadequate evidence for the type-sequence, when only one coin of Series K, and one related 'triquetras' coin, are provided with a context. All options remain open, and two indirect arguments will

[3] The argument, defended in the chapter on Series J above, that Types 85 and 37 were concurrent issues, has a bearing.

[4] 'This hoard . . . is of the highest importance for comparative chronology . . . the later Kentish issues, e.g. Type 32a, begin earlier than expected'. – S. E. Rigold, in *BNJ* 1960-1.

deserve consideration, even though they are open to differing interpretations.

Some types within the series have a much more widespread distribution than others, and there will be a presumption that they are later. Type 33 has a particularly compact distribution with an emphasis on Reculver, and may be compared with Series V. There are various reasons for thinking that it is early.

Secondly, a stylistic analysis of the knotted wreath-ties produces strong evidence of consistency, and helps to suggest a sequence of types, as well as confirming that different styles were produced separately. Thus in Type 32a the knot is tied either left over right, or right over left. Coins in style 'C-D' show one version, and those in style 'A-B' the other (see the text figure). In Type 42 ('A-B' style of bust) the knot is variable in size,

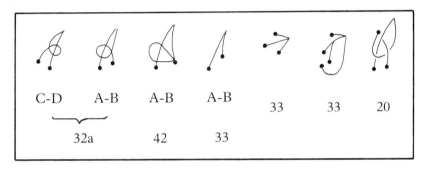

Fig. Knotted wreath-ties in Series K.

showing a wider range than in Type 32a. In at least one specimen with an unusually large knot, it seems not to have been clearly understood by the die-cutter. There are other reasons for thinking that this coin (M. and W.19) may be experimental, and early. Type 33 lacks the characteristic knot of Series K (where, however, it undoubtedly belongs). Instead, it has two straight wreath ties in style 'A-B' or three in 'C-D', accompanied on one specimen (M. and W.7) by a curious extra element. Type 20 introduces a sharp angle into the knot (again, see the text figure), and sometimes shows the ties crossing under or over each other, in true interlace style. The angular knot is also seen in Type 32a, generally on specimens with reverses which have an added torc, or which are muddled. They raise the question whether parts of Types 32a and 20 are from the same workshop or whether the muddled coins could post-date the main issues of Type 32a. Similarly, there is one notable specimen of Type 33 which has a knot in 'A-B' style, and which places a difficulty in the way of suggesting that Type 33 pre-dates the introduction of the knot. Otherwise, the correlation of wreath-tie with type is impressive, and one is encouraged to try to use it as a guide to chronology.

II

Type 33 is known from about a dozen specimens: there have been few additions made to the corpus published in 1967.[5] The obverse has a bust right, with a long cross in front of the face (but no hand). The reverse has the wolf's head, on which Dhénin has commented. It can face either left or right. It occurs in the three main styles, and there are interesting links between style, weight, and provenance, although obviously there are too few specimens to establish a good correlation as regards weight.

Style 'C-D' is the most plentiful.[6] It seems to be significantly heavier. The three known provenances are all Reculver.[7]

Style 'A-B', known from only one pair of dies,[8], has elaborate saddleback drapery of the bust. The wolf's head is again a very careful copy, but it is by another hand (as the obverse, of course, is). The wolf's tongue ends in a (knotted?) circle. The weights are lower, perhaps by chance – or because this is a later issue?

Style 'E-F', that is, the so-called 'Hwiccian' style, is known from two coins, one of which, appropriately, is from the Thames hoard: a London coin with a London provenance.[9] The wolf's head is turned to the left,

[5] D. M. Metcalf and D. R. Walker, 'The "wolf" sceattas', *BNJ* 36 (1967), 11-28.

[6] M. and W. 6, 7a (1.18g), 7b (1.04g), 8 (1.11g), and two more coins which are perhaps similar in style, although the evidence is indistinct: Reculver LVI (illustrated in *BNJ* 1977, pl.2, 23, and

Reculver/Stowe 6 (illustrated from a poor line drawing in *BNJ* 1988, 127).

[7] M. and W. 7a (Reculver XXXIV) and the two coins mentioned in the preceding note.

[8] M. and W. 15a (1.00g) and 15b (0.86g).

[9] M. and W. 30 (1.00g).

Fig. Type 33

and has an extravagantly curled tongue, and pellets to decorate the empty spaces in the field. It is a skilful and close copy of another sceat, but with some creative input from the die-cutter. The other coin was found north of London, at Stevenage. Its obverse die is extremely similar to the first coin, but not the same. Its reverse is difficult to make out, but evidently left-facing.[10]

A coin in much inferior style[11] seems to be a copy of style 'C-D'. It is light in weight and is apparently base. It, too, is from the Thames hoard.

There remains one historically important specimen,[12] on which there has been inserted into the design a hand raised in the trinitarian gesture of blessing. The style is impeccable. The wolf's head, although laterally

reversed, is indubitably by the same hand as M. and W.7 (in style 'C-D'). It even includes the zig-zag ornament in the outer margin. The obverse has knotted wreath-ties in style 'A-B'. The head is obscured by a die-flaw but careful inspection shows that it is in the style 'A-B'. The drapery of the bust is in style 'C-D'. Out of this conflicting evidence, preference should be given to the thought that the two reverse dies were cut at much the same time. The weight and alloy are high.[13]

It has been argued from this coin (which was found in Thames spoil, perhaps from the construction of the Thames barrier), that the archbishop of Canterbury enjoyed minting rights, like his successors in the time of King Offa. Even if its exact date is uncertain, it will fall within the long pontificate of Archbishop Berhtwald (693-731). [14]

[10] 'Coin Register', 77, in *BNJ* 57 (1987), 132, wnr.

[11] M. and W. 41 (0.94g).

[12] Catalogued below.

[13] 1.14g, with 85.8% 'silver', 2.6% tin, and 0.7% zinc. The gold contents are 1.92 per 100 parts Ag,

which is closely matched in Type 42.

[14] D. M. Metcalf, 'A sceat of Series K minted by Archbishop Berhtwald of Canterbury (693-731)', *BNJ* 58 (1988), 124-6.

Might the Kentish king have struck one type in Series K while the archbishop concurrently struck another? It seems, at any rate, unlikely that the king would have granted more than a part share in the privilege of minting. And the archbishop's coins may, like those of Iænberht and Æthelheard (and Ecgberht at York) have been strictly speaking joint issues. That might account for the symbolism of Types 20 and 18/20, where one figure hold a chalice, and the other a hawk.

Could the archbishop have had minting rights at London too, to account for the production of Type 33 in style 'E-F'? The coins are certainly of official quality, and, in so far as the various 'Hwiccian' types can be arranged into a sequence, they probably fit into it at an early point. We shall return to this question later.

Type 33, in summary, seems to be an issue of the archbishop, minted in east Kent and perhaps also in London. The involvement of two or even three skilled die-cutters shows that the choice of motif was made by higher authority.

Only half the known specimens are provenanced, but the half-dozen available find-spots suggest a restricted circulation, which may possibly have been a feature of the earliest years of the secondary phase.

III

Type 42 makes a variation on the theme of wolves. Its reverse type is almost certainly a hound, with a plant or berried vine in the background. How can we be so sure that the canine creature is a dog rather than a wolf? – Because it is wearing a collar. The collar is visible on more than one die. It is not beyond the bounds of imagination, however, that a ruler who was sufficiently obsessed with wolves to seize upon rare Celtic coins as prototypes might also have kept wolves, in some sort of wolf park or menagerie (cf. Charlemagne's elephant?), and that ways might have been found of placing collars round their necks. Against this idea is the fact that the creature on Type 42 tends to have a curled tail which it holds over its back, in a way that grown wolves do not.

The type is known from some two dozen specimens, almost twice as many as were recorded in the corpus of 1967. The sample now includes a fair amount of die-duplication. Of the coins that can be checked, in round numbers 20 include 10 non-singletons,[15] implying an original total of the

---

[15] M. and W. 16a and b, plus two further specimens both from Tilbury; *SCBI Mack* 354 and M. and W. 19; M. and W. 25 and the Bledlow find; two specimens of variety a catalogued below.

order of 30 pairs of dies (evidently in a one-to-one ratio). Of these, 15 or roughly half are known to us.

Type 33, where there are two pairs among a dozen coins, has had a not dissimilar survival-rate: the two proportions are well within statistical limits of being the same.

All the coins of Type 42 are in the portrait style 'A-B' (with the exception of an unconvincing counterfeit from Domburg,[16] and a piece of doubtful authenticity[17]). There are three varieties, which might with some justification have been numbered as separate types. In front of the diademed bust on the obverse there is one of three emblems, namely

> a) a hand holding a plant with berries, or buds on a central spike and two drooping side-shoots, as seen in Series V.[18]
> b) a hawk, normally with its head turned back.[19]
> c) a hand holding a cross-sceptre.[20]

One wonders whether Type 42 could be a joint royal/archiepiscopal issue. The hawk may be taken as a royal symbol. Neither of the other varieties, however, is unambiguously archiepiscopal.

The plant behind the hound shows a good deal of stylistic variation. The versions can be grouped (although not very clearly) into

> i) plant with naturalistic berries and buds (as seen also on obverse a and in Series V).
> ii) modelled plant with S-shaped pair of branches.
> iii) branching plant with pellets; the central spike ends in a single pellet.
> iv) similar to iii but the central spike ends in a group of three pellets.

There seems to be a restricted correlation between the obverse and reverse details, as follows: a is found with ii, b with iii and iv (possibly as two separate phases), and c with i and ii.

That suggests that there is some chronological separation of the obverse varieties, but it leaves plenty of possible arrangements. The problem is to place the coins into the chronological order in which they

---

[16] M. and W. 42.

[17] M. and W. 44.

[18] To the corpus, add the Tilbury find (catalogued below), and Royston 26 (of low weight, 0.79g, and simpler style – the odd man out).

[19] To the corpus add BM, Barnett bequest, 0.97 (illus. as 'Walbury Camp', pl.B), Walbury Camp I (pl, A, 0.99g), Walbury Camp II (*BNJ* 1977, pl.2, 24, 0.93g), the Bledlow find, 0.95g (illus. in *SEC*, pl.10, 20), and the Old Alfriston find, 1.09g (Coin Register 1987/78).

[20] To the corpus add two separate finds from Tilbury, from the same dies as M. and W. 16, and note that 16b is now in the National Museum of Wales (E.014, 72 per cent 'silver').

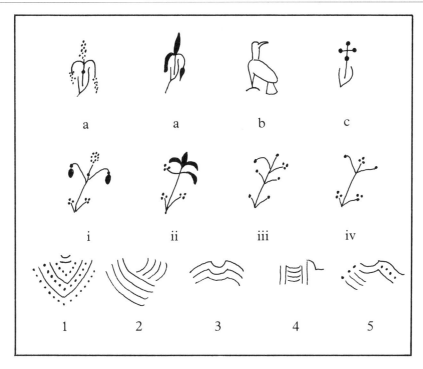

FIG. Type 42: details of the design.

were struck, and we should be prepared to treat it as an open question whether more than one variety was issued concurrently – and also whether the same variety could be resumed intermittently.[21] In the absence of hoard evidence all we can do is to make a provisional classification of the coins, taking into account as many other correlations as possible. If there were any reverse die-links between varieties, for example, their evidence would be important.[22] Other aspects are liable to be inconclusive.

There is some reason to suspect that two weight-standards are involved. If one could demonstrate that that was so, and correlate weight-standards with varieties, it would be a strong argument for chronology. With only 15 or 20 weights, however, distributed among three main varieties, there simply is not enough evidence to define the parameters, given that some variation of weight was tolerated.

With the alloy we are in even worse case, because only three specimens

[21] This might, for example, be a valid explanation for coins which would otherwise be the 'odd man out' in a classification, yet which are evidently of official quality.

[22] How important depends on the context.

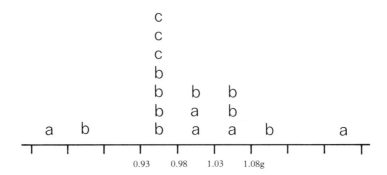

FIG. Type 42: weights of specimens of varieties a, b, and c.

have been chemically analysed. Those three results, however, are very informative. A specimen of the 'plant' variety [23] contains 86 per cent 'silver', a very high figure for a secondary sceat, and virtually the same as the 'benediction hand' coins of Type 33. Series V may have begun as high, but it fell much lower: we can interpret that in one of two ways. A second specimen of the 'plant' variety, badly worn, [24], now contains only 58 per cent 'silver' – although it is apparently from the same dies as the first. And a coin of the 'cross' variety[25] has 72 per cent silver.

On the available evidence, variety a includes a coin with exceptionally high silver contents, and it is in general heavier than b or c; we may therefore guess that it is earlier. Variety b/iv seems to be carefully weight-adjusted, at around 0.96g. Variety c is insufficiently documented.

We can add a further ingredient: the drapery of the bust. In an elaborate and aesthetically successful version, three rounded V-shaped rows of pellets alternate with solid lines (1). One or three pellets may be added at the throat. The concept (later?) undergoes some simplification. Version 1 occurs with all three varieties, a, b, c, but appears to be standard in a, and at its most elaborate there. That again suggests that a is early. A 'shawl' style of drapery (2) is perhaps only a modification of 1. Quite different designs appear with variety b, the 'hawk' coins (3,4,5). These are most commonly found with b/iii, whereas b/iv has drapery closer to 1 or 2.

As these clues accumulate, they encourage one to look again at b/iii, and to notice small differences of general style. The head, and the hawk, tend to be larger; the hound has a larger, rounded ear, and is more

[23] Ashmolean Museum from Tilbury.
[24] Ashmolean Museum, without provenance.
[25] National Museum of Wales, E.104.

Variety **a**   **b**   **c**

rounded in outline.

The knotted wreath-ties also correlate well with the classification: a large knot is characteristic of variety c.

In the end, the number of specimens is not enough to permit a final judgement. One would guess that variety a is early, and that part of variety b is late. But all three varieties may have been introduced, if not concurrently, then within a short time of each other.

Type 42 has a distribution-pattern falling mainly south of the Thames, with two or three finds, interestingly, from Sussex.[26] Its dispersion is significantly wider than that of Type 33.

IV

A unique coin from the Barking Abbey excavations draws its inspiration from Type 42. The reverse is perhaps the 'badge' of another eclectic series of which this is, as yet, the only known specimen.

V

Type 32a is known from over forty specimens, among which there are at least 14 non-singletons.[27] It is demonstrably from more than one mint-place. The regular styles 'A-B' and 'C-D', exactly matching other types in Series K, have a compact south-of-Thames distribution, and are doubtless both from east Kent, whereas another large group of specimens

[26] Variety a: Southampton (BM), Tilbury, Royston 26. Variety b: Wootton Bassett (M. and W. 25, incorrectly said to be from Oxford), Walbury Camp (2), Bledlow, Old Alfriston. Variety c: Reculver, Tilbury (2).

[27] The Margate find is from the same dies as M.

and W. 1. The Hanford (Hod Hill) find is from the same dies as the Stourmouth find. Hamwic 96 and *MEC* 698 are from the same obverse. M. and W. 3a-d and 9a-b have already been noted. The Grimsby and Bradwell-on-Sea finds are die-duplicates.

with stylistic features in common has an almost exclusively north-of-Thames distribution. Rarely does one see such a clear separation of stylistic groups on the ground. The difference in distribution between the two categories is much greater than it is between Canterbury and London pennies in the ninth century. It establishes beyond any doubt that coins of the same basic design were struck at more than one mint. However historically surprising and puzzling it is to discover apparent harmonization in the work of mints lying in different kingdoms, the distributional evidence is unambiguous. The south-of-Thames distribution matches that of Series V or Types 33 and 42, while the north-of-Thames coins are a new feature: a tail, as large as or larger than the dog. Twelve of the 14 non-singletons are in the regular styles, among two dozen specimens. The northern issue seems to have been the larger part, but to have had a lower survival-rate. It high-lights the absence of northern copies in Type 42.

Before embarking upon the detail, we should dot the i's and cross the t's of the above argument by pointing out that there is only one provenance for the 'A-B' style (Reculver), but that its attribution to an east Kentish mint can be justified from the finds of Types 33 and 42 in the same style. One should not multiply mints *praeter necessitatem,* but in any case it is safe to assume that both styles 'C-D' and 'A-B' are east Kentish. Secondly, the northern coins are by no means as compact a group stylistically, and one would hesitate to say, from the evidence of their style alone, that they were all from the same mint. Again, however, one should not multiply mints. The simplest hypothesis is that they are all, or nearly all, from London. Even if a few of them are imitations from elsewhere, the distributional contrast is so great that the conclusion would still stand even if it were to be shown that some specimens had been placed in the wrong category. Thirdly, the same point applies to the 'C-D' group, where a few specimens with left-facing wolf-worm or with an added torc, [28] which may be imitative, have been mapped as official coins – partly on the grounds that their distribution is, in any case, the same.

When the 'wolf' sceattas were studied in 1967, three main styles were recognized, and some coins of Type 32a were catalogued as belonging with the 'E-F' group which, in the case of Type 33, is very clearly by the same hand as the 'Hwiccian' coins of Series L. The large 'northern' group discussed here includes the coins listed as 'E-F' in 1967. It now seems doubtful, however, whether they are by the same hand. The 'E-F'

[28] See below.

MAP. Single finds of Series K, Types 33 and 42 (square symbols), Type 32a in regular style (dots), and Type 32a in northern style (crosses).

and 'northern' busts share a strongly-modelled neck which extends right up to the base of the skull, narrowing in a sugar-loaf shape. On the 'E-F' and 'Hwiccian' coins it is aligned vertically and is symmetrical, whereas on the 'northern' coins it tends to be sloping and to follow the line of the jaw. Probably two die-cutters were attempting the same feature. In their minds, or in the mind of the second of them, he was achieving the same or a similar effect. The slight difference of style was of no importance; but it is useful to us as a diagnostic detail.

FIG. Type 32a: characteristic 'E-F' and 'northern' busts.

If that stylistic analysis is correct the dilemma it presents is to know how the 'northern' style of of Type 32a relates chronologically to the 'Hwiccian' style of Series L and Type 33. If Type 32a in 'northern' style is a London coinage – and so many dies are involved that it seems difficult to attribute it to any nearby place north of the Thames – did it precede Series L? If it did, where do we place the two known specimens of Type 33 in 'E-F' style, to avoid separating them chronologically from Series L? One would be reluctant to imagine that type 32a and Series L were struck concurrently at London, when both are issues on such a large scale. The only way out seems to be to suggest that type 33 in 'E-F' style is later in date that Type 32a in 'northern' style. Perhaps it is a posthumous copy of the archiepiscopal issue, standing right at the beginning of the *œuvre* of the 'Hwiccian' die-cutter. If that were correct, one would have to revise one's view of Type 33 as a design produced concurrently at two mints, and demote the very scarce London variety to the status of a copy. So many of the arguments on which sceattas are classified are ambulatory, or turn out to rest on concealed assumptions – in this case that the different styles of Type 33 are concurrent. Even the general argument by which Kentish and London coins are distinguished by the presence or absence of knotted wreath-ties turns out to be partly incorrect, since Type 32a includes a northern version with the knot. (This means that the proportions north and south of the Thames respectively, set out above in the course of our general consideration of

Series K and L, understate the case.) The great value of the distribution-map for Type 32a is that there are no concealed assumptions which could possibly put what it tells us back into the melting pot. Or so one ventures to believe.

The strength of the case rests on all the detailed information taken up into an analysis of the three styles. Some additional comments are necessary to supplement what was said in 1967, partly to take account of the recognition of the Celtic prototype, but mainly to reconsider some of the 'imitative' coins and to re-define the 'northern' style, recognizing it as being by a different hand from the 'Hwiccian'.

It is the coins in style 'C-D' which offer a close copy of the Celtic *Rolltier*. The 'A-B' reverses are, presumably, a rather free reinterpretation of the 'C-D' version, adding fine lines to represent fur along the creature's back. These fine lines terminate in small pellets which, on the most distinctive dies, are staggered in length.[29] (There are three varieties

in style 'A-B', one corresponding with the model, one which adds diminutive forelegs, and one with both forelegs and hind legs.) The sequence of the three varieties is not clear: the version with four legs has a wolf's head closest in style to the 'C-D' style – and has an obverse with unusual (experimental?) drapery.[30]

M and W. 10 (*SCBI Copenhagen* 43) is at first sight an 'A-B'/'C-D' mule. That is no longer the problem that it seemed to be in 1967, when the two styles were attributed (incorrectly, as it now appears) to separate mints. The coin is, however, the lightest on record, weighing only 0.76g, and the wolf-worm has 'fur' on its back. Whatever it is, it is not a true mule, because the 'C-D' reverse has 'A-B' features.

Lateral reversal is common enough among coins in the 'northern' style, but is of limited occurrence in styles 'A-B' and 'C-D'. In the latter, M. and W. 31 (*MEC* 698), with lateral reversal of the wolf-worm, can now be closely matched by Hamwic 96 (from the same obverse die?) and another recent find from Hamwic (SOU 258).[31] The reverses are rather

---

[29] See *SCBI Hunter* 99, (M. and W. 11).

[30] M. and W. 14 (with four legs) has a panel of 4 pellets ornamenting the bust. The cross is large and is defined by 5 pellets, instead of the usual 4. The wolf's head is in 'C-D' style, M. and W. 12 (*SCBI Mack* 351) is stated in the Sylloge to weigh 0.90g.

When re-sold, *Num.Circular* 1989, item 4581, its weight was given as 1.04g.

[31] This raises the question whether a batch of coinage reached Hamwic, coins from which were in due course lost on separate occasions. One cannot, needless to say, tell from only two specimens.

FIG. Hamwic 96   M and W. 1

variable in style, but as all three coins are from south of the Thames, and as Hamwic 96 is of excellent alloy (82 per cent 'silver'), there is no case for separating them out.

A similar coin which adds an animal-headed torc to the reverse has been excavated at Burrow Hill, Suffolk. It is better regarded as a clever and deceptive copy of the 'C-D' style. Once one has decided to distrust it, one will notice the weak modelling of the head above the eye, the bend in the wolf's tongue, and (on the obverse) the absence of a knot in the wreath-ties.

FIG. Burrow Hill.

(As a curiosity one may mention that the illustration of the obverse of M. and W. 9 was laterally reversed in the printing house, after leaving the authors' hands. How this could happen, photographically, remains one of life's mysteries.)

Lateral reversal of the reverse is almost the rule in the 'northern' style – including the four-legged wolf of M. and W. 34. It is also normal to find a thin wire animal-headed torc added to the design – wrapped around the wolf-worm. The animal heads are seen from above – as on Offa's pennies by the moneyer Alhmund. (One or two coins in the 'C-D' style also have the wire torc.[32]). On the most devolved of the 'northern'

FIG. Grimsby. M. and W. 28

coins, e.g. a pair of die-duplicates from near Grimsby and Bradwell-on-Sea respectively, [33] the wolf-worm's body, its tongue, and the torc are all woven together into a continuous arabesque. Variability within the

[32] M. and W. 4, and *Num.Circular* 1989/3992 (a Tilbury find).
[33] *Sceattas in England and on the Continent*, pl.14, 8.

output of the 'northern' mint is hardly in doubt: on the St. Albans find the wolf's tongue is forked and ornamented.[34] On the obverses, the knot of the wreath-ties regularly has an extra angle, as in Type 20 and 18/20, and the question arises whether this is a chronological development, or simply the style of the 'northern' mint. The distinctive shape of the neck has already been described.

The alloy of the 'northern' coins is often very debased – a far cry from the 85 per cent silver standard which the Kentish mint aimed at, and more in keeping with Series L. The Shakenoak find, and another specimen catalogued below, contain only 35-40 per cent silver, and the Cambridge find is estimated at approximately 20 per cent. It is hard to see how such coins could have been accepted at par with the Kentish prototype. Gresham's Law seems not to have applied, however, as they had essentially separate areas of circulation. We should therefore hesitate to think of monetary cooperation between two independent kingdoms. A useful analogy from later in the middle ages might be the Serbian imitation of the Venetian grosso. The debased northern copies may, in other words, have been a Mercian initiative taken without any consultation with the Kentish king – and probably displeasing to him.

The naturalistic four-legged wolf of M. and W. 33 and 34, with its tongue ending in a trefoil of pellets, is very difficult to locate

Fig. M. and W. 34.

chronologically. M. and W. 33 (catalogued below) has been analysed, and found to contain 51 per cent 'silver', but the fabric is wholly corroded, and the tin contents are excessively high (5.6 per cent). The result may therefore not be reliable.

The 'northern' style is, in summary, a good reminder of the ambiguities of many of the arguments by which sceattas are attributed. It contradicts the basis on which Series K and L are distinguished, by using knotted wreath-ties north of the Thames. Rigold, prescient in all he

---

[34] *Coin Register* 1987, no.75. Cf. the ornamented tongue of the curled (4-legged) wolf on M. and W. 34.

wrote about sceattas, made provision for the problem when he wrote, 'In order to describe the anomalous or irreducible the letters can be used much as type-numbers: if the coin is apparently a 'mule', not so much between types as between a range of types, and the fabric is uncertain, it can be provisonally classed, e.g. as K/L; if the type is that usual for K but the fabric out of place there, but *apparently* more typical of L, then it is nevertheless classed as 'K(L)'; if almost certainly a product of L with borrowed types, then it becomes L(K)'.[35]

As a scheme, that sounds rather too convoluted to be practical. Moreover, one needs not to lose sight of the element of uncertainty in one's judgements. It is still in order to admit that one cannot be sure exactly where or when the 'northern' coins were minted. They were produced on such a large scale that London seems to be the only plausible context for them; and they presumably preceded Series L. The Thames hoard includes a good range of types belonging to Series L, with

three coins assigned to Series K, namely M. and W.34 (in 'northern' style), 41 (an imitation of Type 33, 'C-D'), and 30 (Type 33 in 'E-F' or 'Hwiccian' style). The hoard is not large enough to provide conclusive evidence, but one possible reading of it is that M. and W. 34 is a stray from an earlier issue than Series L.

VI

Type 20 has on the obverse a bust holding a chalice, and on the reverse a standing figure in a boat-shaped curve holding a long cross and a hawk. On the more elaborate specimens the cross has a triangular base of three pellets. The hawk faces the standing figure, in contrast with Type 42, where she turns her head away. The wreath-ties on the obverse are

[35] *BNJ* 47 (1977), 24.

MAP. Type 20 and 20/18

knotted, with an angular knot as in the 'northern' variety of Type 32a. On the best specimens it is carefully represented to show the ties passing under and over each other. The style of these coins appears to be 'A-B'.

There is a variant which Philip Hill published as a Type 20 var./18 mule. In the space below the hawk there is a T-shaped element, possibly a perch for the hawk. It is not invariable, either on Type 18 or on 20/18. The latter is not, in reality, a mule. The significant difference is that there is a cross or a group of four pellets above the chalice. The style is 'northern', and sometimes very close to the 'Hwiccian'.

We appear to have the makings of a parallel situation to that in Type 32a, and the first question is whether the distribution of finds shows that

Type 20 belongs south of the Thames while Type 20/18 is from north of the Thames. There are, unfortunately, far too few provenances to give a clear answer. There is, apparently, a find of Type 20 from Reculver (Stone 7, known from a line-drawing), and one from Tilbury. A specimen from the Isle of Grain, with inner wire borders on both obverse and reverse, is probably imitative.[36] There is at least one example of Type 20/18 from Tilbury, and two more from north Essex. Royston 22 (Type 20/18) is in mature Hwiccian style. So far as the evidence goes, it is in harmony with a double distribution.

Metal analysis has yielded three results close to 50 per cent silver, and a fourth of only 32 per cent.

Die-duplicates are surprisingly plentiful in the small available sample.[37]

There is an imitative coin from very small dies, distinguished by an outer wire border outside the dotted border. It, too, is known from more than one specimen. The wreath-ties are not knotted. The example in the National Museum of Wales contains 31 per cent 'silver' and 9 per cent tin.[38]

---

[36] *Sceattas in England and on the Continent*, p.199 and pl.10, 16.

[37] In the 'A-B' style, *BMC* 107 (1.11g), *SCBI Hunterian* 89 (1.10g), and a coin catalogued below (1.12g, 48% silver) are from the same dies. *SCBI Hunterian* 90 (1.04g) and a Tilbury find catalogued below (1.21g, 54% silver) are duplicates. Coins in the 'northern' style are apparently lighter: *BMC* 106 (0.92g) and a north Essex find (pl.1,13) are duplicates, and an Ashmolean coin is apparently from the same obverse (1.02g, 47% silver).

[38] *SCBI Mack* 342 (now Cardiff, 0.67g) and BM, ex Carlyon-Britton 163b (Hill, pl.6, 5, 1.17g) are very divergent in weight but the EPMA analysis of the Cardiff specimen is perfectly satisfactory as regards authenticity.

VII

Type 18, which is close in style to Type 20/18, is discussed as part of Series L.

A 'mule' between Type 20 and the 'Archer' type is mentioned in the section devoted to the latter.

VIII

The question whether any of the four types in Series K were issued concurrently in east Kent remains open. If Type 33 was struck for the archbishop, it seems likely *a fortiori* that coins were also struck for the king. Evidence could only emerge from the age-structures of hoards, which are lacking.

If we try to place the types in sequence on the evidence of their styles, the result is as follows:

	C-D	*A-B*	*Northern*	*Hwiccian*
33	x	(x)		(x)
32a	x	x	x	
42		x		
20, 20/18		x		x

Type 42 is here placed after 32a because it is found only in the 'A-B' style. The lower weight standard which seems to occur within Type 42 can be construed in the same sense. The absence of 'northern' copies of Type 42, when they are so plentiful in Type 32a, could be because the London mint persisted with a design which had become familiar and acceptable, or it could mark the introduction of Series L. Type 33 in 'A-B' and 'Hwiccian' style fits awkwardly into the chronological scheme, and it is tempting to think that it was reissued intermittently.

SERIES L

THE BASIC London designs, *obv.*, bust, *rev.*, standing figure, are found with variations in the accessories on a range of types and styles of sceattas, which at best contain about 50 per cent and at worst negligible amounts of silver. Die-duplication, within and sometimes between types, is not uncommon, and suggests that the available sample of coins reflects a significant proportion of all the dies originally used. At the same time, new minor varieties continue to turn up. It seems, therefore, that the die-cutters exercised freedom to vary the designs in detail, and that some formal varieties only ever existed in two or three pairs of dies. From the point of view of the users of the London coins, the subtleties of the design cannot have mattered. From the point of view of the numismatist, searching for clues to the correct ordering of the coins, the concept of 'types' should not be allowed to dominate his understanding of the series.

I

The hand of one accomplished die-cutter has been recognized in the so-called 'Hwiccian' style. In 1976 the available provenances were so heavily concentrated in the territory of the Hwicce as to prompt the suggestion that the coins were minted there, rather than in London.[1] That claim was in error, as subsequent finds have made perfectly clear.[2] The 'Hwiccian' coins belong to London, where they form the largest and most varied group within Series L. The face and neck are the distinctive feature of the obverse. The cheek is heavy and full, and is modelled by the die-cutter with a swelling roundness. The eye, a pellet in an almond-shaped outline, is set back towards the middle of the profile, giving the head a startled or nervous look. The nose is Roman, the lips are far forward, as if making a *moue*. The neck is modelled as a prominent tapering column. The wreath-ties are straight, and there are generally three rather than

[1] D. M. Metcalf, 'Sceattas from the territory of the Hwicce', *NC*[7] 16 (1976), 64-74.

[2] M. A. S. Blackburn and M. J. Bonser, 'Single finds of Anglo-Saxon and Norman coins – 3', *BNJ* 56 (1986), 64-101, at p.74.

two. The drapery of the bust is normally made up of four or five shallow Vs or shallow curves, alternately wire and dotted. Occasionally these are replaced by a curving outline or by a pattern copied from Series K.

One specimen, catalogued below, on which neither the face nor the drapery are characteristically 'Hwiccian' is nevertheless thoroughly Hwiccian in fabric and alloy, and is from a regular reverse die. The symbol before the face is a three-branched sceptre.

A miniature version of the bust is used in order to accommodate a legend (ƎVIOႰ or similar), on two or more very similar obverses.[3] One is

seen on *BMC* 91 and (probably the same die) *MEC* 701 (found near Cambridge), while another was found at Badsey, near Evesham. A fourth specimen came to light at Ford, near Old Sarum.[4] Type 32a with a somewhat similar legend, probably related, has a full-sized bust.[5]

The obverses demonstrate the connection between reverses in two quite different styles, which one would not otherwise have ventured to

place close to each other. In one style, the upper part of the body is rectangular with angular shoulders and is cross-hatched, while the skirt is straight, plain, and divided into two modelled curves draping the thighs.

These 'culottes' dies are of distinctive and careful workmanship. The horizontal bars of the crosses are at unequal levels, the left-hand cross

[3] *NC* 1976, pl.12, 9 and 10.

[4] D. M. Metcalf, 'A "porcupine" sceat from Market Lavington, with a list of other sceattas from Wiltshire', *Wiltshire Archaeological Magazine* 83 (1990), 205-8, with enlarged drawings of the two finds from Ford.

[5] *BNJ* 36 (1967), pl.7, 34.

being normally well below shoulder-level. The man's arms are correspondingly elongated. The back of the helmet is elongated and ends in a large pellet beyond the shoulder, and within the upper quadrant of the cross. The Cambridge find, for example, conforms to these particulars.

On a few specimens, the crosses are smaller and higher, their horizontal bars being at or above shoulder-level. This small change in style is probably of value as a chronological indicator. The coins with higher crosses, such as that from Shakenoak, would seem to be later. They include the specimen with irregular drapery and a three-branched sceptre, mentioned above.

In the other style, the shoulders are rounded, the two halves of the rib-cage are modelled separately, and horizontally hatched, the skirt is triangular or flaring, and outlined. The feet are turned outwards.

This round-shouldered style is known from a die on which the standing figure has a facing head, with (?) wreath ties standing out to left and right almost horizontally.[6] The associated obverse die is in impeccable 'Hwiccian' style, with elaborate drapery of the bust. There seems to be no question of its being imitative. It is extremely close to the obverse die of Type 33, M. and W.30. Both these unusual varieties will presumably belong either early or late in the 'Hwiccian' sequence. Even though the former coin weighs only 0.88g, one's instinct is that they are early.

A third style of standing figure again has a facing head, long moustaches, and a simplified tubular garment slightly flared at the hem. The obverse has a Kentish plant in front of the face, and is in good 'Hwiccian' style. The coin looks very coppery.[7] Its place in the sequence is problematic.

The formal varieties that are known in the 'Hwiccian' style are sketched in the diagram below. The tally may well be incomplete.

The silver contents, even of the better-looking specimens, are very low. A coin of Type 16 in Cardiff contains 21 per cent silver plus 4 per cent tin. Three coins catalogued below have even less silver: Type 16/15b, 15 per cent plus 7 per cent tin, Type 18, 20 per cent plus 7 per cent tin, Type 15a, from Shakenoak, 8 per cent, plus 9 per cent tin.[8]

---

[6] *NCirc* 97 (1989), item 3995 (found at Tilbury). 0.88g.

[7] Catalogued below.

[8] EPMA analyses by Dr. J. P. Northover.

The coppery appearance of some of the Tilbury finds may belie similar silver contents, and may, on the basis of figures like these, have more to do with leaching and soil conditions than with an even further decline in silver contents in the course of the 'Hwiccian' issues.

II

Types 12 and 13 carry a legend which is a blundered attempt at LVNDONIΛ+. Usually it is no better than VИOOИИ+. Type 13, which was known from a single specimen in the Thames hoard of 1860, remained unique until 1992, when a second specimen came to light.[9] It seems to be from the same dies. The reverse makes a careful attempt to portray the king seated on a chair with an elegantly scrolled back. He holds a long cross with his left hand, and looks back over his shoulder at a hawk on his right wrist. On the obverse the hair is cross-hatched and there are three wreath ties.

An obverse die-link with Type 12 is provided by a second coin from the Thames hoard.[10] The reverse is now the routine standing figure on a boat-shaped curve, holding two crosses. The torso is cross-hatched.

Other specimens of Type 12 have hair represented more conventionally by fine parallel lines. The drapery of the bust is simplified, until little can be seen except a curve of four or five bold pellets resembling a necklace. Triple wreath ties are standard.

Because of their legend, coins of Type 12 tend to have long pedigrees and to have been illustrated repeatedly. They are by no means as plentiful, however, as familiarity might suggest, and the relatively short list of specimens includes some further die-links. *MEC* 700 (ex Mack 339, ex Lawrence) is from the same obverse as *BMC* pl.2, 16 (= *BMC* 90

[9] *BMC* 92. The second specimen is now in a private collection in the United States. I am indebted to Mr. J. P. Linzalone for details.
[10] *BMC* 88.

not 91). An Ashmolean specimen is from the same obverse as *SCBI Norweb* 57 (ex Lockett, ex Grantley, ex Montagu, ex Marsham). *SCBI Hunterian* 85 shares an obverse die with a find from Middle Harling (MH 62), and is certainly from the same reverse die as *Norweb* 57. Rashleigh 22 is close in style to *BMC* 90.

The Ashmolean coin has been analysed, and found to be 51 per cent 'silver', with a further 4 per cent tin. The Middle Harling coin has also been analysed, by M. R. Cowell; it contains 53 per cent 'silver' (including 4 per cent lead), plus 13 per cent tin (XRF on a polished section of the edge). Other specimens, discussed in the next section, help to suggest that there was a deliberate alloy standard of *c.*50 per cent silver.

Another coin catalogued below contains only 28 per cent 'silver', with 8 per cent tin. It is from the Thames hoard. A die-duplicate in the Lawrence collection is also said to be from the Thames. The style is looser, and the coins may be slightly later in date.

The pattern of die-linkage (which differs from the usual one-to-one ratio) and the half-silver standard point to a brief phase of well-planned and probably brisk output.

III

Coins of Type 12 by another hand are seen in *SCBI Hunterian* 83 and 84, which have curiously similar reverses (from the same die) but are from different obverses. *BMC* 89 is from the same obverse as *Hunterian* 83.

Another coin in the British Museum from the same obverse, but yet another reverse, has been dismissed as a modern cast (Hill, 1953, pl.6,4) but should perhaps be given the benefit of the doubt, at least until its original is identified. A find from South Weston, Oxon., catalogued below, is closely related to *Hunterian* 83: there is a 'crest' outlining the head, and a nose worthy of Cyrano de Bergerac.[11] The coin has been analysed, and found to contain 48 per cent 'silver' plus 5 per cent tin. The soft obverse die of *SCBI Hunterian* 84 is seen again in a Tilbury find, coupled with a reverse in the style of the preceding group. It lacks the base-line within the curve but is, at the least, a very good copy. Another find, from Chipping Warden, Northants, [12] is again similar in style to *Hunterian* 84. The coin, which is now in the National Museum of Wales,[13] contains 49 per cent 'silver' plus 6 per cent tin.

A coin reading LVN·· UΛN (*NCirc.* 1983, 3872) is either from the same workshop, or a good copy.

A coin formerly in the Grantley collection has an obverse related to the

group described above, coupled with a reverse apparently in the style of *BMC* 88, etc.[14]

The two little stylistic groups of Type 12 have features in common. They may have been produced by two die-cutters working side by side.

A die-link into the **MONITASCORVM** group would come as no surprise.[15]

IV

A distinctive reverse style which is presumably the work of another die-cutter in Series L shows the standing figure in a high-waisted, smock-like garment, the lower part of which is outlined. An important specimen

formerly in the Elmore Jones collection has a short legend, perhaps intended as LV.[16] The bust is strongly reminiscent of others in Series K, Type 20/18, and elsewhere, and could well be by the same hand as the 'northern' style.

[11] *BNJ* 56 (1986), 8f.
[12] ibid.
[13] E.029.
[14] *NCirc* 78 (1970) p.407, item 11183, illus.109,

Elmore Jones colln., ex Grantley 680.
[15] Cf. the bust of the specimen catalogued below.
[16] *NCirc* 1970, p.407, item 11185, illus.111.

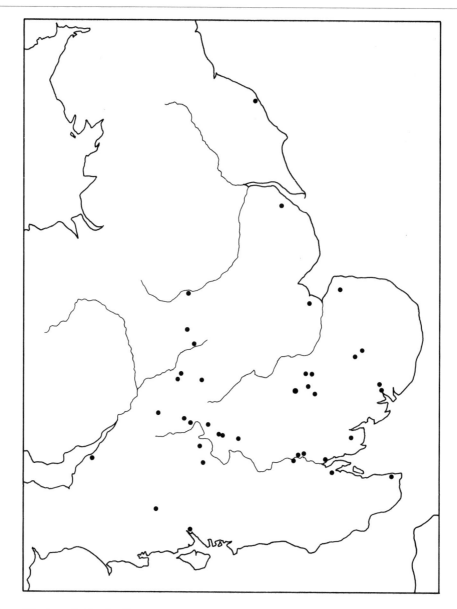

MAP. Finds of Series L.

The smocked figure, with a distinctive curved arm holding the cross, is coupled with a left-facing bust in Type 19 (*BMC* 105), and with lateral reversal of the reverse on a find from Putney.[17]

V

Another style of obverse bust can be recognized in Type 18, in a little handful of coins which resemble the 'northern' style of Series K, but without the distinctive columnar neck. They include, for example, *SCBI Hunterian* 88 (1.02g), Whitby XII (0.65g), and a coin from Rochester catalogued below. Another specimen which may be from the same hand is of Type 15a, but the standing figure has large feet turned outwards and, apparently, a facing head.[18] Variability seems to be a feature of this die-cutter's *œuvre*. More specimens are needed, however, to construct a sequence securely.

Type 18 also includes coins, such as *BMC* 101, with a columnar neck, in the 'northern' style.

VI

There are, inevitably, some oddments which cannot be matched up into groups. A coin from the Thames hoard, catalogued below, has a standing figure with a well-defined waist, holding two symmetrical berried plants.

A similar coin, from different but clearly related dies, has been found at Domburg. Another coin, more debased in every sense, has pyramidal drapery of the bust. It is from Tilbury, and is also catalogued below.

---

[17] *BNJ* 56, 1986, pl.1, 6-8.
[18] *NCirc* 97 (1989), 3994. 0.84g.

VII

In summary, Series L falls into two unequal and dissimilar parts. The flag-ship varieties with the LVNDONIA+ legend, Types 13 and 12, seem to reflect a short but intensive phase of activity by two teams or two workshops (but with a reverse die-link), producing sceattas of about 50 per cent silver. More than one reverse die was coupled with each obverse die.

The other part of Series L is dominated by a wide repertoire of varieties all by the same accomplished hand, forming a series that was originally labelled Hwiccian. The silver contents are generally only 20 per cent or lower.

The division into two parts is not quite as tidy as that. Coins with a 'smocked' figure on the reverse fall, no doubt, into the second and larger part, and are of various types (15, 18, 19) but include an unskilled attempt, on one die, at an obverse legend.

There are various other coins in styles that are difficult to assess or to arrange in groups. They seem to centre on Type 18.

Whether the Hwiccian coins, with their lower silver contents, were a later issue than Type 12 is not clear. Both kinds certainly circulated together, presumably at par, as the Thames hoard of 1860 shows us. The hoard also includes the 'smocked' style and Type 18.

The chronological relationship between Series L and Series K is equally uncertain. Series K includes coins of much better silver, but one cannot be sure that they are therefore earlier. One's instinct is that the 'northern' style in Type 32a can only be from London, and that it precedes the introduction there of the 'Hwiccian' style. There are none of the authentic Kentish issues of Series K in the Thames hoard, with the very doubtful exception of M. and W.41 (*BMC* 159).

VIII

The ideas available to us from regression analysis of ninth-century pennies suggest that the finds of Series L in 'Hwiccian' style, which are so relatively plentiful in Hwiccian territory, reflect long-distance trade out of London. The corresponding absence or paucity of the varieties that generally contain *c*.50 per cent silver may point to the date at which the trade rose to importance.

Overseas finds of Series L hint at London's trading connections. The

Domburg finds have been listed as including 6 specimens of Series L, plus two from the 'rosettes' group (Type 12/34), as against only two of Series K.

THE C ARIP ECLECTIC GROUP

BECAUSE it shows beyond any doubt that types borrowed from different series were copied by a single die-cutter, the C ARIP group is the *locus classicus* for eclectic groups of sceattas – which directly challenge the concept of series.

I

The earliest known coin in the C ARIP group combines a diademed bust with an artistic copy of the 'bird and branch' reverse.[1] To left and right of the bust is the legend C ARIP , the second part reading outwards. The lettering, which is vaguely reminiscent of 'Hwiccian' legends on Types 32a and 12, is executed with the utmost care, with delicate seriffing, although not quite in the best classical style. The meaning of the legend

remains tantalizingly unclear. The bird is so exactly copied from Series U, Type 23b/d, that one can point with some probability to the particular die that was the prototype – Hamwic 107, with its hatched and scrolled wing, and its prominent splayed crest. The vine at which the bird is pecking is correctly delineated; the only fault is that the bird's body and tail are in the more easterly style.

A second coin, with a bust manifestly by the same hand, has the same inscription in a blundered version.[2] The letter C is still seriffed, but the other letters terminate in pellets or lack any tidy ends. The IP has degenerated into a meaningless pattern. The reverse has a distinctive version of curled creature, more worm than wolf, but possibly derived from Type 32a, curled wolf-worm with fur. Its curled tongue is delicately

---

[1] Type 63. Ashmolean, ex D. M. Metcalf, ex Firth ex Lockett ex Grantley ex Montagu ex Marsham.   1.10g.

[2] Ashmolean. Found near Chichester, 1989. 1.01g.

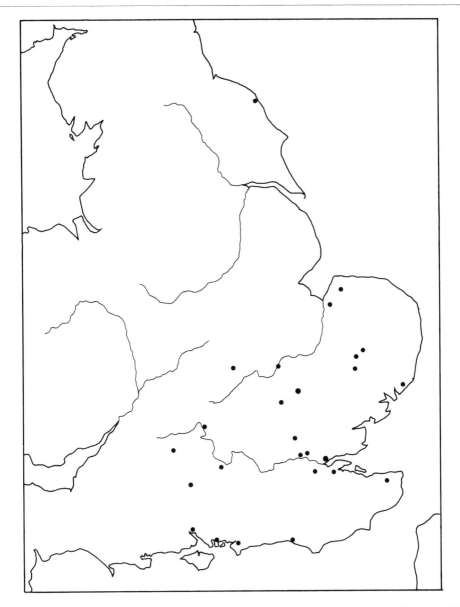

MAP.   Finds of six eclectic groups (to show the general correspondence of their distribution with Series K and, especially, L).

indicated. Exactly the same combination of types occurs on an excavation-coin from Barking Abbey. The curled animal has the same distinctive tongue. The C of the legend is given prominence, and ARIP is blundered in a new way.

The same creature, laterally reversed, is paired with a saltire-standard,

in a unique coin in the Hunterian Museum.[3] It is not obviously by the same hand, but it perhaps belongs with the C ARIP sequence.

A fourth type, which reverts to the bust with legend, is of the highest interest because it allows one to witness the process of stylistic deterioration in the work of an illiterate die-cutter. The formula ARIP is still visible, although it now reads inward. The letter R, however, has fallen apart into two sinuous elements, resembling C ɔ (see Fig.). The P has become a linear, perhaps pseudo-runic letter. The reverse type is a

standing figure with two crosses, much as Series L, Type 12 or 15, with a straight base-line and no feet.[4] The style is good, but not, one would judge, good enough for there to be any question of a borrowed die.

A similar coin from the Royston site is problematic, but is certainly connected with the C ARIP group, as we may judge from the pseudo-runic P.[5]

The regular style of bust is resumed on two specimens (from the same dies) on which the legend is even more blundered. The S C can be recognized, now in reverse order, and there is a rounded version of the P.

On the reverse die the standing figure holds only one long cross, but he holds it with both hands, reaching across his body to do so. To the left there is an elaborate branch with berries (see the catalogue below). The long cross stands on a base, indicated by a triangular group of pellets.

[3] Type 61, *SCBI Hunterian* 46, ex Hunter. 1.31g.
[4] Ashmolean. 1.07g.
[5] Royston 27. 0.89g.

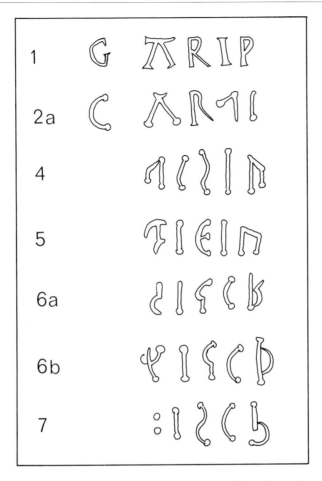

FIG. Disintegration of the C ARIP legend. Sketches of the lettering as seen on the specimens referred to by footnotes 1, 2, 4, 5, 6a, 6b, and 7.

The torso is cross-hatched, and the skirt indicated with four vertical rows of pellets.[6]

Another pair of dies with exactly the same types shows yet another deformation of the legend, including the letters ᒿ C and a deformed P. The reverse is well preserved, and shows clearly that the standing figure has a facing head, with two eyes and a nose.[7] The feet are turned outwards.

Yet another reverse die (the obverse is too obscure for one to be certain whether it is different) also has feet turned outwards.[8]

[6] a) Dutch Royal collection, Hill's photo no.432.
b) Ashmolean. Found at Tilbury. 0.98g.
[7] Hill, Type 15b, var. (i). British Museum, ex

Roach Smith. Found in London. 1.11g.
[8] SCBI Hunterian 92, ex Hunter. 0.93g.

419

The three pellets at the foot of the cross are a regular feature of this last variety. They occur again on a variant of Type 15 with rosettes and a quincunx added on the obverse (e.g. *SCBI Hunterian* 91). Coins of this variant also have a facing head, and neat little feet turned outwards.

Provenances for the C ARIP group are still too few to be of much help in localizing it. Coin no.2a is from near Chichester, no.2b is from Barking Abbey, no.5 is from near Royston, no.6a is from the Netherlands and 6b from Tilbury, while no.7 is a London find. If the pattern is maintained by future finds (which one should be cautious to assume!) it will perhaps prove to be less widespread than that for Series L. That might be

420

construed as evidence that the coins originated elsewhere than London, at a smaller mint-place less involved in long-distance trade. But that is merely theorizing.

The 'bird and branch' coin has been analysed, and found to contain only 31 per cent 'silver', with 3.9 per cent tin and 2.8 per cent zinc. The fourth coin in the series has 35 per cent 'silver', with 3.6 per cent tin and 2.2 per cent zinc.[9]

Weights are for the most part quite high, with three specimens at 1.07g. or above. The Royston coin, which fits least happily into the series, weighs only 0.89g.

II

The standing figure reaching across his body to hold the staff of the cross with both hands is seen again on a coin (catalogued below) which is nominally of Type 23a. It is likely to have been copied from a C ARIP prototype; the monster with curled tail was quite widely copied and is less indicative.

The curled creature, reminiscent of both wolf-worm and porcupine, is copied on a debased imitation of indifferent workmanship. The coin, catalogued below, came from Hertfordshire.

FIG. Duxford find

[9] Analyses by EPMA by Dr. J. P. Northover.

THE 'TRIQUETRAS' ECLECTIC GROUP

FOUR triquetras joined into a cruciform interlace pattern, with rosettes in the angles, make a distinctive design reminiscent of the 'celtic cross' design. A dozen specimens are known, of which all but two have geographical provenances. A south-of-Thames origin, probably in or near east Kent, is strongly indicated.

The progressive simplification of the interlace pattern is the only guide to the chronological ordering of the various types which are copied. An especially neat and elaborate interlace, with a group of five pellets at the centre of the pattern, probably stands at the head of the series. It is paired with a copy of the 'bird and branch' design, – which is a pointer to an early date. The bird's body is in the 'Kentish' style, but the hatched wing is reminscent of the more westerly style of Type 23 b/d, suggesting that both varieties were familiar to the die-cutter. The die is, in any case, imitative.

This and the second coin listed below, and also no.3b, are distinctively badly off-centre in their striking. The reverses of the first two are so similar in style that there can be no doubt that they are by the same hand. They therefore offer strong evidence that the 'triquetras' group is eclectic in character.

If these two coins are indeed early in the group, and close to each other in date, they offer an intriguing hint of a relatively early date for the beginning of Series L, in spite of its lower silver contents than Series U. The standing figure with two crosses is, it is true, a very basic design, but its style suggests that it has been copied from Type 12 or Type 13.

The knotted wreath-ties of the Type 52 obverse (nos.4-7 and 9 below) are Kentish in inspiration and show that the coins post-date the introduction of Types 42 or 32a in Series K (whichever is earlier). The duplication of the ties, so that they stand out on either side of the head like a girl's plaits, does not of course make sense.

The saddleback drapery of the bust on no.8 is related to Type 33, but the wreath-ties are not those of Type 33.

Only three coins in the series have been analysed chemically. A

MAP. Finds of the 'triquetras' eclectic group.

'Victory' coin was found to contain 47 per cent silver, and the Walbury Camp find, which is weathered, contained 54 per cent. An intended standard of half silver seems possible. The Hamwic find, no.7, is too corroded for accurate reconstruction of its original silver contents. A figure of 39 per cent has been tentatively proposed.

The weights of the flans seem to be rather carefully adjusted, with many specimens falling into the range 0.96–1.03g.

There is one pair of die-duplicates.

The later specimens in the series have simpler reverses, engraved more boldly. The Normanby find (no.8) is the odd man out. Taking its provenance and weight into account, one may suspect that it is a northern imitation.

1. *Obv.* Imitation of rev. of 'bird and branch' design (in 'London' style). *Rev.* Cruciform interlace with 5 pellets at centre. The rosettes are carefully executed, with 12–14 pellets. Found in north Essex 1980-3. Stewartby colln. *BNJ* 56 (1986), 7 and pl.1, 17.

2. *Obv.* Imitation of rev. of Type 12 or 15, standing figure with two crosses, head and feet turned left (i.e. the type is laterally reversed. Herringbone pattern on body. No boat-shaped curve. *Rev.* Interlace, with single pellet at centre. The rosettes have *c.*12 pellets. Found at Lewknor. 0.96g, Ashmolean Museum.

3. *Obv.* Facing winged figure. *Rev.* Interlace, single pellet at centre, rosettes of 9–10 pellets. a) 1.02g, Ashmolean Museum, ex Mack. b) 0.97g, *SCBI Yorks.* 952.

4. *Obv.* Facing bust with knotted wreath ties in 'A-B' style, half-circle drapery. *Rev.* Rough copy of 'bird and branch' design. Found at Walbury Camp. 0.96g, Ashmolean Museum (weathered).

5. *Obv.* Similar. *Rev.* Interlace. Rosettes nearer the edge of the coin. Found at Richborough. 1.01g., British Museum, *NC* 1953, pl.6, 10.

6. *Obv.* From a very similar die. *Rev.* Similar? (worn). 0.66g, Hamwic 98.

7. From the same or an extremely similar obverse die but apparently a different reverse. York, Fishergate hoard.

8. *Obv.* Imitation of Type 12 or 15, head and feet turned right. Sketchy pattern on body. *Rev.* Interlace in bolder style, rosettes with 9–10 pellets. Found at Tilbury. 0.96g, Ashmolean Museum.

9. *Obv.* Cf. 4 and 5, 'saddleback' drapery, wreath-ties in 'A-B' style. *Rev.* Interlace without rosettes. Bolder style of engraving, with five single pellets. Found at Reculver. 1.03g, *BMC* 198 (Type 52).

10. *Obv.* Bust, **+C ∧VNOOIII∧+** (copy of Type 12). *Rev.* Interlace of unskilled workmanship. The 7–8 pellets of the rosettes are very small and faint. The outer points of the triquetras are heavily pelletted. Found at Normanby, Li. 0.77g, *SCBI Mack* 341 (pl.56).

An eleventh variety, recently found at Wye, Kent, combines a **MONITASCORVM** obverse with a triquetras reverse.

THE 'CELTIC CROSS WITH ROSETTES' TYPES

ASSIGNING type-numbers to a miscellany of coins is easy enough, but we are not necessarily much the wiser when we have done it; understanding where and when each coin was minted can still vary from difficult to impossible. It is as well to recognize that, in the case of those types with a celtic cross with rosettes as one of their designs, the task is at present impossible. Many of the coins are obviously London-related, and the best of them have a careful legend corresponding with that of Type 12: ELVNDONIA+. Intriguingly, the legend is more literate than it is on Type 12.

The celtic cross design is technically so easy to copy that it offers little opportunity for secure stylistic analysis. The associated obverses (or reverses) show little stylistic coherence. Even within a single type, busts in quite different styles may be found.

We can at least draw a firm distinction between the Hamwic coinage, Type 39, which always lacks a pellet in each arm of the celtic cross, and all the other types, including Type 48 (discussed separately above), which add pellets.

The types to be considered are known in very small numbers, usually from one to three of each type. New varieties may well still turn up. The list of associated obverses, with their derivation, at present stands as follows:

93	Bird and branch (Series U, Type 23 b/d).
14	Bust left, ELVNOOIIV+ (Series L, Type 12).
16/34	Bust right, branch before face (Series L).
14 var.	Bust right, ELVNDONIΛ+ (Series L, Type 12).
58	Two stdg.figs., cross between. (Series N).
34a	Bust right, three-branched sceptre (Series L).
106	Stdg.fig. holding 2 crosses (Series L, Type 15).

With linear cross superimposed:

23/34b	Bird and branch (Series U).
–	Bust left, legend ΛIIΛ (Series L).
34b	Bust right, three-branched sceptre (Series L).

Because of their scarcity, and because they include a 'bird and branch' copy, one will suspect that these types form an eclectic group, similar in their scale and variability to the C ⅄RIP or triquetras groups. When one attempts to arrange the 'celtic cross' dies into a stylistic sequence, however, it appears that there are two or three distinct varieties. The bird and branch design occurs with two of these varieties, as does the distinctive obverse of Type 34, suggesting that they were concurrent.

The finds are predominantly from north of the Thames, but they are very scattered, and it is in any case not clear that we are justified in combining all the evidence into a single pattern.

What follows is merely a set of working notes on the various types – first those with the standard version of the celtic cross, and then those which have a cross superimposed on it.

I

Type 93, published by Hill as a 23c/34 mule, is a London find formerly in the collection of Roach Smith. The pecking bird, imitating the

'London' style, is laterally reversed, and there are three miniature clusters of berries. The celtic cross is of balanced proportions, with a central rosette.[1]

II

BMC Type 14 has an obverse which is laterally reversed, including the otherwise careful legend. The head is outlined in five pellets suggesting a

helmet or crest. The celtic cross is well proportioned, and similar to Type 93, but with only a pellet at the centre.[2]

---

[1] *NC* 1953, p.104 and pl.6, 18, 0.95g.
[2] *BMC* 93, ex Thames hoard, 0.94g.

427

III

A Type 16/34 'mule' found in excavations at Rochester, near the cathedral, has straight triple wreath-ties, and drapery which would fit in with some of the miscellaneous coins listed with Series L. The

(simplified) bow-like branch which defines Type 16 is normally seen on dies in 'Hwiccian' style. The celtic cross has five boldly modelled bosses, one in each rosette, and one at the centre of the design.[3]

IV

Type 14, with right-facing bust, is known from two specimens (one from Cosham, Sussex) from the same dies.[4] The bust is a talented copy, which merges the 'northern' and 'Hwiccian' styles. The legend is fully literate.

On the reverse, the arms of the cross converge to a single line. The five main pellets are quite bold, and the rosettes are made up of as many as 15-17 fine pellets.

V

Type 58. Three specimens by the same hand but from different dies show two standing figures, copied no doubt from Series N but not closely similar to any specific variety. The earliest of the three is a Tilbury find on which it can be seen that the heads are both in profile, turned towards

[3] *BNJ* 1977, 46 and pl.2, 30. 1.17g, 'looks base or plated'.

[4] For the Cosham find, see *BNJ* 1977, 38 and pl,2, 29. 1.06g. The coin was reported as a garden find from 1, Mansvid Avenue. Some unease has been expressed about the provenance. The other specimen, *SCBI Mack* 343, is chipped and weighs only 0.46g. It has been incorrectly published as being of Type 34.

each other (as on Type 41a). Each figure is pointing the toe of his inner foot. The reverse is important because it shows traces of 'rosettes within rosettes' – a few tiny pellets around the central bosses (and also around the pellet at the centre of the design). The rosettes are neat and carefully executed with a large number of pellets – 15 or 16. The arms of the celtic cross converge to a single line, as in Type 14. It would occasion no surprise if a die-link were to turn up between Types 14 and 58. They appear to reflect a separate sequence of production from the other 'rosettes' types.

The other two specimens of Type 58 are worn or less clearly struck. On one the right-hand cross appears to have a triangular head, and the central cross to stand on a semi-circular base, as if the die-cutter had some independent ideas about the design he was creating, and was not merely copying it from another coin. The celtic cross is bolder and less careful, with rosettes of only 9-10 pellets.[5]

VI

Type 34a is better exemplified by a find from Tilbury than by *BMC* 161. The bust, with three straight wreath-ties, is reminiscent of the 'northern'

style in Type 32a. In place of a cross in front of the face, there is a three-branched sceptre. This is, in some sense, an official part of the design: it recurs in Type 34b (below).

BMC 161 is an imitative piece, with a crudely executed bust. The knotted wreath-ties have grown into a triquetra – evidence of influence

from more than one other type. The celtic cross is well proportioned, and encloses very small rosettes, with a fifth, which looks similar, at the centre.[6]

---

[5] *SCBI Hunterian* 112, 1.03g, and BM (Hill, *NC* 1953, 109 and pl.7, 5). 1.15g, worn.
[6] The weight is only 0.76g.

VII

Type 106 is known from two die-duplicate specimens, one excavated at Whitby, the other excavated at Canterbury. They are patently imitative. The standing figure is copied from a version with a facing head, and

wreath-ties sticking out to left and right. In this case they are drawn as a single line, reminiscent of an oriental sun-hat. The celtic cross has a rosette at the centre.[7]

VIII

The coins which have a linear cross superimposed on the celtic cross apparently form a separate sequence, possibly from another workshop. A fine, bold pecking bird combines the hatched and scrolled wing of the

best western-style specimens, with a 'Kentish' body and tail. The celtic cross design, too, is boldly executed, with five pellets defining the linear cross, and a further cluster of four pellets at the centre of the design.[8]

IX

A puzzling coin from Wangford, Suffolk has a left-facing bust with a pseudo-inscription ΛIIΛ. The reverse is of poor proportions and lacks the

cluster of four pellets at the centre.[9]

[7] NC 1953, 104 (described as Type 12/34), and pl.6, 15. 0.87g, and Canterbury VIII, from 77-9, Castle Street. 1.03g.

[8] NCirc 97 (1989), 232, item 4580 (illus.). 1.45g, from Tilbury.

[9] Originally recorded as being from 'Wangford, near Bury St. Edmunds', in 1983 or earlier. See Proc.Suffolk Inst.Arch.Hist. 25/4 (1984), 325. The coin, broken and repaired, came back on the market in 1989 (NCirc 97, 1989, item 3996,) with the weight given as 0.834g.

X

Type 34b with superimposed linear cross is known from several specimens, including *BMC* 162,[10], and a puzzling coin (catalogued below) from the same obverse and almost certainly the same reverse die,

obtained at Brighton before 1940.[11] The bust is in the 'northern' style, and the cross on the reverse has triangular serifs. The alloy of the Brighton coin has aroused misgivings.[12]

A specimen said to be similar to *BMC* 162 is reported from Burghfield, Berkshire.

A find from Burrow Hill, Butley has several distinctive features. On the obverse the sceptre appears to terminate in a fleur-de-lis. On the reverse there is a small diamond-shaped central panel. This coin has been analysed by M.R. Cowell, and found to contain 40 per cent 'silver', plus 7 per cent tin.[13]

A Tilbury find (catalogued below) adds further variety. The bust is

very clearly crested, and the symbol in front of the face is, equally clearly, a cross on a stand. On the reverse the linear cross springs from a central circle.

XI

The 'celtic cross with rosettes' types remain very problematic. There would seem to be three main stylistic sequences, which are likely to run in parallel. One cannot envisage a single sequence. There is, in addition, the 'triquetras' group, which is superficially similar. One wonders whether there can have been a phase of the coinage when 'rosettes' types were adopted simultaneously in several workshops. When might such a new design have been introduced? Can it have been after Series L, Type

[10] 0.83g. Enlarged illustration in *BNJ* 1986, pl.1, 15.

[11] 1.10g. The piece is in very fresh condition, and is superior to *BMC* 162 – which must be in its favour.

[12] EPMA now shows 19% 'silver', with 3% tin and an unparalleled 10% zinc. The gold-silver ratio is acceptable.

[13] M.R. Cowell, in *BNJ* 55 (1985), 47.

12 had become familiar, yet while Series U, Type 23b/d was still available as a prototype? (Were sceattas with such different silver contents in use at the same time?) And where were the 'rosettes' types struck? Mainly in London? – or in the commercial orbit of London? Some of the busts show close stylistic affinities with the 'northern' style seen in Series K(L) or L(K), Type 20/18.

In general, the whole cluster of types seems to be rooted in Series L, Type 12. *BMC* 161, with its triquetra-like knotted wreath-ties, is a red herring.

The connection with Series N, Type 41a may hold further clues, pointing towards a mint-place other than London, north of the Thames, for at least one stylistic sequence.

If the hypothesis of multiple origins is correct, we are not justified in drawing conclusions from the geographical pattern of finds as a whole; and there are far too few provenances to allow us to map each stylistic sub-group separately, to any good effect. Die-linked specimens from Canterbury and Whitby are a warning against drawing conclusions from insufficient evidence.

There is no reason whatever to look for a link, in terms of die-cutting, with Series H, Type 48, which is a relatively plentiful substantive type (*c.* 20 specimens), in which the design is perceived somewhat differently, with the emphasis more on the rosettes and less on the celtic cross. Type 48 is itself problematic, but there seems to be a connection of some sort with Hamwic. The Series L-related 'celtic cross with rosettes' types are not found at Hamwic. There are, however, a couple of (slightly suspect) provenances from Sussex. There are also two finds reported from Domburg. That, again, hints at multiple origins, as in Series J.

Considerably more provenanced material will be needed before we can hope to understand the 'celtic cross with rosettes' types.

COINS WITH ROSETTES IN THE OBVERSE FIELD
(TYPES 32B AND 68)

FOUR eccentrically ornamented sceattas are known which combine a distinctive obverse bust with reverse types borrowed from either Series K or Series L. They are perhaps the first evidence of another little eclectic group.

BMC Type 32b has a left-facing bust, with a rather flat profile and a small, pointed chin. In front of the face are two rosettes, each with 8 pellets and a rather larger central pellet. Behind the head, and below the

two short, straight wreath-ties, is a third similar rosette. The reverse has a copy of the 'northern' style of wolf-worm with an added torque. The coin weighs 0.93g.

A similar flat profile, right-facing, and fairly obviously by the same hand, is ornamented with a quincunx and rosette in front of the face, while behind the head is a similar finely drawn rosette. The reverse has a standing figure holding two crosses, the die being cut, no doubt, by the same hand as the obverse. Both crosses have pyramidal bases composed of three pellets. The head is facing, and the torso is ornamented with herring-bone hatching. The coin, which weighs 1.08g, appears to contain hardly any silver. It is catalogued below.

An extremely similar coin, on which the rosette behind the head is indistinct, has a standing figure with facing head and out-turned feet,

who holds, to the left, a cross with triangular base, and to the right, a staff ornamented with pellets. The die-cutter may clumsily not have left himself enough room for the bar of the second cross. The coin, now in

433

Glasgow, is from the Lockett collection (*SCBI Hunterian* 91). Philip Hill lists it as his Type 68.

He adds a fourth specimen, sold in London in 1952, and described as having in front of the face 4 pellets and pellet in circle, and behind the head 5 pellets.

Can a die-cutter have had such a restricted output that we now know of his work from only four coins, or might they link with some other group? The distinctive modelling of the face, which should be recognizable if it occurred elsewhere, has not been identified. The triangular base of the crosses can be matched elsewhere, but it may be an indication of what such crosses were like, rather than a stylistic mannerism. The herring-bone shading is a better criterion, which again has not been identified elsewhere.

SCEATTAS READING MONITASCORVM OR SCORVM

A FIND from Eastcote, Northants (about a mile north of the line of Watling Street) bears a general resemblance to Series T (bust/porcupine), but the obverse has the legend, in small, neat letters, MONITASCORVM+. The bust is distinctly reminiscent of an early die belonging to Series Q. The profile has the same hooked nose, and the outer wreath-tie curves around the inner one in a way that is so unusual

as to suggest that the die-cutter had a coin of Series Q in front of him. The spine of the porcupine is less bold than in Series T, and the annulet is omitted.[1]

The legend is intriguing. It has been tentatively expanded by Miss Archibald to *moneta sanctorum*.

A crude and garbled imitation formed part of the Bird collection. The obverse legend appears to be ᴟᴧVᴧᴧV.[2]

Another unique and highly interesting coin of essentially the same design reads ..]ELVNDONIA on the obverse, in neat lettering, and SCORVM on the reverse, squeezed into the edge of the design in small letters. It

was said to come from near Thetford, but the information does not command much respect. One can be perfectly sure that it is an English find, and no doubt it is from East Anglia or the east midlands.

A third MONITAZCORVM coin from Wye, Kent, has a triquetras reverse.[4] This coin, illustrated here, is now in a private collection in

---

[1] *NC* 1953, pl.6, 28. *British Museum Quarterly* 15 (1952), 54. 1.10g. There are three adjacent hamlets in Pattishall, named Astcote, Eastcote, and Dalscote, and the second of these is presumably the find-spot.

[2] Glendining 20 Nov.1974, lot 25. 1.28g.

[3] 1.13g.

[4] I am indebted to Mr. Bonser for information on this find, weighing 1.19g.

FIG.   MONITASCORVM types

America.[5]

A fourth, catalogued below, matches Series L in its types.

One cannot be quite sure that all four coins were struck in the same place, even though their legend is so unusual. The link with Series T seems to be the strongest part of the evidence.

Type 46, which is linked with Type 70i, reads   + MONITASCORVM. It tends to reinforce the suspicion that the legend was used at more than one mint-place.

[5] Its weight is virtually the same (1.18g). It was sold as having been found 'near Canterbury'.

436

THE 'ARCHER' GROUP

FIVE sceattas are now known which have in common the type of a bird, right, with its head turned back to peck at a berried vine. The theme is familiar from Series V and Series U, Type 23 b/d, but the handling of the design is distinctive.

On three of the five coins, moreover, the bird, which would normally be considered as a reverse type, is paired with another reverse design of great charm and novelty, namely a kneeling archer, drawing his bow. The head of the arrow is a large round knob, not a pointed tip. Arrows of this type were used by hunters to stun birds. Behind the figure is a berried plant.

The first 'archer' sceat was found near the iron-age hill fort of Walbury Camp in 1975. A green road runs through the hill fort, which is at the

highest point in southern England. The ground falls steeply to the south, with extensive views.[1]

EPMA analysis shows that the coin contains 55 per cent 'silver', with perhaps as much as 6 per cent tin. The weight is 1.13g. The archer is wearing a wreath with two straight wreath-ties. No garments are

[1] The coin was reportedly found 'within half a mile of the hill-fort . . . apparently washed out by heavy rain', i.e. the finder asserted that it was a single find at some distance from any other of the Walbury Camp finds. He later sold the coin at auction, with the intention of giving the proceeds to charity for the benefit of handicapped children. The coin was bought by the Ashmolean with generous help from Mr. D. R. Walker.

depicted. The finger and thumb of the hand holding the bow are distinguished, and fingers can be made out on the clenched hand holding the bow-string. The heel of the rear foot is shown. In short, the figure is delicately and elaborately drawn. The plant has five branches, each of which ends in a cluster of berries.

The bird is roundly modelled throughout. The vine springs from the lower left margin, as on Series U, Type 23.

A second specimen came to light in 1983 at Middle Harling, Norfolk. It is in rather weathered condition, but can be seen to be essentially very similar to the first, although from different dies. It did not form part of the Middle Harling hoard, but was found singly about 100m to the south-west of the seventh/ninth-century settlement site.[2]

On a third specimen, possibly from the same 'archer' die as the first, the bird is laterally reversed. There is no provenance.[3]

The same bird is seen in combination with another reverse type, the standing figure with long cross and hawk (Type 20, etc.), on a coin from Great Bircham, Norfolk.[4] The bird is less roundly modelled, and the coin is double-struck, in such a way that the bird's neck is missing from the impression, being replaced by a row of pellets that belongs to the outer

border. The style of the standing figure (which might, in principle, provide a link to some other group of coins) is not easy to assess, because of weak striking. He appears to be raising his shoulders. The large head is turned to the right; the hawk is long and thin, with a small head; the feet are below the boat-shaped curve. The tunic flares sharply at the hem, and there seem to be two small pellets at the waist-line. The upper half of the

[2] M. M. Archibald, 'The coinage of Beonna in the light of the Middle Harling hoard', *BNJ* 55 (1985), 10-54, at p.15 and pl.2 (MH 63); for the exact find-spot, see p.37.

[3] *Dans le commerce.* I am indebted to Mr. Derek Chick and Mr. M. J. Bonser for their kindness in

drawing this coin to my attention, in September 1991.

[4] M. A. S. Blackburn and M. J. Bonser, 'Single finds of Anglo-Saxon and Norman coins – 3', *BNJ* 56 (1986), 64-101, at pp.87f., no.99. The exact site is confidentially recorded.

tunic is perhaps cross-hatched. There are no obvious comparanda, and the die may very well be a copy of a familiar type, by another workman and at another mint-place than that of Type 20.

A fifth coin was published by Roach Smith as a Reculver find.[5] The bird is in combination with a dog-like monster with, apparently, a triple

tail. One cannot say much more on the evidence of a sketchy line-drawing. The proportions of the pecking bird are, however, persuasively the same as on the other three coins; and because the group is scarce it is unlikely to have attracted imitation.

The four provenances are so widely scattered that one should defer judgement on the region of origin of the group. More weight should be given to the two finds from Norfolk, which was in some sense peripheral, than to the coin from Reculver, where trade-routes converged and many sceatta types mingled.

I

Who is this archer? Would users of the coins have recognized him as the same person, in another role, as the standing figure with two crosses, or with cross and hawk? – In the case of Type 13, showing a seated figure with cross and hawk, one can be confident that the same person is intended as on Type 12, because there is a die-link, and because the seated figure seems to depict a real-life situation. Our general conviction that sceattas were royal coinages makes it easy to believe that he is a person of authority, and of secular authority (because of the hawk) – in a word, that it is an icon of the king.

Mary Morehart has discussed the problem of attaching political meaning to sceatta types. She has argued forcefully against seeing the archer as a royal figure, and has offered a wealth of comparative material from sculpture and manuscript illumination, to show that he was a familiar motif in Anglo-Saxon art, usually shooting at a bird. He is merely one more of the denizens of the inhabited vine-scroll, from which several other sceatta types are drawn.[6]

[5] C. Roach Smith, *Richborough, Reculver, and Lympne*, pl.7, 3.

[6] M. J. Morehart, 'Anglo-Saxon art and the "archer" sceat', *Sceattas in England and on the Continent*, ed. D. Hill and D. M. Metcalf, Oxford, 1984, pp.181-92.

'VICTORY' SCEATTAS

A ROMAN coin with a winged Victory advancing right, holding a wreath, is the model from which *BMC* Type 22 was closely copied. Some such coin must have been found in the soil, and brought to the attention of the die-cutter. He seems to have understood the figure as male and (on some dies) to have reinterpreted the wing as a long banner, although the staff of the banner is not clearly drawn, and it is difficult to make out what is intended. The wing or banner is always divided into two segments, of about a third and two-thirds. The dividing line is often a continuation of the forearm. Either the figure is holding the staff (omitted) of a banner, or it is winged, as on the model, in which case the angle of the arm probably indicates forward movement. In front of the figure, quite prominently, there are either pseudo-letters, or alternatively a cross potent on a mount.

There are two associated reverse types, of which one is a routine full-length figure with two crosses, as found in Series U and L. The head and feet are turned to the right, and the legs are well apart, as though a walking rather than a standing figure were intended. The other reverse type is richer and stranger in content. It shows a standing, facing figure in a triple boat-shaped curve, strongly incurving. The figure has – without doubt – outspread wings. The head, turned to the right, is helmeted or long-haired as usual. In the world of ideas current in the eighth century a winged figure can presumably only be intended to represent an angel. There are crosses symmetrically to left and right.

Was the 'Victory' type merely a Roman design that caught the die-cutter's fancy, or was there some more specific contemporary significance? – Some solemn occasion of state? It need not be a military victory, or a victory of any sort: the wreath may not have been understood, even, as a wreath. There is usually a pellet, or a small cross in the centre of it. We should curb our enthusiasm before envisaging eighth-century commemorative issues (cf. Alfred's London Monogram type?), while recognizing that there are sceattas which bring iconography close to real occasions, notably Type 13 which shows the king seated on a scroll-backed chair, holding a hawk and a long cross.

We cannot date the 'Victory' coins at all accurately. To search the historical record for an appropriate occasion when they might have been struck would therefore be deplorably speculative. It should be mentioned that the Hamwic find came from an unexpectedly early archaeological context, on a street surface which the excavators dated to 700-725, with a porcupine nearby.

There is another, completely separate type, known from two die-duplicate specimens, which has already been discussed as part of the 'triquetras' group. It does not show Victory advancing, but its obverse has a standing, facing winged figure, possibly female. There is, of course, no evidence that it was struck at the same date, much less for the same reason, as the other type.

The 'Victory' coins are *c.*40-50 per cent fine, and weigh 0.95-1.14g.

I

If the legends have any significance, they have so far guarded their secret with complete success. By comparing one specimen with another we can, however, discern some common features, which serve to link the two reverse types. The Hamwic, Hinton Parva, and Bawsey specimens are all

1   2   3   4   5

FIG. Legends on the 'Victory' sceattas, Type 22.

attempting the same pattern. The British Museum specimen (sketched from a cast) may be distantly related. The Royston find, which from its style could be the earliest in the series, has sketchier pseudo-letters, and it is not clear whether they end with a ∆.

The cross potent on a box-shaped mount would, later in the middle ages, be iconographically suitable for Golgotha. One suspects that it had a specific meaning in the context of Type 22, which remains elusive.

II

The tally of specimens of the 'Victory' type is as follows. Their correct chronological sequence is far from clear. The specimen with cross potent has been placed last, because its silver contents are the lowest of the three coins that have been analysed.

Rev. Standing figure with 2 crosses

1. Royston 30, 0.95g. *BNJ* 56 (1986), 74, no.30, and illus., p.97. The Victory's head appears to be copying the style of the Roman model. On the reverse, there are some unexplained details to the right of the right-hand cross.
2. Hamwic 101, 0.97g. EPMA 51% 'silver' (reconstruction), with 6.6% tin and 0.6% zinc. The first pseudo-letter is joined to the figure's arm.
3. *BMC* 110 = Type 22. 1.10g. There is a delicate x in the wreath.

Rev. Facing, winged figure in boat-shaped curve.

4. Hinton Parva find, 1.14g. The (?) banner on the obverse and the wings on the reverse are ornamented with a herringbone pattern. The heads on obverse and reverse are noticeably alike. EPMA analysis, part corrected, shows 53.9% 'silver', with 4.5% tin and 0.3% zinc.
5. Bawsey find, *BNJ* 56 (1986), 74, and illus. as 30A, p.97. Sotheby, 19 July 1984, 113.
6. Ashmolean. Found near Hitchin. 0.91g. *Obv.* with cross potent. *Rev.* from the same or a very similar die to no.5. EPMA analysis shows 37.0% 'silver', with 5.3% tin and 1.3% zinc.

III

It would be puzzling to imagine that a small mint, or a single moneyer, struck the 'Victory' types and nothing else. Could they be part of a longer sequence of issues from one source? Our only chance of answering that question is through finding a die-link connecting nos.1-3 above with some other type, or at least finding convincing similarities of style to make the link. The body of the standing figure is the most revealing feature: a rectangular outline, within which the body is modelled in quite high relief, with irregular criss-cross shading. Sometimes there is a horizontal line of division superimposed at the waist. There are no obvious candidates among the main styles found in Series K and L.

A K/N-RELATED ECLECTIC GROUP

SMALL dies with neat double or triple outer borders composed of a dotted border, an outer wire border, and sometimes an inner wire border as well create such a distinctive appearance, in a small group of sceattas, as to suggest that they are from a separate workshop. They include coins corresponding exactly with Series K, Type 20, and others on which a Series L standing figure with two crosses is coupled with a monster with curled tail. The latter were classified in *BMC* as Type 23a. Other coins have subsequently been listed as Type 23a which are in another style, and seem to belong more closely with the C ARIP group.

Two finds from among the few recorded from the territory of the West Kentish kingdom prompted the speculation that the style belongs to a mint at Rochester.[1] There is far too little evidence for this to be anything but a guess, especially since one of the two finds[2] does not conform with the stylistic criteria very closely.

The coins in question are:

1.   Type 20, with knotted wreath-tie. Inner wire border, and outer dotted border. Found in or near the Isle of Grain. 0.64g. EPMA analysis of the coin, which is corroded, shows 40 per cent 'silver' and 12 per cent tin. (Catalogued below).

2.   Type 20, with two straight wreath-ties. Inner dotted border and outer wire border, on both obverse and reverse. a)1.17g. BM, Barnett bequest ex Carlyon-Britton.[3] b)Cardiff, E.017, from the same dies.[4] EPMA analysis of the coin, which is corroded, shows 31 per cent 'silver' with 9 per cent tin.

3. Type 15/41, monster right. The standing figure has a cross-hatched tunic. There is a base-line joining the two crosses. The feet point outwards. Inner dotted and outer wire border. On the reverse, note the animal's drooping crest. Triple outer border (wire, dotted, wire). 1.10g. Found at Tilbury. (Catalogued below.)

4. Similar. Found at Cooling, near Hoo, Kent.[5]

5. Type 15/41, monster left. Triple border on obverse and reverse. Found at Bradwell-on-Sea, Essex.

6. Type 16/41, monster right. a) Montague colln. b) Thames hoard (same dies), catalogued below.

[1] D.M. Metcalf, 'Twenty-five notes on sceatta finds', in *Sceattas in England and on the Continent*, pp.193-205, notes 19 and 20.

[2] No.1 below is larger, and has knotted wreath-ties.

[3] *NC* 1953, pl.6, 5.

[4] Off-centre striking, cf. the Tilbury find.

[5] Metcalf, loc.cit., note 20.

THE 'ANIMAL MASK' ECLECTIC GROUP

WHAT is this creature with large staring eyes set in the front of its head, prominent ears, and whiskers? On the left of the design we see its neck or shoulder, while to the right and above there are normally anything from two to five pelleted annulets in the field. Six specimens are known, from five different reverse types. The style varies considerably: one certainly could not claim that all the dies were by the same hand. Nor do the obverses

complement each other in style, to convey any clear idea of the creature that is intended. One looks like a donkey, another like a fox, a third suggests a cat. It is hard to think that any of these animals is dignified enough to be chosen as a coin type. Perhaps a lion was intended, and the die-cutter, never having seen one, used his imagination.

Presumably all six coins are from the same workshop or the same place. Their provenances are widely scattered, and do not serve to indicate the region of origin any more closely than Middle Anglia or the Thames valley. It seems that all the coins are of very base metal. Their sequence is a matter of guess-work.

A specimen catalogued below was probably found near Oxford, and not (as has been stated) near Marlborough.[1] Its reverse type is the monster with foreleg folded under the body (cf. Series N) but with a delicately modelled

---

[1] In *BNJ* 1976, at p.8, it is suggested that two provenances became confused, probably while the coins in question were in the cabinet of Lord Londesborough.

MAP. Finds of the 'animal mask' eclectic group.

canine head, and a curled tail. EPMA shows 28 per cent 'silver' plus 5 per cent tin.

Royston 46 copies the reverse of Series K, Type 20, etc. (standing figure with cross and hawk). The obverse is indistinct, but the modelling of the animal mask can be made out, with rosettes to the right.[2]

A somewhat similar coin was classified by Hill as his Type 76. The reverse has a standing figure with two crosses, and Hill rightly drew attention to the similarity of the die to *BMC* 117 (Type 23a).[3]

A find from near St. Neots has an entirely new reverse design, of four letters T in the segments of a circle.[4]

Finally, a coin from Horton Kirby, near Farningham, Kent, and another

from Cheriton (Hants.) have on their reverses a bird which is perhaps imitated from the 'sea-gull' of Series Q.[5] The dies of the Horton Kirby find are small, and both obverse and reverse have a double outer border. The outermost border on the obverse is irregular. The dies of the Cheriton find are obviously by the same hand.

---

[2] The illustration of the obverse appears to be upside down.

[3] This coin, described as base, was in the collection of Mr. F. Baldwin.

[4] I am indebted to Mr. Bonser for preliminary advice on this find.

[5] Again, I am indebted to Mr. Bonser, to the finder, Mr. G. Burr, for a photograph, and to Mr. Chick for casts of the coin, which is in very fine condition. Its weight is 0.99g, and it is described as base.

K/R 'MULES'

FOUR specimens are now known which combine the wolf-worm of Type 32a with a 'standard' reverse. They are thus 'double reverse' coins. The fact that there are four of them is intriguing, and makes it difficult to dismiss them simply as opportunist forgeries. They are stylistically diverse, only two of the eight dies being obviously related. The coins, with their provenances, are:

1. A coin that came to light in 1971 and has been assumed to be the same as one found in a field near Winchester in 1839. The reverse has a cross with annulets. *BNJ* 1977, pl.2, 26.

2. Lakenheath, Sf. 1977 or earlier. *BNJ* 1977, pl.2, 27, and in the catalogue below. The wolf-worm has a certain amount of 'fur' on its back, which implies an acquaintance with style 'A-B' as well as style 'C-D' of the prototype. 0.96g, 59% 'silver'.

3. Great Wilbraham, Ca., *c.*1980. 'Single finds, 2', no.30, 0.97g.
4. No provenance (English find), 1991, 0.69g.
Nos. 1-3 have been thoroughly discussed by Blackburn and Bonser,[1] who point out that nos.2-3 may well be from the same workshop. Nos.1 and 4, with annulets, are not obviously related.

An East Anglian or, more probably, Middle Anglian origin is plausible. Blackburn and Bonser rightly point out that the Winchester

---

[1] M. A. S. Blackburn and M. J. Bonser, 'Single finds of Anglo-Saxon and Norman coins – 2', *BNJ* 55 (1985), 55-78, at pp.62f.

find may be from a different workshop, the similarities of type being coincidental. One could find a matching situation in the standard-saltire series (Type 70). It is only prudent to add that we cannot be certain that the 1971 coin is the nineteenth-century Winchester find.

It is possible that some or all four of the coins are part of larger eclectic groups. That could only be proved through die-linkage or close stylistic similarity. No links have so far come to notice, and we should not expect any in Series K proper: these are not true mules.

The reverse types, particularly those with annulets, are more likely to yield a link, perhaps into Type 70, which (so far as one can judge of such an easily copied design) may be by the same hand. The unique and enigmatic *BMC* 188 (Type 46) seems to be an imitation muling the saltire-with-annulets in standard, with an early, inscribed version of Series O, Type 40, [2] – a coin from very early in the secondary phase.

One thinks of the Garton-on-the-Wolds grave-find, in which a coin of Type 32a is associated with a Series R coin with an unusual annulets reverse.[3] It always seemed surprising that the annulets design was in existence at such an early date. The K/R 'mules' perhaps have a similar, relatively early context, dating from a time when Type 32a was sufficiently prominent to attract copying.

[2] Blackburn and Bonser draw attention to Type 46, which there is no positive reason to assign to Series O.

[3] *BNJ* 30 (1960-1), pl.4, R2z.

SERIES L, TYPE 23E

A WHORL of three wolf-worms is coupled, in Type 23e, with a London-derived standing figure with two crosses. The type stands in no discernible relationship to either Series H, Type 48 or Series S. The distribution of finds, so far as one can judge from small numbers, is in conformity with Series L, with provenances from as far afield as Temple Guiting, Glos., and East Garston, Berks. The type was present in the Thames hoard. It is absent from east Kent, and from the site near Royston. Intriguingly, there are three specimens from Tilbury.

The standing figure lacks a boat-shaped curve: there is a straight line joining the bases of the two crosses. The tunic normally flares outwards at the hem-line.

There is more variability in the whorl. It can rotate either clockwise or anti-clockwise. The three tongues which meet at the centre-point of the design can be shown as solid lines or as rows of pellets. There can be an extra outer wire border. The most interesting variation is the addition of diminutive legs to the wolf-worms (as seen in style 'A-B' of Type 32a).

The most elaborate and careful die has a design rotating anti-clockwise; the wolf-worms have legs. Two specimens are known, from different dies.[1]

Another specimen with legs, but with a clockwise whorl, is catalogued below. It is not clear what its place in the sequence is, but it is heavy.[2] Its silver contents are 31 per cent, with 4 per cent tin.

[1] *SCBI Mack* 348, 0.92g. A coin from Tilbury is extremely similar, and is perhaps from the same 'standing figure' die.

[2] No provenance. 1.07g.

A find from Tilbury,[3] and another from Temple Guiting[4] seem to be run-of-the-mill coins with anti-clockwise whorls. The East Garston find has dotted tongues.[5]

The Thames hoard specimen has a clockwise whorl, and a rather fuller standing figure.[6]

I

The imitations are of variable quality. A coin from Barrington, catalogued below, is struck from a small obverse die, and the standing figure is diminutive.[7] It could be a late member of the series, or – more probably – a poor but honest counterfeit. Its weight is only 0.78g, and its silver contents are 24 per cent, with 4 per cent tin.

The Lakenheath, Suffolk find is exceptionally unconvincing in style.[8]

On the Cimiez coin the standing figure is laterally reversed, and a berried branch has been added to the right. The whorl, interestingly, is imitated from Type 48 rather than 23e.[9]

On an extraordinary coin from Tilbury, catalogued below, the standing figure is again laterally reversed, and the crosses are replaced by irregular

twig-like branches. These appear to grow out of the ends of the man's arms, making him a hybrid between Struwwelpeter and the Green Man. The whorl is clockwise, the tongues are dotted, and diamonds of pellets are inserted into the design.

It is curious that a type which is so scarce today, and evidently so debased, should have attracted copying.

[3] *NCirc.* 1989, 4006, 0.938g, and information from Mr. M.J. Bonser.

[4] *SCBI West Country* 243. 0.69g.

[5] *NCirc.* 1989, 4005, 0.937g, and information from the finder, Mr. B. Cavill.

[6] *BMC* 117. 1.08g.

[7] The coin is ticketed as being from Malton.

[8] *Seaby's Bulletin* 1978, E.239 (illus.)

[9] Le Gentilhomme 75, Cimiez 325, 0.69g.

SERIES M

THE NEED to find a home for Type 45 (Series M) raises basic questions about the number and location of mint-places in southern England, and also about the reliability of arguments from typology. The coins are of a design not closely related to any other sceatta types. On the obverse is a sinuous animal, usually with a curled tail and a curled tongue. On the reverse is a distinctive spiral branch with berries. From the nine or ten recorded provenances, it is clear enough that it circulated south of the Thames, in Kent and north-eastern Wessex, and that it was, effectively, absent at Hamwic and absent everywhere north of London, including East Anglia.[1] The Tilbury evidence rules out an East Saxon attribution.[2] Had it been a London coinage one would have expected, among nine or ten finds of the type, to see more signs of its circulation northwards, e.g. at Royston. There will be a presumption that it is Kentish rather than from an inland mint in the middle Thames valley, but it is in principle very difficult, and in this case virtually impossible, to deduce from a distribution-map the point of origin of coins within their circulation area.

Could Series M be from east Kent? Its types are completely unrelated to those of Series K, and one would be reluctant, therefore, to think that it was concurrent with K at the same mint-place. Since K first appears at the very beginning of the secondary phase, it would seem that M could only be late secondary, if it were from the same mint-place. Analyses show that it was struck on a 50 per cent silver standard, – but in one instance, apparently, contained 68 per cent silver. Could coins of very good weight and with that amount of silver be late? The later stages of Series R and L fall well below 50 per cent silver: could a small, contemporary south-of-the-Thames issue, circulating like L in the south-eastern corridor, have maintained so much better a silver standard than the dominant series ? – One might hope that a major new hoard from the middle Thames valley, falling late in the secondary phase, would put the chronology of various southern series into a much clearer light, and allow us to dispense with complicated hypotheses.

---

[1] There are 3 finds from Reculver (see sub-section IV), and single coins from Canterbury, London, Hamwic (very worn), Walbury Camp, Knighton, Brk (also published as 'in the vicinity of Swindon'), and Tilbury.

[2] One find, cf. large numbers of Series S.

(The Thames hoard of c.1860 is unambiguous, but is too small for the absence of particular types to be considered as negative evidence).

Series M, with its own characteristic if rather nondescript designs, in a range of minor varieties, looks like the product of a separate mint, which worked only on a small scale, but for long enough to need several separate batches of dies. That is, on the face of it, an argument merely from typology. In reality, it is the bottom line of a more protracted consideration: it expresses a judgement that the alternative interpretations are untenable for archaeological reasons and reasons of the alloy, and also a conviction that the idea of a minor mint keeping to its own distinctive and recognizable design chimes in with what we know, more securely, about the habits of other sceatta mints.

Series L and K clearly represent the activity of the two major minting centres of London and east Kent. Series M, N, and O (and various other smaller groups of coins that have hitherto been swept up into L or U) also circulated in the south-eastern corridor, and they are, as one might say, surplus to the requirements of our ideas about the concentration of minting in coastal wics. They push us towards envisaging, reluctantly, that there were more mints in the region than survived into the early ninth century.

I

Series M is known from about twenty specimens, among which there are several pairs and obverse die-links,[3] pointing to the use originally of as many as forty to fifty obverse dies. There are half-a-dozen varieties, one of which might reasonably have been given a separate type-number, as it shows a winged animal. The varieties exist in very unequal numbers. As some are known from only one specimen, it is possible that further varieties may still come to light. The estimated total of dies implies that the scarce varieties may originally have been struck from only two or three dies.

The sequence of varieties is very difficult to guess. The basic type is an animal with arched back and raised head, with forelegs extended – the gesture of a dancing or prancing dog inviting another dog to play. It has a curled tail and a long curled tongue. (For the tongue, compare Series K, Types 32a and 33.) The arched shape of the body and the angle between body and neck are sometimes exaggerated to the point of caricature. Variations on the basic type are a triple-forked tail (cf. Series Q), a forked

[3] *SCBI Hunterian* 106 and 131 are from the same dies, and the Canterbury find is from the same obverse. *BMC* 187 and *SCBI Mack* 364 share an obverse. BM, Hill 1953, a and b are stated to be from the same dies. The obverse links offer some confirmation that the animal design was on the lower die, and they imply that more than one reverse die may have been used with each obverse.

454

tongue, no tongue, the addition of wings, lateral reversal, and the tucking of the foreleg back under the body (cf. Series N and X). The reverted foreleg strikes one as a significant modification to the design, whereas the other variations may be merely whimsical.

The obverse varieties, with the numbers of specimens recorded, are:

a) Winged animal right, curled tail, curled tongue.[4] (3)
b) Animal right, forked tail, curled tongue.[5] (1-2)
c) Animal left, forked tail, forked tongue.[6] (1-2)
d) Animal left, with ear, curled tail, curled tongue (neat die).[7] (1)
e) Animal right, forked tail, no tongue, head points upwards.[8] (3)

f) Animal right, with ears, curled tail, curled tongue, foreleg with long toes, tucked back under body as on Series N or X (neat dies).[9] (*c.*8)

g) Animal left, as f but stylistically very schematized.[10] (1)

There is no clear inner logic to the variations, such as would support a sequence. Experimentation, reflected by scarce types, is perhaps more likely to have been early, while the die-cutter's more settled habit is seen in variety f (among 8 specimens of which there are, however, at least 5 non-singleton dies). We cannot even be certain that the scarce types were strictly sequential.

The reverted foreleg shows the influence, probably, of Series N or X.

[4] *BMC* 187, *SCBI Mack* 364, Ashmolean.
[5] Walbury Camp; Hamwic?
[6] *BMC* 186; BM, Hill, c?
[7] *SCBI Hunterian*. 107
[8] *MEC* 702 (Reculver), Ashmolean (London),

Knighton.
[9] *BMC* 184, 185, Hill a and b. *SCBI Hunterian* 106, 131, Canterbury (Castle Street), Canterbury (Longmarket), *MEC* 703 (Reculver), Ashmolean.
[10] *SCBI Hunterian* 132 ex Lockett 264, 1.02g.

Variety g, which copies f, perhaps stands right at the end of the sequence, but its evidence is inconclusive, because it might be merely an unofficial imitation.

The spiral branch with berries which is the 'badge' of Series M can be analysed by art-historical criteria, to reveal two separate styles. In variety f, there is an annulet in the field, and the branch consists essentially of a continuous coiled stem, with side-shoots on its outer side, alternately leaves and groups of three bold pellets representing clusters of berries. Variety g conforms. Varieties a to e have a segmented branch. Each segment ends in a V-shaped pair of shoots, from the middle of which the next segment springs. This can be studied on a clear specimen of variety a, catalogued

Fig. Series M. Two styles of spiral branch.

below. The pellets are much smaller, and are found on either side of the branch. The berries may be in groups of five or six, or (on the less elaborate dies) there may be as few as two.

On some less careful dies, the outer arm of the segmental V is drawn as a continuation of the line of the stem, the next segment being turned inwards at an angle, to create the spiral. The underlying concept, however, is the same.

The two distinct styles are almost certainly the work of different die-cutters, presumably in sequence. If we had a larger corpus, the fine details of the segmented style would perhaps enable us to suggest the order of the scarce types. *SCBI Hunterian* 107 (variety d) is a key coin, from careful dies. It shows a curious resemblance to some of the East Anglian animal types of Series Q, with numerous pellets scattered in the field. That can hardly be through shared die-cutting, since the two distribution-patterns (for M and Q) are as separate as they well could be.

II

Type 45 appears to be on the common weight-standard of *c.*1.05g. Several specimens reach as much as 1.17g.

MAP. Finds of Series M.

The alloy can be judged only provisionally, from the three available EPMA analyses. Specimens of varieties b and f are approximately 50 per cent silver, with significant amounts of tin. Variety e is problematic: it gave a measurement of 69 per cent silver. One would be reluctant, on grounds of style, to place it at the head of the series.

III

Type 62 has sometimes been assigned to Series M. There is very little justification for doing so: the animal has a curled tail. There are better parallels among varieties assigned to Series L.

A uniface sceat from Whitchurch, Bucks has also been identified as belonging with M, taking account of the animal's curly tail. It is at best imitative (and from north of the Thames).

IV

Series M is more compact, both in its range of styles and in its geographical distribution, than N. In the quest for its region of origin, it can usefully be compared with Series O.

If the choice lies between Kent and north-eastern Wessex, the former seems more likely. One would guess at a lesser trading centre on the Wantsum Channel, although that raises questions about the political authority under which the coins were struck. If M were from such a lesser wic, and if in the future we were fortunate enough to obtain a series of site-finds from the mint-place, they might be expected to show a preponderance of coins of Series M, even though diverse coinages mingled very freely in east Kent. The sample would need to be large enough for the contrast with east Kent as a whole to be statistically significant.

In that context one notes that five finds are said to have come from Reculver or Thanet. Five among 57 may be compared with two among fourteen finds from Canterbury, and none among nine at Richborough. The numbers are quite inconclusive, and in any case it seems very probable that two of the nineteenth-century finds from Reculver have been reported twice, and that there are really only three.[11]

[11] The Roach Smith coins are 'either ex Battely or from a few preserved in the collection of Dr. Faussett of Heppington, where they are marked as having been procured from Reculver'.

SERIES N

THE QUESTIONS 'where' and 'when', addressed to Series N, are more than usually open. The type (two standing figures/monster with head turned back) belongs to southern England, certainly, and there are numerous single finds which define the area over which it circulated.[1] It was distinctly plentiful in east Kent,[2] less so in the London area,[3] and it occurs at Hamwic[4] and further north in Wessex.[5] There are also significant numbers of more northerly finds, from Middle Anglia[6] and Norfolk.[7] The type is, however, virtually absent from the rest of East Anglia, Lindsey, and Northumbria.[8] Its distribution is thus comparable with that of Series M south of the Thames but extends north of the Thames too. Many of the more northerly finds appear to be imitations. Even if it is debateable where one should draw the line, on grounds of style, between official and unofficial coins, some of the northerly finds are of such poor style, or weight, or alloy (or all three) as to leave very little doubt that they are opportunist copies. They include more than one pair of die-linked coins which point to an unexpectedly localized circulation. The full extent of the area within which Series N has been found may therefore not be the best guide to its region of origin. More weight should be given to the coins in the best style, – several of which, unfortunately, are unprovenanced, but which include those from Walbury Camp (Berkshire), Old Sarum, Canterbury, and Royston. There are wide margins of uncertainty, but one thinks of a parallel situation with Series C, with its swathe of northerly imitations, springing up to meet a

---

[1] A corpus was included in D. M. Metcalf, 'Sceattas found at the iron-age hill fort of Walbury Camp, Berkshire', *BNJ* 44 (1974), pp.1-12. Numerous additions can now be made.

[2] Reculver, M.9, M.19 (= Stowe 14), M.E (= *MEC* 706), M.15, Richborough M.10, Canterbury X, Canterbury (Marlow site, 41b/41a), St. Nicholas-at-Wade.

[3] M.17 (= M25?), another broken Roach Smith coin (London X), Barking Abbey, Tilbury.

[4] Hamwic 103.

[5] Walbury Camp, M.3 (= Check-list, VI) and Check-list V (illus. in *BNJ* 1977), Old Sarum (with some doubt, but the coin now in Salisbury Museum (M.5) is doubtless a local find even if it is not (as it probably is) the Old Sarum find).

[6] Royston 33 and 34 (but 35 is perhaps another type), and 82, Totternhoe.

[7] Binham, Hindringham, and Caistor St. Edmund.

[8] Malton, Y.

monetary need.

When the series was studied in 1974,[9] a dual distribution pattern was detected, and a westerly origin was tentatively proposed for the coins in the best style, emphasis being laid on the proximity of Walbury Camp and Old Sarum. A second find from the Walbury Camp area, but about two miles distant from the first, is either from the same workshop or is a very close copy. The Hamwic coin is a less skilled copy, but is evidently based on a similar model.

The canon of English single finds has now grown, impressively, from nine to over thirty. The general arguments against inland mints (with the re-attribution, e.g., of Series J), and the more recent finds of coins in the best style from Canterbury and Royston, should prompt a reconsideration. The prudent attribution for the coins in the best style might seem to be to a mint somewhere in east Kent, giving due weight to eight finds from the area. Only one of the eight, however, is in the best style; and the attribution would immediately raise the question of the relationship of Series N to Series K. In appearance – fabric and style – it is very different. Even if the significance of the two standing figures is not clear, we can say that the design of N is distinctive (as is the style), and that it can hardly be accommodated alongside the 'bust' or 'standing figure' types of Series K and L. Could it, therefore, be either earlier or later in date? That further question brings into the discussion hypotheses about progressive debasement, and one's doubts whether the coinage alloys used at different mints were necessarily kept in step with each other. Series N can hardly be late: it is on a heavy standard, and it was imitated by coins of another series which are demonstrably early.

The 'two standing figures' motif might, like other sceatta designs, have been drawn from non-numismatic sources. The E/N 'mule' in the Hallum hoard could have adopted the type independently, and may therefore be judged inconclusive evidence for an early date for N. But a 41/40 'mule' in Series Q is quite clearly imitated from an actual coin of Series N, as the minor details of its style reveal. As it is 83 per cent silver and is firmly tied into the early phase of Series Q, it is of crucial importance for the interpretation of Series N. (Having registered that point, we may note that there is another early type of Series Q in the Hallum hoard; we may for that reason be disposed to accept that the E/N 'mule' does in fact reflect an acquaintance with Series N.)

Early though it is, Series N cannot precede K at Canterbury: the association of K with J in the Garton grave-find and in the York (Fishergate) hoard enforces an early date in the secondary phase for K.

---

[9] Metcalf, loc.cit.

MAP. Finds of Series N. Coins which are plated on a base-metal core, or which are palpably imitative, are shown by triangular symbols.

FIG. The E/N 'mule'.

Even though both those finds are small, so that the absence of N from them might be merely by chance, the early origin of K simply does not leave room for as extensive a series as N to precede it at the same mint. It seems, then, that N originates at much the same date as K, or only a little later, but that it is from another mint somewhere in south-eastern England.

The most economical hypothesis would be that that mint is London. Series L runs in parallel with K, at least in part (e.g. Types 18 and 20/18, discussed above), and has obvious affinities of design. It may well have begun rather later than K, however, as its range of alloy seems not to extend above *c*. 50 per cent, and it does not include a matching type to set alongside Series K, Type 42 – or an equivalent for Series V.

The arguments for and against a London attribution are these: N appears to have been a substantial issue, and its mint-place is accordingly likely to have been an important commercial centre. Further, and more cogently, it attracted so much imitation as to suggest that it was perceived by users (particularly north of the Thames) as enjoying a high commercial status. That, again, points to the probability that it belonged to a major centre. Against London is the fact that it is less plentiful there than in east Kent. Two London provenances have been published: one broken specimen weighing 0.76g, and another coin (41b/41a) weighing 1.12g.

I

Series N comprises Types 41b, 41a, and 41b/41a. The varieties do not correspond satisfactorily with the classification of the type, giving a false impresssion of its structure. Such as they are, the distinctions between them are as follows:

41b Two identical facing standing figures, on a base-line, hold three long crosses. (The middle cross soon degenerates into a small cross at shoulder height, and the two arms which hold it, one belonging to each man, are ludicrously elongated to touch the base-line.) Monster l., with head turned r. Beak-like jaws. Long crest hanging down from the back of the head. The body is outlined with pellets. Foreleg tucked under body, with long toes pointing upwards. Hind leg with toes pointing down.

41a Two profile standing figures, turned towards each other, with arms bent at the elbow, holding a single long cross between them. A row of pellets to l. and r. No base-line. Monster r. (i.e. laterally reversed), with head l., as in 41b but with sexual member as in Series X.

41b/41a Two standing figures, facing, but with heads in profile turned towards each other, on a base-line, hold three long crosses (or degenerated as 41b). Monster l., with head turned r., or laterally reversed.

Hill[10] listed 41b/41a as a mule (regarding the monster as the obverse) but it would have been more exact if he had called it 41b/41a var, because the two standing figures combine elements of both 41a and 41b. Although 41a is of careful workmanship, it seems doubtful whether it is a substantive variety, as it is very scarce.

Types 41a and b are clearly not two varieties from a single workshop. A corpus suggests that what in fact we have is a substantive variety in a uniform style (to be found among the coins of Type 41b, and the only uniform group), plus a wide variety of imitations (in all three types), sometimes with lateral reversal of the monster.

The substantive variety is in a coarse style, with the simplest of turnip-heads on which are superimposed two very large pellets for eyes and another blob for the nose. The effect is of two men wearing gas-masks. It was noted and imitated (e.g. in Series Q) although rarely with the heavy-handed panache of the original.

Another fairly consistent group of coins has a wire border and an outer border of coarse pellets, on both obverse and reverse. This distinctive feature is matched on Series X. It too was imitated. An excavation-coin from Richborough, which strikes one as belonging firmly with the group,

[10] In *NC* 1953.

is linked by its reverse die with a coin from Cimiez[11] with a much simplified obverse.

Yet another little group of specimens has a monster with a re-curving tail. It includes an obverse die-link of Type 41b/41a.[12]

It is possible that two or three die-cutters worked in the same town, each producing his own style of a common type, either concurrently or successively. If that were the case, a respectable proportion of Type 41b might be regarded as official. How might one hope to prove or disprove such a hypothesis? – By patterns of weight, or of alloy, perhaps, if enough specimens were available, but in practice more easily by distribution. When we see, for example, a coin in eccentric style from Hindringham,

Norfolk,[13] and its die-duplicate from Malton, Yorks,[14] the chances are that those two coins from the north-eastern fringes of the area where Series N circulated are local imitations. A third coin from Barton, Cambridgeshire[15] (catalogued below) shares some stylistic features, and possibly belongs with them. A die-duplicate of it has been found at the Royston site,[16] only ten or fifteen kilometres away.

A fifth coin, from Binham, in middle Norfolk,[17] has two penguin-like

standing figures, without arms and with heads in profile wearing (?) helmets. These distinctive figures are reminiscent of those on the

[11] M.11 (illustrated by Le Gentilhomme in *RN* 1938, pl.4, 70).

[12] M.17 and 18 – of which only 18 has the re-curving tail.

[13] Information by courtesy of Mr. Bonser. The coin, in fresh condition, weighs only 0.60g.

[14] Information circulated at the 'Productive Sites' symposium in September 1989 by Mr. Blackburn and Mr. Bonser.

[15] 'Coin Register', *BNJ* 57 (1987), no.81.

[16] Royston 82.

[17] 'Coin Register', *BNJ* 58 (1988), no.133.

Hindringham and Malton finds. Binham and Hindringham are within three or four kilometres of each other, and the coins were found within a couple of months of each other, by the same detectorist. The monster of the Binham coin has a distinctive pellet-in-annulet head, probably by the same die-cutter as another Norfolk find, from Caistor-by-Norwich.[18]

The Caistor coin and another with the same pellet-in-annulet feature (both catalogued below) are both plated, i.e. *prima-facie* forgeries.

A picture of much interest for monetary history is beginning to emerge, of pairs of die-linked or similar imitative coins found close to each other on the northern fringes of the circulation-area of Series N. A little chain of varied but linked styles is part of this picture, with its focus in Norfolk. It is quite separate from Series Q,[19] but perhaps helps to explain Q's copying of N. In date it must be contemporary with R1.

If other pairs of provenanced coins came to light, they might serve to detach more of the apparently imitative varieties from the official series.

II

The two standing figures motif is found again in Types 30a and b and Type 51 (discussed in another section). Those types may have a bearing on our interpretation of Series N. Types 30a and 51 offer another permutation of design: the head of the senior figure is facing, and moustached, while that of the junior figure is conspicuously in profile, and diademed, with jutting nose and mouth. As well as recognizing copying, therefore, we should be ready to consider that the motif may have had an independent existence, other than as a coin design, and – possibly – some contemporary political significance. There is no obvious classical prototype for the design.[20]

The sensible way to interpret it will be first to determine where and when it was minted, and only then to ask whether there was an appropriate historical context. A London attribution has been tentatively suggested above. The date of origin will be within a few years of 720, on the accepted chronology. Facts about the political control of London at

[18] Catalogued below.
[19] Note Q's distribution is west Norfolk, e.g. Series Q, cf. Type 41b from Great Bircham.

[20] J. P. C. Kent, 'From Roman Britain to Saxon England', in *Anglo-Saxon Coins* (ed. R.H.M. Dolley), 1961, pp.1-22, at p.12 (and pl.2, 1).

that time are just enough to hint at complexities which we do not fully understand.[21] Although Essex was sometimes ruled by two kings concurrently,[22] there is nothing known that would encourage us to think of joint rule of a kind such as might be represented by the design of Series N. In light of the ecclesiastical attribution of Series K, Type 33 and a similar interpretation suggested (above) for Series J, Types 85 and 37, we ought perhaps to venture to ask ourselves whether the two standing figures might represent the king and his bishop. Iconographically it is not impossible.

There is no way in which we can usefully test the hypothesis, other than by referring again to the occasional differentiation of the two heads, – and by asking how it might fit in with a wider range of numismatic evidence. Series O, Type 40 is a one-man version of Type 41b, quite close in style to the substantive variety. It is treated separately in the following section, and we can summarize at this point by saying that it is less plentiful than N, and more compact in its stylistic range. It has its own version of the monster, with foreleg raised to touch its head. In so far as one can guess from style, and the few recorded provenances, it could be from the same mint as the substantive variety, but whether it was concurrent, earlier, or later in origin is very difficult to guess. The crucial coin of Series Q, already mentioned, is quite clearly a 41/40 'mule', i.e. it imitates both types.

Types 30 and 51 can neither be dated nor localized independently enough to contribute to the argument.

III

Five specimens of Series N have been chemically analysed.[23] They show an alloy standard close to 50 per cent silver, and also reveal the existence of plated copies. The analyses are not as informative as they might have been, because no coins in the best style have been analysed. One should bear in mind that, if they were, it is quite possible that, as in Series O, Type 40, some specimens would prove to be better than 50 per cent. The analyses thus fail to throw light on the relative chronology of the origins of Series N and K. And because the imitative specimens of N are presumably from a variety of sources, the information from the analyses is not cumulative in its value.

---

[21] K. Bailey, 'The Middle Saxons', in *The Origins of Anglo-Saxon Kingdoms* (ed. S. Bassett), 1989, at pp.113f. and 135f.

[22] ibid., pp.136f..

[23] The four catalogued below, and Hamwic 103.

The three coins with around 50 per cent silver also include around 4 per cent tin. The two plated specimens are on copper cores (with small amounts of tin), and may originally have had surfaces with roughly 50 per cent silver, which are now corroded.

IV

The monster looking over its shoulder, as on Type 41, has an existence independent of coinage, as part of the general stock of Germanic imagery. It is seen in Series X, and appears on various other sceattas. In a few cases it is evidently imitated from Type 41, e.g. on a Whitby find. No 'mule' has come to notice which shares a die with a straightforward coin of Type 41, nor are there any stylistic similarities which are so close as to imply that a 'mule' was probably from the same workshop as a Type 41 imitation – although it would not be surprising if such a coin came to light.

SERIES O

THE DISTINCTIVE obverse design of Series O, a bare head with shoulder-length hair, usually enclosed in a heavy cable border, is found with several reverse types. In the perspective of the sceatta series as a whole, it is, one would assume, the 'badge' of a particular mint-town. The crested bird on the reverse is, on at least one die, clearly pecking at the berries of a vine. It may merely have been copied from Series U, but it is more probable that Series O is the product of yet another mint involved in the concerted coinage at the beginning of the secondary phase (discussed more fully in the chapter on Series U). Most of the provenances are in east Kent, with a secondary distribution in the Thames valley. Where, then, was Series O minted? South of the Thames, surely, for it shows no sign of following a London pattern. It might seem that the find-spots are directing us towards east Kent. One at least of the earliest coins of Series O is of excellent silver, posing the dilemma of either an early date or the restoration of a very pure alloy. A late date is not a serious possibility; the pecking bird motif is a strong indication of an early secondary date, and there is also an interesting imitation which 'mules' the Series O obverse with (almost certainly) the SAROALDO reverse. If it is early, Series O jostles for space in east Kent with Series V and K. Can there have been more than one mint-town in such a tiny region? What would be the political implications if two such different series were issued concurrently in the same kingdom? Could the distribution-pattern be deceptive because east Kent was a cross-roads of international trade, where sceattas from many English regions arrived? Might Series O be from some lesser *wic* with access to the Thames estuary, from whereabouts we have too few single finds for Series O to show up? Statistically, that would be perfectly possible, if Series O had been an issue of even moderate size. One would then have to say that there was not enough find-evidence to permit the conclusion that it must belong to east Kent (and therefore, presumably, to a secondary *wic* on the Wantsum Channel). The amount of die-duplication in Type 38, however, suggests that there were only ever about twelve or fifteen pairs of dies. Greater interest attaches,

MAP. Finds of Series O. (Series U, Type 23c is also shown, by open circles.)

therefore, to the two finds from Richborough, out of a total of only nine from the site. Regrettably, the excavation report does not make it clear whether they were two separate finds (when they would amount to strong evidence) or a mini-hoard (when they would not). Patience is in order, to await a larger body of finds. One other clue: there is a close link of type with Series U, Type 23c, which has an essentially West Saxon distribution, and thus reinforces the view that Series O belongs south of the Thames.

The series includes Types 38, 21, 57, and 40. The first three obviously belong together, but Type 40 is not connected with them in style. As it has a more northerly distribution-pattern, there seems to be no justification for supposing that it is from the same mint-place. It is therefore treated separately, in another chapter (and the general remarks made so far refer, in fact, only to Types 38, 21, and 57). Type 38 is known from ten or a dozen specimens, including at least five non-singletons. All four known specimens of Type 21 are from the same dies. Type 57 is known from only three specimens.

I

Within Type 38 there is considerable stylistic development. The type begins with coins which are heavy, of good silver, and with legends of pseudo-letters on both sides. The legends are soon abandoned, to be replaced by a bold cable border. The reverse type is a bird, enclosed within a heavy torc. As the bird is crested, on the earlier specimens, we may suspect an affinity with the pecking birds of Series U, etc.

The coin which stands at the beginning of the sequence was found at Lewknor, Oxon., in 1987, and is catalogued below. It weighs 1.26g and is 94 per cent 'silver', with no tin and virtually no zinc. On the obverse the head has a grotesque peg-like nose, turned up at the tip, and an annulet

to represent the eye. The head is attached by a slender neck to an ornamental curve possibly representing the breast. The pseudo-letters of the legend appear to be quite meaningless. On the reverse the tousled bird is no doubt intended to be crested. Its toes and tail-feathers are treated rather similarly. The feature of the design which on subsequent specimens is a torc seems to have been misunderstood, and is treated as a circular panel interrupted by the bird's head. One may compare the treatment of the legend on Type 46.

A second coin has an obverse legend but a chain of overlapping ∽ symbols in place of the reverse legend.[1] The nose, the eye, and the back-to-front ear are by the same hand, and the treatment of the bust is

recognizably related. On the reverse, too, the bird is no doubt by the same hand as that on the first coin, although the knob-headed torc is now a clear part of the design, emphasized by a dotted outline.

On *SCBI Mack* 352 the bust is represented by a large annulet with central pellet. On the reverse there is no pseudo-legend, and the central type fills the flan. There is a symbol in front of the bird, possibly a branch or vine. Another pair of dies, lacking the branch or vine but otherwise extremely similar, is represented by a find from the excavations of Eynsham Abbey, Oxon.[2]

The order of the remaining dies is not easy to judge from their style. Various elements in the design are modified or replaced, in a way that makes it difficult to arrange the coins into a single sequence. It would not be worth struggling over, except that it has a considerable bearing on the relationship of Type 21 and 57 to 38, and (to a lesser extent) on the view we take of the SAROALDO 'mule'.

BMC 169, and a die-duplicate from Tilbury (catalogued below) are rather intrusive in the sequence, because they have a bust with

conventional drapery, a small cross with central pellet added on both obverse and reverse, and a bird with a long crest reminiscent of the monster of Series N. The main reason for wishing to place these two specimens early is that they have a simple cable border of well-spaced ∽ symbols; but the symbols would have been easy enough to imitate as a later revival. The weights are 1.07 and 1.12g respectively.

[1] Carlyon-Britton 168.
[2] Mack, ex Lockett, ex Grantley 693, ex Rashleigh
31, 0.82g. Eynsham 1990, 1.22g.

SCBI Hunterian 117 has a head, not a bust, and an irregularly linked chain-like pattern all around. On the reverse there is a larger bird, with a crest of three lines ending in pellets (as in Series U, etc.), and pecking at the berries of a vine. The torc (but not the bird) is laterally reversed. The weight is 0.94g. A British Museum coin, ex Barnett, is probably similar. It weighs 0.98g.[3]

Two die-duplicates from the Richborough excavations of 1924-5 are from a very similar obverse die to the foregoing, perhaps from the same batch, and from a more normal reverse, with a large pellet near the bird's beak.[4] A third coin, from Tilbury (catalogued below) is almost certainly from the same dies. It contains 61 per cent 'silver' plus 3 per cent tin.

The weights are still high – 1.18, 1.10, and 1.14g. They raise the question whether the chronological order of the dies should not be reversed, *SCBI Hunterian* 117 being later.

Lockett 255a shows a simplification of the obverse design, by the omission of the cable border. There is a double dotted border. The

heads, so far as one can judge, could be by the same workman as the preceding coins. There is a sketchy cross in front of the face. On the reverse, the bird is very similar in style to the Mack coin, above.

As we already know roughly half the dies that were used for Type 38, it looks unlikely that a more complete picture would alter our impression of variable detail, within a recognizable style.

II

Type 21 is known from four specimens, all apparently from the same

---

[3] Hill, in *NC* 1953, 100-1, Type 38,a.
[4] ibid., b and c. Illustrated in *BNJ* 1977, pl.2, 33.

FIG. The repertoire of style of Type 38.

dies.[5] The two that are provenanced are from Reculver and Tilbury. On the obverse, the bust is laterally reversed from Type 38. It has the distinctive peg nose of the earliest coins, in combination with a rough annulet to represent the drapery of the bust, and an irregular cable border, roughly matching the later dies of Type 38 (which no longer have a peg nose). The eye is a large pellet. This combination of features does not fit into the sequence of stylistic development of Type 38. The recorded weights are 1.07, 0.81, and 0.86g. Taking the provenances into account, one is inclined to accept that Type 21 is the work of the same die-cutter as Type 38, perhaps at a later date, – rather than a clever imitation.

The reverse die has a standing frontal figure holding two crosses, all within a curve. It is made distinctive by the large curled moustaches. Careful inspection of the Tilbury find shows that they spring from the face, i.e. they cannot be understood as long hair curling outwards from the back of the head.

The same moustached figure appears on Type 23c. One is obviously a close copy of the other , but which is the original? Both types are scarce: is a single die likely to have provoked imitation? Type 23c bears more of the hallmarks of copying, and it has a more peripheral distribution. The type which is concentrated in east Kent is thus more likely to be the prototype.

III

On Type 57 the characteristic obverse of Series O is paired with the monster of Type 40 or with a similar monster. Three or four specimens are known, of which one is from Reculver, pre-1756, and one is from recent excavations at Woolwich. A third example, in the Ashmolean Museum without provenance, has been analysed, and found to contain 57 per cent 'silver', plus 3 per cent tin.

SCBI Hunterian 118 corresponds well with a line drawing published by Withy and Ryall, and in view of the extreme scarcity of the type, there need be no doubt that it is the Reculver find.[6] The border is made up of

---

[5] *BMC* 108 (1.07g) and the very similar *BMC* 109 (0.81g), Ashmolean, ex Tilbury (0.86g), and a fragment from Reculver (Reculver XX = *MEC* 706a, known also from a line drawing, made when the fragment was larger than it now is).

[6] There is also a line-drawing in the Stowe MS. The correspondence is less good, but that may be put down to poor drawing.

reversed recumbent ∽ symbols. The snub nose ends in a pellet. The workmanship is quite close to that of *BMC* 169 (Type 38). The treatment of the bust is indistinct because it is partly off the flan, but seems to be a pellet-in-annulet. The reverse is so close in style to Type 40 that it would seem perverse to treat Type 40 separately, if its distribution-pattern were not so different.

The Ashmolean specimen apparently has a bust with conventional

drapery, and a simple, continuous interlace border. The monster is laterally reversed, and the leg scratching its head is misunderstood.[7]

The Woolwich find may well be by the same hand: the shape of the cheek corresponds, and the neck is shown, in a way not seen in Type 38.

The drapery of the bust is composed of some disjointed curves, reminiscent of early specimens of Type 38. The cable border is irregular, and is perhaps copied from the die of the Richborough coins. On the reverse, there is a different version of the monster, with a tightly curled tail.[8]

The status of Type 57 is doubtful.

IV

An imitative coin picks up several early features from Type 38, in particular a pseudo-legend and an annulet as the bust. The design is

laterally reversed. The reverse type, with a large standard containing a saltire, is probably borrowed from the **SAROALDO** type, rather than Type

---

[7] Ex Evans, 1.02g.

[8] From excavations by Mr. B. Philp, 1988.

70 (which has a smaller standard). This coin weighs 1.07g and appears to be of good silver.[9]

BMC Type 46 is more problematic. It belongs with a southern version of the standard-saltire types, and is discussed there. The bird is not closely similar to any in Type 38: its head is turned back.

There is a Merovingian copy of the bird and torc of Type 38, probably

from northern Francia.[10] Taking Type 23c into account, the fact that a type as scarce as Type 38 should attract so much copying is probably best explained if Series O belonged to a *wic* – from which we have few or no finds.

[9] Photo courtesy of Mr. P. Finn, Spink and Son Ltd.

[10] *MEC* 631, 1.23g, *c.*74 per cent silver. The reverse has the Parisian *croix ancrée*.

SERIES O, TYPE 40

BMC TYPE 40 is a one-man version of Series N, Type 41. Its similarity of style to the substantive group of that type suggests that it might well be from the same region. Its distribution coincides, so far as one can judge, with that of Type 41. An early date in the secondary phase is indicated by an imitative coin of Series Q (mentioned previously) which 'mules' the two standing figures of Type 41 with the monster of Type 40. If Type 41 is a London coinage, then Type 40 probably is too: it has a far-flung distribution, both north and south of the Thames.[1] Like Type 41, it was copied, although perhaps not quite so much.

Type 40 is unconnected with the group of other types making up Series O. Its general appearance is different, as is its distribution. The ostensible link is the reverse type, the so-called 'wyvern'. The term is heraldic and therefore anachronistic – as Rigold was well aware, when he bestowed it jocularly, with porcupines in mind.[2] A wyvern has wings, and forelegs with eagle's claws, but no hind legs, and a serpent's tail. The point of the name as applied to Type 40 was merely that the dragon-like creature lacks a leg. In Type 41 the foreleg is folded back under the body, with the long toes or claws pointing upwards. In Type 40 the monster at first sight has only a hind leg (although with a series of decorative parallel lines where the toes of the foreleg would have been – suggesting that if the design was derived from another sceatta type, rather than from some other artefact, the prototype of Type 40 was Type 41 rather than vice versa).

On closer inspection the whole business turns out to be a misconception:

[1] When Sutherland prepared his check-list, the only certain provenance for Type 40 was Hemel Hempstead: the evidence is reviewed in D. M. Metcalf, 'A sceat of *BMC* Type 40 found near Canterbury, and another from Thanet', *BNJ* 44 (1974), p.12. The list can now be considerably extended, and comprises: 'a hop garden near Canterbury' (before 1747), Reculver XL = Stowe 12 = Locket 256b, Tilbury, Hemel Hempstead, Lakenheath, Sf., Royston 83, Hamwic 104 and 105, and Bidford-on-Avon.

[2] S. E. Rigold, 'The principal series of English sceattas', *BNJ* 47 (1977), pp.21-30, at p.29, where wyvern is defined as a 'similar creature [to a dragon] without foreleg, but spine or small hump on back'. Rigold is taken to task by Mary Morehart in 'Female centaur or sphinx? On naming sceat types: the case of *BMC* Type 47', ibid., 55 (1985), pp.1-9, at pp.2-3, where she notes that this form of dragon (with wings, serpent's tail, and eagle-like claws) was in general use in medieval art from the early Norman period. No-one is suggesting continuity from the eighth century: the creature of Type 40 is not a wyvern.

the monster has another leg. It is raised above its back, and the creature appears to be scratching the top of its head. The claws of the raised foot can be seen clearly on *SCBI Hunterian* 122 and on a coin catalogued below, which are probably from the same die. The leg is attached to the body rather vaguely, perhaps because of the exigencies of the design, but the intention seems to be to represent a foreleg. The modelling, particularly on the Hunterian coin, encourages this interpretation.

The raised leg was understood as a standard and necessary part of the design of Type 40. It was reproduced on imitations. On the 40/41 'mule' in Series Q the die-cutter has apparently tried to represent the creature scratching its head with its *hind* leg (as quadrupeds generally do).

I

An apparently unique sceat published here for the first time has a monster on one side, so very similar in all its detail and in the well-rounded quality of the modelling to that of Type 40 as to suggest that it is by the hand of the same workman. The monster is scratching the back of its head in the approved manner. The other side of the coin, which one would take to be

the reverse, has a four-lobed wire outline, with a large pellet in each circle, and groups of pellets between, all in a double pelletted border. The monster die has an inner wire border inside the boldly pelletted border, a feature sometimes found on Type 40. The alloy is much the same as that of Type 40 – 61 per cent silver, with 1.7 per cent tin. The weight, 1.16g, is on the high side for Type 40.

The reasons for thinking that this coin stands at the head of Series O, preceding Type 40, are, first, that there is unlikely to have been a change of design in the course of a notably uniform issue, and secondly that it seems to be the model for an otherwise puzzling imitative coin in the Garton-on-the-Wolds grave-find, 'muling' the obverse of (the early) Type R1, with a cross-and-annulets reverse in a triple-pelletted border. The quality of workmanship of the 'mule' is mediocre, and is even poorer on another specimen, Ruding pl.2, 17, which again has *epa* facing inwards. The context requires a date very early in the secondary phase for the Garton

MAP. Finds of Series O, Type 40.

coin, when there is no other model in sight for the cross-and-annulets design. One would be reluctant to give the die-cutter of the Garton coin the credit for originality.

II

The standing figure has a crudely drawn head with large pellets for eyes and another for the nose, giving the appearance of someone wearing a gas-mask, as in Type 41. The feet are turned to the viewer's left. There are vertical rows of pellets in the field – three or four pellets to fill the spaces between the crosses and the dotted border, two or three pellets below the arms, which are bent at right angles, and sometimes one between the legs.

The monster's beak-like jaws end in bold pellets. It has a short tail curling up over its back, but it has no crest.

III

A range of counterfeits of Type 40, of varying deceptiveness, present the numismatist with the usual problem of knowing where to draw the line: what to admit as variations within the official series, and what to reject as unofficial.

A couple of coins with a diamond of four pellets between the monster's beak and its back are easy to reject. *BMC* 112 has a profile head right, and feet turned to the right. It may well have been influenced by Series U, Type 23b/d. Lockett 256b is similar, apparently again with a profile head: it is very probably the same coin as the pre-1756 find from Reculver ('Thanet').

SCBI Hunterian 121 arouses misgivings, although its faults are not very obvious. The monster's eye is not encircled by an annulet forming the outline of the head, and the foot of the raised leg seems to be omitted.

SCBI Mack 345 (the same specimen as Lockett 256a and Carlyon Britton 170) and a die-duplicate catalogued below are more difficult to judge. The inner wire border counts against these coins, which unfortunately are unprovenanced. On the obverse, the eyes are very large and they are encircled, giving an owl-like appearance. There is an excessive number of pellets in the field. Hamwic 104 (in worn condition) could be by the same hand.

A find from Bidford-on-Avon, in worn condition, seems to be very close in style to the original, and may be authenticated by future finds. The only details over which one should hesitate are the number of pellets in the obverse field, and the way the lower half of the monster's beak is attached to its head. The raised leg is attached to the body nearer the rump than is usual.

Even if it were not so difficult to be sure where to draw the line between official and unofficial coins, there would still be insufficient evidence to show whether the latter had a different distribution pattern from the former.

As between an attribution to east Kent or to London, the available provenances are nevertheless clearly in favour of London. The Reculver find is imitative, whereas those from Tilbury and Hemel Hempstead are entirely convincing.

IV

The three specimens catalogued below have been analysed. The two just mentioned, of the substantive variety, contained 47 per cent silver (Tilbury) and an estimated 69 per cent (Hemel Hempstead) respectively. The coin with an inner wire border has 58 per cent silver. Tin contents are 2 - 2.5 per cent (Tilbury, 5 per cent).

Hamwic 104 was somewhat corroded. A tentative reconstruction of its alloy based on EPMA gives 57% 'silver', with 3.3 per cent tin and 5.6 per cent zinc – the last figure unexpectedly high.

The evidence is thus reasonably clear that some specimens of Type 40 contained well over half silver – as might be expected if they fall early in the secondary phase.

A MONSTER/INTERLACE TYPE (*BMC* TYPE 43)

THREE specimens are recorded of a type which cannot safely be assigned to a series. It combines the 'wyvern' of Series O, Type 40 with a quatrefoil interlace. It is presumably English.

Royston 45 and *BMC* 182 are from the same dies, while a third specimen *dans le commerce* is from different dies.[1]

[1] The type is discussed, and both pairs of dies are illustrated, in M. A. S. Blackburn and M. J. Bonser, 'Single finds of Anglo-Saxon and Norman coins – 3', *BNJ* 56 (1986), 64-101, under no.45.

SERIES Q

SERIES Q is an east-coast coinage which has been found widely in East Anglia, but particularly in the western half of Norfolk. Its most characteristic coins have a quadruped on one side and a bird on the other. The series is of medium rank, accounting for about 2 per cent of the English finds (cf. Series R, with about 6 per cent), but it was struck over a period of probably not less than thirty years, as the Hallum and Cambridge hoards demonstrate. It was a long-lasting and extremely varied series, for which little batches of dies would seem to have been cut on numerous occasions. That presumably tells us something about the nature of the demand for the moneyers' services, and may have some bearing on the most intriguing question which the series presents, namely where it was struck.

The distribution of finds of Series Q makes it abundantly clear that it is English (there are just two finds from Domburg), and that it is from north of the Thames, with a pronounced East Anglian emphasis. It does not, however, coincide with the distribution for Series R and, in so far as both sets of data discount the uncertainties of the modern find-records in the same ways, the contrast between them ought to be evidence of excellent quality. Series Q is, in short, more heavily represented in western Norfolk, and less so in eastern Suffolk, than is Series R. We should look not just at the pattern of symbols on the map, but also at the proportions of Q to R at the major sites, in particular Ipswich and Barham, Caistor St. Edmund, the Thetford area, and (further afield) the site near Royston. Brandon attracts particular attention as a site where Q is plentiful. In western Norfolk and the adjacent areas as a whole, Q amounts to around 25 per cent of all the recorded finds (cf. *c.* 2 per cent for England as a whole), whereas in eastern Norfolk there is only one doubtful provenance among 63 single finds. There was evidently a north-west/south-east axis in the monetary affairs of East Anglia, linking the two regions from which archaeological finds of all kinds are most plentiful. As finds of Series Q occur in both regions, we must postulate movements or transfers of coinage along the axis. The main centre of political power in East Anglia lay, almost certainly, in the south-eastern coastlands, and it is understandable enough, if the coins of Series Q originated in western Norfolk or thereabouts, that some should have been found in eastern Suffolk. Drift in the opposite direction is, perhaps, less to be expected.

Further, it is improbable that Q was minted (like R) in eastern Suffolk, if only because it should then have been carried to eastern Norfolk to a similar extent to Series R, given the duration of the series.

Besides, the style and content of the types are as different as they well could be. Both develop over a long period, practically throughout the secondary phase, and must therefore have been concurrent. Series Q is as varied, pictorial, and inventive as R is uniform and conservative.

A little group of coins which appear at first glance to be Q/R mules – true mules – and which might be thought to argue for a common place of origin, are better interpreted (from a detailed consideration of their style) as forming part of Series Q, but copying the distinctive obverse of R. The runes on these Q/R coins are always *er* retrograde, or similar. There are also scarce coins with that legend, matching Series R in both obverse and reverse. They have the same distribution-pattern as Q, and are in all probability from the same mint as the Q/R 'mules'.

The obvious hypothesis, then, is that the mint-place of Series Q lay in western Norfolk or nearby. There are still three difficulties about that, one political, one commercial, and one numismatic. Politically, it seems strange that two such different coinages as Q and R should have been minted in the same kingdom, – unless East Anglia was partitioned or under joint rule before 749 in ways that we know nothing about. The reply to that might be that our expectations could be mistaken, and that coin series were distinctive to the place or the region to which they belonged, but not necessarily to the kingdom within which their mint-place lay.

Another, and more serious problem is that there is no obvious place within western Norfolk where Series Q might have been minted. Brancaster may have been a crossing-point to Lindsey in the eighth and ninth centuries, but it does not commend itself as the sort of place where there would have been a commercial need to strike coinage in the very substantial quantities represented by Q. Thetford and its vicinity have yielded enough sceattas for it to be reasonably clear that it was not the home of Q. There is no other archaeologically obvious district within the frontiers of the East Anglian kingdom, consistent with the pattern of finds.

As the area where finds of Q are most heavily concentrated looks westwards, topographically, towards the fen edge, we ought probably to consider whether the mint-place might not have been a river-port on one

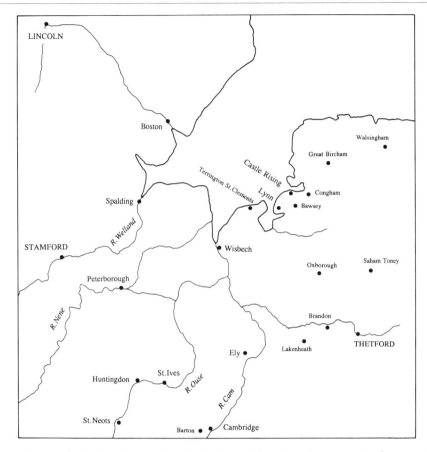

of the rivers draining into the Wash, with the character of a medium-sized wic. Kings Lynn would be the modern analogy, but Lynn was a hamlet of no importance until at least the time of the Domesday Survey. If we are casting around for a place which might have fulfilled a similar function to that of thirteenth-century Lynn in middle Saxon times, we should remember that the drainage system in the Fens was then substantially different. The Lynn estuary drained quite a small area, and the Ouse reached the sea by way of the Wisbech estuary.[1] Could the mint have been located as far west as Wisbech? – The finds from Cambridge (on a tributary of the Great Ouse) and from nearby Barton, and the conspicuous absence of finds from the productive site near Royston, offer some encouragement.

We may, on the other hand, be searching for a place which no longer

[1] H. C. Darby, *The Medieval Fenland*, Cambridge, 1940, pp.93-100; E. Carus-Wilson, 'The medieval trade of the ports of the Wash', *Med.Arch.* 6-7 (1962-3), pp.182-201.

exists as a town, or even as a settlement. There is, for example, a site at Hey Green (Terrington St. Clement) where archaeological surveying has recently revealed an unusually large middle Saxon settlement, from which there have been recovered over a thousand sherds of Ipswich ware, from thirteen fields covering more than 7 ha.[2] Parts of the Hey Green site, however, have been thoroughly searched with metal-detectors, with negative results.[3]

It is intriguing that Castle Rising has had, since at least the sixteenth century, a legend of having been a port long before Kings Lynn.[4]

In the end, we have to admit that the whereabouts of the mint-place of Series Q, within the west Norfolk area, remains completely elusive. Its monetary context, however, was clearly that of a place with access to the sea, and to east-coast shipping, by way of the Wash. There are three interesting Northumbrian provenances for Series Q (York, 2, both in worn condition, and Carlisle) which probably reflect an early phase of contacts by sea between the Wash and the Humber. Although the coins are partly explicable as being early secondary issues of good silver, which travelled more freely than the later, debased coins, nevertheless finds of the corresponding early, good-silver coins of Series R from Northumbria are by no means plentiful.[5]

The third difficulty is numismatic: two distinct styles are found in Series Q, and their distribution patterns do not match perfectly. The different styles are easily recognized, and will be labelled simply 'linear' and 'modelled', although the 'linear' coins may comprise a cluster of styles by two or three different hands. The clear differences between the two styles, in the range of types they use, as well as in fabric and in the technique of die-engraving, will inevitably raise the question whether there were two mint-places for the series, one (the 'linear') in the west Norfolk area, and the other ('modelled') perhaps in east Suffolk, where it seems to be relatively more plentiful. The numbers of provenances are too few for this division to be better than very conjectural. The obvious difficulty with it is that it involves the minting of Q and R concurrently in the same region. An alternative might be to place the two styles end to end, as a single series, the modelled coins being late. There are severe difficulties in the way of that hypothesis, too, as coins in the 'modelled' style are apparently of better alloy than the worst of the 'linear' coins. Abundant hoard evidence would settle the chronology and might thereby resolve the problem, but of course it is lacking. The 'linear' style certainly begins early in the secondary phase, as it is represented already

[2] R. J. Silvester, *The Fenland Project, Number 3: Marshland and the Nar Valley, Norfolk* (East Anglian Archaeology, Report No.45), Dereham, 1988, at pp.37 and 174f.

[3] Pers. comm., A. Rogerson, Norfolk Museums Service.

[4] id.

[5] York, Fishergate no.4909; Nether Poppleton.

in the Hallum hoard, for which Blackburn suggests a date not later than *c*. 720. A hoard found in or near Cambridge in *c*. 1894 shows both styles still in use alongside very debased specimens of Series R. Neither style was present at Middle Harling. The Q/R 'mules' fall to lower weights and, eventually, lower alloy standards than any other variety.

As always, one should hesitate to multiply mints. On the other hand, the common-sense view is that the two styles of Series Q will not fit easily into a single chronological sequence, and that their slightly divergent distributions at least raise the question whether two mints may not have been at work. Perhaps they were both in the hinterland of the Wash.

The weights of the coins are individually variable. The intended standard seems to have been in the region of 0.95/1.05g for the linear style, and 0.85/1.05 for the modelled varieties. The Q/R 'mules' tend to be lighter. The silver contents, from a surprisingly high starting-point of *c*. 80 per cent, were reduced eventually to *c*. 30 per cent or even less. Altogether, Q seems to match the pattern of declining intrinsic value of R quite closely; and the Q/R 'mules' seem to be among the latest coins in the series.

I

Series Q includes an exceptionally rich variety of types, particularly in the early secondary phase, when it shows eclectic tendencies, before settling down into its more characteristic bird/beast combinations. Several types are known from only two or three surviving specimens, and it is quite possible that new varieties may still come to light. Itemizing the varieties has not so far prompted any ideas of value for an understanding of the mint, other than the general point that it did not at first opt for a distinctive type as its badge or logo, in the way that most most mints did.

In the 'linear' style or styles there are at least sixteen varieties. Arranging them into a chronological sequence is a speculative exercise. The linking of obverse or reverse designs, and their stylistic devolution, help to suggest an order. High silver contents are a good indication of an early place in the sequence. There is no useful evidence for an absolute chronology, but one may guess that the early, eclectic types were all struck within a short period.

One can begin to introduce some sort of order by grouping the varieties into small blocks. The first, in quite good silver, is markedly eclectic. The second is firmly linked to the first by its reverse type. In the third and fourth blocks it is not clear which is the obverse and which the reverse die: the bird has been taken as the reverse type, as it seems to be in the second. There are three different styles of bird in the third block, namely one with a V-shaped tail, one looking remarkably like a sea-gull, and one with long, drooping tail-feathers, like a cockerel. The fourth block introduces a bird with a solid triangle as its tail, and also introduces a triquetra in the obverse field or even on both dies. The beast has a triple-tipped tail on some varieties in both the third and fourth blocks (cf. Series Z). The Q/R 'mules' (part of the fourth block) make up a rather more plentiful issue.

To repeat: the sequence is conjectural at various points.

First block. This is full of numismatic interest, as it includes a medley of obverse and reverse types, obverse links which conclusively prove the close association of quite different reverses, and links which do the same in the other direction. One can see the die-cutter experimenting, and the stylistic interpretation of a type becoming devolved over what was almost certainly a very short space of time. It looks as if the types were being varied even within the period of use of the very first dies to be cut, as 'earlier' and 'later' dies are paired up in ways that cannot be disentangled into a regular sequence of development.

Series Q would seem to have begun with imitations of Series N and O/Type 40 (which as prototypes would have been available in the currency of Middle Anglia, and probably in Norfolk too), but then almost immediately to have embarked upon its own repertoire of types. The logical starting-point is a Great Bircham find (QIA, 1) copying Series N, Type 41. Series N is notorious for the amount of copying it attracted, and there are other styles from the same general region. On this coin the

FIG. Type QIA, 1 and 2.

head of the right-hand figure is not absolutely clear, but one can make out the diagonal line of the diadem which confirms that the head is in profile, as on Type 41b/a.[6] The distinctive feature which betrays the die-cutter's hand is the 'bevelled' linear treatment of the arms and shoulders. The feet of each standing figure are angled outwards. On the reverse the crested monster is a thin and angular affair, but its fore- and hind leg are clearly modelled as on Type 41, not Type 40. The coin weighs 1.07g.

[6] Blackburn and Bonser, 'Single finds – 3', pp.85f., no.96. The writer has studied a rather better print from the same negative, and is persuaded that the head is in profile.

488

Another specimen from the same obverse die has the monster of Type 41, but laterally reversed and in a deplorably crude style (QIA, 2). As Blackburn and Bonser remark, it is salutary to find two dies of such different style linked by the same obverse: one would not otherwise have ventured to connect them with each other.[7]

Another very similar obverse, manifestly by the same hand, is coupled (Q1B, 1) with a monster that is copied from Series O, Type 40.[8] A close comparison shows that the die-cutter had a specimen of Type 40 in front of him, and did his best to copy almost every detail of it, although without achieving the full and rounded quality of the modelling of the original. The monster is lifting its hind leg to scratch the back of its head, and the Series Q coin shows the leg jointed, and with toes – an improvement, almost, on the prototype, where, however, the same raised leg is a standard part of the design. The monster's long, beak-like jaws

FIG. Types QIB, 1 and 2.

are reproduced, and it is given an ear, also terminating in a pellet, which is not on the prototype. The coin, which is reported to have been found at Barton, near Cambridge, weighs 1.09g, and is of 80 per cent silver.

These three specimens, linked as we shall see in a moment to a coin in the Hallum hoard, provide important evidence that both Series N and O/Type 40 were in existence and available to be copied at an early stage in the secondary phase. Metal analyses of specimens of N and O/40 have not produced any figures as high as 80 per cent. That may be by chance, for silver standards seem to have fallen off very quickly at the beginning of the secondary phase; but it might also be that Q used a rather better alloy than its prototypes. It is in any case clear from the continuity and linkages of style further into Series Q that what we are looking at is the borrowing of designs at a newly-opened (or re-opened) mint, rather than any sort of fraudulent imitation.

A fourth coin, from the same obverse die as the third, is nominally of the same reverse design, although laterally reversed.[9] The design has however become routine, and betrays a complete lack of intelligent interest on the part of the die-cutter (Q1B, 2). Between the raised rear leg (no longer understood) and the neck, a large pellet has been added,

[7] Metcalf 22 (*BNJ* 1974, pl.2), BM ex Barnett ex Carlyon-Britton 173.

[8] Catalogued below.

[9] *SCBI Norweb* 61 ex Lockett 257b, ex Rashleigh, 21 June 1909, 33.

489

presumably as the monster's eye. The three lines ending in pellets, for the monster's jaws and ear, are also copied mechanically, with no sign of understanding. It would be difficult to imagine that the same workman cut both dies – and yet they are die-linked. The Norweb specimen weighs 0.98g.

The two pairs of obverse die-linked coins are sufficient to show that the 'two standing figures' design was on the lower die – and to suggest that, from the very beginning of work at the mint which struck Series Q, more than one reverse was being used with each obverse. Evidently a brisk demand for the moneyers' services was expected.

The monster of Series O/40 is reinterpreted again, on a coin with the enigmatic label 'L. Sutton' (provenance, or owner's name?). The style is not such as to assign it firmly to Series Q: it could perhaps belong with the other 'standard' types such as Type 70.[10] It is, however, very

FIG. Type QIx (perhaps not from the mint-place of Series Q?).

probably from Norfolk or the Fens (Long Sutton is just to the west of the Wisbech channel),[11] and its alloy is 75 per cent silver, which suggests that it is early in date. We may provisionally classify it as QIx.

A monster very obviously related to that of the Barton find, but laterally reversed, is paired with an obverse with bust right, on a coin from the Hallum hoard.[12] The two lines of the beak-like jaws taper to a point, unpelletted. The coin is presumably by the same workman as the Barton find. A die-link and some related specimens with provenances serve to connect it with the Norfolk area. It may be classified as QID.

The same obverse die is paired with a reverse design of a standing bird, left, with raised wing and drooping tail-feathers, long legs, and large, three-toed feet. Two die-identical specimens are known (QIE, 1a and b) both weighing c. 0.81g, of which one is from Lakenheath, Suffolk.[13] Series Q has now severed its links with Series N and O, and is free-standing. Hill records three more specimens of what was evidently a

[10] See, for example, *NCirc.* 1983, illus. 3870.

[11] Rigold noted that the coin, in the Norwich Castle Museum, had been found wrapped in a piece of paper annotated 'L. Sutton', and suggested that this was possibly the name of the original owner, W. Lincolne Sutton, of Eaton near Norwich, who was active in the Norfolk Archaeological Society c. 1900-25. Long Sutton is in Lincolnshire, just. The coin has now been republished as *SCBI East Anglia* 1001.

[12] Hill, Type 67a. *RBN* 1870, pl.D, 31. Dirks records twenty specimens, but that is obviously a confusion with his pl.D, 30.

[13] Spink auction 63 (28 March 1988), 308, ex Spink auction 31 (12 October 1983), 82, from Lakenheath; Spink auction 20 (31 March 1982), 50, ex Bird colln., ex Seaby 1967. This is Hill Type 67b. He notes having seen it around 1950.

larger-scale issue. Another pair of dies, where the bird is certainly from the same workshop, and the distinctive bust presumably so (although its treatment is superficially different), is known from duplicate specimens found at York in 1886 (in very worn condition: mentioned above) and (again) at Lakenheath, Suffolk in *c.* 1977 (catalogued below). The latter is 86 per cent silver and weighs 1.09g. In place of a cross in front of the face, this obverse die has a symbol which may be a pseudo-rune. Another

FIG. Type QID. E and F.

worn coin, lacking a find-spot, *SCBI West Country* 244, is from a different but similar obverse, and perhaps the same reverse. (There is apparently a specimen from Barham). *BMC* 163 (Type 35), with yet another distinctive version of the bust, may be part of the same *œuvre*. It weighs only 0.88g.

Exactly the same reverse variety, the bird certainly by the same hand, is paired with a standing figure holding two crosses (QIF). Four specimens are known,[14] from at least two obverse and three reverse dies, without die-linkage to the preceding variety, although a die-link might well turn up, if one is to judge by the closeness of the dies. The specimen catalogued below contains 68 per cent silver.

There is next an apparent gap in the continuity of style and types. We come to a type with a facing head on the obverse and, instead of a bird on the reverse, a long-legged quadruped (QIG). It has been pointed out that the facing head is very similar to that of the standing figure of QIF – an enlarged detail of that design, as it were. For many years the type was known only from a unique specimen found near Carlisle in the nineteenth century, and which passed through the Batty and Ready collections.[15] For some time it was assigned to Series Z, – which has essentially the same facing head. QIG may indeed be deliberately recalling the primary type struck at the same mint. In about 1988, after more than a hundred years, a second specimen came to light, from 'a site

---

[14] Hill Type 71, listing three coins, of which the F. Baldwin specimen, ex Montagu, is now in the Ashmolean collection. *NCirc.* June, 1983, adds a fourth.

[15] Type 59, 0.98g.

near Thetford'. The exact location is doubtful, but may safely be assumed to lie in or near East Anglia. The new specimen, which is a die-duplicate, weighs 1.13g.[16]   A similar pairing of provenances between

FIG. Type QIG.

Northumbria and East Anglia, which we have seen in QIE and QIG, occurs again, with a type related to QIG, that was (again) for long known only from one worn specimen, found at York in 1885.[17] Another, in extremely fine condition, and from different dies, came to light at Saham Toney, Norfolk, in 1986 (QIH). A half-length figure, right, holds a cross; on the reverse, there is again a long-legged quadruped, left, with head turned back (a cross between a monster and a hound!). It is generally

FIG. Type QIH.

very similar to the quadruped on QIG, except that it is the creature's tail, and not its crest, which curves between its legs. The Saham Toney coin[18] contains 72 per cent silver. Two more specimens have recently come to light, the first apparently from the same obverse as the York find, the other thoroughly garbled, laterally reversed, and with a long crest between the quadruped's legs.

FIG. *BMC* 163 (Type 35).

II

The second block quickly abandons the use of human figures, and adopts the distinctive bird/animal or animal/bird combinations of Series Q. It is difficult to be sure which is the obverse and which the reverse, as both birds and animals were used on the reverses of the first block. These later

[16] Offered for sale by Spinks and believed now to be in America.

[17] Illustrated in *BNJ* 1977, pl.3, 37.
[18] Catalogued below.

492

Fig. Series QI.

coins have the anonymous character of 'double-reverse' types: whether that has any political significance, we do not know. No metal analyses are available to show their range of fineness. One would guess from their appearance that they may be somewhere in the 60-40 per cent range. Their absence from the Cambridge hoard suggests an intermediate date.

A Reculver find known only from an eighteenth-century line-drawing[19], has a standing figure with two crosses as its obverse, paired with a bird left with forked tail, with a cross at an angle in the field above, and numerous pellets. One strongly suspects that an obverse and reverse which do not belong together have been accidentally associated by the engraver, and that the obverse is that of a coin of Series U, Type 23d – recognizable in *SCBI Hunterian* 120. As a formality, we may record the Withy and Ryall coin as QIIz, but in fact reject it as a variety. Its reverse no doubt belongs with a regular coin of Series Q, – perhaps even another Hunter coin, on which it is paired with a quadruped left, with long tail curved between its legs. The creature's foreleg is raised, and there is a diagonal line in the field above, which may be an incomplete cross (QIIA). The long tail is reminiscent of coins in the first block. The coin[20] is of good weight, at 1.14g.

The bird with forked tail – looking like a seagull – is paired with yet another (?) obverse, on which the animal, right, with raised foreleg, has a short curled tail, and looks more canine than equine (QIIB).[21]

FIG. Types QIIA and B.

Two more varieties in much the same general style can be listed with the second block, although their designs are slightly different, and their place in the sequence is conjectural. A more elaborate 'seagull', with displayed wings, and with one or two crosses in the lower field, is paired

FIG. Type QIIc.

with a long-legged quadruped, left, with head turned back, and with a long tail curved first over its back and then between its forelegs. One foreleg is raised. The head has only a short snout, and pointed ears

[19] R. Withy and J. Ryall, *Twelve Plates of English Silver Coins*, 1756, supplementary plate. Reproduced in *Sceattas in England and on the Continent*, p.259, the third coin on the seventh row.
[20] *SCBI Hunterian* 130.
[21] Lockett 246.

(QIIc). A find from Congham, Norfolk, weighs 0.98g.[22] A coin from a different but similar pair of dies is without provenance.[23]

Finally, there is another version of the bird, more like a cockerel, with two long, drooping tail feathers, and no raised wing (QIID). As in QIIA there is a cross placed at an angle in the field above the bird – in fact, where its wing might have been – and another cross in front of the bird. The animal, left, is of the canine variety, and is distinctive because its tail, curving above its back, ends in a cross: a variant of the triple-tipped tail. Two pairs of very similar dies are known. Their provenances are

FIG. Type QIID.

peripheral for Series Q: Walton, near Aylesbury, and 'bought in London, 1894', but their general style links the variety firmly into the series. The Aylesbury find weighs 0.89g.[24]   A Brandon find (5103)[25] which has affinities with both the second and third blocks, but which is apparently 87 per cent silver, and yet weighs only 0.50g, has no clear place in the series. At the risk of being proved too sceptical by future discoveries, one may leave it on one side as an unofficial copy.

III

Some and perhaps all of the varieties in the third block are severely debased, containing only *c.* 30 per cent silver. The animal and bird designs are often embellished with a triquetra above, and the animal has a triple-forked tail. The significance of the three-fold elements is unknown (three-fold partition of the East Anglian kingdom?) but there are exact parallels in the Northumbrian coinages of Aldfrith (animal with triple tail) and of Eadberht (triquetra, on his varieties D, E, and F). Both these precedents were available when the coins of the third block were struck.

The bird differs from earlier versions in having a solid, triangular tail. It serves to link the two otherwise separate obverse designs of the third block (QIIIA and B). Although one is right-facing and the other left-facing, they are identical in their treatment of the design.

The strange animal of QIIIA has a long, thin beak or snout, an eye, and

---

[22] Found by a resident of Congham in 1987.

[23] Lockett 270b ex Grantley 717 ex Montagu, allegedly weighing 1.67g.

[24] D. M. Metcalf, in *Sceattas in England and on the*

Continent, pp.200-2 and pl.10, 17 (Aylesbury) and 19 ('bought in London').

[25] Analysis by Dr. J. P. Northover.

FIG. Types QIIIA and B.

a long, curved neck, but virtually no head. One foreleg is raised to scratch the back of this diminutive head – a gesture which takes us right back to QIB. Its tail is curled almost into a circle, over its back and between its hind legs.[26]

The die-cutter modified the design slightly, on another die, by changing the raised foreleg into a crest (leaving an amputated stump of a foreleg) and by leading the tail straight into a triquetra, in the field above the animal.[27]

The same bird, laterally reversed but doubtless by the same hand, is next coupled with essentially the same animal as on QIID, that is to say,

FIG. Great Bircham find.

with a raised foreleg and a triple-forked tail. The tips of the tail are now curved, however, rather than cruciform; and the ear ends in a pellet instead of tapering to a point (QIIIB). There are at least two pairs of dies (Cambridge hoard 3 and Brandon 4318, same dies; Lockett ex Grantley 720, with cross added). The Brandon coin contains 32 per cent silver, plus 8 per cent tin (enriched?).

This animal with forked tail now persists for the rest of the series in 'linear' style, although whether as the obverse or reverse is difficult to say. It is found with another version of the bird, right, with raised leg, jaw-like beak, and no triquetra, in the Cambridge hoard (QIIIc). XRF

FIG. Type QIIIc.

analysis showed about 50 per cent silver, plus 7 per cent tin, but one may suspect that the figure for silver is exaggerated by surface enrichment.[28]

Finally, the Q/R 'mules' (Hill Type 73) couple the animal with forked tail with a copy of the obverse of Series R. The variety of R that is copied

[26] Birmingham City Museum (Finney Loan 181).
[27] Hill Type 64 (F. Baldwin colln.).
[28] Metcalf, Merrick, and Hamblin, analysis O.79.

FIG. Series QII–IV

497

is also only about 30 per cent fine. The variety was struck from a number of different dies, and specimens tend to be distinctly lighter than the average for Series Q. That is the best reason for placing Q/R as the last of the varieties in 'linear' style. A Brandon find (4320) of very poor

FIG. Type Q (R).

workmanship and base alloy would point to the same conclusion provided it is official.

Was there any political reason for the amalgamation of designs proper to Series Q and R? Might the change signal an extension of East Anglian political control over the mint-place of Series Q? We do not know.

An unusually elaborate Q/R coin from the Burrow Hill excavations (SF 317) has a complicated and delicate pattern of letters and pellets behind the head, and rows of fine pellets within the runes. It may be an early die, as the animal is very close to that of QIIIB.

There is a general tendency for the animal die to be smaller than the bust die. *SCBI Mack* 327 (weighing only 0.72g, and in rather sketchy style) shows this feature.

Q/R coins regularly carry the runes *er*, retrograde. The bust is sometimes laterally reversed, as on the specimen catalogued below. There are also coins ostensibly of Series R, Group 8, with the same obverse legend. Two have been found at Bawsey. They raise the question

FIG. Type R8, with runic legend *er* (from the same workshop as Type Q (R)?).

whether these *er* coins may not have been minted in the west Norfolk area, i.e. at the mint of Series Q. There is a conceptual problem in drawing the boundary between Series Q and R: should we be prepared to think of the *er* coins as part of Series Q, even though they correspond formally with Series R, Group 8? Or should we envisage Series R as 'taking over' the Q mint at a late stage in the sequence? A more thorough survey of provenances, in particular for Ipswich, is needed before the attribution of Group 8 coins reading *er* to a different mint can be regarded as secure. Their style varies considerably. One of those catalogued below is eccentric (e.g. the lips), as is *SCBI American* 100 – but the designs are so simple that they would not have been difficult to copy deceptively. In Rigoldian algebra the type will be labelled Q(R).

IV

In the modelled style, the deeply rounded torso and skilfully indicated fur make the quadruped look like nothing so much as a clipped poodle. The brush at the end of the tail suggests that it may have been understood as a lion. The bird, on the most elaborate of the dies is pecking at berries on a vine, and thus is attempting the same motif as the 'bird and branch' coins of Series U, Type 23b/d. The assumption is that the die-cutter had either seen a coin of that type, or was acting on similar instructions. He could not have taken the idea from QI-III.

On what is, apparently, the earliest variety (QIVA) the pecking bird has an ornamental triple tail. The lion has a long tongue and – inappropriately – the bird's feet. Two coins from the same dies are known.[29] The

Fig. Type QIVA.

die-cutter quickly pulled himself together, and went on to become very accomplished, achieving a dense, compact style of gemstone quality. Some of his other early quadrupeds have one or even two ears.

In the later development of the modelled series, small, neatly grouped pellets are scattered over the field on both obverse and reverse. QIVB is similar to A but with the animal facing right.[30] QIVC has the pecking

Fig. Types QIV C, and D.

bird, still with berries and vine, laterally reversed, and the animal as on QIVB.[31] QIVD lacks the berries and vine. The bird is again left-facing, and has an elegant lily-like tail, reinterpreting the earlier triple form. The lion, usually tongueless, has gaping jaws. There are several specimens.[32]

QIVE combines two very similar animal dies, in an irregular fashion. The style, however, is impeccable.[33]

[29] *SCBI Norweb* 67 ex Lockett ex Carlyon Britton 172; *BMC* 183 (= Type 44). An eighteenth-century drawing of a Reculver find, ostensibly bird/bird, may perhaps have been a misunderstood specimen of this variety.

[30] Burrow Hill 61-12.

[31] *SCBI Hunterian* 128 ex Lockett; BM ex Barnett = Hill, 1953, pl.6, 9.

[32] Cambridge hoard, 1; Ipswich; *SCBI Mack* 363 ex Grantley; Whitby; several others.

[33] Lakenheath, 0.81g; Barham, 0.97g.

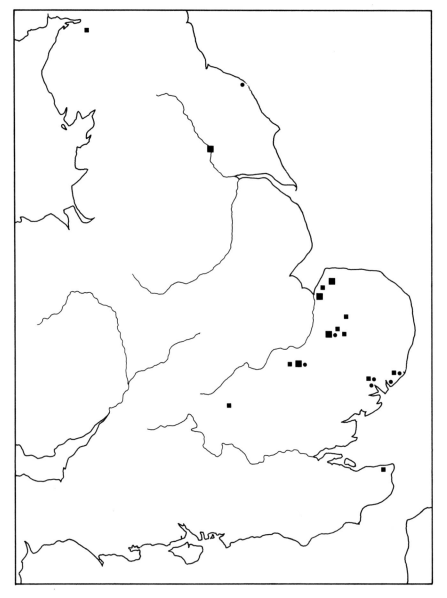

MAP. Finds of Series Q. Square symbols: QI-III, Q(R) and R8,*er*. Round symbols: QIV.

FIG. Type QIVE.

V

The main unresolved problem in Series Q is whether QIV is from the same mint as QI-III, and if not whether QIV should also be located somewhere towards the north-west of the East Anglian kingdom – i.e. whether it was a lesser mint within the commercial orbit of the mint of QI-III.

EAST ANGLIAN SCEATTAS: SERIES R

THE RUNIC sceattas of Series R, which were minted in large quantities over a period of several decades, were the principal coinage of the kingdom of the East Angles.[1] The distribution-map of single-finds shows clearly that their use, particularly in the later stages, was concentrated in Norfolk and Suffolk.

Coins attributable to Series R occur already in the Aston Rowant hoard in small numbers, suggesting that their issue began $c.705$-10. The very latest varieties are found in the Middle Harling hoard ($c.760$-5) alongside coins of Beonna. It is unparalleled that a single basic design (radiate bust/standard), begun in direct continuation of the primary runic design, Series C, should have been maintained without change to the very end of the sceatta coinage, even though in other regions of England primary types were replaced by completely different and more varied designs. The East Anglian coinage, in short, was very conservative. The earliest issues of Series R are of good silver, while the latest are more debased than any other sceattas.

A considerable variety of scarce types have also been assigned to Series R, on grounds of the general similarity of one or other of their designs, or of typological links. It should be understood that this is generally a catch-all classification which does not rest on any rigorous proof. For most of the types in question, there are hardly enough provenances to demonstrate their area of circulation. They will be discussed below in separate sections, leaving the question whether more than one basic kind of coinage was struck in East Anglia to be decided there. One can see, meanwhile, that the same general historical question might arise as has been identified in the Thames valley, namely whether regular series and eclectic groups (royal coinages and free-lance coinages?) were in use or even were in issue concurrently.

The main primary and secondary runic series is quite complicated enough on its own, without confusing the picture by introducing untested assumptions about coins which may in fact belong to other regions. A stylistic analysis, in conjunction with chemical analyses and average weights, quickly clears the ground and shows that almost all

[1] Again, Rigold's scheme contrived to be mnemonic.

MAP. Single finds of Series R, Type 1-6. Types R1 and 2, which are early coins with a wide distribution, are shown by open circles. R3-4 are shown by round symbols. R5 (*spi*) is shown by square symbols. R6 (? not East Anglian) is shown by crosses.

specimens of Series R belong to one or another of about a dozen coherent and readily identifiable groups. There is a good correlation between alloy, runes, and style in the more plentiful groups. The series falls into two parts, namely coins with a bust, i.e. a head with a neck, and those with just a head. The former are of better silver, varying from *c.*95 per cent down to about half silver. The latter are mostly below 40 per cent, falling eventually to as little as 2 or 3 per cent. The distinction between bust and head is, obviously, chronological: it defines two phases.

After that, the pattern becomes a little untidy. There is a weight reduction, undertaken at the main mint fairly early in the first phase. Thereafter, the weights seem to be stable. But not enough information can be assembled, from which to construct useful histograms. The scarce groups are less adequately defined, even in terms of their style, and sometimes only one specimen has been chemically analysed.

Even from the limited body of material available, which is not rich in die-duplication, it is possible to show with very little room for doubt that more than one mint struck Series R. It seems self-evident that the main mint was at Ipswich or nearby. There is some reason to suspect that a second, less important mint may have been at Thetford, and that there was a third, minor mint at or near Norwich.

The groups are described below in roughly the descending order of their silver contents, which seems to correspond at least broadly with their chronological ordering. In the final phase we see two named moneyers, Wigræd and Tilbeorht, each striking coins in his own style. It deserves to be considered whether they were working in different places – if only because a similar claim has been made for the succeeding coinage of Beonna. Miss Archibald has mapped the finds of his coins by the moneyers Wilræd and Efe separately (and also the 'interlace' type), and has given us an exemplary discussion of the patterns (and of the scarce coins of Beonna's early moneyer Wærferth). She draws attention to Thetford as a possible location for a second mint.[2]

The runic sceattas may well have been produced under similar administrative arrangements, at least in the final phase. In the earlier phases the great majority of the coins read *epa* (much discussed, but not demonstrably a moneyer's name). A few read *spi*, and there are others, equally scarce, with related readings such as (apparently) *rhy* (although this make no obvious sense to runologists). In Series Q there are runic obverse dies which regularly read *er* retrograde. Whether or not these legends can be construed as moneyers' names, the different versions are likely to be the work of different moneyers. As a separate proposition,

[2] M. M. Archibald, 'The coinage of Beonna in the light of the Middle Harling hoard', *BNJ* 55 (1985), 10-54, at pp.27-31.

MAP. Single finds of Series R, Types 7-12. Type R7 (*rhy*) is shown by triangular symbols. R8 and 10-12 are shown by round symbols. R9 (*spi*) is shown by square symbols.

ᛗᛉᚠ   ᛃᛉᛁ   ᚾᚺᛗ

some of the moneyers may have worked elsewhere than east Suffolk.

In order to discover whether that was so, one would have to apply the same method within Series R as, for example, between Series K and L: two districts of origin, among coins which mingled freely in circulation, could only be proved by establishing a contrast in the geographical pattern of finds, probably in a numerical form. If any such contrast exists, we might expect it to be between the estuarine region of east Suffolk, and the west or north-west of East Anglia. The scarce varieties of the runic type which are candidates for attribution to a minor mint or mints cannot as yet be firmly localized, because there are too few provenances on record. We should bear in mind, however, that the dozen groups are not necessarily to be arranged into an unbroken chronological sequence.

Nor is it absolutely certain that silver contents steadily declined. It has been suggested, for example, that an eclectic grouping of R and related types, particularly Type 70, on an enhanced silver standard, appears to be the immediate forerunner in East Anglia of the coinage in the name of Beonna.[3] But this hypothesis rests merely on typology.

The list of groups tabulated below is possibly still incomplete. It excludes obvious forgeries in poor style.

We can discern three substantive coinages, represented by groups 3, 8, and 10-11. Within each the silver contents vary, either because they were inconsistent or because there was a decline during the issue. Between the substantive varieties there are, nevertheless, distinct breaks in the alloy. The silver contents are approximately halved between groups 3 and 8, and halved again between 8 and 10-11.

Between groups 3 and 8 there is, moreover, a sharp reduction in the average weight of the sceattas.

If there is a second mint, the search for it will focus on groups 5 and 9.

Group 7, which is apparently of better silver than group 8, the substantive issue whose style it copies, includes a Group7/Type 70 'mule'. The idea that it reflects a late enhancement of the silver standard (and weight standard) leading directly into the coinage of Beonna encounters the difficulty that one would have expected the transition to be made from the later Groups 10-11.

[3] M. Blackburn and D. Sorensen, 'Sceattas from an unidentified site near Cambridge', *Sceattas in England and on the Continent*, pp.223-7, at p.225.

1–6. *Bust with pyramidal neck*

	Rigold type	Runes		'Silver'	Weight
1	Rigold –	ᚹᚳᚻ	(*epa* outwards, retrograde)	91–95%	1.20–1.25 g
2	R1x	ᛏᚹᚳᚻ	(similar)	88–96%	1.15–1.20 g
3	R1z	ᚷᛗᚳᚾ	(substantive issue)	*c.* 90–*c.* 70%	1.05–1.15 g
4	R1z/R1b?	ᛗᚳᚾ	(imitative? ᛇ behind head)	90%	*c.* 0.70 g
5	R1x/R1b?	ᛗᚳᛈ	or ᚾᚳᛁ (Norfolk?)	60–75%	0.8–0.9 g
6	R1z copy	ᚾᛗ	(bold style; lateral reversal)	*c.* 45%	*c.* 0.9 g?

7–12. *Head, with no neck*

	Rigold type	Runes		'Silver'	Weight
7	R2/R1z copy	ᚢᚻᛘ	(*rhy* or similar)	*c.* 50%	0.8–1.1 g
7x	Gp. 7/type 70		(similar; also laterally reversed)		
8	R2	∘ᛗᚠ	(substantive issue)	*c.* 38– *c.* 24%	0.7–0.9 g
8R	,,	,,	(laterally reversed	,,	,,
9	R2	ᚼᚳᛁ	(*spi*)	*c.* 35%	0. 7–0.9 g
10	R2, late	ᛈᛁᚷᚱᚪᛗ	(*wigræd*)	*c.* 13%	0.7–0.9 g
10R	,,		,, (laterally reversed)	,,	0.7–0.9 g
11	R2, late	ᛏᛁᚷᛒᛗᚱᛏ	(*tilbeorht*)	*c.* 11–7%	
12		Very late phase, continuing 10 and 11, but even more debased?			

I

Groups 1 and 2 differ in their fabric, but have many details of their
design in common. Specimens of each are catalogued below. They are the
only groups on which the runic legend is inverted and retrograde. They
are the earliest varieties to read *epa*. (The coins of Series C, from which
they are copied, read *æpa*.) Both groups were represented in the Aston
Rowant hoard. Both have vertical, rather than splayed, letters I, I in the
votive formula. Group 1 has the standard design-elements of an inverted
ᚪ behind the head; Group 2 relaces it with ᛏᚪᛏ or ᛁᛏᚪᛏ (repeated,

507

probably, from the border of the reverse), and for good measure adds another T before the runic legend, T *epa*.

The attribution of both groups to East Anglia is debateable. Series A is evidently Kentish. Series C, reading *æpa*, is arguably Kentish, with a numerous fringe of copies north of the Thames. The distribution of finds of the authentic coins of Series C is, however, by no means restricted to regions south of the Thames (cf. the Kentish and 'northern' styles of Type 32a), and it does not rule out of court an attribution to East Anglia. Series R, Group 3 is certainly East Anglian. Groups 1 and 2 belong in the transitional phase. If Series C were to be given to East Anglia, then obviously Groups 1 and 2 would go the same way: if Series C is judged to be Kentish, then Groups 1 and 2 remain debateable. The discontinuity in design between varieties C2 and R1-2 is an argument for an interruption in mint-output and a new beginning. The transitions from TIC to *æpa* and from *æpa* to *epa* are each puzzling, whatever the context in which they occurred. In the end, we do well to return to the straightforward argument, namely that the place of origin of Groups 1 and 2 can best be decided from a comparison of distribution-patterns (A, C, R1-2, R3). The comparisons will need to be made, probably, against the background of an expanding zone of monetary circulation. At present there is not enough information from which to reach a decision. Time will tell, as more finds accumulate. The distribution-patterns are not as compact as they become in the later stages of Series R. The good-silver coins were carried beyond East Anglia more freely. More find-evidence will therefore be needed than would have been the case with a purely regional currency.

A C/R 'mule' provides a cautionary tale. The writer found it in Dr. P.V. Hill's cast collection, mounted on a board and labelled as being from the F. Baldwin collection. In fact, the obverse and reverse of two different coins had accidentally become associated at some stage.

The sequence of Groups 1 and 2 is not clear. At first sight, 2 is copied from 1. It may be, however, that the broader and flatter fabric of Group 1, which matches Group 3 better, is the later version.

II

The large-flan coins of Group 1 have been found as far afield as York and near-by Nether Poppleton,[4] Hamwic,[5] and also in north Essex.[6] Their fineness is 91-95 per cent 'silver', and their weights are carefully adjusted

[4] York (Fishergate) 4909; for Nether Poppleton see *Yorkshire Numismatist* 2 (forthcoming).

[5] Hamwic 1.

[6] *BNJ* 56 (1986), 7, no.9 and pl.2, 20.

at 1.20-1.25g. There is no tin in their alloy, and very little zinc.

The York and Nether Poppleton finds taken together, in conjunction with the absence of Series C at York and Whitby, point to an East Anglian source for the R 1 coins reaching Northumbria (cf. the presence there of early coins of Series Q). That amounts to an oblique argument in favour of attributing R 1 to East Anglia rather than to Kent.

Coins of Group 2 are apparently a little lighter (1.15-1.20g) and less exactly adjusted.[7] Their fineness also may be rather more variable (88-96 per cent), and they contain marginally more zinc, but still no tin. The

only English provenances appear to be Wollaston, Northants, Telscombe, Sussex,[8] and a recent find from East Anglia.[9]

None of this provides any clear indication of origin as between Kent and East Anglia. One might even consider the possibility that Group 2 is an imitation of Group 1, from some other region. There are half-a-dozen reasons why that does not seem plausible – the newness of Group 1, the relative proportions in which Groups 1 and 2 survive, the borrowing of elements from the Group 2 design in later East Anglian runic issues, and so on. There are, however, a couple of Group 2 coins in the Paris cabinet; and there is the Telscombe find. The tally of English finds will have to grow before the theory of imitation can be dismissed out of hand.

III

Group 3 is completely straightforward – consistent and distinctive in style, with large, carefully drawn runes, now the right way round, and beginning with an X. Is this a stray symbol, or is it a runic (soft) g? The workmanship suggests the latter. There is often a pellet in the rune *e*. Behind the head are the symbols ΛO, again often with a pellet in the Λ. On the reverse, the border is distinctive, with ·|· on each side.

The reading *gepa* would call to mind the theory that the runes refer, not to the name of a moneyer, but to the mint-place – Ipswich. *Gipeswic*

[7] There are not enough weights for it to be clear whether this is an objective difference, or an effect of the Aston Rowant hoard.

[8] *BNJ* 47 (1977), pl.1,7; *BNJ* 56 (1986), 10, and pl.2, 30, with references to other specimens.

[9] Inf. courtesy of Mr. M. A. S. Blackburn.

is first attested in the late tenth century, and its etymology is conjectural. This suggestion, put forward in 1976, found no favour, but the regularity of the X or *g* is perhaps an added reason to consider it. Æpa is generally assumed to be a hypocoristic personal name.[10] If it were in fact a place-name it would, obviously, provoke a reconsideration of the mint-place of Series C. The distribution of finds of coins of Series C in good style will be decisive – when enough have accumulated to provide an answer.

The weights are around 1.15-1.05g, and the alloy shows a technical innovation: it now contains deliberate additions of tin (*c*.1.5 per cent) and zinc (*c*.1 per cent). Four chemical analyses show 'silver' contents of 94, 80, 74, and 61 per cent.[11] Does this reflect variability, or decline? The analysis of style allows us to address that question. The coins appear to fall into two sub-groups, a) with linear pyramidal neck, and added pellets in the field of the standard, and b) dotted pyramidal neck and no added pellets, but with a pellet in the central annulet. Sub-group a) gave the results 94 and 74 per cent, sub-group b), 80 and 61 per cent. Group 3a seems to be heavier.

Provenances include Brandon (3b)[12] and Caistor-by-Norwich (3a).[13]

A derivative coin in the Garton-on-the-Wolds grave-find, with an intriguing cross-and-annulets reverse, reads *epa* (inverted) exactly as on Group 1, but is otherwise more like Group 3 (in particular the annulet behind neck).[14] The curving dotted hair-line and the small zig-zag top and bottom suggest that the coin is not from the workshop of Group 3.

Its dies may well have been cut, however, when Group 3 was already in existence. (There are no precise conclusions for chronology, because one cannot be sure that the coin was not older than the other specimens in the grave-find.) *SCBI Hunterian* 15, with a garbled obverse design, is essentially of the same variety as the Garton find, with a triple dotted

[10] D. M. Metcalf, 'Twelve notes on sceatta finds', *BNJ* 46 (1976), 1-18, at pp.14f. Cf. R. I. Page, *An Introduction to English Runes*, 1973, p.125. B. Dickins, 'The *epa* coins', *Leeds Studies in English* 1 (1932), 20-1 suggests that Eppa = Eorpwald (617-28), an attribution which can quite safely be dismissed on the evidence of chronology.

[11] Coins catalogued below.

[12] From excavations by R. Carr, BRD 018-34001.

[13] Catalogued below.

[14] *BNJ* 30 (1960-1), 49 and pl.4, R2z.

border on the reverse. Perhaps the border betrays the influence of Series J.

A plated forgery from Caistor-by-Norwich combining a Group 3b obverse with a porcupine-style reverse is, on the other hand, so close to the original that it could even be from a purloined or misused die.[15]

IV

Group 4, which is less homogenous, appears to be a continuation of Group 3, into a period of less intensive or sporadic mint-output. Some specimens are virtually identical with Group 3 except that they lack the X or *g* in the legend, and are significantly lighter in weight – e.g. *BMC* 33, 0.87g, and a coin from the same obverse die, catalogued below, 0.67g. The ∧ behind the head is generally duplicated, to appear as a large zig-zag ornamented with pellets. The Ashmolean specimen contains a surprising 90 per cent silver, with 2 per cent tin.

The reverse design is modified, to become a diagonally mirrored pattern in the standard on coins which are from obverse dies so similar to

the foregoing that they could well have been cut as part of the same batch. *MEC* 709 (0.71g) and Whitby II (0.71g) are in this category.[16] The latter adds a large annulet at the end of the legend.

It seems likely that the average weight of Group 4 was deliberately reduced, by about a quarter, but there is not enough evidence to show whether the change was immediate or progressive.

One coin catalogued below with Group 4 will fall under the suspicion of being imitative. It is in debased style (crude lips, and less careful runes), and contains only 26 per cent silver.

The only provenance so far recorded is Whitby.

V

Group 5, which is characterized by the legend *spi*, and which leads directly into Group 9 (with no neck, but also reading *spi*), has every

[15] Catalogued below.

[16] Whitby II has been claimed, erroneously, to be from the same obverse die as *BMC* 33. So has the Woodbridge find, but this seems to have been simply confusion. A coin in the British Museum ex Barnett ex Bruun 10 ex Carlyon-Britton 153 is again similar.

appearance of being from a separate mint. The sequence modulates through a number of formal varieties, and there are hardly enough specimens to demonstrate that they are all from the same workshop, although one would judge that that is the case. The early members of the series, which are of better silver, read *epi* or *eps*. They have a distinctive radiate crown of two triangles, and a group of three pellets above or before the legend. Behind the head are the letter T or AT, borrowed (along with the radiate crown) from Group 2 (ITAT). The early reverses have four Ts within the standard, again evidently derived from Group 2. As the runes are not outwards, however, and as there are pellets within the *e*, the influence of Group 3 can be detected. An early coin of Group 5 of which P.V. Hill made casts from the F. Baldwin collection reads TAT in the reverse margins to left and right. The legend on the obverse is *epa*, and the radiate crown has three triangles. Another early coin has slightly blundered runes (*ep* followed by a partial repetition of *p*), and a

FIG. Type R5, ex F. Baldwin and ex *NCirc.* 1983.

distinctive reverse with symmetrical patterning of the borders, which is however 90⁰ out of phase with the standard.[17] The first coin catalogued below is closely related. It contains 67 per cent silver plus 7 per cent tin (corroded, however, which makes the measurements a little uncertain). The second, which is obviously by the same hand again, contains 59 per cent silver with 6 per cent tin (likewise corroded). The design in the standard is completely different: it could perhaps have been copied from a porcupine sceat. The margins of the reverse are ornamented with four crosses, copied perhaps from R1 with influence from C2.

The third specimen below has an obverse with many points in common with the preceding coin, but the T behind the head has become a cross,

FIG. Type R5, reading *spi* (from Binham).

and the runes now read *spi*, with some extra lines inserted. The first rune is certainly not *e*. The associated reverse is very distinctive, with a diagonally mirrored design in the standard, and a tufa with ∧, ∧, ∧, in the margins – again copied from Groups 1-2.

A similar reverse (*SCBI American* 77) links a modified obverse with

[17] *NCirc* 91 (1983), p.160, item 3890.

FIG. Type R5, *SCBI American* 77.

three bold annulets in the design. The first rune could be construed as a blundered *e*; the third is clearly *i*.

Another similar reverse provides a close link between Group 5 and Group 9 (below).

The provenances of the second and third coins mentioned above are Weeting (near Brandon) and Binham (north-central Norfolk) respectively – a small pointer, perhaps, towards a Norfolk mint-place for the coins reading *spi*.

VI

Three distinctive coins with laterally reversed obverses, in a coarse style of engraving, and runes resembling **MN** or **MNI** (laterally reversed; *es* or *esi*), are almost certainly by the same hand. As such, they may be separated out as Group 6. One, from Caistor-by-Norwich, has a reverse

copied from Group 3. It contains 45 per cent 'silver' and 4 per cent tin. Another, found near Cambridge, has an unrelated reverse type, with four annulets interrupting the outer border. A third coin, found 20 miles further into Middle Anglia, at Langford, Beds., seems to be from the same workshop. The obverse has many features in common with the

FIG. Type R6. Finds from near Cambridge and from Langford.

Cambridge find, in particular the large pellet for the eye. The reverse is another version of the 'standard', possibly influenced by a porcupine variety[18]. One will begin to suspect that Group 6 is Middle Anglian

[18] The Caistor find is catalogued below. For the find from near Cambridge, see M. Blackburn and D. Sorensen, 'Sceattas from an unidentified site near Cambridge', *Sceattas in England and on the Continent*, pp.223-7, and pl.13, 6. The Langford find is illustrated in the W. Allen sale, Sotheby, 14 March 1898, lot 171. There are various Langfords in different counties, but the next two lots include coins found at Sandy and at Hitchin, so Bedfordshire is plausible. There is no Langford in East Anglia. The coin reappeared as Lockett 210.

rather than East Anglian.

It has been suggested that the Cambridge find is a late revival, on the basis of a specimen from near Ipswich, also with annulets in the outer border, providing a link into Type 70.[19] Another similar specimen has subsequently been reported (rather surprisingly) from Eastdean, Sussex.[20] The link seems strong, for the outer border with four annulets is distinctive, but it is another question whether these coins are as late as has been claimed. The model for the obverse bust is early, and shows no influence from Group 8, let alone any later groups. One thinks, also, of the (eight) annulets in the outer border of the 'L.Sutton' find (provisionally classified as QIx, i.e. early).

A coarse reverse corresponding with that of the Caistor find is coupled with an equally coarse obverse, with a right-facing head with no neck (*SCBI Norweb* 48). The runes are blundered, possibly *pi*. This coin is so

crude that it is difficult to judge it in isolation. Perhaps one ought not to say more than that its affinities are with Group 6.

Similar uncertainty attaches to Lockett 210.

VII

The scarce coins of Group 7 have their own style and their own three-rune legend, of which the middle rune is certainly *h*. The legend has been tentatively read as *rhy*, outwards. Whatever was intended, the versions seen on different dies are related, as may be judged from the drawings.

Fig. The runic legends of Type R7. Top row: nos.408 and 409. Bottom row: finds from Caister-by-Yarmouth and Caistor-by-Norwich.

The obverses are crowded, with a large head with full, modelled cheek. A specimen from Caister-by-Yarmouth [21] and one catalogued below are

[19] Blackburn and Sorensen, loc.cit., at p.225. The coin in question was found in or near Ipswich, and was shown to Miss Archibald in 1981. The interpretation is reiterated in the publication of the Eastdean find (below).

[20] 'Coin Register' 1987, 92, 0.90g.

[21] *SCBI East Anglia*, pl.52, B. Coin found 1932, now missing, and illustrated from casts; also illustrated in *BNJ* 1960-1, pl.4.

from extremely similar but different dies. Their reverses are nondescript, with crosses in the borders. A similar obverse (also catalogued below) links into Group 7 an unrelated reverse with a simple saltire in standard. The same reverse die is also coupled with a laterally reversed obverse, from Caistor-by-Norwich.[22]

The Ashmolean derivative coin contains 48 per cent 'silver' plus 3 per cent tin. As on the other specimens of Group 7, the obverse has a head with no neck. If this were copied from Group 8, the first substantive variety with no neck, it would be strange that the copy should have higher silver contents than the model. A more probable explanation is that Group 7 is from a separate workshop: it copies the radiate crown of some earlier variety, but omits the neck.

The two provenances and the negative evidence from elsewhere, hint at an origin in eastern Norfolk.

VIII

Group 8 is a plentiful issue in crude but consistent style. It probably represents a recoinage, on a new and distinctly lower silver standard. The runic legend is reduced to an annulet followed by *ep*, or by a characteristic ligation preserving something of the *p*. There are two prominent annulets behind the head, separated by ʌ. The profile is rectangular, and the lips are heavy and elongated, sometimes ending in pellets.

The reverse has four crosses in the margins. The pattern in the standard varies, and will eventually merit a stylistic analysis, correlated with the weights of the coins, which are generally lower – in the range 0.7-0.9g. The silver contents vary from *c*.38 to *c*.24 per cent. Analyses of die-duplicate specimens would show how far that arose from mere carelessness or indifference: the Cambridge hoard (below) suggests that there was a decline during the course of Group 8. The coins in the hoard

[22] Photo by courtesy of Mr. M. A. S. Blackburn.

are engraved with some delicacy. At the other end of the stylistic range there are specimens of exceptionally coarse workmanship. These may show small variations from the basic design, e.g. the use of a cross behind the head, and irregular patterns in the standard, on coins which one would nevertheless hesitate to dismiss as copies. The examples shown are

from the Lockett sale, lot 209, l and k respectively.

Coins with a left-facing bust, and with the runes also laterally reversed, are generally similar, e.g. in the placing of the three prominent annulets, and their silver contents are in the same range. It is difficult to judge whether they could be from the same workshop. A reverse die-link between 8 and 8R would go some way to proving a connection.[23] One sees vestiges of a radiate crown more commonly in Group 8R, and diagonal

mirroring of the reverse design is less usual.

Provenances for Group 8 include the Cambridge hoard (*MEC* 708, and a specimen catalogued below from the same obverse die, but from a reverse of a different design; also another coin catalogued below), Caistor-by-Norwich,[24] Ipswich 1966,[25] Thetford, and Normanby.[26] The

FIG. Type R8R. Lakenheath find.

obverses of the Cambridge coins are of more delicate workmanship, and two specimens analysed by EPMA gave 36 and 38 per cent 'silver' with 4 and 5 per cent tin respectively. If the sample in the hoard is representative, it implies a t.p.q. part-way through the issue of Group 8.

[23] The Lakenheath find (below) looks as if it might eventually provide a die-link.

[24] Christies, 4 Nov.1986, lot 370.

[25] Line-drawing reproduced from *Proc.Suffolk Inst.Arch.*, in *BNJ* 46 (1976), 14.

[26] Thetford, 1985; 'Single finds of Anglo-Saxon and Norman coins – 2', *BNJ* 55 (1985), p.71 and item 65. Normanby, ibid 46 (1976), pl.1, 12, 1.04g, catalogued below.

Provenances for 8R include Lakenheath[27] – a coin of neat workmanship that could well be from the same phase as the Cambridge hoard coins.

A coin from Middle Harling (MH54) imitates the obverse of Group 8, with blundered runes *æea* outwards. Its reverse design has probably been influenced by a secondary porcupine. This coin is one of the very few obviously imitative, unofficial pieces based on Series R.

IX

The legend *spi* is resumed in Group 9, on coins with no neck on the obverse. One that has been analysed shows 35 per cent 'silver', matching the reduced standard of Group 8.

A stylistic link between Groups 5 and 9 is provided, apparently, by a coin from the Cambridge hoard with a similar distinctive reverse to the Binham coin, but with a simpler and more normal obverse.[28] The reverse

FIG. Type R9, ex Cambridge hoard.

differs from that of the Binham coin in the ornaments of the reverse border – here with tufa on one side, and pellets copied from Group 3 on the other three. There is another coin, in the British Museum ex Barnett, which is from the same obverse die with the same die-flaw in the diadem, and from an extremely similar reverse, with the design in the standard rotated through 90° in relation to the tufa.[29] A third coin, found at Woodbridge, is also from the same obverse die, but from a simpler reverse design.[30] It is intriguing that the Woodbridge coin should lack the die-flaw; but the various reverse dies will presumably have been cut within a very short period, and the unexpected order need not invalidate the link between Groups 5 and 9, which in any case rests principally on the use of the runes *spi*.

The coin catalogued below has a closely similar obverse, again with only one annulet coupled with a more normal reverse design. It was found in the Norwich area. It contains 35 per cent 'silver' plus 5 per cent tin. A find from Burrow Hill (BH9) is from very similar dies.

Another stylistic link between Groups 5 and 9 is seen in a coin in the

[27] See now 'Coin Register, 1985', 35, 0.84g.

[28] J. Evans, 'On a small hoard of Saxon sceattas found near Cambridge', *NC*³ 14 (1894), 18-28, pl.2, 7 = *SCBI Mack* 324 ex Hill ex Grantley 752 = *NC*⁶ 13 (1953), pl.6, 25, 1.10g = *NCirc* 91 (1983), 160 item 3891.

[29] Hill, *NC*⁶ 13 (1953), pp.105-6, coin g. Hill's cast collection.

[30] ibid, h, and see now *MEC 721*, 0.87g.

British Museum, ex L. A. Lawrence, which has a Group 9 obverse reading *epa*. This represents a reversion to the use of *epa*. One asks oneself, of course, whether it could be an unofficial copy, but the style is so exactly that of Group 9 as to leave no room for doubt. The reverse, too, has features of the *spi* sequence, namely Λ, Λ in the margins.

The problem coin in Group 9 is one excavated at Caister-by-Yarmouth in 1954.[31] Its reverse is close in style to that of the preceding coin from the Norwich area. Its obverse conforms with Group 8, except that the

reading is clearly *spi*. We are reduced to asserting that the die-cutter, whose output was in any case varied, has made a fair copy of the style of Group 8. The coin contains *c*.30 per cent 'silver', plus a (possibly exaggerated) 5 per cent tin.

Group 9 thus seems to have silver contents in line with Group 8, while Group 5 was in line with Groups 3-4. Groups 5 and 9 together have a strong claim to be considered as the work of a second mint. Taken as a whole, the series is well represented in Norfolk. Its occurrence at Ipswich and Barham remains to be established, but it should be possible in the near future to settle the question on a very adequate statistical basis.

X

The legend *er* (retrograde) is found on Q/R 'mules' and also on coins similar to those of Groups 8 and 9. Two such Series R coins from Bawsey raise the question whether the *er* coins are the work of a moneyer in the west Norfolk area. They are discussed in the section on Series Q, above.

XI

Groups 10 and 11 belong to a still later stage of the East Anglian issues, and introduce two new runic legends which are (for the first time) certainly personal names – Wigræd and Tilbeorht. The flans tend to be large, and the silver contents are very low, with high tin contents. Differences of style and detail between the coins of the two moneyers show that their dies were cut separately.

Wigræd's coins copy the general design of Group 8. The three annulets

[31] *SCBI East Anglia* 1005, 0.84g.

are now less prominent, and are pelletted. The appearance of the obverses is dominated by the long runic legend, in particular the elongated X for *g*, echoed by the ornamental interlocking XX replacing the drapery of the bust. The rune *æ* is usually omitted. The reverse dies are of the basic design.

Specimens on which the obverse is laterally reversed are listed as Group 10R. *SCBI Hunterian* 17 and *MEC* 715 are from the same dies, and both are at the upper end of the weight-range for the variety: 0.89 and 0.86g. *MEC* 714 has the same slightly irregular design in the

standard, with two unjoined pellets, and again is heavy: 0.84g. One would guess that these carefully made coins are Wigræd's earliest efforts, and stand at the head of the sequence. They have not been chemically analysed.

Two sceattas of Wigræd were published by Evans in the Cambridge hoard. Others, such as *MEC* 714, and one or more coins now in the British Museum ex Carlyon-Britton, could perhaps be from the same source.[32] The Ashmolean specimen contains 13 per cent 'silver', plus 6 per cent tin. Two specimens from Burrow Hill contain similar amounts of silver (Ag) but are heavily leaded, and with large amounts of tin (BH8: Ag 16%, Pb 4%, Sn 9%; BH9: Ag 14%, Pb 12%, Sn 8%).[33] A British Museum coin, BMA 11, has 16 per cent silver and only 2.4 per cent lead, with 10 per cent tin.[34] The evidence is difficult to interpret sensibly in terms of 'silver' (silver plus gold plus lead), but the intended contents were clearly less than in Group 8, and may have been a quarter 'silver', subsequently reduced to an eighth, or thereabouts.

Two coins from Middle Harling illustrate a later phase, when the 'silver' contents had fallen to 5-6 per cent (having been halved yet again?) and the actual silver (Ag) was only 2-3 per cent.[35] The style is crude, and the reverse designs are diagonally mirrored. On a specimen catalogued below the first rune, *w*, can be seen to have degenerated into a single stroke.

[32] There were none in *BMC*, but Hill (*NC* 1953) lists six specimens, of which four were in the Carlyon-Britton sale (lots 144b and 145a, b, and c). The weights which he quotes are those of a carefully adjusted coinage: 0.72, 0.72, 0.78, 0.78, 0.91. See also the two specimens from Burrow Hill (0.61 and 0.92g), *SCBI American* 99 (0.79g), and Lockett 209j. No die-duplication has been reported.

[33] Analyses by M. R. Cowell in *BNJ* 1985, 47.

[34] ibid. It is not stated what the BMA numbers refer to.

[35] MH 55 and 56, weighing 0.81 and 0.78g respectively.

A find from Burgh Castle, with 4 Ls within the standard, is perhaps later still.

XII

Tilbeorht's obverses are dominated, even more than Wigræd's, by the sprawling line of large runes, in which his name is usually spelled *tiberlt*. The characteristic reverse type, differing from Wigræd's, has four Ts in a rectangular alignment (a). The alloy is at best *c*.10 per cent silver, without the heavy leading that is found in Wigræd's sceattas. It declines to 6-7 per cent (with relatively more lead) in coins that are still of good style. They contain 8-11 per cent tin.

Two other, more traditional patterns are found in the standard (b, c). There is no obvious way of arranging the varieties into a declining series in harmony with their silver contents, unless perhaps one could regard a specimen of variety b as early and experimental, taking account of the quality of the modelling, the badly-judged rune *b*, and the positioning of

the ear (see catalogue below). The lead contents are exceptionally low: Ag 9.3%, Pb 0.5%, Sn 5.6%. Variety a would follow, spanning the transition to a lower alloy (the broken coin below has Ag 9.2%, Pb 1.7%, Sn 8%, whereas MH 59 has Ag 3.7%, Pb 2.2%, Sn 11.3%). Variety c would then be the last of the three, as its sketchier modelling encourages us to suppose: Ag 4.4%, Pb 2.8%, Sn 7.9%. New evidence might easily disturb this arrangement.[36]

Two coins from Middle Harling apparently share an obverse die;[37] and at least one other die-link has been noted.[38]

XIII

Two other coins of Tilbeorht from Middle Harling (MH 57-8), which also share an obverse die, are quite different in style, and will fall either at

[36] Three coins catalogued below have been analysed by Dr. J. P. Northover. MH 59 was analysed by Dr. M. R. Cowell.

[37] MH 59 and 64.

[38] A coin offered to the Ashmolean but declined as a duplicate.

57   58

the beginning or the end of the main sequence. An attempt was made to analyse one of them, but it was unfortunately too corroded to yield an acceptable result.[39] Miss Archibald has drawn attention to the close similarity of one of the reverses with a coin of Beonna. The natural reading of the evidence will be that these are the very latest sceattas of Series R.

A coin found at Barham, from the same dies as MH 57, has, unusually, a clear *h* (reversed) in *tilberht*.[40]

A coin from very similar dies to MH58 was found at Ipswich in 1973: it was published as 'R2 derivative, ep, broken', although it very clearly reads *til*.[41]

XIV

If Wigræd and Tilbeorht were working in different places – as Wilræd and Efe and their colleagues seem to have been doing a few years later, under Beonna – Tilbeorht will have been in the more northerly location. The find-evidence is not yet quite sufficient to allow us to reach a judgement, although the extensive series of finds from Ipswich should in due course provide a good reference point. As things stand Barham has produced one coin of Tilbeorht and 3 of Wigræd, and Burrow Hill in 1980-1 produced two of Wigræd, whereas the Middle Harling hoard contained three of Tilbeorht against two or three of Wigræd (late varieties); there was a further find of a Tilbeorht discovered 50 or 60 metres away from the hoard, which may represent secondary redeposition from the hoard after disturbance in the tenth or eleventh century, but which so far as one can judge is more likely to have been a separate loss. In the latter case it should be scored separately as evidence for the frequency of the two moneyers. The third Wigræd mentioned above was found subsequently, in 1987. It is from dies similar to MH55, i.e. very debased in style.

Another Tilbeorht that certainly antedates the hoard was said in 1977 by an intermediary to have been found at Deptford. Although it is not impossible that a very late coin of Series R should be found in Kent it is so unusual that one wondered whether he had not misheard or

[39] MH 58.

[40] For a full discussion of the runes, see R. I. Page, 'The legends of the coins', in *BNJ* 55 (1985), 37-40.

[41] *Proc.Suffolk Inst.Arch.* 33 (1973-5), 100. Identified now from casts made at the time by S. E. Rigold.

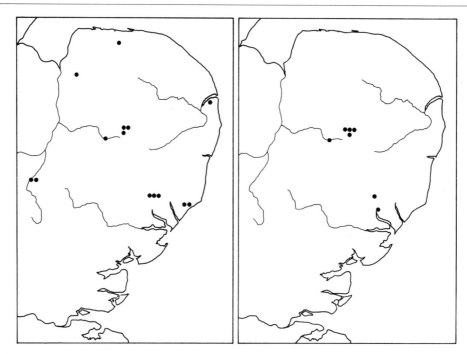

MAPS. Finds of coins of Wigræd (left-hand map) and Tilbeorht (right-hand map).

misremembered its true provenance of Thetford. The writer was offered this coin in 1985, and it is now in the Ashmolean.[42]

In summary, Wigræd's coins appear to be more widely distributed than those of Tilbeorht; but they are more plentiful, and that may account for the contrast in the present distribution pattern. In addition to the finds from the south-east coastlands, there is one specimen of Wigræd from the Red Castle excavations at Thetford,[43] one from within the walls of Burgh Castle,[44] and one from Binham.[45] (See the map.)

Tilbeorht's distinctive reverse type of four Ts in a rectangular alignment may well be a deliberate reference back to the early coins of the *spi* series, Group 5.

The absence of coins of Tilbeorht from the Cambridge find is perhaps to be explained by the date of deposit: their issue had not yet begun. Their absence might, on the other hand, be by chance in such a small group. The hoard as published contains 6 sceattas of Series R, of Groups 8 (3), 9 (1), and 10 (2).

[42] *BNJ* 47 (1977), 39 s.v. Deptford, and pl.3, 40. The coin was not correctly identified at the time, – before the Middle Harling coins had been found.

[43] *SCBI East Anglia* 1006.

[44] ibid, pl.52, A (late variety with 4 Ls).

[45] Found November 1987. Photos courtesy of the Norfolk Archaeological Unit.

XV

The simplest hypothesis for the interpretation of Series R is that there were at least two and in all probability three separate sequences, from different mint-places. The main sequence included, over a period of about fifty years, Groups 1-4, 8, and 10. Their runic legend is *epa* or (in one group) X *epa* or *gepa*, and whatever that means, their mint-place is likely to have been Ipswich or Woodbridge. The debased coins of Wigræd are the final phase of this coinage, before it was replaced by better silver pieces in the name of King Beonna. There is a well-evidenced minor sequence, which at first imitates the *epa* sceattas of Group 2, but later changes to the legend *spi*. It begins not much later than the main series, perhaps during the issue of Group 3, with reasonably high silver contents, and continues, perhaps intermittently, into the phase of debasement. Tilbeorht's coins may well be a continuation at the same mint-place, somewhere in the north or (less probably) the north-west of East Anglia. Groups 5 and 9, and probably 11 constitute this sequence. A small group of coins with a runic legend *rhy* appears to be separate, and may belong in the Norwich area, and to an intermediate date: they are classified as Group 7. Coins with the retrograde legend *er* may be another separate issue, related to Series Q. That leaves another small group of coins, Group 6, which are not certainly East Anglian.

TYPES 30, 51, AND THE SALTIRE-STANDARD TYPES

IN THE DESIRE to find a place for everything within Rigold's alphabetical scheme of classification, Types 70, 77, 78, and 79 have been labelled R, and numerous other types (mostly known from single or from very few specimens) have been grouped as 'related or derivative types' of Series R. They include Types 51, 56, 61, 73, 80, 81, 86, and 87.[1]

The label may create the impression that some or all of these 'types' are judged to be East Anglian. If that were so, it might seem that coinages of very different designs from the main issues of Series R were being produced side by side with them in the East Anglian kingdom. There might in that case be some sort of analogy with the coinages of Kent, the Thames estuary, and the Thames valley, where eclectic groups of issues were minted alongside the regular, and presumably official, coinage in east Kent and at London. Series R proper, the runic series, which persisted with the same basic designs for half a century, was in all probability the coinage of King Aldwulf (663/4-c.713) and of his son King Ælfwald (c.713-49). Although it did not bear the royal name it was just as much a royal coinage as the reform issues, on a better silver standard, of King Beonna. Were all these other typologically distinct issues, which have in the past been designated 'R-related', also East Anglian royal coinage – or were they free-lance coinages tolerated by the king?

Or can one escape from the difficulty by arguing, as Miss Archibald and others have done, that the coins of Type 70 are late varieties on a restored alloy standard, i.e. precursors of Beonna's reform, or even contemporary with it? The comparison that has been drawn is, specifically, between the form of the saltire on MH 58 (a late die of Tilbeorht) and on Type 70.[2] Even though this design element was the simplest in the world to copy, and might have evolved independently, we should not underestimate the propensity of die-cutters to pick up features

---

[1] I. Stewart, 'The early English denarial coinage, c.680-c.750', in *Sceattas in England and on the Continent*, ed. D. Hill and D. M. Metcalf, Oxford, 1984, pp.5-26, at p.15 ('various other adaptations later appear. . . in the final stages. . .'), and p.26.

[2] M. M. Archibald, 'The coinage of Beonna in the light of the Middle Harling hoard', *BNJ* 55 (1985), 10-54.

from the earlier issues of their mint. In the preceding section we saw that there is a case (not fully proved) for locating Tilbeorht at a northerly or westerly mint-place in East Anglia.

The obvious difficulty in seeing Type 70 as a very late East Anglian issue of sceattas is their absence from the Middle Harling hoard, which included a few survivors from the end of Series R.

Was Type 70, in fact, East Anglian? That is the first question to be asked, and it would be decidedly premature to embark on historical speculation about the extent of royal control over the currency of East Anglia until it has been answered.

There are two groups of types to be considered. In one group a large, thickly pelletted saltire-standard, reminiscent of that seen on the primary **SAROALDO** type, is coupled with a variety of obverse or reverse types. (The status of the two designs is often ambiguous.) On the assumption that all these varieties belong together, i.e. that they were minted in the same place, the saltire-standard design of Type 51 might be supposed to be the distinctive 'badge' of an eclectic series. An exceptionally valuable die-link[3] connects Type 51 with the scarce Type 30a – which is evidently the earlier of the two types. They share the 'two standing figures' motif which is associated with series N. In Type 30, a facing moustached and bearded ('Wodan') head occupies the place later taken by the saltire standard. The Wodan head seems also to have served as the badge of a particular mint-place, for it can be traced back into Series BZ, and to a date earlier than the concealment of the Aston Rowant hoard.[4] The crucial die-link thus serves to link Series BZ, and Types 30 and 51 with their related varieties, into a single sequence. Type 30 is known from only three or four specimens, and Type 51 is itself quite scarce. We may be looking, then, at the (sporadic?) issues of a minor, northerly mint – where the designs of the primary and secondary sceattas were loosely connected. To say that, however, is to run on ahead of the detailed evidence on which the case rests.

Types 51, etc. have an average weight of $c.1.1g$. Three specimens which have been analysed contain 94, 82, and 70 per cent 'silver' respectively – significantly better, and also somewhat heavier, than even the best of Beonna's coins, which are more usually around half silver.

The other group is even simpler in its designs, which vary considerably in detail, around the theme of standards with saltires, annulets, etc. They were all classified, or (more accurately) lumped together as Type 70 by

[3] Discussed and illustrated in M. A. S. Blackburn and M. J. Bonser, 'Single finds of Anglo-Saxon and Norman coins–3', *BNJ* 56 (1986), 64-101, at p.76, and nos.44-44A.

[4] The hoard included Series BZ.

Hill,[5] but his varieties a-j probably include two distinct groups in terms of mint-output. Most of them form a single series, to which stylistic analysis can be applied with some success, but a few seem to be separate, and may even originate south of the Thames. One coin is perhaps an unofficial copy.

The weights of the main group are closely controlled, at around 0.9-0.95g. The silver contents are again high. Two specimens have been analysed: one shows 87 per cent 'silver', the other, 72 per cent, but its authenticity is problematic. On the evidence of one coin, then, it seems that Type 70, like Type 51, is of a much better alloy than the coinage of Beonna.

Again, however, the prior question is 'where'. In order to discover their region of circulation we need to map the finds, but before we can do that, we have to group the varieties that are to be mapped together. Stylistic analysis of such simple designs may be thought to yield uncertain results, and possibly false groupings. Let us, however, examine the typologically related varieties on the working hypothesis that they form coherent groups. That should show, at least approximately, the regions to which Type 30-51 and 70 respectively belong.

Type 51 and its derivatives have been found at Tilbury (at least 3 specimens) and Royston – at both of which major sites Series R is effectively absent. The presence of such a scarce type as 51 where the much more plentiful East Anglian issues are absent gives strong reason to doubt whether the scarce type can be East Anglian.

Type 30 and 51, etc. are also recorded from North Ferriby, on the northern shore of the Humber; Alkborough, on the southern shore of the Humber; Alford, Lincs.; Lewknor, Oxon.; West Ilsley, Oxon.; 'the Thetford area' (allegedly within 5 miles of Thetford); Minster-in-Sheppey, Kent; and an unnamed productive site near Canterbury. Together with Royston and Tilbury that amounts to a scattered distribution, which will require a larger number of coins to define its centre of gravity adequately. Already, however, it is fairly clear that the types are so much less plentiful in East Anglia than elsewhere, that it is unlikely they are East Anglian. The northerly finds point us towards the east midlands.

So the historical problem turns out to be a quite different one from that which was first perceived. It is hard to imagine what place in the east midlands might have had a mint in the eighth century. There are no obvious coastal locations, but there may have been a few trading centres that could be reached by water.

[5] In NC[6] 13 (1953), at pp.112f.

MAPS. Types 30, 51 etc. (left-hand map). The (earlier) type BZ is shown by open circles. Type 70 (right-hand map). Types 46 and 70i are shown by open circles.

Type 70 has been found at Burgh Castle, and at the other end of Norfolk, in the Heacham area. There is also apparently a find from the Ipswich area from 1981 (not seen). Further provenances are Elloughton (near Brough, on the northern shore of the Humber); West Leake, Notts.; and East Dean, (?West) Sussex.[6] More than half the known specimens of the type, unfortunately, are without provenance. The few find-spots that are listed could hardly be said to support an origin in east Suffolk. Nor are they in harmony with the regionally restricted circulation of Beonna's coins. A Norfolk origin is not, however, completely out of the question, on the evidence of the finds.

I

The 'Wodan' head of Type 30 is an echo or a continuation of Series BZ. The two standing figures are the same as those found in Series N, and

[6] For the St. Albans find, see below.

527

one wonders whether they may have had some political significance.

The obverse has crosses to left and right of the head, which are presumably borrowed from Series X, the Jutish series (where they are a standard part of the design). That would imply convergence: the die-cutter was familiar with both Series BZ and X, which he recognized as being of a common design.

In Type 30, the same types occur in two very different styles, which are distinguished as Types 30a and b. Of these, Type 30b, in coarse style, seems to stand near the head of the series. On the reverse, the two standing figures are symmetrically identical. There are two specimens: *BMC* 146 and a coin catalogued below are from different but extremely similar dies. They are heavy, weighing 1.15 and 1.22g respectively. The second coin contains 91 per cent 'silver', with only a trace of tin.[7]

A modern forgery of Type 30b was reported in 1988.

An obverse which is certainly by the same hand is linked with an individualistic 'standard' reverse, in a coin from North Ferriby, weighing 1.15g.[8] Another obverse, almost certainly by the same hand again, has a standard reverse with four Ls. This coin, once more weighing 1.15g, has been described as a 30b/8 mule.[9] It is probably the specimen found at Minster-in-Sheppey in *c*.1809. The reality is that four or five similar obverse dies of Type 30b are known, in association with three reverse types. As the 'two standing figures' reverse is taken up by Type 30a, it would seem likely that the 'standard' reverses are earlier.

Type 30a is much more delicately engraved. *BMC* 145 is from dies which may be judged experimental, because of the outline of fine pellets

around the crown of the head – a detail subsequently omitted. The obverse mimics that of BZ, in particular the lens-shaped eyes or eye-sockets, and the angle of the moustaches.[10] There are crosses composed of pellets to left and right of the face, and these too seem to be an early feature within Type 30a.

[7] EPMA analysis by Dr. J. P. Northover.

[8] E. J. E. Pirie, 'Some Northumbrian finds of sceattas', in *Sceattas in England and on the Continent'*, pp.207-15, at p.208 and pl.11,14.

[9] R. C. Lockett sale (Glendining, 6 June 1955, 241) = Hill (*NC* 1953), pl.6, 19.

[10] One can conveniently compare *BMC* pl.3, 14 and 16.

FIG. The so-called 'Wodan' head in different styles.

The two standing figures on the reverse of *BMC* 145 both have facing heads, but they are already differentiated: the senior figure, on the left, has long moustaches.

A specimen from Tilbury (below) is from different dies. The head of the figure on the right is now shown in profile, diademed. The two crosses on the obverse are each reduced to a row of 3 pellets. The

specimen which provides the die-link, Lockett 240a, is from another similar obverse die, and a coarser reverse, again with a profile head to the right.

Two specimens from coarse obverse dies in the style of Type 30b are problematic.[11] The modelling of the head, instead of being egg-shaped, is broad and extends only down to the moustaches: half a larger egg. There are pellet crosses again to left and right. One's first instinct might be to think that they were imitative, but there are two of them, very similar to

each other, and they are coupled with reverses that seem quite acceptable as the work of the die-cutter of Type 30a. Because there is an early version of 30a, with two facing heads, it appears that the differentiation of the heads was introduced part-way through the issue of 30a. If these two specimens are 30b/30a mules (for once the term might be appropriate) how is it that they already show a profile head? Perhaps all the coins in question were produced within a relatively short time, and we should not look for a completely rigorous logic in the development of the type by a second die-cutter. Perhaps the concept of two different heads for two rulers of different status had a non-numismatic origin. The one 30b/30a coin for which a weight is available is heavy (1.16g) – which is in its favour.

The other half of the 30a-51 die-link is Type 51, which is known from as many as four die-duplicate specimens (*BMC* 197, and finds from

---

[11] *SCBI Copenhagen* 41 (1.16g) and Lockett 240b.

Royston, Thetford, and Alford[12]), another pair of similar dies (the Lewknor find[13]), and a further pair of dies which are sketchier, and on which the head of the *left*-hand figure is in profile. The right-hand head is almost entirely off the flan, but one can see part of the moustaches (probably). If that is correct, it means that the whole design has been

laterally reversed.[14] Instead of all four feet trailing to the right, they trail inwards to the mid-line of the design. The rectangular lines of the arms and shoulders, and the two pellets on each chest, suggest that the die is by another hand.

The saltire of Type 51 is continued right into the corners of the standard, with a very regular pattern of 4 or 5 pellets forming each arm of the saltire, and groups of 3 pellets in the quarters. It is seen in a rather

looser style on a coin with a monster as its obverse (or reverse?) – borrowed, no doubt, from Series N, like the two standing figures type.[15]

Better workmanship informs the saltire-standard in a new variety where it is coupled with a double croix ancrée. Two specimens are known, one from Tilbury[16] and the other from a productive site near

Canterbury.[17] The ornaments in the margins of the saltire-standard appear to be four tufas – unlike Type 51, which seems to have just a pellet or a couple of pellets. There is a third similar coin from Domburg.

Another style of saltire is slightly smaller than the standard. One cannot be dogmatic that it is by the same hand, because the design would have been so easy to copy. It is seen in combination with a bust (with pyramidal neck) copied from the earlier half of Series R, probably from Group 3. The runes and the annulet behind the head are replaced in each case by a cross with a pellet in each quarter. The Alkborough find[18] is

[12] Royston 44; Coin Register 1987/90; *BNJ* 1986, p.184, L3. Their weights are 1.07, 1.07, and 1.00g respectively.

[13] Catalogued below. 1.08g. The design apparently includes the male members.

[14] British Museum (P.V. Hill casts: presumably =

NC 1953, p.102. 1.26g).

[15] *NC* 1953, Type 23a/51, F. Elmore Jones colln., 0.94g = *NCirc* 78 (1970), 407, item 11181, illus.107.

[16] Catalogued below. 1.33g.

[17] Inf. courtesy of Mr. Bonser.

[18] 0.90g.

catalogued below. Because it has the same two pelletted crosses, *SCBI Hunterian* 14,[19] laterally reversed, may be considered a copy of the same

variety. It is surprising that such a scarce coin should have attracted copying. The quality of the dies of the Hunter coin is unimpressive, and one would be reluctant to see it as part of the series.

Two other coins with obverses borrowed from Series R, namely *SCBI Hunterian* 13 [20] and a so called *epa*/51 mule in the British Museum,[21]

remain problematic. Both have tufas in the margins of the reverse.

A variety with a similar reverse, from Domburg,[22] has an obverse type of cross with annulet terminals, which recalls a variant of Series R in the

Garton grave-find. It is said to be base. Again, it is of interest that an imitation should be found on the continent.

All the affiliations of Types 30-51 are in the later primary and early secondary phases. The weight and alloy, and the widespread distribution, are appropriate to an early secondary type. One may suspect that the mint-place was the same as for Series BZ.

II

The characteristic obverse of Type 70 has a small standard, surmounted by an empty tufa, flanked symmetrically by two crosses or lines, and with a row of three pellets below. In the standard is a small saltire with single

[19] 1.08g.

[20] 0.88g. The quality of the reverse die, in particular, is very acceptable. *NC* 1953, pl.6, 23.

[21] *NC* 1953, pl.6, 11. 0.92g. Study of Hill's plaster cast makes the writer think that there are only two runes, *ep*.

[22] ibid., pl.7, 23 (i.e. Type 70j). Cf. also *SCBI Hunterian* 15, of dubious style.

pellets in the quarters. One can arrange the obverse dies into some sort of order: the two crosses are simplified and become merely lines; the standard becomes smaller; the three pellets are reduced to two; the pellets are omitted from the quarters of the saltire. That interpretataion is to some extent confirmed by the reverses, which are of several varieties, beginning perhaps with 70c, with a more elaborate saltire similar to that of Type 51, etc.[23] This coin is said, however, to be base. From its photograph, it could well be by the same hand as the Alkborough coin. If it really is base, there will be some doubt whether it may not be imitative.

FIG. Type 70, Hill varieties c, b, a, d, f, e, and g.

The style of the obverse is much in its favour. It is the link, if one accepts its official character, which tends to show that Types 30, 51, and 70 form a continuous series – with a weight reduction coinciding more or less with the introduction of Type 70.

The next reverse variety is a distinctive standard with a zig-zag (radiate crown) attached. As well as Hill's 70b[24] and 70a [25] there is a find from near Heacham, in the north-western corner of Norfolk, from the same obverse die as 70a and an extremely similar reverse.[26] There is also a find from Elloughton,[27] and an unprovenanced specimen in the Ashmolean.[28] This last is 87 per cent 'silver' with perhaps 2-3 per cent tin. It shows the zig-zag reduced from ΛΛΛ to ΛΛ, and the crosses replaced by simple lines. The four symbols in the standard are reduced to two angles (70d). This little batch of specimens probably reflects an active phase of mint-output, perhaps with a die-ratio in excess of 1:1.

The same two angles are seen on a coin with four crosses, or rather four Ts, in the margins (70f).[29] The Burgh Castle find is similar, but with a diagonally mirrored pattern (70e).[30]

At the end of the sequence a new reverse design is introduced, with 4

[23] ibid., pl.7, 19. 0.92g.

[24] 0.93g.

[25] ibid., pl.7, 18. 0.76g.

[26] Inf. courtesy of Dr. B. Green. 0.86g.

[27] Found December 1984. Inf. courtesy of Mr. J. Booth.

[28] Ex G. E. L. Carter, ex Lockett, ex Grantley = Hill 70d. 0.94g.

[29] *SCBI Yorks*, 947, ex Lockett 225a, ex Carlyon-Britton. 0.90g (according to *SCBI*).

[30] Lockett 226b, resold as *NCirc* 1989, 4000. 1.022g.

annulets set in the outer dotted border (70g).[31] There are two very similar dies, one being a find from Eastdean, Sussex.[32] The obverses are simplified, with two dots instead of three below the standard, or without pellets in the quarters of the saltire.

Some element of doubt attaches to a similar coin, with complete crosses on the obverse,[33] especially in view of the existence of a forgery in somewhat similar style (discussed in section III).

Blackburn and Sorensen have suggested that a Cambridge find classified above as Series R, Group 6 might belong with Type 70g, as it shares the 4 annulets.

There is a closer, but still uncertain parallel in Type 56, with 8 annulets set into the outer (wire) border. It has been tentatively classified above as QIx.

These two uncertain pieces apart, all the above varieties of Type 70 obviously come from the same mint. Their absence at Middle Harling is probably sufficient to rule out their being late East Anglian coins. The weight-standard of 0.9-0.95g suggests a mid-secondary date.

III

A specimen of Type 70 in the National Museum of Wales containing a plausible 72 per cent 'silver' will nevertheless fall under the suspicion of being a modern forgery, on the grounds that the minor constituents of its alloy are extremely irregular. The trace of gold per 100 parts of silver is only about a quarter of what one would expect, the lead contents are far too low, and there is no tin in the alloy.

The coin's style commands no confidence either.

IV

Type 46 [34] (imitating Series O) and a find from near St. Albans[35] have obverses which, if not identical, are extremely similar, and which in any case serve to link the two different reverse types just as securely as a die-identity would. A third coin, with yet another reverse design, (70i) is catalogued below: it appears to be debased and very corroded.

[31] NC 1953, pl.7, 20.

[32] Coin Register 1987, 92, mentioning Capt. B. E. Forrest. 0.90g. I am indebted to Mr. M. J. Bonser, who has clarified that the find-spot is a minor productive site at Eastdean near Eastbourne – not East Dean inland from Chichester.

[33] NCirc 91, 1983, item 3870. 1.03g.

[34] BMC 188, which remains unique. 0.98g.

[35] Coin Register 1987, 91. 0.80g.

These three unique coins appear to be the harbingers of an eclectic series, on which little comment is yet possible, except that it seems to be early, on the grounds that the prototype in Series O belongs very early in Type 38. One of only two known specimens of 38 with legends, rather than cable borders, has silver contents of 94 per cent.[36]

The legend of Type 46 is MONITASCORVM.

The K/R mule from Winchester has a formally very similar standard-annulets obverse. Although it is not demonstrably by the same hand, it may belong to the same mint-place as Type 46, etc.[37] If so, it gives another indication of date.

Our guess as to where that place was might be modified or confirmed by even one more piece of evidence. The three terms in the equation at the moment are O, St. Albans, and (?) Winchester. Series O almost certainly belongs south of the Thames, and so may Type 70i.

V

Type 70h, formerly in the F. Baldwin collection, is said to be base[38] and may (to judge from its types) be imitative.

h

A coin from the Brandon excavations is unfortunately in very decayed condition, but could be from the same source.

[36] It is catalogued below.
[37] It is discussed in the section on K/R mules.
[38] *NC* 1953, pl.7, 21.

Type 70j, the remaining Hill variety, has already been included in the discussion of Type 51.

VI

A single distribution-map of all the varieties that have been discussed here, including Series BZ, but excluding Types 46 and 70i, covers the whole of eastern England. The only prospect of localizing the mint-place is to calculate, for various regions, the proportion of sceatta finds which Types BZ-30-51-70 make up. The percentages direct us towards the regions from around the Wash and northwards – but excluding York. As with Series J, the numerical differences are not great. Perhaps if we had a good series of site-finds from the mint-town itself, they would show a clear proportional lead. The choice appears to be between a site on south Humberside, and Lincoln.

EAST SAXON SCEATTAS: SERIES S

SERIES S consists of only one type, the distinctive 'winged female centaur', *BMC* Type 47, which was previously interpreted as a sphinx (whence the mnemonic S). It is strongly localized in the area of the East Saxon kingdom, as many as 20 specimens having been found at the productive site of Tilbury, and others at Maldon, Southminster, Bradwell-on-Sea, north Essex, Watford, – and at London. It is, on the other hand, absent or virtually absent among the numerous finds from East Anglia and from east Kent. It is absolutely clear that the Tilbury finds are stray losses; and there is also an interesting lead impression from another Tilbury site, with an obverse impressed in intaglio on each side.

One other major site has yielded Series S in quantity, namely Royston, from which there are no fewer than 6 specimens. The exact location of the Royston site has not yet been disclosed; it is close to, if not actually within, the modern county boundary of Essex. The territorial extent of the East Saxon kingdom in the eighth century can be glimpsed from charter evidence in only the most fragmentary fashion. Mercia, it seems, was encroaching upon Hertfordshire and Middlesex; but the north-western salient of Essex may have remained under East Saxon control. That is what the numismatic evidence suggests, and it seems that there is nothing else available which could contradict it. If the Royston site was, in fact, near the East Saxon boundary, the frequency of Series S among the finds may be judged to provide support for a political interpretation of the sceattas: the type was carried thus far (but no further), precisely because it was the coinage of the East Saxon kings.

A sample check for die-duplication suggests that there were originally something of the approximate order of 60 obverse dies, with a higher number of reverse dies.[1] Type 47 is a secondary type, with silver contents of a half or a little less. The weights vary widely, from 0.7g to 1.1g with no obvious correlation with style, and with some sort of peak at *c*.0.9g.

Professor Morehart has established very clearly that the type is best

---

[1] This may turn out to be an underestimate. It is based on a triplet and two pairs among twenty-odd coins.

described as a winged female centaur, and she has given ample evidence that there are both classical prototypes and Anglo-Saxon parallels.[2] She is not disposed, therefore, to accept that the model for Series S was a Celtic coin of Cunobelin showing a (male) centaur carrying a leafy branch[3] – partly on the grounds that she knew of no instances where secondary sceat motifs were borrowed from Celtic coins. Morehart has chided the writer[4] for seeing in the mythical creature a local symbol of political independence from Mercia – occupying the place in the coin's design which would otherwise be occupied by the helmeted standing figure of Æthelbald, whose hegemony extended almost everywhere south of the Humber. The argument has now moved on, to the extent that the beginning of the secondary phase has been re-dated to a time probably before Æthelbald's hegemony was established.

There are various strands to the argument: whether the model can be identified; whether the type was believed to allude to Cunobelin; whether the sceattas were minted in Essex (and if so where); whether they are a coinage produced under royal authorization; whether the (female) centaur's (male) head was deliberately borrowed from another sceatta type, or just copied without any particular purpose; whether the classical motif was invested with any contemporary meaning.

Several of these questions are incapable of receiving conclusive answers, but even since 1985 it has become increasingly clear that the distribution of finds of Series S is concentrated within the kingdom of Essex.[5] The attribution of the type to King Selered (*ob.*746) or possibly Swæfberht (*ob.*738)[6] rests on wider considerations involving the whole of the sceatta coinage.

The reverse design is a whorl of four wolf-worms advancing clockwise, with fangs, and with chains emerging from their throats to meet at the central point of the design, marked by a larger pellet. The four chains form a sinuous cross, which the die-cutter evidently laid out carefully so that it should be regular.

The typology, deriving presumably from Series K, Type 32a, is close to that of Type 23e, which however has only three wolf-worms. The region of origin of that type, within south-eastern England, is uncertain. In Series H, Type 48 (*not* from Hamwic) the three chains follow the

---

[2] M. J. Morehart, 'Female centaur or sphinx? On naming sceat types: the case of *BMC* Type 47', *BNJ* 55 (1985), 1-9.

[3] D. M. Metcalf, 'A sceat of *BMC* Type 47 from Houghton Regis, Beds.: the East Saxon sphinx', ibid. 46 (1976), 8-13, and pl.1, 8-11 (with the coin of Cunobelin).

[4] Morehart, loc.cit.

[5] The pattern is mapped in *BNJ* 56 (1986), at p.6. Numerous new finds from Tilbury have subsequently been reported to Mr. M. J. Bonser.

[6] On the history of Essex see B. Yorke, 'The kingdom of the East Saxons', *Anglo-Saxon England* 14 (1985), 1-36.

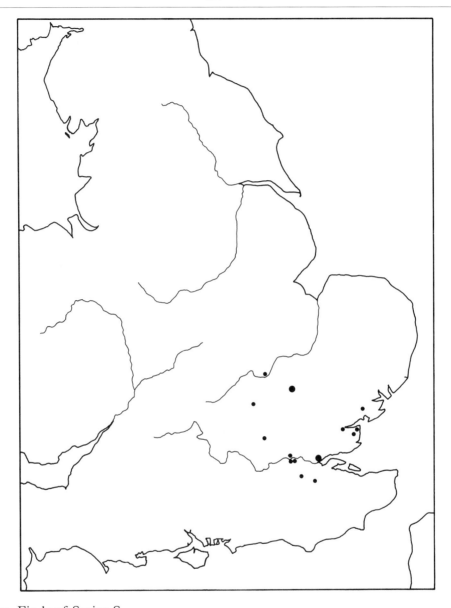

MAP. Finds of Series S.

profiles of the creatures' heads, and do not meet at the centre of the design. Again, the region of origin of Type 48 is uncertain.

I

The type comprises two main varieties, of which one is relatively uniform and makes up the great bulk of the issue, while the other is very scarce and perhaps reflects a later resumption of striking at the same mint.

A stylistic analysis of the centaur in the first variety will pay attention to the care with which the feathering of the wings is drawn, and to the centaur's S-shaped tail. The rib in the middle of each wing is sometimes marked with a row of prominent pellets. There are normally about 11 pairs of feathers on each wing. The S-shaped tail is a more flattened curve, on coins that are presumably later (because less careful): it normally consists of 12-14 pellets, but occasionally there are fewer, e.g. 10. The final pellet is usually somewhat larger. The centaur's body and haunch are a distinctive shape, scooped out where the neck should be, to follow the curve of one breast. This concavity becomes less pronounced. The neck, shown as a third swelling circle, looks goitred. There is, all told, not much evidence of stylistic devolution within quite a large block

540

of dies. The Maldon and Bradwell-on-Sea finds are among the die-cutter's best (and earliest?) efforts. One important piece of evidence is a coin from Tilbury on which the reverse is laterally reversed. The same obverse die is used with two other coins (both from one reverse die), both also from Tilbury. One would assume that the lateral reversal is in this case an early, experimental feature.

A very minor variation shows the neck as an upright cylinder, the back of the helmet standing out at an angle, and a jutting chin.[7]

In a more significant variation, the centaur is shown with a similar head and neck, and with two thin haunches, and a linear tail ending in a prominent pellet. The protome is not scooped out to accommodate the breast. An associated reverse die has fewer pellets than usual in the four chains. A coin found in the Rhine at Hilversum is apparently similar, although the detail is indistinct.[8] Again, the chronological place of this variety is not at all obvious. Is it the work of the same die-cutter who made the main batch of dies, or of someone else working alongside him, – or working at a later date?

Three or four specimens are known which are laterally reversed, or bungled and of poor quality, or both. The poor coins are probably

[7] See for example a coin catalogued below.
[8] Hill photograph.

541

FIG. Sketches to show the shape of the centaur's body, a) in the best style, and b) with thin haunches.

FIG. Two die-linked specimens from Tilbury, the first showing lateral reversal of the reverse type.

FIG. The Bradwell-on-Sea find.

FIG. Unbalanced designs on a specimen from Tilbury.

counterfeits rather than late members of the series. An interesting example has all the right ingredients of the designs, but gets the balance wrong.[9] Another, catalogued below, with lateral reversal of the obverse, is more obviously a forgery. The two London finds of which Roach Smith published line drawings are in sorry condition, but one can see that they are palpable forgeries.

The Roxton find,[10] which unfortunately is broken, is more difficult to assess. Both dies are laterally reversed, and the reverse appears to be of

[9] Found at Tilbury.
[10] 'Coin Register', 1987, no.93.

542

fine quality. Could it be another early, experimental coin? The obverse tells against that idea: the wing is a mere row of pellets, and the forefeet are not pelletted at the toes. The lower jaws of the wolf-worms also vary from the standard design.

Two specimens [11] of the standard variety have been analysed, namely the Houghton Regis find, and a Tilbury find with cylindrical neck. The former was found to be corroded, with heavy surface enrichment. Its core contains 47 per cent 'silver', plus 6 per cent tin and 1 per cent zinc. The Tilbury find is also 47 per cent 'silver', with 4 per cent tin and 1.5 per cent zinc.

II

The other main variety is known from only three or four specimens. The wolf-worms appear to be by the same hand on all three, and the centaurs clearly are. On the most distinctive example (catalogued below), the chains are omitted, and there is a rosette of 9 pellets at the centre of the

reverse; on the obverse the centaur's hind legs trail back at an impossible angle, and are truncated. The tail ends in a trefoil of three pellets. One foreleg is bent at a sharp angle. There is an outer wire border on the obverse. A find from Royston[12] has a similar obverse, with spiky rays

around the head. The reverse is more normal; it is not clear whether this or the first coin described is the earlier. The third specimen, *SCBI*

[11] Below.
[12] Royston 40.

543

Norweb 64, has a reverse which is laterally reversed. It shares the feature of wire borders. On a fourth coin, possibly related, (*SCBI Hunterian* 105) one can see similar modelling of the centaur's body, and the same bent foreleg – with lateral reversal.

SCBI Hunterian 103 may be an imitation of this variety.

The Ashmolean coin has been analysed, and found to contain only 42 per cent 'silver', plus 4 per cent tin, and 2 per cent zinc.

Presumably the coins of the second variety are East Saxon, – but the only provenance so far recorded is Royston.

III

In summary, Series S may be classified as follows:

S1x (Experimental reverse die, with lateral reversal).
S1a, i The standard variety.
S1a, ii – with cylindrical neck.
S1b – with thin haunches.
S2a Reverse with central rosette.
S2b Similar, but with normal reverse.

Almost nothing can be said about the chronology of the series. The high proportion which S makes up among the Tilbury finds suggests that it was in use there for a significant length of time. If the available analyses are representative, the alloy was quite well maintained. A date of origin when Series K, Type 32a was already familiar is probable. We might look to a phase when an alloy of *c*.50 per cent silver was in use at the nearby mint of London, for Series L, Type 12. Without hoard-evidence, however, everything is speculative. The Wrotham grave-find, in which two battered and pierced coins were associated, one each of Series S and T,[13] tells us little. T also is about half silver, and one wonders whether there was some moment when an effort was made to coordinate the issues of several mints.

[13] *BNJ* 47 (1977), 50, s.v. Wrotham, and pl.3, 42- 3.

SERIES T

SERIES T, which has been found at Stamford and Breedon-on-the-Hill, consists of a single type (*BMC* Type 9), and stands on its own as the product, probably, of a small mint in the east midlands. It is a stylistically distinctive and compact issue, of which about twenty specimens survive,[1] reflecting the original use of about two dozen obverse dies.[2] The mean weight for the type appears to be *c.* 1.03-1.04g, and its silver contents are in the 40-50 per cent range.

The obverse has a London-based bust with the outward-facing legend +LEL or +LELN꙯. The final letter, represented here as ꙯, is in fact shaped more like a comma, and is perhaps a pseudo-letter or sign of abbreviation. There is one specimen (from Domburg) on which +LEL is replaced by TΛNVM+.[3] A Lockett coin which was described in the sale-catalogue as reading TИΛՐ or something similar was misread: it is in fact from the same obverse die as the Domburg specimen, and from an extremely similar if not the same reverse die.[4] The underlying meaning of the legends, if they have a meaning, remains elusive.

The standard version has sometimes been transcribed as +LEV or +LEVN꙯. The seriffing of an L and a V ought to be different, but in Series T the two letters in the legend are normally treated in the same way. One limb of the letter is usually slightly longer than the other. The best guess seems therefore to be LEL.

The reverse has a laterally reversed 'porcupine' design, with in one variety an added annulet. Within the curve of the porcupine are four parallel lines. They could have been copied either from the VICO variety, or from a later, 'secondary' porcupine, although in either case the bold knob is an innovation.

---

[1] They are noted below.

[2] Die-links include the following: *MEC* 717 (from Stamford) and Ashmolean (from Tilbury) share an obverse die. *SCBI Norweb* 58 and Ashmolean (also from Tilbury) are die-duplicates. Lockett 278 and the Wrotham find are die-duplicates. The Domburg find and *SCBI American* 101 are from the same obverse and perhaps the same reverse.

[3] Hill, *NC* 1953, pl.6, 14.

[4] British Numismatic Society photographic record. This coin is now published as *SCBI American* 101.

I

There are three varieties of Type T, all by the same hand. The treatment of the mouth is a distinctive feature. On the more elaborate, the bust is crested or helmeted, and the curved 'spine' of the porcupine is bordered by a matching curve of small pellets beneath. On the simpler variety these are omitted, as is the helmet, allowing room for a longer legend. The drapery is reduced to a necklace of pellets. Which variety is the earlier? – The more elaborate treatment of the drapery of the bust, and the careful seriffing of the initial cross, suggest that the crested version stands first. One such coin from what are evidently experimental dies, has the 'porcupine' laterally reversed.

There are transitional specimens, without the crest but with the row of pellets.

The often somewhat pretentious treatment of the Є in LЄL attracts attention. The central bar is elongated, and all three endings are prominently seriffed.

The coin reading TΛNVM+ belongs with the simpler variety.

The type may be classified as follows. It should be borne in mind that there were only a couple of dozen obverse dies.

1.   Crested or helmeted bust / row of small pellets added to porcupine. (seriffed initial cross, LЄL).
   - a)   'Head of porcupine to right (experimental).[5] Careful drapery of bust. Tall, rectangular Є, unseriffed and smaller second L.
   - b)   'Head of porcupine to left (as in all later varieties). i) Helmet with dotted crest,[6] ii) with linear crest.[7]

2/1   Bare-headed bust / row of small pellets added to porcupine.
   - a)   Seriffed initial cross, LCLᴧ (bar of Є omitted).[8]
   - b)   Cross pommee, LЄLN.Wᴧ,[9]

[5] A Tilbury find.
[6] *BMC* 85, *SCBI Hunterian* 48, Royston 41.
[7] *MEC* 717, Ashm. 1.06g.
[8] West London (National Gallery site).
[9] *SCBI Hunterian* 47.

2. Bare-headed bust / porcupine without extra pellets. The quills are straighter, and there are one or two fewer of them.
    a) Cross pommee. LELN.[10]
    b) Similar, but two pellets in place of cross pommee.[11]

3. As 2, but legend TΛNVM+, annulet added on reverse.[12]

There is a little stylistic puzzle which this scheme of classification creates. The Є with long central bar occurs in both varieties 1 and 2, but so does a more rectangular Є, seen on the experimental variety 1a and again on 2b.

II

The style of the bust is reminiscent of the 'Hwiccian' style at London. The neck is prominent and modelled in high relief, giving the appearance of a thryoid condition. Series T, however, is not by the same hand as the 'Hwiccian' group. Indeed, the stylistic separateness of the coins of Series T from all other sceattas, their clear identity as a group, and the high quality of their workmanship have prompted the hypothesis that they are the products of a separate small mint.[13] Their northerly provenances, in particular Stamford[14] and Breedon-on-the-Hill, Leics.[15] suggest that their mint-place should be sought well to the north of the Thames, e.g. possibly at Stamford. Those two finds are of special interest because they come from a region where there are relatively few finds of secondary sceattas of any kind, but two swallows do not make a summer. Obviously, several more finds from Five Boroughs territory would be needed to make a strong case. That is all the more true, because the evidence of the major sites is problematic. Although there are no specimens of Series T

[10] *SCBI Norweb* 58, Ashm.1.17g.

[11] Lockett 278, Wrotham.

[12] Domburg, *SCBI American* 101 (0.77g).

[13] D. M. Metcalf, 'Monetary circulation in southern England in the first half of the eighth century', *Sceattas in England and on the Continent*, pp.27-69, at p.39.

[14] *MEC* 717.

[15] A. Dornier, 'The Anglo-Saxon monastery at Breedon-on-the-Hill, Leicestershire', in *Mercian Studies*, ed. A. Dornier, Leicester, 1977, pp.155-68, at p.164.

from east Kent or Hamwic, and only one from East Anglia (Thetford area), six have been found at Tilbury, and three are recorded from London.[16] Could T be, after all, (a) an East Saxon issue, or (b) a London coinage, the two northerly finds being merely outliers? In either case, one would have to be prepared to suggest how room could be found for the series alongside others, of quite different designs – S in the case of Essex, and L in the case of London. The Tilbury evidence may not be quite as strong as it seems: three[17] of the six specimens were found in the same season, and it is possible that they reflect a small, scattered hoard.

Rigold, in his scheme of classification, deliberately kept Series S and T close to each other, on the strength of the grave-find from Wrotham, Kent. Its evidence for monetary circulation is inferior, however, because both the coins are pierced and battered.[18]

In spite of the significant number of finds from Tilbury, an East Saxon attribution remains problematic. Types S and T are very different in appearance, and would have to be seen as successive. Which should be placed first? The corresponding distribution-pattern for S (which has similar silver contents to T) lacks a northerly component, and is much more widespread in Essex. T seems to be heavier, and more closely controlled. Moreover the ratio of finds per die at Tilbury – the recovery rate per die at that particular site – appears to be significantly higher for S than for T.[19] The true explanation might be that T was from a region which, in the secondary phase, looked towards London for its commercial contacts with the wider world – but which also had some special link with Tilbury. The two monastic find-spots attract attention, and one wonders whether Cedd's monastery could have had some unexpected contacts with a Mercian or Middle Anglian house, e.g. Medeshamstede (Peterborough), which was also in touch with Breedon. That is, however, highly speculative.[20] The most one can say is that, because it is difficult to see how the type could be prominent in Five Boroughs territory and in London without leaving more traces at the Royston site,[21] some sort of long-distance contacts are worth considering.

[16] A fragment in the Roach Smith collection, of variety T2, reading +LЄ. . . (Hill, *NC* 1953, at p.98), a specimen in the collection of Dr. Ian Stewart, and an excavated coin from the National Gallery site.

[17] Or even four. The Ashmolean acquired three on one occasion, and subsequently exchanged one of them for another type.

[18] There are other pierced coins from the edges of the Weald.

[19] This argument hinges on the difficulty of recognizing die-identities in Series S. See the preceding section.

[20] There is the (much earlier) case of coins minted at Lieusaint-en-Brie, and arguably reaching Folkestone because of the link with Farmoutiers and other royal nunneries in Brie: see S. E. Rigold, 'The Sutton Hoo coins in the light of the contemporary background of coinage in England', in R. Bruce-Mitford, *The Sutton Hoo Ship Burial*, vol.1, 1975, pp.653-77, at pp.663 and 672 (two if not three finds from Folkestone and one from near Lincoln).

[21] One find only.

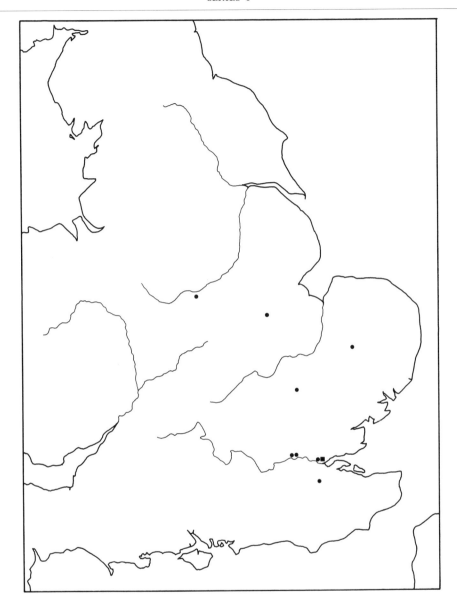

MAP. Finds of Series T.

A London attribution for T is typologically unlikely, and it might have been expected to generate a wider scatter of finds along the Thames corridor. As much of Series L falls below 50 per cent silver, T would presumably have to be earlier if it were from the same mint. The balance of the argument should become much clearer as new finds, particularly from the east midlands, accumulate year by year.

Provisionally, there seems to be no likely alternative to the east midlands as the home for Series T. We should note, however, that there are no finds so far from west Norfolk or Lincolnshire.

We are, perhaps, entitled to bear in mind the MONITASCORVM+ imitation from Eastcote, Northants.[22]

III

Three specimens of Type T have been chemically analysed,[23] namely two of variety T1b and one of T2a. One of each variety has silver contents very close to 50 per cent (51.3, 49.7[24]), plus about 3 per cent tin and 2 per cent zinc. The third coin, which on grounds of style one would say was the earliest, has only 41 per cent silver, but 7 per cent tin, and 2 per cent zinc. There was nothing in the analysis to suggest that the coin had suffered particularly from corrosion and leaching, and it is of good weight – 1.06g.

The alloy of Series S is similar, but the evidence, so much as there is, suggests that the standard may have been more closely controlled in Series S.

IV

Type T, which stands on its own, is difficult to interpret convincingly. It seems to belong to the east midlands, but it has London and East Saxon links. It was a substantive type, of good secondary weight, and has had quite a high survival rate. Our knowledge of its silver contents (c.50 per cent) rests on the analysis of only three specimens, – although both main varieties are included. Its date-range is difficult to judge, but is unlikely (from the number of dies, and their stylistic homogeneity) to have been very long.

[22] On or near Banbury Lane (the 'Jurassic Way').
[23] By Dr. J. P. Northover, using EPMA.
[24] This coin (not from Tilbury) was previously analysed by XRF (0.45), without adequately overcoming the effects of surface enrichment – 60 - 74 per cent 'silver'.

FIG. Series T.

551

SERIES U

LET US begin by trimming the fat from Series U. Rigold included in it Types 63, 23b and d, 23a, 23e, 23c, and the 'archer' type. Of these, 23b and d are the basis of the series. The essential point for their interpretation is that they are uniformly of good silver: at around 80 per cent, consistently better than anything else in the secondary phase. All the other varieties that have been assigned to Series U belong elsewhere. Type 63, although a deceptively good imitation, is only 31 per cent silver, and in any case is certainly part of an eclectic group (C ARIP) whose affinities are with Series L. Type 23a is a scarce London-related variety, much debased; Type 23e seems to be a substantive type, but its alloy, again, is much debased, and its geographical distribution is unlike that of the basic type, 23b/d. Only Type 23c has a claim to be considered along with 23b and d. It apparently 'mules' Series O (Type 38) and U, in silver of much the same quality as Type 23b/d. But a die-link from Hamwic established that 23c is imitative.

We are left, then, with only Type 23b/d, the 'bird and branch' or (better) 'pecking bird' type.[1] Because its silver contents are so high, there is a presumption that it belongs very early in the secondary phase – although we should guard against assuming any exact correlation between date and alloy. There is no hoard evidence to guide us. One may mention, if only to dismiss, the possibility that it is a late revival on a restored alloy standard, with a limited regional circulation. The fact that it was copied, e.g. by Type 63, and imitated, e.g. by Type 23c, and that it is the model for Series QIF (another regional 'bird' type) effectively rules out a very late date.

It seems that the obverse of Type 23b/d (a standing figure, with head right, holding two long crosses, all within a semi-circular curve) became an archetypal motif, used with variations for much of the London series – sometimes as the obverse but often apparently as the reverse. The reverse of Type 23b/d shows a bird walking to the right, characteristically

---

[1] D. M. Metcalf, 'The "bird and branch" sceattas in the light of a find from Abingdon', *Oxoniensia* 37 (1972), 51-65, giving a survey and corpus of the type as then known.

crested (a peacock?[2]), pecking at berries on a plant or vine. This 'pecking bird' motif was used on the early secondary sceattas in more than one kingdom, notably in Wessex (Series H, Type 39, and subsequently Type 49) and in east Kent (Series V). As between Series U, H, and V there is no question of one coin type being copied, with some variation, from another coin type. Rather, it appears that in each case the die-cutter created his own version of a concept that was, perhaps, known from stone-carving or metal-work or textiles – part of a general stock of motifs, many of which were ultimately derived from classical sources.[3]

The suggestion has been made that Series U is the Mercian version of a coin type which reflects a concerted attempt to create a new currency for southern England after the cessation of minting of primary sceattas: a brave beginning to the secondary phase. The obvious political context for such joint action seemed (before Grierson and Blackburn established an 'earlier' chronology for the sceattas by redating the Cimiez hoard[4]) to be that described by Bede in the early 730s, namely King Æthelbald's growing hegemony everywhere south of Humber. It was tempting to see the standing figure of Type 23b/d as Æthelbald himself.[5] The corresponding coins of Series V and Series H, Type 39 lack any human figure.

The absolute chronology is something of an obstacle to this 'political' interpretation of the coin types. Æthelbald's overlordship became possible only after the death of Wihtred of Kent and the abdication in 726 of Ine, king of the West Saxons. Most of the arguments by which the secondary sceattas are dated are uncertain or speculative. The Aston Rowant hoard, in which all but the very latest primary issues are already present, is dated by Blackburn to c.705-10. There may have been a gap before the secondary phase began, but the entire phase, in all its complexity, has to be accommodated before the coinage of Beonna was introduced, soon (though not necessarily immediately) after 749. Identifying gaps in minting in a scheme of relative chronology is in principle very difficult. It would seem problematic, however, to push the beginnings of the secondary phase as far forward as 726. The Hallum hoard, for example, would become difficult to understand.

If the origin of the various 'pecking bird' types lies in the 710s, the political initiative for cooperation will have been taken by the senior

---

[2] Few large birds are crested: cranes are the only others that come to mind. The raised wing might be a misrepresentation of the displayed tail-feathers – although Type 23b/d clearly shows a tail as well.

[3] These may well have included peacocks.

[4] M. Blackburn, 'A chronology for the sceattas', *Sceattas in England and on the Continent'*, pp.165-174, locating the main output of Series U in the decade 710-20.

[5] Metcalf, loc.cit.

figures of the day, Wihtred and Ine. Mercian involvement, under Ceolred (709-16) or the youthful Æthelbald (716-), is unexpected.

I

In Series U there are two versions or styles of the pecking bird, which are about as different from each other as either is from the Hamwic version. As their geographical distribution also looks distinctly different, there is a *prima-facie* case for thinking that they are from separate mints.

As well as two groups of specimens recognizably of regular style, there are also one or two problematic coins which seem to be unofficial (although it is difficult to be quite sure of their status), a few inferior specimens which are very obviously forgeries, and a surprising number of 'mules' in the eclectic groups associated with Series K and L. It is usually quite clear which of the two versions of the pecking bird has been copied, although the copyist has sometimes included details borrowed from the other version – thus showing that he was familiar with both. In any case, one can be perfectly sure that such coins have been copied from another coin, or other coins, rather than from a motif used elsewhere.

Series U, then, is known from twenty-odd specimens of Type 23b/d, together with which one should consider the five or six known specimens of Type 23c. The corpus includes an above-average number of die-duplicates. In the two official styles, eight non-singletons among 16 specimens imply an original total of roughly two dozen pairs of dies, which were used in a one-to-one ratio. The official issues were thus quite a small coinage, and the forgeries were even fewer.

The two main styles are easily recognized and told apart, from many characteristic small details. The styles of obverse and reverse correlate, and it is fairly obvious that in each case the two sides of the coin are by the same hand. No mules are known.

In Type 23b the standing figure has a large head, shoulder-length hair, a short tunic, feet shown naturalistically and pointing to the right, and hands like bunches of bananas. On the more elaborate or earlier specimens the bird is crested, and its raised wing is hatched and scrolled. It strides forward, and its beak gapes open to peck the berries from a vine which encircles the lower half of the bird's body.

In Type 23d the standing figure is much more angular and elongated, the crosses are pommee with four pellets not three, they sometimes have groups of three pellets as their bases, and the curve within which the

Fig. Sketch of the two main styles in Type 23b/d.

figure stands lacks pellets at its ends, which taper. On the finest (and earliest?) die the head is delicately engraved, and there are *two* fine lines sticking out behind – intended presumably to represent wreath-ties. These lines were subsequently reduced to one, giving rise to the suggestion that the figure is wearing a helmet – the *cynehelm*.[6] It is still possible that that is what other die-cutters intended when they copied the design, but the proof that the standing figure is royal looks less secure, in light of the die with wreath-ties (although they too, of course, are a sign of dignity). The entire balance of the bird is different from that on Type 23b. Its neck and tail consist of matching and opposed curves, to give a shallow S-shaped outline. The raised wing, ending in a curl, is less prominent and is at a much flatter angle. The bird's beak prolongs the curve of the neck. Its legs are closer together. On the earliest die the place of the vine is taken by two berried spikes, both springing from a point in the outer border at about 8 o'clock. This die has very obvious affinities with the plants on Series V and Series K, Type 42.

There are differences in fabric between the two styles. The earliest coins of Type 23b are on noticeably small flans. Type 23d is often struck on characteristic squarish flans.

[6] For early references to the *cynehelm*, or helmet-crown, see W. A. Chaney, *The Cult of Kingship in Anglo-Saxon England*, Manchester, 1970, pp.137f.

Type 23b has been found at Dorchester, Abingdon, and Moulsford – all on the upper Thames within 20km of each other – at Hollingbourne (Kent), at Hamwic (2 specimens), and at a site near Scunthorpe. Type 23d has been found at Canterbury, Reculver (2 specimens) and Houghton Regis, Beds. There is an imitation of 23d from Hamwic. Major sites such as Tilbury and Royston contribute negative evidence. A dozen finds are too few for the pattern to be considered completely secure, but they are not negligible. The concentration in east Kent is pronounced. We may note also that, so far as the upper Thames region is concerned, the three specimens of 23b still account for a large proportion of all the secondary sceattas that have been found there. On the find-evidence that has accrued so far there is a good geographical separation between the two styles. Both fall within the 'south-eastern corridor' that has been described in connection with Series K and L.

Where was Series U minted? The suggestion was made as long ago as 1972 that the two main styles were struck at two mints, one in the Dorchester-Abingdon area, the other in the south-east, presumably either in east Kent or at London. Part of the case was that there was a similar distributional contrast between Series B and J. The idea that Series J was minted in the upper Thames region has now been shown to be erroneous, and the claim concerning Series U must stand or fall on its own. The numerous single finds which have been brought to light in the last twenty years, and which have modified the earlier distribution of Series J, have as yet done little to falsify the curious pattern of Type 23b.

Both style and provenance point to east Kent rather than London as the mint-place of 23d. The early years of the secondary phase in east Kent, however, already seem very crowded, with Series V and K (Types 33, 42, and 32a, all known in good silver). And the political implications of two mints striking the same distinctive type, one in the upper Thames valley and the other in Kentish territory, are such that one would wish to be extremely sure of the facts before basing any far-reaching historical conclusions on them. Æthelbald's successor Offa is thought to have minted all his coins in Canterbury, London, and East Anglia, and none, so far as we can tell, anywhere north or west of London, i.e. none in Mercia proper. The pennies of the first half of the ninth century, where the mint-attributions are a good deal more secure, repeat the pattern of minting in the south-eastern coastlands, with no mint north or west of London, although of course coinage circulated freely throughout the Thames basin and the south and east midlands.

The political status of the Oxford region in the early eighth century is

556

MAP. Finds of Type 23b (round symbols), 23d (square symbols), coins that are judged to be imitative (open circles), and Type 23c (triangles).

not absolutely clear. Stenton, in his essay on St. Frideswide, wrote, 'in 735, the traditional date of St. Frideswide's death [*rectè* 727], the land on each side of the Thames at Oxford seems to have been under the direct rule of Æthelbald . . . During the next 100 years every powerful West Saxon king asserted a claim to this territory, but the Mercian kings more than held their ground until their dynasty came to an end, and it was not until the middle of the ninth century that the debateable land was finally divided between them, Berkshire and northern Wiltshire becoming West Saxon, and the plain of central Oxfordshire remaining Mercian'.[7] If a date earlier than 726 is even a possibility for Type 23b, we should admit that its political context is uncertain. Blair has constructed a view of the princely dynasty, holding power in the middle and upper Thames valley, to which Frithuswith no doubt belonged.[8] Whether the overlordship of the region was Mercian or West Saxon, one hesitates to pronounce. But it certainly was not Kentish, and the conundrum of a coin-type apparently struck in two mints, under two separate kings, still demands an answer.

There are difficulties in seeing both Type 23b and Type 39 as West Saxon, which are not easily resolved except on the hypothesis that there was a gap of some years between the laying out and development of Hamwic,[9] and the establishment of a mint there. The attribution of Type 39 to Hamwic is certain. The idea that the three versions of the 'pecking bird' are Kentish, West Saxon, and Mercian has a symmetry that is tempting. But it bristles with difficulties.

The most radical difficulty, as regards Type 23b, is that a disturbingly similar problem of attribution can be seen in Series L, where in the 1970s an inland mint was proposed for sceattas in the 'Hwiccian' style. These were recorded as finds from London, but mainly from the Cotswolds and beyond, where they made up a very high proportion of all the secondary sceattas from the region. On the strength of the contrast in distribution-patterns within Series L, a political interpretation of the coins in that particular style was offered, namely that they belonged to the sub-kingdom of the Hwicce and were presumably minted in the Hwiccian

[7] F. M. Stenton, 'St. Frideswide and her times', *Oxoniensia* 1 (1936) 103-12; M. Biddle, G. Lambrick, and J. N. L. Myres, 'The early history of Abingdon, Berkshire, and its abbey', *Medieval Archaeology* 12 (1968), 26-69; T. Hassall, 'The Oxford region from the conversion to the conquest', in G. Briggs et al., *The Archaeology of the Oxford Region*, Oxford, 1986, pp.109-14.

[8] J. Blair, 'Saint Fridewide reconsidered', *Oxoniensia* 52 (1987), 71-127; id., 'Frithuwold's kingdom and the origins of Surrey', in *The Origins of*

Anglo-Saxon Kingdoms, ed. S. Bassett, 1989, pp.97-107.

[9] B. Yorke, 'The Jutes of Hampshire and Wight and the origins of Wessex', ibid., pp.84-96. A date of *c*.700 or just before has been mooted for the laying out of the regular grid of streets of Hamwic, specifically in the Six Dials area, and there is a dendrochronological date of *c*.710 from the planks lining a nearby well. See D. M. Metcalf, 'Nyt om sceattas af typen Wodan/monster', *Nordisk Numismatisk Unions Medlamsblad* 1986, 110-20.

province in imitation of London coins. New stray finds since 1976 have made that view completely untenable. The pattern is now seen to be more complex, with dispersion of the 'Hwiccian' sceattas in various directions from London – e.g. into Middle Anglia, and into southern Wessex – even if the secondary coins from Hwiccia are still (puzzlingly) predominantly of Series L and of this particular style. Regression analysis of ninth-century pennies has shown that coins of the London and Canterbury mints were characteristically carried over long distances, presumably in the course of trade. Finds from the Cotswolds and beyond may have been carried there to pay for wool, and a similar context may explain the 'Hwiccian' sceattas.

It appears therefore that although the distributional evidence available in the 1970s was clear-cut, it was deceptive, and the question should occur to us whether the same might not be true of Series U, Type 23b, in the 1990s.

The parallel between the cases of Series L and U is not exact, because the curiously restricted pattern of Type 23b has at least withstood the very large accession of new material. It may be that it is typical of the earliest years of the secondary phase, when Series V and Series K, Type 33, for example, have a compact distribution, arising perhaps from a still rather sluggish monetary circulation, at the end of a recession.

If there was, exceptionally, an inland mint in the Abingdon-Dorchester area, its *raison d'être* may have been in the context, not of the east-west route up the Thames valley, but of the north-south route from Hamwic. A find of Type 23c from Walbury Camp (sharing a die with a Hamwic find) suggests a half-way house along that route. Hamwic was a major mint in the first half of the eighth century, as it certainly was not in the time of Offa and later, and the currents of monetary circulation into the south midlands may for a few decades have been significantly different from their later pattern. (Hamwic coins were not carried northwards into Mercia or Middle Anglia, but perhaps Mercian silver was minted near the southern frontier, to be carried southwards and spent in Wessex.) This argument merely points out a possibility, but if one rejects it there is some onus to explain the occurrence of no fewer than five specimens of Series U at Hamwic (cf. seven of Type 39): namely two of 23b out of only ten or eleven known, one of 23c, none of 23d, one imitation of 23d, and one blatant forgery.[10] There is also a find of 23c from Hanford, Dorset.[11]

---

[10] D. M. Metcalf, 'The coins', in *The Coins and Pottery from Hamwic* (Southampton Finds, vol.1) edited by P. Andrews, Southampton, 1988, at pp.49f.

[11] Illustrated in *Proc.Dorset NHAS* 101 (1979), 138.

FIG. 'As well as two groups of specimens recognizably of regular style, there are also one or two problematic coins which seem to be unofficial (although it is difficult to be quite sure of their status), a few inferior specimens which are very obviously forgeries, —

560

— and a surprising number of 'mules' in the eclectic groups associated with Series K and L. It is usually quite clear which of the two versions of the pecking bird has been copied, although the copyist has sometimes included details borrowed from the other version – thus showing that he was familiar with both.'

561

If the find-evidence for the place of origin of Type 23b is hazardous, that for 23d is relatively straightforward. Type 23a, b, and c taken as a whole is predominantly found south of the Thames; 23d is recorded from Canterbury, Reculver (two finds) – and Houghton Regis. The last-named find-spot is the odd man out, and perhaps too much should not be built on it.

The evidence of style tends the same way. The berried spike, seen on an early die in Type 23d, is so similar to that of Series V and Series K, Type 42 that it would be difficult to imagine that it is not the work of the same die-cutter. Die-cutters can migrate, or supply dies to be used elsewhere; but the straightforward reading of the evidence is that 23d is from east Kent. If that conclusion is correct, it is highly unlikely that it was struck for the benefit of the Mercian king. If the standing figure is indeed royal, our thoughts should turn in the first place to Wihtred.

Type 23b/d was a small but influential issue: more widely copied than Series V or Type 33, for example. (And Type 42 seems not to have been copied at all.) The extent of copying may eventually tell us something about the place of Series U in the sequence of types – or it may have a more political explanation.

II

Type 23d is known from eight specimens, which include two pairs of die-duplicates. The finest dies show the standing figure with wreath-ties, and holding crosses with triangular bases, while there are three delicately modelled clusters of berries on the reverse, and the bird is crested. A beautiful specimen in the Hay collection[12] is from the same dies as *SCBI*

Hunterian 120.[13] Withy and Ryall illustrated what is almost certainly the obverse of the Hunter coin, incorrectly paired with the reverse of a coin of Series Q.[14] We may safely assume that it was found near or at Reculver. The Houghton Regis find (catalogued below)[15] is from the

[12] 1.04g. I am indebted to Mr. Hay for allowing me to photograph the coin.

[13] 1.25g.

[14] Reproduced in *Sceattas in England and on the Continent*, at p.259. Note the (very unusual) wreath-ties, the three pellets at the base of each cross, and

the dotted border visible around the upper part of the flan.

[15] 0.93g. D. M. Metcalf, 'The "bird and branch" coin from Houghton Regis, Beds', in *Sceattas in England and on the Continent*, at p.195.

same dies as *SCBI Mack* 346.[16] The reverse die already shows more vine-like foliage – less spiky, although evidently having evolved from the berried spikes.

Another Ashmolean coin still has the root-stock of the vine in the margin at 8 o'clock, and, although the impression of the die is indistinct, one can see that an attempt has been made at two modelled clusters of berries.[17] On a find from near Canterbury,[18] and on *MEC* 718 (also from

Reculver)[19] and *BMC* 114[20] the vine originates at 10 o'clock.

Of Type 23d, three specimens were analysed by XRF in 1978, – of which the first is no longer available for study. It was found to contain 87 per cent 'silver' plus 4.8 per cent tin. The other two, analysed in exactly the same way, have subsequently been re-analysed by EPMA. That allows us to judge to some extent the reliability of the figures for the first coin, with high silver contents and surprisingly high tin contents. The second coin, namely the Houghton Regis find, showed 67 per cent 'silver', plus 6.0 per cent tin (XRF), but was found by EPMA to be severely corroded, with 57 per cent 'silver' out of a total count of only 80 per cent: the tin contents were 7.5 per cent. The third coin (also catalogued below) gave 80 per cent 'silver' plus 1.6 per cent tin (XRF), or 78 per cent 'silver' plus 2.4 per cent tin (EPMA).[21] In short, the XRF analysis of the first coin appears to be acceptable for comparative purposes. The tin contents of the first and second coins are high in comparison with sceattas of *c.*80 per cent 'silver' in Series V and K, but not impossibly so. The use of bronze as the alloying material represents a sharp change of practice from the primary phase; but it does not seem to offer any clear guidance on the more detailed chronology of the early secondary phase in east Kent.

The weights are variable, and there are not enough to give a reliable

[16] 1.14g. Resold in *NCirc* 1989, item 4004, where the weight is given as 1.16g.

[17] 1.09g.

[18] Canterbury III, 0.90g, found in a brickfield near Canterbury before 1950.

[19] 0.64g (broken).

[20] 1.07g.

[21] D. M. Metcalf, 'Chemical analyses of English sceattas', *BNJ* 48 (1978), 12-19, at p.18. The silver contents as measured by XRF tend to be too high. M.14 was exchanged. O.59 and M.15 are catalogued below, and have been re-analysed by EPMA.

average. It seems to lie in the region of 1.05-1.10g.

III

Type 23b begins with two specimens on unusually small flans, and of such low weight as to make one think that the issue was introduced on a lower weight-standard, which was soon raised. The first coin, Hamwic 107, has many features which suggest that its dies are experimental.[22] On the obverse, the feet are shown with exceptional care. The enclosing curve is duplicated in its central part. The head is large, with clumsy lips, and (?) long hair curled at the ends. On the reverse, the bird's head and in particular the eye-socket are carefully drawn. The crest is fan-shaped. The vine originates at 8 o'clock. The weight is only 0.81g, and the silver contents are estimated at *c*.70 per cent, with 2 per cent tin, and a relatively large amount (1.5 per cent) of zinc.

The Hollingbourne find has the same carefully drawn, naturalistic feet.

The obverse die is generally very similar, but of clumsier workmanship. The associated reverse die is discussed below, in connection with *BMC* 113 and a coin from the Barnett bequest.

SCBI Mack 347 is a similar, rather small coin, weighing 0.78g. The Abingdon find, which is generally similar, again has an elaborately

hatched and scrolled wing, and a fan-shaped crest.[23] It is catalogued below.

The die-cutter of the C ARIP eclectic group certainly had a specimen similar to these in front of him.

SCBI Hunterian 119[24] and *SCBI Norweb* 59[25] are die-duplicates, from

---

[22] Illustrated in Metcalf, loc.cit. (note 10 above). 0.81g.

[23] Metcalf, loc.cit. (note 1 above). 1.07g.

[24] 1.10g.

[25] 1.18g.

an obverse and a reverse die extremely similar to those used for another pair of coins, one found at Dorchester-on-Thames,[26] the other at Hamwic.[27] On both obverses the figure is shown with large feet which trail down to the right. The pecking bird on the reverses lacks any hatching on the wing, and lacks a crest.

A closely related bird, with linear wing and lacking a crest, is seen again on *BMC* 113 and on a find from near Scunthorpe (which are from the same pair of dies).[28] The bird has a hooked beak, which is closed, and

it is bending its head sharply dowwards in order to peck at the berries.

These two coins prompt careful reconsideration of two more which are very similar in style and content, but of decidedly rougher workmanship. The first of them, which entered the British Museum as part of the Barnett bequest,[29] was dismissed by the writer in 1972 as imitative. Dismissing sceattas as imitative is a tendency that should be resisted as far as possible. A second specimen, almost certainly by the same hand as the Barnett coin, has now come to light at Hollingbourne. The outer border of pellets on the reverse is widely spaced, and the bird is clumsy. The standing figure's feet, however, are exactly as on Hamwic 107. For that reason, one should be inclined to place the coin as early as possible in the sequence.

The pecking bird of the Moulsford find[30] is obscure (being weakly struck, or from dies of poor metal?) but evidently conforms with the Barnett and Hollingbourne specimens. In short, all these coins should be accepted as being from the same source, even if the quality of their workmanship varies.

Five specimens have been chemically analysed by EPMA. Their silver and tin contents are as follows:

⋆Hamwic 107	70%	2.2%
Abingdon	79%	2.5%
⋆Dorchester	82%	1.7%
⋆Hamwic 108	76%	4.8%
⋆Moulsford	89%	1.5%

[26] 1.15g.

[27] Hamwic 108. 1.10g.

[28] *BMC* 113: 1.21g. Metcalf, loc.cit, pl.1, 3.

Scunthorpe: 1.15g.

[29] 0.82g. ibid., pl.1, 12.

[30] 0.82g. Catalogued below.

The four results marked with an asterisk needed adjustment to allow for the effects of corrosion, and some of the variation in silver contents may be extraneous. In so far as one can detect a trend, the earlier coins seem to contain a little less silver.

The pattern of weights of Type 23b is intriguing. There is such a clear separation as to suggest two distinct weight-standards, the earlier coins

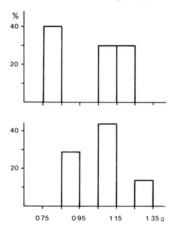

FIG. The pattern of weights of Type 23b (above) and 23d (below). Ten and 7 specimens respectively.

being at least 25 per cent lighter. The confirmation of a few extra weights would be welcome, because the evidence is puzzling. It does not follow securely that, because Type 23b began on a lower weight-standard, it was introduced before Type 23d; but the anomaly does offer some support for the hypothesis of a second mint, not in east Kent.

IV

Hamwic 109 is a good example of a coin of problematic status.[31] Its reverse might be accepted as an early die of Type 23d, with berried spikes and a crested bird. The alloy, 81 per cent 'silver', and the squarish flan are both thoroughly acceptable. The obverse, however, is of very poor artistic quality, and has a short, dumpy figure quite unlike the work of the regular die-cutter. Are we justified, for that fault alone, in saying that the coin is unofficial? Might it not have been produced by another,

[31] 0.91g.

566

less active moneyer in the same mint-town as Type 23d? Only as more specimens come to light will it perhaps be possible to give a firm answer.

A find from Barking Abbey imitates Type 23b in many particulars – the vine, the bird's wing and head, the standing figure's hair – but the

general execution is loose, the flan is irregular, and the striking is off-centre. Confirmation that this is a copy is provided by the lateral reversal of the standing figure.

Obvious counterfeits of Type 23b/d include a plated coin on a base-metal core, Hamwic 111.[32] The obverse appears to draw on the style of

23b, while the reverse is quite closely copied from 23d. There is one coin of which the obverse is so similar that one may judge it is probably by the same hand, from Bradwell-on-Sea, Essex.[33] The bird's crest has become a mane. Another specimen from the same obverse and an extremely

FIG. Type 23b/d (imitative). The Hollingbourne and Bradwell-on-Sea finds.

similar reverse comes (again) from Hollingbourne, Kent. A fourth, of somewhat better workmanship but in the same vein, is (again) from Barking Abbey. The ultimate in clumsy copying is seen on a Low Countries find, ex Boogaers, on which the enclosing curve has been transposed, to appear above the standing figure.[34]

[32] Hamwic 111

[33] Inf. courtesy of Mr. P. M. Barford.
[34] Metcalf, loc,cit, (note 1 above), pl.1, 13.

V

Type 23c, which is known from only five or six specimens, has a very distinctive variation of the standing figure with two crosses. Instead of the normal version, on which the head and feet are turned to the right, we see a frontal figure, with feet turned outwards, and with what it is permissible to interpret as enormous curled (and waxed?) moustaches. One may ask whether they are not really curling locks of hair; but careful examination of the dies shows that the lines spring from beneath the nose. Moustaches are intended, even if the effect is of extreme caricature.

This same figure occurs in another series, namely Series O, and is listed in *BMC* as Type 21. Types 21 and 23c are manifestly related, but it is not obvious which is copied from which. A 23b/23c mule from Hamwic contains 82 per cent 'silver', while a specimen of 23c from Walbury Camp, from the same reverse die, contains only 57 per cent. The silver contents thus offer ambiguous evidence as regards affinity with Series O or U. The provenances, however, and the mule point very clearly to an association of some sort with Type 23b. The muling of types hints at an unofficial or opportunist workshop.

On the Walbury Camp find,[35] the pecking bird is laterally reversed. It appears to have been copied from *BMC* 113 or something like it (discussed above as a problematic example of 23b) – notice the cluster of three berries near the bird's beak. The bird's crest has been misunderstood and exaggerated.

The same reverse die is also used with a more straightforward imitation of the obverse of Type 23b/d, of rather indeterminate style. For good measure the outer border of this obverse is changed into a serpent-headed torque.[36] The eclecticism, and lateral reversal, are quite enough to stamp the coins as unofficial.

BMC 115 is from an extremely similar reverse die – possibly even the same die with some recutting. The bird's distorted crest can be studied

[35] Catalogued below.

[36] Hamwic 110. 0.98g. Note that this coin was found in the same pit as Hamwic 109, probably implying that it was in use at the same date.

from it. The weight is low.[37] On the obverse, the curve within which the figure is enclosed is asymmetrical.

The place of origin of Type 23c, on the evidence of finds from Hamwic, Hanford, Walbury Camp, and   Jarrow, seems to lie along the same north-south axis as has been conjectured from the finds of Type 23b.

FIG. The Jarrow find.

[37] 0.80g.

SERIES V

THE SHE-WOLF and twins type occurs only once in the sceatta series, as the distinctive design of a scarce issue, *BMC* Type 7, which makes up the whole of Series V. The reverse has a bird pecking at berries (related to Series K, Types 42 and 42 var.) The absence of a bust gives the type an anonymous look. It is artistically powerful and is unusually well struck.

The Roman motif (copied presumably from a chance find of a coin of the fourth century[1]) offers a text-book example of the need to separate out the classical source of the motif, with its original significance, from the significance attached to it in the eighth century. Dirks, writing long ago about sceattas, allowed himself to comment on the place held by the wolf in Anglo-Saxon imagination. The frequency with which the element 'wulf' occurs in personal names makes the point. The she-wolf and twins, however, is much more specifically a classical motif, associated with the city of Rome – and, for eighth-century Anglo-Saxons, with what Rome meant for them. When Charlemagne brought the handsome bronze statue of a she-wolf to adorn his new capital at Aachen, he was promoting ideas of a second Rome and a new empire, in the context of a renaissance.[2] When the moneyer Lul struck silver pennies for King

[1] J. P. C. Kent, 'From Roman Britain to Saxon England', in *Anglo-Saxon Coins*, ed. R. H. M. Dolley, 1961, pp.1-22, and pl.2, 7, identifying the prototype as the very plentiful Constantinian *'Urbs Roma'* type.

[2] E. G. Grimme, 'Karl der Grosse in seiner Stadt', in *Karl der Grosse. Lebenswerk und Nachleben*, Dusseldorf, 1965, vol.4, pp.229-73 at p.271. The statue was almost certainly brought to Aachen by Charlemagne. Whether it was originally intended to represent a she-wolf or a she-bear is uncertain.

Æthelberht of East Anglia with the she-wolf and twins as their reverse type, perhaps shortly before the king was murdered by Offa in 794,[3] what was he thinking of? Was he asserting an (ill-starred) independence from Mercia? Or is there a clue in the fact that one of the three known specimens of this coinage was found at Tivoli?[4] Was the coin-type, through a punning allusion, recalling the days of East Anglian greatness under the dynasty of the Wuffingas?[5] Why were the wolf and twins chosen as one of the scenes carved on the Franks casket, in association with Germanic mythology?[6] These questions are speculative. What the numismatist can usefully add is that Series V long antedates Charlemagne's removal of the statue to Aachen, and that the coins are certainly not East Anglian. The type has a very clear south-of-Thames distribution,[7] and was doubtless minted in east Kent.

About twenty specimens are known, nearly all from different dies.[8] The style is relatively uniform, and all but the earliest and latest issues may represent a brief phase of mint-activity. Metal analyses give results which are difficult to interpret. EPMA results in the 40s and 50s suggest an alloy standard of roughly half silver, but there are also some much higher values, in the 80s and even apparently in the 90s. Although these may be to some extent distorted by corrosion, they are careful EPMA analyses, and should not be lightly discounted. They are not compatible with a standard of half silver.

The practical problem of interpretation posed by Series V is to decide how it relates to Series K, which appears to have been struck at the same mint-place. Does V precede K, – or interrupt it? Could the ruler of more than one kingdom have enjoyed minting rights at the principal mint of east Kent? The average weight of Series V is about average for the secondary phase, at $c.1.00$-1.15g.

---

[3] Brooke's suggested Kentish attribution should now find no support. See C. E. Blunt, 'The coinage of Offa', in *Anglo-Saxon Coins*, pp.39-62, at pp.49f.

[4] The coin was found at the foot of the walls in Tivoli, in 1908. It passed from the Carlyon-Britton collection to Lockett and is now in the National Museum of Wales.

[5] The Larling, Nf. bone casket (or book-cover) is illustrated in *The Anglo-Saxons*, ed. J. Campbell, Oxford 1982, p.67, where Campbell points out that by the late eighth century the claim was made that Caesar was one of the ancestors of the East Anglian royal house. His statement that the twins appear 'on East Anglian coins and on them alone' is contradicted by the find-evidence for Series V.

[6] J. Beckwith, *Ivory Carvings in Early Medieval England*, 1972, p.17 and illus.5 (*not* derived from a coin).

[7] Provenances are Canterbury, Wingham, K, Reculver, Richborough, Eastry, K, Reading, Bitterne (*Clausentum*), Southampton, London (Covent Garden), Barking Abbey, and Tilbury (2).

[8] *SCBI Mack* 361 is from the same dies as the Canterbury find.

I

The pecking bird has frequently been described as being in a vine, and thus one of those creatures copied from an inhabited vine scroll. This generalization should not prevent us from seeing that, unlike Series U, Type 23b, where a curving vine is intertwined with a pecking bird, the reverse of Series V is symmetrical apart from the head, and consists of the spread-eagle bird flanked by two separate plants, each consisting of a simple spike terminating in an upright cluster of berries, with two lateral drooping similar clusters of berries. Exactly the same plant is held by the figure on the obverse of Series K, Type 42 var.[9] In botanical terms, what is it meant to be? Clusters of grapes do not stand erect on a spike. What plant was of sufficient symbolic significance to be interchangeable with the falcon held by the same diademed figure on Type 42? Is the plant a symbol of the king or of the archbishop? No answers are forthcoming to these questions. The one firm conclusion is that Types 7 and 42 var. are closely associated.

II

If we attempt a stylistic analysis of the available specimens of Series V, we can look at the row of pellets between the twins (4, 2, or none), the degree of elaboration in representing the six bunches of berries, the groups of space-filling dots on either side of the bird's tail (3, 2, 1, or none), the shape of the bird's beak, the treatment of its feet, and so on. A survey of these various elements in the designs serves to reveal an odd man out: on a coin now in Cardiff,[10] the she-wolf's head is lowered, with the muzzle almost touching her fore-paw. All the other coins in the sample have a stylized head turned sideways in order to look solicitously back at the twins. The Cardiff coin is different also in that the plant consists of a single spike, with no drooping lateral bunches of berries. The delicate treatment of the claws of the bird's feet seems to be an early feature. When we add that the silver contents of the Cardiff coin are 89 per cent, it seems safe to conclude that it is from experimental dies, and that it stands very early in the series. The rest of the series is difficult to put in order. On most specimens the bird's body shows a distinct cleavage between the wings, as if seen from the back, but on others the

---

[9] Catalogued below.
[10] E 022, ex Lockett 224.

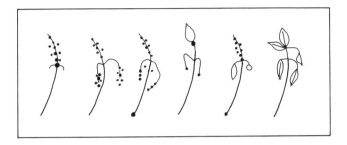

FIG. Series V. Different versions of the berried spike.

body is rounded, as if one is looking at the breast. On an unusual specimen with a rounded body, from Tilbury, the plants lack berries, and instead have leaves, 4 on the left-hand spike and 5 on the right.[11] They are stylistically related to, but not identical with, the plant behind the hound on the reverse of Type 42 var. On most specimens the bird has an open or even a gaping beak, but on this same Tilbury coin the lower half of the beak is omitted. At least one other specimen has a mixture of berries and leaves: berries on the central spike, but leaves as the drooping laterals.[12] Yet another has a big fat bud on the central spike – for which again a parallel can be found in Type 42 – and sketchy laterals.[13]

All this variability cannot be arranged neatly into a single line of stylistic development. Tentatively, one may suggest the following sequence:

V1. Wolf with head lowered.

V2. Wolf with head turned back.

    a) bird with gaping beak, elaborate treatment of berries; wolf's head stylized, with large eyes and ears.

    b) beak shown as two roughly parallel lines; berries, or berries and leaves, or large fat bud.

V3. Similar, but wolf's head is smaller. Bird with rounded breast, single beak; numerous leaves.

It would be rash to assume a regular, linear connection between silver contents and date. The evidence is nevertheless reminiscent of that

---

[11] This coin also shows, unusually, a diamond of 4 dots between the twins. The wolf's head is small.

[12] Paris 46.

[13] Reading (illustrated in Metcalf, Merrick, and Hamblin 1968, pl.1, O.46 bis).

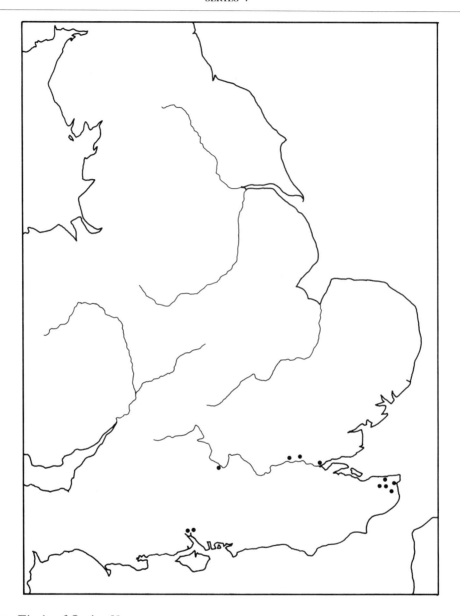

MAP. Finds of Series V.

relating to Series O, and suggests that Series V began (on a small scale?) very early in the secondary phase.

The high initial silver contents make it possible to postulate a parallel between the pecking bird of Series V and the pecking bird of Series U, Type 23b, which is about 80 per cent fine. A specimen of Series K, Type 42 var, on which the ruler holds the same plant, has silver contents of 86 per cent, and an example of Type 33 has the same. As Series V falls to below 50 per cent (and Series K does so too), we should envisage either the concurrent minting of V and K, or more probably rapid fluctuations in the alloy standard, with a decline or variability during the issue of V, followed by the abortive restoration of a higher standard in the earliest phase of Series K.

III

It seems possible that Series V stands at the very beginning of the secondary phase in east Kent, where it marks a new initiative, perhaps after a period when minting was in abeyance. A cluster of EPMA results in the 80s for various types suggests that new types were introduced in other regions at much the same date. Clear evidence of the relative chronology of the types could only come from a major hoard, of similar importance to Aston Rowant, but concealed ten or fifteen years later.

An absolute date for the introduction of Series V is impossible to demonstrate. Was it before or after the death of Wihtred? There is at present no evidence which would allow us to answer that question. The occurrence of Series K, Type 32a in the Garton-on-the-Wolds grave-find, alongside Series J, should encourage us to look for as condensed an arrangement of the early stages of Series K as possible – and, by extension, to see Series V as falling within a brief period.

FIG. The Eastry find of May, 1992.

NORTHUMBRIAN SCEATTAS: SERIES Y

THE LETTER Y in Rigold's scheme stands for York, which was presumably the mint-place of the distinctive sceattas struck in the name of the Northumbrian king, or in the joint names of the king and his archbishop. The series begins in the reign of Eadberht (738-57), whose coinage was so plentiful that it is likely to have been introduced in the earlier part of his reign, and it continues with the issues of Æthelwald (759-65), Alchred (765-74), Æthelred I (first reign, 774-9), and Ælfwald I (779-88).

The obverse of the royal sceattas is non-pictorial, consisting simply of the king's name in a circular legend around a cross. The coins of King Aldfrith are the only English precedent. The distinctive reverse type shows a horse-like animal, with long toes and long erect ears which are sometimes interpreted by the die-cutter as horns. The foreleg is raised at a sharp angle. The animal has a prominent crest or mane, a long tail, and sometimes a protruding tongue. This creature is akin to the monsters and other imaginary quadrupeds of King Aldfrith's coins and of Series N and Q, but it is *sui generis*, with no exact parallels south of the Humber. Perhaps it was recognized at the time as some sort of royal or Northumbrian device, and was displayed in other forms. Be that as it may, it was used as the exclusive badge or identifying device of the royal Northumbrian sceattas for nearly half a century.

On the joint issues of King Eadberht and his brother Archbishop Ecgberht, the quadruped is replaced by a standing figure of the archbishop, in a short tunic and sometimes diademed, holding two long crosses, or a cross and crozier. His name and sometimes his title are added. Differences in the obverse:reverse die-ratio between Ecgberht's coins and those of Eadberht suggest that they were minted independently – as seems to have been the case with the king's and archbishop's issues in the ninth-century styca coinage, and as it certainly was later in the middle ages at York. Joint issues were continued by King Æthelwald and for a short time by King Alchred, still with Ecgberht (765 x 766). Their coins carry the two names, but with no pictorial device.

Only one coin of Æthelwald is known today: in the second half of the century the issue of sceattas was probably intermittent.

Series Y has been very thoroughly studied by Booth, who has published a corpus of 160 specimens.[1] At least a further 20 specimens have subsequently been found at Newbald,[2] and a few more elsewhere.[3] We are thus in a position to answer the basic questions 'where', 'when', and even 'how many' with a degree of confidence that would be misplaced for most other series of sceattas: Series Y was minted in Northumbria, and doubtless at York; it lasted from a date not long after 737 until c.785; and it was struck from an estimated 1,070 upper dies (subject to margins of statistical uncertainty).[4] We can state as a plain fact that all these coins were royal or joint royal/archiepiscopal issues, whereas for the southern series their issuing authority is a matter of historical opinion. Historians may well think that the element of certainty more than compensates for the rather broad limits within which some of the statements about Series Y are true. They would do well to ponder the fact that the various coinages minted south of the Humber were in aggregate far larger than that of York.

I

We are also exceptionally well supplied with scientific evidence for the alloy of the Northumbrian sceattas, although it is less easy to draw secure conclusions from the data about the intentions of the moneyers. Early work by X-ray fluorescence spectrometry[5] gave results for the silver contents of the coins which were sometimes much too high, because the problems of surface enrichment were not overcome. The work has recently been re-done and extended, using the more refined techniques of scanning electron miscroscopy[6] and electron probe micro-analysis.[7] Duplicate analyses of the same specimens continue to reveal serious difficulties of accurate measurement because of corrosion, leaching, and

[1] J. Booth, 'Sceattas in Northumbria', in *Sceattas in England and on the Continent*, edited by D. Hill and D. M. Metcalf, Oxford, 1984, pp.71-111.

[2] J. Booth, 'The coins from Newbald', (forthcoming).

[3] These include the York (Fishergate) and the Whithorn excavation finds, and a few single finds published in the 'Coin Register' of the *BNJ*.

[4] D. M. Metcalf, 'Estimation of the volume of the Northumbrian coinage, c.738-88', in *Sceattas in England and on the Continent*, pp.113-16.

[5] D. M. Metcalf, J. M. Merrick and L. K. Hamblin, *Studies in the Composition of Early Medieval Coins* (Minerva Numismatic Handbooks, 3), Newcastle-upon-Tyne, 1968, at pp.31-2 and 50-2. Not all the specimens published there have been re-analysed.

[6] M. M. Archibald and M. R. Cowell, 'The fineness of Northumbrian sceattas', *Metallurgy in Numismatics* 2 (1988), 55-64.

[7] Analyses by Dr. J. P. Northover.

inhomogeneity.

It is nevertheless clear that the great majority of coins of Series Y contain between one half and two-thirds silver, alloyed with copper and almost always with 2-5 per cent tin and/or 1-3 per cent zinc. Detailed discussion of the figures dwells, inevitably, on the questions whether the earliest varieties were meant to be better than two-thirds silver (or whether the data are distorted by surface enrichment); whether there were intended standards for particular varieties (e.g. half-silver or two-thirds silver), and whether variability or a falling-away from the prescribed standard was tolerated. This last question can only be answered empirically on a statistical basis. Even though the experimental evidence is unusually full, it is insufficient and its exact accuracy is questionable.

We should rely on common sense, therefore, and hold on to the main point that the variability of the figures between about a half and two-thirds continues much the same in later reigns as in Eadberht's, – and, indeed, beyond Series Y into the 790s. It is improbable that the authorities would keep alternating between standards of a half and two-thirds, and we should be predisposed to explain the variation in terms of inefficiency or indifference.

Archibald and Cowell have argued that Eadberht's earliest issues, on somewhat smaller flans, were intended to be three-quarters fine, but that the standard was soon abandoned in favour of a two-thirds standard. The common-sense view that has just been expressed does not, in principle, have any bearing on their hypothesis: early experimentation is always a possibility. They detect a 50 per cent standard in several other of Eadberht's varieties, and accordingly propose a chronological arrangement based on the hypothesis of a general downwards drift.

An alternative hypothesis is that the classes (A-G) of Eadberht's coinage are essentially each the work of a different moneyer, and that they are mostly concurrent. A substantial hoard concealed part-way through the issue might show clearly enough which hypothesis was nearer the mark – although if most varieties were present in the hoard there might be disagreement over its date of concealment. No such hoard is available.

There appears to be an inverse correlation between the silver contents in Series Y and the tin/zinc contents of the coins. That would automatically be the case if the base-metal component of the alloy were added in the form of a standard low-grade bronze or brass. On the other hand, an inverse correlation between tin/zinc as a proportion of the base-metal component, and silver contents would suggest that a deliberate

MAP. Finds of coins of King Eadberht (circles) and Archbishop Ecgberht (square symbols).

attempt was made to improve the colour of an inferior alloy. That would almost certainly imply that the decline in the alloy was progressive over time.

Unfortunately it is quite clear that the measured tin contents are exaggeratedly high in sceattas affected by corrosion, and one must suspect that they are subject to significant errors even when corrosion is not obvious. Further, replicate analyses by SEM and EPMA of the same specimens show a disquietingly poor agreement as regards tin contents. The historical significance of the tin contents should therefore be treated with great caution, and the correlation should perhaps be discounted.

The weight-standard or standards of Series Y is a topic similarly beset with technical difficulties arising from the corrosion and leaching of stray losses. Much of the variation in the weights recorded in Booth's corpus is secondary.[8] In the absence (again) of a substantial hoard it is impossible to establish the original average weight of the sceattas accurately, or to make accurate comparisons between varieties. The Hexham hoard provides a warning that there may have been small differences from one variety to another.[9]   Again, our starting-point should be that there is a similar degree of variability in Eadberht's coins and in those of later kings – and in the following series in the 790s, for which it is possible to quantify a significant loss of weight by comparing specimens from the Hexham hoard with others from the Whitby excavations. Broadly it seems that there was a single weight-standard of about one gramme throughout Series Y.

The suggestion has been made that the new coins of King Eadberht were of a better alloy than the imported southern sceattas which they replaced. The argument would be untenable if southern sceattas continued to be imported and to circulate after Eadberht's reform, because it would not be clear from the evidence of stray finds what the currency was like on the eve of the reform. The Newbald site seems to offer very good evidence of a controlled currency from which southern coins were strictly excluded. If the same controls applied at Whitby (from where there is a range of southern sceattas), the currency by c.740 was indeed bad enough to provoke a political response – not least because it was so varied and included so many fraudulent imitations. The alloy of Eadberht's coins may not have been better than the best of what it replaced, but the new Northumbrian currency was certainly more reliable.

[8] D. M. Metcalf, in *Coinage in Ninth-Century Northumbria*, 1987, at pp.83f.
[9] ibid., at pp.383-90.

FIG. Series Y.

II

What remains to be done in classifying Series Y? The possibilites are greater for the reign of Eadberht than for the years 759-*c*.785, mainly because the available sample is larger (126 specimens compared with 35) but also because the coins bear more signs of complex organization. Booth has established a scheme of classification into 7 main groups (Classes A-G) with many sub-groups, plus two groups for the archbishop. The classes are, in general, defined by the ornaments which are added to the basic design. It remains formally necessary to show that the ornaments correlate with the style of the dies, or in other words that the classes are separate and distinct in terms of their die-cutting. Once that correlation has been established the question arises of the purpose of the ornaments. They could have been added to allow those in authority to distinguish between successive issues; or (more plausibly) they could have served to identify the work of different moneyers.

There may be further clues, in differences between the classes, to the ways in which minting was organized. In particular, the obverse:reverse die ratio varies from class to class, and it seems that the king's name was on the upper die in some varieties and on the lower die in others.

One should keep an open mind on the question whether (as common sense suggests) all the varieties were struck in York, or whether one or more of them could, on the basis of contrasting distribution-patterns of single finds, be assigned to some other region of Northumbria.

III

Class A of Eadberht's coinage is a relatively large group, on which his name is spelled with Ꜳꝺ rather than ᴏᴛ – EAꝺBERhTVᴦ – and is the only variety to do so. That suggests that it belongs either at the beginning or

the end of the series, although the spelling could in principle be merely the idiosyncrasy of a particular die-cutter/moneyer. The animal faces right, and almost always has a tongue. Two SEM analyses show 66 and 72 per cent 'silver' respectively, that is, at the upper end of the range found among Eadberht's coins. A replicate analysis of the second coin by

582

EPMA, however, shows only 64 per cent silver. The suggestion that Class A was an early issue on a 75 per cent standard [10] should therefore be treated with great reserve.

The stylistic variation within Class A is not great: one can recognize minor differences in the spacing of the legend around the cross. Out of two dozen specimens, there are two with the variant reading EⱭƏBEREhTVᴦ, and in a perceptibly different style. On one of the two there are apparently pellets in two angles of the cross, which is plainer, and without a central pellet. Booth 17 could be by the same hand. The animal lacks a tongue. Two pairs of die-duplicates and one obverse link have been noted. That suggests that the obverse was the upper die.

Finds are from York (4), Newbald (6), Whitby (2), Malton (2), Lindisfarne, and Whithorn.

IV

Class B is the other big group, with over 30 specimens now recorded. It reads EⰞTBEREhTVᴦ around a cross (Bi) or around a cross enclosed in a circle of pellets (Bii). The animal faces left, and lacks a tongue. Analyses show 63 and 65 per cent 'silver' in specimens of Bi, in the first case with 4.7 per cent tin and a little zinc, and in the second case with 2.9 per cent zinc and a little tin. For Bii, silver contents of 78, 61, and 62 per cent

have been measured, as usual with small amounts of tin and zinc, but predominantly one or the other. The suggestion that the coin with 78 per cent 'silver' (Booth, B17) reflects an initial issue on a three-quarters fine standard and on slightly smaller flans [11] should again be treated with caution, as being based on insufficient evidence.

A stylistic comparison reveals no obvious differences between the animals of Classes B and A, except, perhaps, that the triangular tip of the tail is often larger in Class B. Nor are there obvious differences between the obverses of Bi and A. The obverses of Bii may be compared with those of Archbishop Ecgberht, variety v, which are arguably his earlier substantive issue, and the question comes to mind whether Bii could be an early, unsigned joint issue.

[10] Archibald and Cowell, loc.cit.
[11] ibid.

A specimen has recently come to light with the letters A, R inserted into the reverse design. Its stylistic affinities lie with Class B. It would seem to belong to a joint coinage.

Booth B1, 2, and 3 share an obverse die but are from different reverses. That is a strong indication that the obverse die, with the royal name, was the lower die (its traditional place) in Class B. In Bii there are three die-duplicates (dies Ll), and two specimens are now recorded from die M.

Varieties Biii and iv, with added pellets on the reverse, lateral reversal, and the obverse cross placed on a boss, are problematic. The alloy of Biii is acceptable – 70 and 63 per cent 'silver' – but Booth 23 (Biv) is only 53 per cent 'silver' – compensated, it seems, by a substantial amount of tin (6.6 per cent).

An apparent B/A 'mule' in very clumsy style is undoubtedly a forgery, but it is not certain whether it is a modern or a contemporary forgery – if only because of its peculiar alloy, which contains 9.5 per cent gold, plus 0.4 per cent tin.

Provenances for Class B are York (4), Newbald (5), Barmby Moor, Whitby (3), and Jarrow.

V

Class C has two distinguishing features. Within the loop of the (left-facing) animal's tail there is added the ornament of an annulet with central pellet. And on most (but not all) specimens, the central cross on the obverse is replaced by a tribrach, with pelletted rather than properly seriffed terminals. Is the tribrach merely ornamental, or is it an allusion

to the pallium? One's guess is that the cross was not replaced by another symbol lightly. From the style of the coins it is clear that those with a tribrach and the few with a cross belong together. The narrow R and the very narow h are distinctive to Class C, and demonstrate a separate phase of die-cutting, indeed very probably a different die-cutter. The alloy is somewhat poorer than in Classes A and B, (56 and 49 per cent 'silver'), and both analyses show more zinc than tin. The spread of weights is not significantly different from Classes A and B, so far as one can judge from a small sample. Among only 9 specimens, 3 share an obverse die (used with two reverses), and there is another pair of die-duplicates. Finds come from York (2), and Newbald (1), with one from Dorestad.

VI

Classes D and E are more conspicuously ornamented, with a seriffed cross in the loop of the animal's tail, and a triquetra below its body. In D the animal is left-facing, and in E it is right-facing. In E, moreover, the obverse legend is always retrograde (not laterally reversed: the letters are the right way round, but in the wrong order). Whether their identical ornaments allow us to infer that D and E were closely related in terms of organization is a delicate question. It seems clear that they are by

different die-cutters, and such evidence as we have suggests that their average weights were not the same. There is a coin which has been published as a D/E mule; its reverse die certainly belongs with Class E, and the obverse probably does too – but not, in any case with Class D. The coin does not, therefore, demonstrate a close connection between D and E. There is no significant difference in the distribution of single-finds of the two classes.

In Class D, the coins tend to be large, with large lettering and a large central cross, which lacks a central pellet. Some specimens have the uprights of the letters Γ, T, and h, and sometimes R, aligned with the arms of the cross. The weights are higher than usual, with an average of around 1.05–1.10g.

Class E is the only variety with a retrograde legend. It tends to omit a letter, usually reading E□TBERETVΓ or E□TBEREhTΓ. The 'mule' reads (forward) E□TEREhTCΓ. The bar of the Γ is bent down, after the fashion of a rune. Two long opposed Ts aligned with the cross are a characteristic detail. The central cross is much smaller than in Class D, and usually has a central pellet. On the reverse, the animal's mane is widely spaced, and its hind leg is at a distinctive angle to the body. The muzzle is often pointing downwards. All told, D and E are evidently by different die-cutters; and both dies of the 'mule' belong to Class E. Presumably it stands at the end of the sequence. Booth 8, with the additional ornament of a circle of pellets, – and with a very fat triquetra – may then be early.

Class E (unlike D) is heavily die-linked. A sample of only 10 specimens includes 4 from the same reverse (and two obverses), and another 3 from a shared obverse (and two reverses). The weights are normal. Finds of Class D are, as usual, from York, Newbald (5), Barmby Moor and Whitby (2), and of Class E, from York, Newbald (6), and Whitby.

VII

Class F stands completely aside from the other varieties in its use of the letter-forms H and S. The lettering, which is of decent, Roman proportions is virtually unseriffed, the ends of the letters being marked out by small pellets. The coins read EꟼTBREHTVS or EꟼTBERHTVS, around a circle of pellets containing a cross and pellets, or sometimes around a boss with either one or two circles of pellets. The reverse has a triquetra beneath the animal, and occasionally there is also a cross in the loop of the tail, or a circled boss in the same position, or scattered pellets in the field. On one die the triquetra is upside-down and is ornamented with pellets. The style of the animal, with very long ears or horns, is distinctive.

The Whithorn find, on which the obverse type is a boss, suggests that that variant is early. The coin is the only one with a reversed Ƨ. The tail is made up of a chain of dots (as it is on Booth 11), which seems to be an experimental treatment. The triquetra, too, is drawn with great care, each lobe being 'eared'. The immensely long horns sweep backwards, as they do on Booth 11 and 12. If Fvi and vii in fact belong at the beginning of the sequence, the story they tell is of a die-cutter beginning his work by copying the coins of Aldfrith (which have a reversed Ƨ), and later coming into line with other die-cutters using a cross as their obverse type.

The weights of Class F are normal, and the only available analysis shows 65 per cent 'silver', with a modest amount of tin.

Here, if anywhere, are the coins of a second mint. The variability of design within what is obviously the *œuvre* of a single workman suggests that he was not constrained, by the nearness of colleagues, to keep to 'his own' ornaments. The recorded provenances for Class F are Newbald (2), Whitby, Hayton, Malham, Whithorn, Caistor-on-the-Wolds (Lincs.), and Epworth (Lincs.). The two distant finds, and the two from Lincolnshire, are intriguing, but more evidence is needed before any secure conclusions can be drawn. If there were a second mint south of the Humber, one would expect its products to circulate into Yorkshire, and to be found at the major sites. One is looking for a shift in regional emphasis, as measured in the proportion of all the finds of a particular class which are *not* from York, Newbald, or Whitby; and as a correlative a peripheral concentration on a particular variety or varieties, e.g. south of the Humber. The regularity of the York-Newbald-Whitby pattern in each of Classes A to E is part of the evidence. The weakness of the case is that the total number of finds from Lincolnshire, etc., is small.

VIII

Class G manages to find room for four ornaments around the animal, normally four identical annulets with central pellet, the annulet being composed of pellets. Variant dies have three annulets, and a cross in the loop of the tail, or two annulets, a cross, and a group of four pellets. The style of the animal is similar to that of Class F, with long ears or horns, but note the swan-like neck, and the angle of the hind leg. The obverses

are variable, in the size of the central cross, and otherwise unexceptionable. Apart from one very heavy coin (Booth 1), the weights are typical. Three specimens have been analysed: the heavy (experimental?) coin shows 44 per cent 'silver', and two others both have 52 per cent. Two of the three add substantial amounts of tin. It is tempting to accept the theory of a half-silver standard. The finds are again unusually scattered, coming from Newbald, Thwing, Piercebridge (Durham), Wetherby, and Caister-by-Yarmouth.

IX

The joint issues of Eadberht with Archbishop Ecgberht are known from about 30 specimens, which fall into two broad groups, distinguishable by the style of the standing figure of the archbishop. In one (Booth 1-9a) he holds a cross and a crozier and is shown as a stick-like facing figure, with head turned right. In the other (Booth 10-27) he holds two crosses, and is shown in a more modelled style, and in profile, diademed, and with knees flexed (as if he were skiing). The two groups seem to be separate in terms of their die-cutting, but their chronological relationship is difficult to decide. In each group several upper dies were used with each lower die. The lower die carried the standing figure. The estimated die-ratios are roughly 3:1 for Booth 1-9a and (unusually) 6:1 for Booth 10-27. The former ratio in particular is based on a small sample and may well be imprecise. There is also an apparent contrast in the survival-rate: roughly 0.5 coins per (upper) die for Booth 1-9a, but only *c.*0.15 for Booth 10-27. It is by no means clear what we should conclude from these contrasts. Out of 15 English provenances, it is curious that none is from York.

Variation within each broad group may eventually yield some clues to their interpretation. B.1-9 are quite uniform. The legend is normally EᴄGBERhT (cf.-BEREhT on the obverse). B.5 is an odd man out, with modelled torso and the longer legend EᴄGBERhTΛR.

B.10-27 are a more varied group, including two quite different obverses, namely B.iv and B.v-vi. B.v has the obverse cross enclosed in an inner border of pellets. B.vi is similar, but with a larger, neatly-seriffed cross with a pellet in each angle. It includes a careful specimen (B.26) reading ⊓TBEREhTΛΓ· (the Λ inverted) and with a base-line joining the feet of the two long crosses. The archbishop's legs and feet continue below the base-line. B.v includes a coin from a stylistically similar reverse die (B.23), with a laterally reversed obverse. It also includes a blundered legend, ⊓TBEREVΓTEΓ· (B.21). These three coins are presumably the early work of an inexperienced die-cutter, but it does not follow with certainty that Bv/vi is earlier than Bi/ii. Biv includes the most characteristically large, modelled figures, and usually adds ΛR to the legend.

B.9a is a clumsy coin, with crozier but with a profile, diademed figure, and a base-line between the crosses. It does not fit in convincingly with Bv/vi, its only possible place in the sequence. Perhaps, therefore, it is derivative from Biv, but also from Bv/vi and (for the crozier) Bi/ii.

The average weights seem to be much the same as for the royal coins. The alloy, which is attested from 6 good analyses, varies between 50 and 65 per cent silver, plus 3 to 5 per cent tin, showing an inverse correlation, as the royal coins do. The tolerated variability may, again, have been quite wide, but the two available analyses for B.1-9 are at the lower end of the range for silver contents – which is perhaps a pointer to their being later in date.

X

The issues from the period 759–*c*.785 are known from only 35 specimens in Booth's corpus[12] – to which two or three recent finds can be added. Die-estimation shows, however, (within rather broad limits) that as many or even more upper dies were used as for Eadberht's coinage. That is puzzling. It could be because the coins had a lower loss-rate (although it is difficult to see why, unless there was a contraction in the area where a monetized economy flourished) or because the average output of an upper die was much lower. But if die-output was lower, why were several upper dies used with each lower die?

Some of the uncertainties can be discounted from the evidence of two major sites, both of which continued in use into the ninth century. At Newbald the numbers of single finds from the time of Eadberht and from 759–*c*.785 are 35 and 7 respectively,[13] and at Whitby 14 and 1. Lacking hoard-evidence, we do not know to what extent Eadberht's coins remained in use until 785, but on any interpretation it is likely that mint-output declined sharply. Otherwise, one would expect numerous finds from the period 759–*c*.785 in York itself (in relation to the number of finds of Eadberht from York), which is not the case.

Perhaps a balance-of-payments deficit developed, leading to outflows of York coins from the region, to be melted down and recoined elsewhere.

XI

The attribution of a unique coin as a joint issue of Æthelwald (759-65) with Archbishop Ecgberht has recently been vindicated by Stewart.[14]

[12] Booth, loc.cit. (note 1 above.

[13] Booth, loc.cit. (note 2 above).

[14] I. Stewart, 'A Northumbrian coin of King Ethelwald and Archbishop Ecgberht', *NC* 151 (1991), 223-5.

XII

The coins of Alchred (765-74) with Ecgberht (734-66) can be dated to the brief period of overlap, 765-6. The fact that seven specimens are known, plus an eighth from the York (Fishergate) excavations, from at least seven different (upper?) dies suggests that a prompt and vigorous effort was made to strike for the new ruler.

The workmanship of the dies is poor. The legends are often retrograde. The weight and alloy are nevertheless of about the usual standard, the silver contents being between 50 and 55 per cent. The alternation between tin and zinc as additives, in a pair of die-linked coins, shows that it was a matter of indifference.

Two specimens are from York, and one from Richmond.

XIII

Alchred's own coins are more legible. They are distinguished from any of Eadberht's varieties in having a cross beneath the quadruped. Fifteen

specimens are almost all from different dies. A few make some attempt at modelling the animal's body (Booth 5, 7, 15) but most are simple and stick-like. Omission of the initial cross on the obverse seems to correlate with a mane of only two spikes (Booth 8, 9, 11, 14). Only one specimen of this latter variety has been analysed. It is of better-than-average silver (65 per cent). Booth 4, on the other hand, falls as low as 37 per cent, with correspondingly high tin contents.

Map. Finds of coins of the period 759-96.

Three specimens have been found at Newbald, and one is thought to be from Jarrow.

XIV

The Hornsea find of 1875 was for long the only 'animal' sceat in Æthelred's name, and its attribution remained uncertain. If (as now

seems to be beyond question) the moneyer's-name coins of Æthelred belong to his second reign, 790-6, the 'animal' type will fall before Ælfwald's issues, in Æthelred's first reign, 774-9. A second specimen was found in 1989 at Newbald. It differs from the Hornsea coin in having a cross within the tail as well as a triquetra below the animal. The obverse legend has the same distinctive letter R. A third specimen with a severely

blundered but related legend, and an animal in the same style, was seen *dans le commerce* in September 1991.

The Hornsea coin contains 59 per cent silver, with more zinc than tin.

XV

Ælfwald I (779-88) attempted a restoration of the coinage, striking at least five varieties, distinguished by field-marks in ways that are reminiscent of the coins of Eadberht, his grandfather. They include a

left-facing animal (A), a right-facing animal (B), a cross beneath (C), a triquetra beneath (D), and circled pellet in the loop of the tail together with a cross beneath (E). As only a dozen specimens are known in all, there is not much opportunity to judge how closely the style of die-cutting correlates with the varieties. Class E, of which there are five specimens, appears to be quite consistent. The king's name is spelled with an initial runic *æ*.

NORTHUMBRIAN COINS OF ÆLFWALD I AND ÆTHELRED I BY NAMED MONEYERS, AND JOINT ISSUES OF ÆTHELRED WITH ARCHBISHOP EANBALD I

THE ANIMAL type of Series Y, which was revived in five or more varieties by King Ælfwald (779-88), was replaced at the end of his reign by a new style of coinage without a pictorial reverse, naming a moneyer Cuthheard. No coins are known of Osred (788-90), and probably none were made for him. After the restoration of Æthelred I (second reign, 790-6) the moneyer's-name type was resumed. Specimens are known of five if not six moneyers – Æthelræd (unless this is the king's name repeated on the reverse), Ceolbeald, Cuthgils, Cuthheard, Hnifula or Hunlaf, and Tidwulf. There are also coins with Æthelred's name on the obverse and **EANBALD** or **EANBALDA** on the reverse, which continue the precedent of joint issues by the king and the archbishop, in this case Eanbald I (778-96). The series ends with Æthelred's issues: none is known for Eardwulf (796-808). The attribution of Ælfwald's coins by the moneyer Cuthheard has been disputed, but there are difficulties in assigning them to Ælfwald II (808-10). It is more likely that they belong to the 780s. By 796 at the latest, therefore, the minting of coinage seems to have been in abeyance in Northumbria, and it was resumed only in the time of Eanred, that is, in 810 at the earliest, after a gap of at least 14 years. Æthelred's coins mark the end of a chapter.

Booth has recently published a corpus of the moneyer's-name series,[1] to which there are only one or two additions to be made, from Newbald[2] and Whithorn.[3] In all, 7 coins of Ælfwald, about 60 of Æthelred, and 8 of Æthelred with Eanbald are known. They are mostly about two-thirds fine,[4] and they seem to be on the traditional weight-standard.[5] An effort

---

[1] J. Booth, 'Coinage and Northumbrian history: c.790–c.810', in D. M. Metcalf (editor), *Coinage in Ninth-Century Northumbria (CNCN)*, Oxford, 1987, pp.57-89.

[2] J. Booth, 'The coins from Newbald', (forthcoming).

[3] I am indebted to Miss Pirie for photographs of the Whithorn finds.

[4] Booth, loc.cit., p.83, quoting inter alia M. M. Archibald and M. R. Cowell, 'The fineness of Northumbrian sceattas', *Metallurgy in Numismatics* 2 (1988), 55-64.

[5] D. M. Metcalf, in *CNCN*, pp.83f. discusses loss of weight by wear and corrosion.

may have been made to see that the coins were of the full intended weight, of a little over one gramme. Die-estimation suggests that about 130 to 150 pairs of dies were originally used, in a 1:1 ratio. We thus know a little more than a third of the dies. As the level of activity of the six known moneyers was unequal, with Cuthgils and Hnifula represented by only four or five specimens each, and Æthelræd by one, it is possible that one or two new moneyers could still turn up, but unlikely that there will be much change in the balance, namely that 98 per cent of minting was conducted by five moneyers.

I

The seven known coins of King Ælfwald are all by the moneyer Cuthheard, who spells his name CVDhEART, with a round C and a T. The arguments for and against an attribution to Ælfwald I or Ælfwald II respectively are complex. If we opt for Ælfwald I, we must accept that the changes in the coinage were made piecemeal. First, the animal type was dropped and the name of the (sole) moneyer was placed on the reverse of the coins. Cuthheard struck a substantial amount of coinage for Ælfwald, but his activity as a moneyer then ceased during the reign of

Osred. Someone of the same name, but spelling it with a square C, square H, and D, and who may or may not be the same man, then resumed or began production for Æthelred. He may have done so at the same moment as several other moneyers, newly appointed, or he may have preceded them. The legibility and aesthetic quality of the dies used by the new moneyers show a marked improvement, not noticeable in any of Cuthheard's work. One's impression is of a concerted attempt to produce a handsome and literate new coinage by four or five moneyers. The size of the group will recall the five known varieties of Ælfwald's animal type,[6] and will make one consider whether those varieties may not have been the output of a similar-sized group of moneyers (of whom Cuthheard may, of course, have been one). The attribution of his signed coins naming Ælfwald to Ælfwald I necessarily implies that minting was sporadic, and that when the issue of Ælfwald's animal type ceased, there

[6] Discussed in the section on Series Y.

was a lull, during which Cuthheard (working alone) used ten or twenty dies, and then a cessation during the reign of Osred possibly followed by another phase when (the same?) Cuthheard was sole moneyer for Æthelred.

On the other side of the debate, Miss Pirie has argued[7] that CUDhEART is the same man as the moneyer CVDHARD who worked for Eanred. His later coins (i.e. for Eanred) are scarce and they have not been chemically analysed.[8] They may belong before Eanred's reform, along with the work of Tidwine.[9] In order to avoid making his career longer than the evidence demands, and on the assumption that all three Cuthheards are one and the same man, Miss Pirie favours an attribution of Ælfwald II. Her argument would be equally strong or stronger if she limited it to the CVDHEARD/CVDHARD of Ælfwald and Eanred. On her interpretation, the reform of the coinage was accomplished at a stroke by Æthelred, at a similar level of organization (five or more moneyers) as in the immediately preceding animal-type coinage of Ælfwald I (five or more varieties). After a gap, Cuthheard alone [or another Cuthheard?] undertook the striking of similar coins for Ælfwald II, and continued to work at a modest level of activity in the early part of Eanred's reign.

On the evidence set out so far, either scheme seems possible. The Hexham hoard and the Newbald site-finds, however, tip the balance towards Ælfwald I. The contrast between Hexham and Newbald is crucial. The hoard contained half-a-dozen varieties (illustrated by Adamson) of coins of Æthelred I (790-6) and 165 varieties of the first (better-silver) phase of Eanred, but none of Ælfwald.[10] If the Ælfwalds were from 808-10, they might be expected to have had a higher survival-rate at the time of Eanred's reform than if they were from before 788. As there were three Eanred/Cuthheards in Hexham, two or three at least of Ælfwald/Cuthheard might have been expected. The argument is statistical in character, and the numbers are only just large enough to support a case. One may add that the seven known coins of Ælfwald have

[7] E. J. E. Pirie, 'Phases and groups within the styca coinage of Northumbria', CNCN, pp.103-45, at p.110 and pl.6, 1-6.

[8] E. J. E. Pirie, 'Adamson's Hexham plates', CNCN, pp.257-327, at p.260; G. R. Gilmore, 'Metal analysis of the Northumbrian stycas: review

and suggestions', ibid., pp.159-72, notes 2, 3, and 4.

[9] G. R. Gilmore and D. M. Metcalf, 'Consistency in the alloy of the Northumbrian stycas: evidence from die-linked specimens', NC 144 (1984), 192-8, no.53 (Tidwine).

[10] Pirie, loc.cit. (note 8 above).

not had an erratically high survival-rate: they are from six obverse and five reverse dies.[11] Another point to note is that, although Adamson does not give totals, but merely illustrates 'varieties', there are extremely few unprovenanced coins of Æthelred I in existence which could be strays from Hexham.[12] The true figure could be 8 rather than 6. For Eanred, we cannot be as sure that 165 is close to the correct total.

At the productive site of Newbald, North Humberside (previously published as Sancton) the pattern of single finds is very different. In place of 0, 6 +, 165 + for Ælfwald, Æthelred I, and Eanred, we have 3, 7, 10. There are 42 earlier coins of Series Y from Newbald, and 62 later stycas.[13] The site began to be used for cash transactions abruptly during Eadberht's reign (there are no southern sceattas), and its importance declined after the time of Æthelred I. A ratio of 3 coins of Ælfwald II to 10 of Eanred's first phase looks distinctly improbable.

As well as at Newbald, Ælfwald's coins have been found at York and at Thwing.[15]

II

Æthelred's coins show a distinct improvement in the standard of their lettering compared with those of Alchred and Ælfwald. The letters are well shaped, and more attention is paid to their spacing. This may be one small reflection of a new emphasis on literacy in Northumbria.

The six known moneyers, and the archbishop's moneyer, each produced their own characteristic coins. Each may have been his own die-cutter, or may have employed a die-cutter of his choice. That independence makes it difficult to decide whether they were all working concurrently – or whether Cuthheard, for example, might have worked alone before a new coinage was launched.

The levels of activity of the moneyers varied widely. Of Ceolbeald, 25 coins are known; of Æthelræd, one.

The analogies with the coinage of King Eadberht and his joint coinage with Ecgberht make it seem plausible that Eadberht's Classes A-G are likewise essentially the work of six or seven independent moneyers. There is no compelling reason, for either reign, to suppose that coins were minted at different places in Northumbria. It has been suggested

[11] Booth, loc.cit. (note 1 above).
[12] ibid.
[13] Booth, loc.cit. (note 2 above).

[14] Booth, loc.cit. (note 1 above), at p.65.
[15] ibid., pp.76f.

that Ceolbeald's coins have a more northerly distribution than normal,[16] but statistically there is not a clear-cut difference from the distribution of Æthelred's coins as a whole.

Ceolbeald's dies are particularly varied and inventive. He uses a cross with rays or wedges in the angles, and also a cross boxed within a square. The boss circled with pellets is a distinctive feature of Æthelred's coinage. It occurs also in a larger, double form. Another obverse type of wider interest is an R with contraction-mark for *Rex*. It could have been imitated from southern English pennies (and it will be recalled that

Æthelred married Offa's daughter in 792). The initial cross of the legend is regularly at 6 o'clock in relation to the R. The chronological sequence of Ceolbeald's many varieties defies analysis: the alternative spellings CEOLBALD and CEOLBAED are used on closely similar coins of more than one variety.

Tidwulf, the next most prolific moneyer, with 12 coins, is by contrast very unadventurous in his choice of types. The obverse always has a

central cross, the reverse a cross in a circle of pellets. The king's name is mis-spelled, usually as EDELDRE, or at best as AEDLRIEDR (the last two letters uncertain).

Cuthheard is alone in always giving the king his title, with a titulus above the letter R. His types are always cross/cross, and the spelling is regular. Ten specimens are known.

Eanbald has sometimes been listed as a moneyer, but a recent find from Whithorn proves satisfactorily that he is the archbishop: it reads EANBALDA. Another suggestion which has been made is that these are indeed joint issues, but that they are from the first reign of Æthelred I (774-9).[17] As Eanbald's pontificate began in 778, that is chronologically

[16] D. M. Metcalf, 'A topographical commentary on the coin finds from ninth-century Northumbria (c.780–c.870)', *CNCN*, pp.361-82, at pp.375f.

[17] Booth, loc.cit. (note 1 above), at p.69.

possible. The use of a circled boss, however, would seem anachronistic at that date, whereas it is common on Æthelred's later coins. One would expect the archbishop to have had his own moneyer, and that is borne out by the style of his coins, which are the only ones from the reign on which lateral reversal (on the reverse only!) is normal.

Cuthgils is an odd man out. His reverse type is always a triangle surmounted by a cross – in which earlier students, imaginatively, saw a shrine or reliquary. The obverse legend is consistently blundered, with

the initial cross inserted in the middle of the name, as ED+LRED or similar. The reverse legend, in two segments, is CVD CLS for which Cuthgils is a plausible reading. Booth 38 has been analysed and found to contain only 35 per cent silver, plus 6.7 per cent lead, and some zinc and tin.[18] The workmanship is so clumsy, in comparison with the rest of Cuthgils' *œuvre*, that the analysis suggests a contemporary forgery. Indeed, the figure of 6 per cent silver, obtained by neutron activation analysis of the same specimen at Bradford, hints at its being plated.[18] The coin is from the Hexham hoard, and is of good weight. Cuthgils' coins have also been seen as candidates for attribution to the first reign of Æthelred I. There is no way of refuting the suggestion from the coins' style, but it has nothing to commend it.[19]

Hnifula's coins are not unlike those of Tidwulf. The reverse type is either a circled cross or a circled boss.

A coin by Æthelræd has R (without contraction-mark) as its obverse type. It has been interpreted as a double-obverse coin of Ceolbeald, but the legend begins at 12 o'clock, and the general style is not closely matched on any of Ceolbeald's coins.

[18] Archibald and Cowell, loc.cit. (note 4 above).
[19] Booth, loc.cit., at p.69.

III

Archbishop Eanbald's coins are useful as evidence for the share that he enjoyed in Northumbrian minting. There are 7 specimens in Booth's

corpus, plus the Whithorn find, all of which are from different dies. It is possible but unlikely that they have had a lower survival-rate than Æthelred's coins generally. The best available measure of their original quantities will be a *pro-rata* estimate based on the corpus – 8 joint issues against 56 royal coins.

IV

The corpus includes three specimens (Booth 22, and two inserted after 58) which seem to be ninth-century imitations and should be discounted.

THE COINS OF KING BEONNA

NOT MUCH is known about King Beonna.[1] The *Historia Regum* records that, after the death of Ælfwald of East Anglia, 'Hunbeanna and Alberht divided the kingdom between them'. Chadwick proposed the emendation, 'Hun, Beanna, and Alberht'. Of these three, only Beonna placed his name on coins. They were very scarce, only half-a-dozen being known, until a substantial hoard discovered at Middle Harling, Norfolk, in 1980-1, brought some fifty specimens to light. Excavations at Burrow Hill, Suffolk, have yielded five coins of Beonna, and there are two more from excavations at Ipswich. Various single finds have taken the total up to around eighty.[2] Care is needed in their analysis because they are, obviously, not a random sample. The earliest issues may be under-represented. And it has been argued that the coins were struck at more than one mint – a claim for which the distributional evidence needs to be weighed with its bias kept well in mind.

It appears from 'Florence' of Worcester that a Beorna or Beornna or *Beornus* was king of East Anglia variously in 760 or in the time of Offa. We may reasonably assume that the (runic or partly runic) Beonna or Benna of the coins is one and the same with the name spelled in other ways in the sources. It is probably a hypocoristic form of a name in Beorn-.[3] Beonna's coinage will necessarily have begun after 749, and may have continued after 760. Miss Archibald's belief that it began after the death of Æthelbald in 757, as a re-assertion of East Anglian independence, relies in part on the idea that Æthelbald had no coins of his own.[4] The other part of her argument is that one of Beonna's moneyers subsequently minted for Offa at his East Anglian mint. Her proposed dating of the series to 757 x the early 760s thus begins later and is more condensed than the evidence otherwise demands.

Beonna's coinage is a reform coinage, which replaced the extremely debased East Anglian issues of Series R, with coins that were initially

---

[1] What little there is is summarized in M. M. Archibald, 'The coinage of Beonna in the light of the Middle Harling hoard', *BNJ* 55 (1985), 10-54, at pp.33f.

[2] Archibald, loc.cit., pp.34f.

[3] R. I. Page, 'The legends on the coins', in Archibald, loc.cit., 37-40.

[4] Archibald, loc.cit., 33.

about three-quarters fine, but which were soon reduced to about half silver. The king will not necessarily have turned his attention to this reform quickly after his accession. He may, for all we know, have continued for some years to strike sceattas of Series R; or there may have been an interval, on either or both sides of 749, during which minting was in abeyance.

The date of origin of the signed series is of interest in relation to Pepin's reform (755?) and Offa's reform (in the 760s?). We should hesitate, however, to see Beonna's coins as a half-way stage towards pure silver denarii, or as in any sense forward-looking (except that they may reflect the early stirrings of a general monetary up-turn in the North Sea coastlands). There was a sufficient precedent in the Northumbrian coins of King Eadberht (Series Y), of which we may be virtually certain that they antedate the death of Ælfwald. They are signed, and they are of very much the same quality of alloy as the reformed East Anglian issues.

Are Beonna's coins sceattas? They have sometimes been called proto-pennies. They are epigraphic, unlike most series of sceattas. Their broader flans continue a trend already visible at the end of Series R. The fabric may have been influenced by Pepin's new deniers, if the late chronology is correct. It hardly matters what we call them. They are not of pure silver, like Offa's pennies, and they clearly belong to the preceding chapter of monetary history.

I

The names of three moneyers appear on the coins – Wærferth, Efe, and Wilræd. Page suggests that Efe, which is not otherwise evidenced, may be a mutated form of the name Afa.[5] A fourth variety of Beonna's coins lacks any moneyer's name, the reverse being occupied by an intricate knot or interlace design.[6] The numbers of specimens in the corpus are: Wærferth, 2; Efe, 51; Wilræd, 17; 'interlace' variety, 6.

Both Wærferth's surviving coins are c.75 per cent silver. He may have initiated the series. The bulk of the coinage, by Efe and Wilræd, has silver contents with a normal distribution around a modal value of 53 or

---

[5] Page, loc.cit.
[6] It is vaguely reminiscent of the so-called 'Maastricht' type, but there is no particular reason to imagine that it was copied from it.

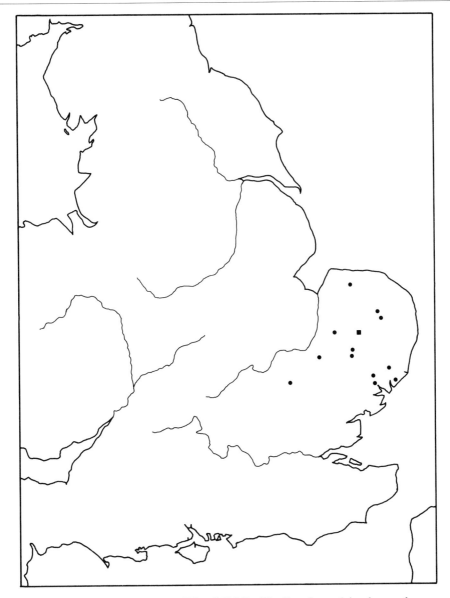

MAP. Finds of coins of Beonna. The Middle Harling hoard is shown by a square symbol.

54 per cent 'silver'. Wilræd's coins tend to lie on the lower side of the peak, and he was also responsible for two surviving (die-linked) coins, with only *c*.25 per cent silver. The 'interlace' coins fall squarely into the 51-56 per cent range. We can postulate successive silver standards of three-quarters, roughly a half, and a quarter. Efe and Wilræd may have worked concurrently in the middle phase; Wilræd perhaps continued for longer. The middle phase is more complicated than this summary reveals, and we will return to it in a moment.

The numbers of dies are small enough to allow us to estimate them with reasonable accuracy. Both Wærferth's surviving coins are from a single pair of dies. Efe's 51 coins are from only 11 obverses, and 23 reverses. Statistical estimation suggests original totals of 12 and *c*.34 respectively – a ratio close to 1:3. Wilræd, it is clear, works differently from Efe, placing the obverse design on the upper die: 14 obverses are known, against 7 reverses. Estimation suggests *c*.48 obverses and *c*.9 reverses, – an even higher die-ratio of perhaps as much as 1:5. The 'interlace' coins follow Wilræd technically, using more than one 'obverse' with the single known reverse. The estimated total for Beonna, of *c*.23 lower dies, and *c*.90 upper dies, may be distorted by the inclusion of a single large hoard in the sample. The results will, if anything, understate the case. We can at least say that the two coins with *c*.25 per cent silver are from the hoard, which may therefore reflect the whole period of issue. Of the non-hoard coins, however, several are singletons from their obverse dies: C.49, 50, and 51 of Efe, C.68 of Wilræd, and C.71 of the 'interlace' variety.[7]

Wærferth's coins may have had a lower than average survival-rate through being withdrawn for their higher silver contents; or the series may have got off to a slow start. The evidence does not allow us to decide between the two hypotheses.

We are exceptionally fortunate in having 56 accurate analyses, by scanning electron microscopy supplemented by XRF for the minor constituents.[8] We are also in the exceptional position of having analyses for up to a dozen coins from the same obverse die. This wealth of reliable

[7] The chances that the next single find will be from a different lower die from the 16 represented in the hoard (out of *c*.23) are complicated by unequal use of dies, but will be less than one in three.

[8] M. R. Cowell, 'Analysis of coins of Beonna and related issues', in Archibald, loc.cit., 42-8.

detail allows us to see that between die 3 and die 4 of Efe there is a difference in the pattern of silver contents which is so clear that it can hardly be other than intentional. There is a corresponding difference in zinc contents. The clinching evidence is that there is also a difference in weight. The coins from die 3 average 1.09g, with a modal value for silver contents of $c.57$ per cent, whereas the coins from die 4 average a more normal 0.96g, with silver contents peaking at $c.53$ per cent. The distributions are compact enough to leave no doubt that two silver standards are involved. The difference in intrinsic value is a quarter greater for die 3. That die is the only one of Efe's which reads *Benna* rather than *Beonna*. We may assume that it was his first. He used it with an exceptional number of reverses – seven. It seems, then, that in the history of Beonna's coins, Efe's die 3 stands somewhere between Wærferth's issues and the bulk of the coins containing about half silver; and that there was a deliberate adjustment in the mint prescription. Yet the coins on the divergent standards were indistinguishable to the users, and will necessarily have circulated together at par.

II

Where were Beonna's coins minted? The map of finds shows a heavy concentration in Suffolk, with relatively few provenances in Norfolk.[9] (The Middle Harling hoard is north of the county boundary, but only just.) Five finds of Wilræd's coins are all in the Ipswich area. The contrast with the distribution-pattern as a whole is persuasive. It points to somewhere in the Ipswich area if not Ipswich itself as Wilræd's mint-place. Wilræd, as we have seen, used the greatest number of upper dies. Efe's coins are more widely scattered. Miss Archibald has suggested Thetford as their mint-place, on general grounds. The technical difference in the positioning of the obverse die certainly supports the idea of two separate mint-places. The Middle Harling hoard (concealed fairly close to Thetford) is weighted with Efe's coins: 36, against 9 of Wilræd, although Wilræd was apparently the more active moneyer (using $c.48$ dies to Efe's $c.34$). Thus, the hoard would support the proposed Ipswich

[9] The finds are listed in Archibald, loc.cit., 28.

and Thetford attributions.

The 'interlace' coins have an inland distribution, in the vicinity of Bury St. Edmunds, but as there are only two of them (apart from the hoard) one should reserve judgement.

Efe and Wilræd were successors to Wigræd and Tilbeorht, who struck sceattas at the end of Series R. The evidence for locating their mint-places is, unfortunately, very unclear, and nothing can be gained by trying to match them with Efe and Wilræd.

III

A unique coin from the Burrow Hill excavations, clearly East Anglian and related in style to the coinage of Beonna, has been published by Miss Archibald (*BM Mag.* 13, 1993, p.19), who interprets it as an issue of King Alberht (who 'divided the kingdom with Hun and Beanna'). The obverse,

however, reads *Ethælbert* in runes, and one wonders whether it may not refer to the same King Æthelberht who struck rare silver pennies with a she-wolf and twins reverse type. The moneyer's name is *Tiælred*, interpreted by Miss Archibald as Ceolræd. If the coin belongs to Alberht it will not necessarily be early, although that would be the way that the negative evidence of the Middle Harling hoard would point. The weight and alloy of the new coin may have a bearing on its attribution, but again will probably not be conclusive.

IV

Beonna attempted to give the East Anglian kingdom a coinage of better quality than the sceattas of Series R had become. For one reason or another, the high silver standard originally chosen (75 per cent) was soon lowered, to *c*.57 per cent and then *c*.53 per cent. Some 90 dies were used. In the end, the standard was halved to a quarter silver. This all happened within ten or fifteen years. The new currency went the way of Series R,

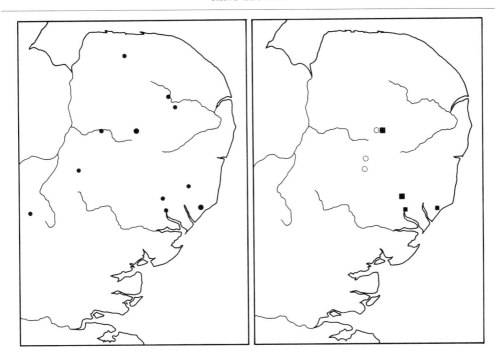

MAPS. Finds of coins of Beonna by the moneyer Efe (left-hand map); and by Wilræd (square symbols) and of the 'interlace' type (open circles) (right-hand map). The Middle Harling hoard is omitted but non-hoard coins from the same site are included. Cf. the distributions of coins of Wigræd and Tilbeorht, at p.522 above.

perhaps for similar underlying reasons. Net inflows into eastern England of the new Carolingian money seem at first to have been minimal: finds of Pepin's coins are extremely few. The scene was set for control by Offa, and another reform of the coinage.

607

A SCEAT OF KING OFFA?

OFFA became king of the Mercians in 757. The date of the earliest of his reformed pennies is uncertain. The new currency began on a small scale in east Kent, possibly around 765, but perhaps later. Might Offa, in the first years of his reign, have minted sceattas? If he did, how should we recognize them? May some mints, outside east Kent, have continued to produce sceattas after the introduction of the first pennies? (That is what happened, of course, in Northumbria, but could it have happened elsewhere as well?)

Questions such as these turn upon the relative chronology and the absolute chronology of the secondary sceattas. Hoard-evidence, which alone could provide secure evidence of an archaeological character, is of little help. The Middle Harling hoard does not contain any stray coins attributable to Offa.

The no-nonsense answer would be that the end of Series L is the obvious place to look for sceattas minted under Offa's authority, but that there is no reason to expect that they should bear his name, or even that they should look any different from the coins of his predecessor.

What, then, of a unique coin, now in Paris, which Miss Archibald and M. Dhénin have discussed in a paper read to the British Numismatic

Society, and which they plan to publish? It has a bird on one side, with a legend that is partly off the flan but seems to read O F F Λ. On the other side are four very similar birds in a cruciform pattern.

If Offa struck this coin early in his reign, it was part of a small issue, for no companion pieces have come to light among the hundreds of single finds of the 1980s.

There are no comparanda close enough in style to suggest that the new coin is the final member of some better-known series of sceattas. Any further comment seems speculative.

CHEMICAL ANALYSES
by Dr. J. P. Northover

WHAT ARE SCEATTAS MADE OF?
HISTORICAL IMPLICATIONS OF THEIR ALLOYS

D. M. METCALF and J. P. NORTHOVER

Introduction

It was the late Stuart Rigold who first saw that the silver sceattas, minted during the late seventh and much of the eighth century, fall broadly into two phases, namely an earlier one, when the coins were of good silver, and a later one, during which they became increasingly debased. He named these the primary and secondary phases.[1] The coinages of the two phases were as a whole very different in character, but each phase lasted for roughly half a century. Their approximate dates in England (subject to margins of uncertainty of a decade or more) were 670-720 and 720-770.[2] Thus they covered the reigns of Wihtred and Ine, and the supremacy of Æthelbald, and stretched into the early years of Offa's reign.

It was Rigold, too, who invented the current nomenclature for the many different designs of sceattas, grouping them into 'series'. The concept was intended to be neutral in relation to the problems of copying and imitation, and flexible in response to the seemingly endless variability which characterizes the secondary phase: each series consists of one design, or a number of typologically related designs but without the intention to imply that all the specimens in a series were necessarily from the same mint-place.[3]

Rigold also introduced the concept of an 'intermediate' phase, when the weight and alloy were still good, but were showing a small decline.[4]

Sceattas were minted mainly at the coastal wics in which the commerce of the North Sea coastlands was focussed. They rarely name their mint-places, which have to be deduced from distributional evidence and on the balance of probabilities.

In contrast with the daunting profusion and uncertainties of the numismatic detail, which have generated a lot of discussion, attempts to explain or to provide a plausible historical context for the process of debasement in the secondary phase have been meagre in the extreme. Rigold linked the flowering of the primary

[1] S. E. Rigold, 'The two primary series of sceattas', *BNJ* 30 (1960-1), 6-53; id., 'Addenda and corrigenda', ibid., 35 (1966), 1-6.

[2] M. Blackburn, 'A chronology for the sceattas', in *Sceattas in England and on the Continent*, edited by D. Hill and D. M. Metcalf, Oxford, 1984 (= *SEC*), pp.165-74.

[3] S. E. Rigold, 'The principal series of English sceattas', *BNJ* 47 (1977), 21-30.

[4] ibid., and Blackburn, loc.cit. Rigold's 'intermediate' category was devised mainly for the porcupines, where 'the case for any royal control is generally weak, but still not negligible'. The criterion was thus not just chronological.

phase in England with the long and successful reign of Wihtred in Kent, and the beginnings of the decline with Frankish destabilization of Frisia in the 730s.[5] Since he wrote, important revisions have been made to our understanding of the chronology of the sceattas, which make this scheme look less tidy.[6] The relative chronology is unaffected by these revisions. It remains true that at the beginning of the secondary phase the silver contents of the sceattas were in the high eighties or better, while at its end we find coins containing as little as 5-10 per cent silver. We have perhaps allowed ourselves to think of a steady decline between these two extremes. In that way the secondary phase could be seen as part of a recurrent pattern of stability, debasement, and reform running from the early seventh century through to the late ninth, with four phases of debasement — of Merovingian gold from the time of Dagobert onwards until its replacement by silver;[7] of the secondary sceattas until their replacement by Offa's pence; of the pennies and Carolingian denarii of the 840s onwards (under pressure from the Viking assaults) until they too were replaced by the reformed, good-silver coins of Charles the Bald and Alfred;[8] and more briefly of the mid-tenth-century coins of Eadred, Eadwig, and Eadgar.[9] The sequence is shown schematically in Fig.1.

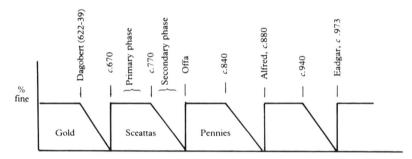

FIG.1   Schematic diagram to show the repeated cycle of stable coinage and debasement in southern England.

Underlying such general historical thinking as there has been about the sceattas, there is the idea that the debasement broadly reflects political responses to the availability of silver, which in turn reflect regional balances of payment, i.e. that commercial requirements dominated the uses of coinage, - if only because the same trends are visible over such a wide area affecting several politically

[5] Rigold, 1960-1 (note 1 above).

[6] Blackburn (note 2 above).

[7] J. P. C. Kent, 'Gold standards of the Merovingian coinage, AD 580-700', in *Methods of Chemical and Metallurgical Investigation of Ancient Coinage,* edited by E. T. Hall and D. M. Metcalf, 1972, pp.69-74; D. Brown, 'The dating of the Sutton Hoo coins', *Anglo-Saxon Studies in Archaeology and History* 2 (1981), 71-86.

[8] D. M. Metcalf and J. P. Northover, 'Coinage alloys from the time of Offa and Charlemagne to *c.*864', *NC* 149 (1989), 101-20.

[9] H. McKerrell and R. B. K. Stevenson, 'Some analyses of Anglo-Saxon and associated Oriental silver coinage', in *Methods of Chemical and Metallurgical Investigation* (note 8 above), pp.195-209; D. M. Metcalf and J. P. Northover, 'Interpreting the alloy of the later Anglo-Saxon coinage', *BNJ* 56 (1986), 35-63.

independent kingdoms at very much the same date, and stretching from Frisia and northern Francia, through southern England and into Northumbria, as well as north-eastwards to Jutland.[10] What is true of the uses of coinage in the secondary phase may well be largely true also of the primary phase (and even of the preceding gold coinages), but the *debasement* during the secondary phase *opens up possibilities of analysis and interpretation* which are not as obviously available in the relative uniformity of the primary phase. The theme of debasement should therefore occupy the foreground of the historian's attention, but he should spare a few thoughts also for the other half of the picture, the other half-century.

Different approaches to the subject have employed sociological models in order to emphasize class-related aspects of the benefits of silver currency.[11] The explanatory power of such models in relation to the numismatic detail seems to be disappointingly limited.

Underlying the enquiry into debasement is the assumption that something like Gresham's Law might be expected to have operated, that coins of worse alloy would have tended to drive out those of better alloy. This could happen if individuals had a choice of mints to which they could take their bullion, so that, for example, they received more sceattas (and could buy more with them) for a pound of silver by going to Hamwic rather than Canterbury. One has only to invent such an example to see that there were heavy constraints on the freedom of choice. In sum, inter-regional transfers of silver stocks were limited by the balance of payments. Also, we know that in the later Anglo-Saxon period, coins of recognizably different intrinsic value were able to circulate together at par, apparently without any malpractices such as culling becoming a problem. So we should not expect any simple or clear-cut explanations to be forthcoming for the sceatta period.

The straight-line graph of the course of debasement in the secondary phase, as shown in Fig.1, is purely conjectural. Its basis is the assumption that things went gradually from bad to worse. To make any progress, we undoubtedly need to get the numismatic facts into sharper focus, in order to create a detailed, well-substantiated description of what happened. By doing so we shall quickly discover that the straight-line graph is a very inadequate hypothesis.

The critical questions are these: first, did coins with different intrinsic values circulate acceptably alongside one another? And secondly, did the debasement in different regions or kingdoms in fact keep closely in step? The first question could best be answered from the evidence of the hoards, which alone can show us what coin types remained in use together. Failing hoards, it is at least possible to discover the range of variability of single types. This calls for the analysis of a

---

[10] D. M. Metcalf, 'A note on sceattas as a measure of international trade, and on the earliest Danish coinage', *SEC* pp.159-64; id., 'The quantities of the coins and their monetary interpretation', in *Southampton Finds*, vol.1, *The Coins and Pottery from Hamwic,* edited by P. Andrews, Southampton, 1988, pp.17-25.

[11] P. Grierson, 'Commerce in the Dark Ages: a critique of the evidence', *Trans.R.Hist.Soc.* 9 (1959), 123-40; R. A. Hodges, 'State formation and the role of trade in Middle Saxon England', in *Social Organization and Settlement,* edited by D. R. Green, Oxford, 1978, pp.439-55; id., *Dark Age Economics,* 1982.

good number of specimens if it is to be statistically reliable, and it can very usefully include die-linked specimens. Much the best way to answer the second question would be, again, by reference to hoards of mixed composition, which could be used to establish the relative chronology of sceattas from different regions. Unfortunately, extremely few hoards are known from the secondary phase; and one, upon which a good deal has been built (Nice-Cimiez) is possibly misleading, because it is known to us only from the general catalogue of a collection which contained a few coins from other sources too. The lack of reliable hoard evidence is just as much an obstacle to establishing the facts about debasement as the lack of chemical analyses would be.

A good range of analyses has been available since 1968, the measurements having been made by X-ray fluorescence spectrometry (XRF) on an abraded section of the edge of the coin.[12] Additional analyses have been published from time to time, and by 1978 the total amounted to more than 150 specimens, including at least one or two from almost all Rigold's series, although N and W were still unexamined.[13]

Pa	5	F	4	N	-	V	2
Va	5	G	5	O	2	W	-
A	8	H	4	Q	1	X	3
B	15	J	8	R	15	Y	10
C	11	K	8	S	1	Z	1
D	9	L	7	T	1		
E	18	M	4	U	6		

Although they were quite enough to give a preliminary impression, most of the secondary series (in which variability is a problem) were inadequately explored. Moreover, the form of XRF analysis that was used is of limited accuracy, for two technical reasons. First, when using an X-ray beam of about 1mm diameter, it is difficult to overcome the effects of surface enrichment, and secondly, because of 'background noise', the minor constituents of the alloy, such as tin, gold, zinc, arsenic, and lead, could not be measured with sufficient accuracy (or even reproducibility) to permit valid comparisons.

We have therefore undertaken new analyses, using what is in practice a more accurate scientific method, namely electron probe micro-analysis (EPMA).[14] By analysing the whole series of coins under exactly the same conditions, one can make comparisons within the sample with a higher degree of confidence in their

[12] D. M. Metcalf, J. M. Merrick, and L. K. Hamblin, *Studies in the Composition of Early Medieval Coins* (Minerva Numismatic Handbooks, 3), Newcastle upon Tyne, 1968, pp.17-33 and 41-52.

[13] D. M. Metcalf and L. K. Hamblin, 'The composition of some Frisian sceattas', *Jaarboek van Munt- en Penningkunde* 55 (1968), 28-45; D. M. Metcalf, 'Chemical analyses of English sceattas', *BNJ*

48 (1978), 12-19.

[14] The equipment and the procedures used are described in *NC* 145 (1985), at p.176. The limits of detection are the same as are indicated there, except that the measurement of bismuth has been improved, by using the Mα line. The new limit is calculated as 0.02%.

validity. The Oxford collection has been considerably enlarged over the last few years, in preparation for cataloguing, and it now includes a wide range of types and scarce varieties, which help to elucidate the internal order of several of the secondary series. In addition, many of the finds from the Hamwic excavations (including numerous specimens of Series H) have been analysed at Oxford under the same conditions,[15] as has the systematic collection in the National Museum of Wales,[16] and a certain number of coins from sites in East Anglia.[17] In all, the corpus of specimens analysed by EPMA now amounts to over 360 specimens. In addition, an important study undertaken at the British Museum has made available a large body of analytical evidence for the East Anglian coins of King Beonna,[18] which stand right at the end of the sceatta series and therefore cast a useful retrospective light on the secondary phase. Many individual coins have now been analysed by different procedures, and it is therefore possible to compare the results and (to some extent) to assess the probable accuracy of earlier analyses that could not be repeated.

The data for Series H and for the coinage of Beonna are both well suited to reveal the extent of variability and the short-term stages of debasement, because the coins are amenable to detailed classification, i.e. they can be arranged into sub-groups in a way which should correspond with the order in which they were issued.[19] The tally of EPMA analyses is now as follows:

Pa	5	F	2	N	6	V	5
Va	4	G	6	O	10	W	2
A	8	H	29	Q	10	X	15
B	11	J	16	R	38	Y	19
C	15	K	16	S	3	Z	6
D	24	L	21	T	3	others	7
E	67	M	4	U	12		

In order to give the reader a preliminary idea of the shape of the enquiry, the intended 'silver' contents (Ag + Au + Pb) of all these coins have been shown diagrammatically in Fig. 2, from which it will be seen that there are some series which appear to span both the primary and secondary phase, and that among the secondary series, variation of as much as 20 or even 30 per cent is commonly found. A lot of numismatic effort has to be expended on trying to decide whether this was variation over a period of time, or whether the sample includes lower-grade imitations or forgeries (of which there are plenty among the sceattas), or

[15] J. P. Northover, 'The EPMA analysis of sceattas', in *Southampton Finds* vol.1 (note 10 above) pp.34-5, and cf. pp.31-3, 36.

[16] We are indebted to Mr. G. C. Boon for his encouragement and support, in making the Cardiff collection available for analysis.

[17] We are grateful, likewise, for the kind help of Dr. B. Green (Keeper of Archaeology, Norfolk Museums Service) and Mr. R. Carr (Director of the

Brandon excavations).

[18] M. M. Archibald, with M. R. Cowell, R. I. Page and A. J. G. Rogerson, 'The coinage of Beonna in the light of the Middle Harling hoard', *BNJ* 55 (1985), 10-54.

[19] The classification of Series H is discussed in *Southampton Finds* vol.1 (note 10 above), at pp.27-31, and the classification of Beonna's coins is discussed in Archibald, loc.cit.

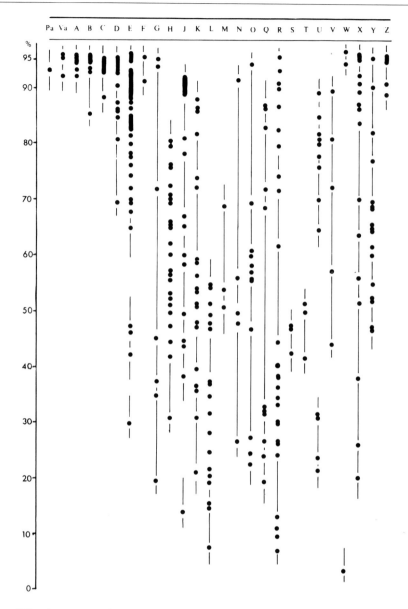

FIG.2 'Silver' contents of the main series of sceattas, to show the range of values encountered in each series. (Some of the values shown in this diagram are affected by corrosion, and may not be accurate.)

616

whether there were intended standards (such as 50 per cent 'silver') which in practice were not always reached, either through technical incompetence or dishonesty at the mint or indifference or unawareness. Historians may be inclined to think that all the numismatic detail is not their business; but in so far as a general historical understanding of the uses of money in the seventh and eighth centuries emerges from the detail, they need at least to be satisfied that the reasoning is sound and persuasive.

That is why we present our interpretation of the data, below, in what may seem an inconsequential order. Instead of speaking first about the transition from low-gold thrymsas to silver sceattas, and then discussing the primary phase, we begin by looking for clear-cut evidence of intention on the part of the minting authorities, and we attempt to proceed from what is clear, towards what is still debateable or still in need of extra evidence. In practice, we shall examine the topic of silver contents more or less in a reverse chronological order, beginning with the latest sceattas and ending with the earliest (sections 1-24). We will then move on to the question of silver sources, analysing the patterns of the trace elements that are potentially diagnostic (sections 25-7). Finally we shall look at minor additions and impurities in the coinage alloy, of which the two that are important are tin and zinc (sections 28-31).

1. *Intended alloy standards in the coinage of King Beonna*

Numismatic evidence of superb quality is available for Beonna's East Anglian coins, struck in the third quarter of the eighth century, which have had an extremely high and altogether unusual survival-rate because so many were found in the Middle Harling hoard. No fewer than 56 specimens have been chemically analysed, in the context of a meticulous die-study.[20] Nearly all the 56 are from Middle Harling, and so they are a sample of specimens that should all have undergone similar corrosion and leaching. The results (Fig. 3) show that the 'silver' contents for most of the coins form a 'normal' distribution with a modal value of about 53 or 54 per cent. Two-thirds of the specimens fall between 50.5 and 56.3 per cent. That is a very respectable level of accuracy. Because any corrosion will have tended to alter the distribution pattern, it gives a *minimum*

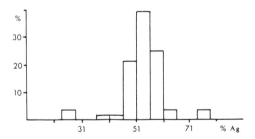

FIG.3   'Silver' contents of 56 coins of King Beonna, nearly all from the Middle Harling hoard.

[20] Archibald, loc.cit.

impression of the accuracy originally achieved by the moneyers. *A convincingly 'normal' distribution offers us self-validating evidence of intention on the part of the moneyers.* Fig. 3 shows that there were two outlying groups, of only two coins each, averaging approximately three-quarters and one quarter 'silver' respectively. The two (die-duplicate) coins with *c.*75 per cent silver are the only two specimens in the sample by the moneyer Wærferth, all the other coins being by the moneyers Efe and Wilræd. The two coins with *c.*25 per cent silver are again die-linked, and are by Wilræd, the silver contents of whose other coins tend to be on the lower side of the central band, and include the specimens in the steps from 36 to 46 per cent. We can envisage that Beonna's coinage began, probably on a very small scale, at a 75 per cent standard, produced by only one moneyer; that the bulk of the issues followed at a reduced standard of a little over 50 per cent, carefully achieved by two moneyers; and that perhaps only Wilræd went on to strike a trickle of late coinage at a 25 per cent standard. There might originally have been rather more of Wærferth's coins, which had been driven out of circulation by Gresham's Law before the Middle Harling hoard was concealed.

The picture, sketched above, of three successive and logically-related alloy standards by which Beonna's coins repeated the process of debasement over a period of only a few years is not completely convincing, but we are exceptionally fortunate in being able to demonstrate that it is inadequate. If we had to make do with many fewer analyses, there would be a temptation to minimize the fact that the peak of the histogram is over, rather than just under, 50 per cent; and one would in any case accept it very cheerfully as a single, 'normal' distribution — not bimodal. But bimodal it certainly is. Among Efe's coins we sometimes have as many as a dozen analysed specimens from the same obverse die. Between die 3 and die 4 there is a difference in the pattern of silver contents (Fig. 4) which is so clear that it could hardly be other than intentional. This is borne out by a corresponding difference in zinc contents. The clinching evidence is that there is also a difference in weight. The coins from die 3 average 1.09g, whereas those from die 4 average *c.*0.96g, which is the normal figure.[21] The intrinsic silver contents for die 3 are thus a quarter greater. Similarly, there seems to be a difference between Wilræd's dies 1 and 3, and 2. Within the *c.*50 per cent silver band, then, there was at one point a modal value of *c.*57 or 58 per cent — distinctly too high to be intended as an approximation to 50 per cent; and there seem to have been differences in the average silver contents *at different times*, not because of a falling-away from the standard intended and originally achieved, but by a deliberate adjustment in the mint prescription. For Beonna, we have evidence of fantastically good quality: it is difficult to see how one could be any more certain about the moneyers' intentions, without documentary evidence. The chronological separation of the slightly different silver contents (struck from different obverse dies, with no die-links recorded between them) is as clear as one could ever hope for. Equally clearly, the individual coins on the divergent standards were indistinguishable from one another, and in the Middle Harling hoard they are found mingled together, valued at par.

[21] ibid., p.26.

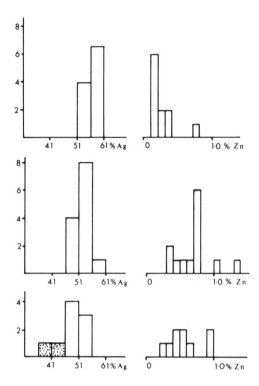

FIG.4   'Silver' contents and the corresponding zinc contents of selected coins of King Beonna, by the moneyer Efe, from die 3 (*top*) and die 4 (*centre*), and by the moneyer Wilræd, from dies 1 and 3 (plain) and 2 (shaded) (*bottom*).

There is always a problem in interpreting the silver contents of coins of about half silver and below, because they seem to have been particularly susceptible to changes suffered by the alloy over the centuries through corrosion and leaching while buried in the ground. One should not therefore dismiss out of hand the idea that the coins were originally much closer to 50 per cent silver than they now are. The best argument seems to be that if corrosion had produced that degree of enrichment, one would not expect to see histograms as tight as those in Fig.4.

Thus Beonna's coins demonstrate that, where we have the benefit of a very high survival-rate, we learn that the facts are not as straight-forward as they might at first glance appear. The successive standards of *c.*75%, *c.*57-8%, *c.*52-3% and *c.*25% accompanied by changes of weight-standard, strike us as illogical, and form a pattern that we could easily have guessed wrongly, e.g. as three-quarters, a half, a quarter. It is salutary always to remember that a sceatta series for which we have only half-a-dozen analyses, giving a range of scattered values, *might well be seen to be as complex and as illogical as Beonna's coins*, if only we had ten times as much information.

At a date right at the end of the secondary phase, coins were being struck to alloy-standards which were accurately achieved. But the standards were being altered very rapidly. Coins on different standards remained in use and circulated at the same face value. This is not what we would have expected from the general theory of progressive debasement over fifty years. Rather, what was happening was an attempt by Beonna to restore a higher alloy standard, which very quickly went into decline again.

Beonna's coinage might in principle represent a radical break away from the alloys and intentions of the secondary phase, a novel development, even if one that rapidly foundered. On the other hand it might be characteristic of what was happening during the secondary phase. At least we should look.

When we do so, we find that the preceding East Anglian coins, Series R, shows an arpeggio of values which could probably be interpreted in very much the same terms as Beonna's coins. And when we look, for example, at Series K (which includes several different types, related to each other by style and content, and presumably not far distant in date) we see what could be construed as the makings of a similar pattern once more:

Type 20:	54%, 53%, 48%, 47%
Type 32a:	74%, 51%
Type 33:	86%
Type 42:	86%, 58%
Type 52:	54%

Percentages somewhat above half-silver are again plentiful. The order of the numbered types is arbitrary, and there are no obvious numismatic reasons against rearranging them into another sequence, e.g. 33, 42, 32a, 20, 52. But if we had half-a-dozen analyses of Type 33, who knows what the silver values would be?

2. The Cambridge hoard and the Thames (A.W. Franks) hoard

Fragments of two old hoards illustrate the composition of the currency at a late stage in the secondary phase, and suggest that there was indeed a period, before Beonna's attempted restoration, when most or all of the coins in circulation were very debased.

Five coins from the Cambridge hoard[22] were analysed. Three are of Series R, and are main-stream East Anglian issues, with legends o ep, o eæ, and *wigræd*. Two are of Series Q, Type 65, which seems to be localized in the north-western part of East Anglia. Their silver contents are:

[22] J. Evans, 'On a small hoard of Saxon sceattas found near Cambridge', NC[3] 14 (1894), 18-28; S. E. Rigold and D. M. Metcalf, 'A revised check-list of English finds of sceattas', SEC, pp.245-68. s.v. Cambridge, speculates on strays from the hoard, MEC vol.1, p.519, attributes only no.708 to the hoard.

Series Q	31%
"	27%
Series R, o *ep*	36%
" , o *e*	38%
" , *wigræd*	13%

The hoards may well have been concealed before the debasement had run its full course, since British Museum analyses of coins of Wigræd[23] show the following 'silver' values (which include substantial amounts of lead):

BMA 9	43%
BMA 11; Burrow Hill 8 and 9	19%, 20%, 26%
Middle Harling 55 and 56	6%, 7%

The specimen with 26% 'silver' in fact contained 14% Ag, 0.8% Au, and 11.5% Pb, as well as the usual addition of tin. If the lead entered the alloy with the silver, all one can say is that the process of cupellation was carried out very inefficiently. But much of it may have been associated with the bronze.

The coins of Series R by the moneyer Tilbeorht are also at the bottom end of the range:

Tilbeorht:	11%, 10%, 8%
" (Middle Harling)	7%

It seems clear that the few coins of Series R that survive into the Middle Harling hoard are the latest and poorest issues of the series, by two new moneyers who had taken over from the workmen of the *epa, spi,* and *rhy* coins, cf. the disappearance of Wærferth during Beonna's coinage.

The Thames hoard[24] included the following four specimens which, again, were all well below half-silver:

Series L, Type 12	28% (corroded)
" , Type 15b	22%
" , Type 15	16%
" , Type 16/15b	15%

East Anglia and London are the only minting regions where debasement is known to have proceeded to such drastic levels. In Wessex, to which we turn next, nothing of the sort happened.

[23] Archibald, loc.cit., p.47.

[24] Rigold and Metcalf, (note 22 above) s.v. London: the Thames hoard.

3. *A traditional standard of c.80 per cent silver at Hamwic, and persistent failure to maintain it*

From very early in the secondary phase, Hamwic minted sceattas of its own distinctive types (Series H) — first Type 39, and then Type 49. The archaeological evidence suggests that they provided a major part of the currency of Hamwic for several decades. This is imprecise evidence for chronology, amounting to little more than a subjective assessment, but what is certain is that Series H was not later replaced, in the currency of Hamwic, by any substantial numbers of more debased varieties of sceattas — whether minted locally or drawn in from elsewhere. Series H may even have continued in use, on a dwindling scale, until it was replaced by Offa's pennies. Either that, or there was a gap of a couple of decades or more during which a sceatta currency had virtually disappeared, and Offa's coins were not yet current.

All this is to say that we have no hard and fast evidence for the length of time over which Type 49 was struck.[25] It would seem from the numismatic details to have been a long time, for the type comprises at least half a dozen different varieties. They have been classified as Varieties 1-6, and the question has been carefully considered whether they are successive or concurrent or a combination of the two.[26] Varieties 1b and 1c, and perhaps 2a, could be concurrent, and one cannot exclude the possibility that Varieties 3 and 4a are concurrent.

Fig. 5 may, therefore, give a somewhat false impression of the extent to which the Hamwic moneyers kept returning to a standard close to 80 per cent silver — which declined just as often to as little as 50 per cent. The evidence of Variety 1a is particularly clear. Even without analytical information, one would unhesitatingly

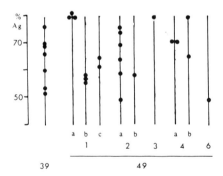

FIG.5 'Silver' contents of coins of Series H, Types 39 and 49. Type 49 is classified into varieties 1-6, with sub-varieties, but it is not certain that there is no chronological overlap between some of the varieties.

[25] P. Andrews and D. M. Metcalf, 'A coinage for King Cynewulf of Wessex?', *SEC*, pp.175-9.
[26] See note 19 above.

place it at the head of Type 49 because of the details of the reverse die. All three specimens are from the same dies. Variety 1a obviously reflects a determined (but short-lived) attempt to impose exacting standards on the alloy, after the variability of Type 39.

Because the coins of any one particular variety cannot be arranged rigorously, on independent evidence, into their chronological order, one cannot say whether the observed range of silver values was a repeated short-term decline or whether it merely reflects variability. One would need the evidence of analyses of a good number of pairs of die-linked specimens to resolve that uncertainty.

In judging the data summarized in Fig.5, one should remember that many of the Hamwic finds were severely corroded, and that the measured silver contents cannot be expected to be as accurate or even as consistent as those for Beonna's coins all from the Middle Harling hoard. Even if one tries to imagine a certain degree of blurring of the evidence there is no reason to suspect a number of successive alloy standards in Series H. This is frankly puzzling, since the moneyers were undoubtedly quite capable, at a technical level, of working accurately to a standard — as Beonna's coins demonstrate.

Coins of Series H are rarely found anywhere else in England than at Hamwic or in its West Saxon hinterland; nor are they found, for example, at Domburg except in minute quantities. This unusual distribution pattern has led to the suggestion that Hamwic enjoyed a favourable balance of trade in the decades when Series H was in use, i.e. that there was little or no net outflow of money from the region.[27] Two conclusions might follow. First, if there was no net outflow of silver from Hamwic, and even an inflow, the underlying economic pressure to debase was absent. Secondly, if the Hamwic coinage was not being used to meet debts on the continent or in other regions, where its intrinsic silver value would come under scrutiny, it may be that there was less incentive for the West Saxon king to maintain exact alloy standards. If he imposed fairly stiff minting charges, coins of varying intrinsic value could have been made to circulate at par, just as they were in later Anglo-Saxon England.

When the problems have been stated, we see that 30 analyses of a single series of sceattas are by no means enough, in this case, to settle the basic questions. If a hoard concealed mid-way through the issue of Type 49 were to come to light, it might remove some of the chronological uncertainties and give the analytical results greater force. Chemical analysis of hoard coins would probably give us a more exact view of silver standards. And die-duplicates, if there were any pairs in such a hoard, should help to show whether debasement within varieties was progressive or erratic. Without new evidence, we should admit that all these questions remain debateable.

4. *A controlled silver standard or standards at York in the 740s and 750s*

King Eadberht of Northumbria (738-57), like Aldfrith before him, issued sceattas bearing his name. There are a number of distinct varieties, which have been

---

[27] In *Southampton Finds*, vol.1, pp.17-25.

classified into seven groups (A to G),[28] which were, at least to some extent, sequential rather than concurrent, as their very different survival-rates indicate.[29] They were all of the same basic design and no doubt circulated alongside each other at par. (There is no hoard evidence.) We do not know the date at which Eadberht began to strike these coins, but on the view that the seven classes are at least partly sequential, it would be reasonable to imagine that the first issues came quite early in his reign, to allow a reasonable length of time for the series. In parallel with Eadberht's own coins, he and his brother, Archbishop Ecgberht, also struck a joint coinage, of which there are several varieties.[30]

Fifteen EPMA analyses are available, covering all the varieties, but (obviously) there are only one or two of each. Taken all together, they suggest silver standards of a half and two-thirds, with a few higher values, — rather than a two-thirds standard imperfectly achieved, cf. Series H. The secondary peak of the histogram, Fig. 6a, b, is visible whether one plots only the EPMA data, or the lowest available figure by whatever method of analysis. There is a natural presumption, depending on how clear-cut the secondary peak is, that *it would not have arisen either from the random effects of corrosion, or from mere inefficiency or dereliction on the part of the moneyers in producing a two-thirds alloy.* One should also take into consideration a few coins of Eadberht's successors Alchred, Æthelred I and Ælfwald, which would contribute to the secondary peak if they were included.

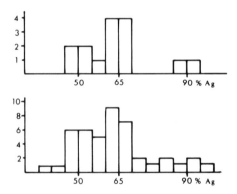

FIG.6 a,b. 'Silver' contents of coins of King Eadberht (alone, and with Archbishop Ecgberht) (Series Y), as analysed by EPMA (*top*), and by various methods, choosing the lowest result (*bottom*).

Over all, the problems and the general historical results of analysis of Series Y thus look rather similar to those for Series H. Instead of progressive debasement, we find a recurrent standard of about two-thirds silver. The stumbling-block to historical interpretation lies not so much in the patchiness or the illogicalities of the analytical data, as in our inability to demonstrate the correct

[28] J. Booth, 'Sceattas in Northumbria', *SEC*, pp.71-111.

[29] D. M. Metcalf, 'Estimation of the volume of the Northumbrian coinage, *c*.738-88', *SEC* pp.113-16.

[30] Booth, loc.cit.

order of Classes A to G, or to date them. The differences from the Hamwic situation are both improvements: the whole range of Eadberht's coins can at least be securely dated within the 19-year period 738-57; and the general trend continues into the reign of Alchred. Secondly, there does seem to be a subsidiary peak in the histogram. One could readily imagine that Eadberht (like Beonna) began by issuing coins of good silver but very quickly changed to a two-thirds alloy, and then later in his reign to half silver, but it is much more difficult to contemplate his switching back and forth between standards. If some varieties were on the higher standard and some on the lower (which is apparently not the case) one could arrange them into a chronological order accordingly. But what if most of the varieties were concurrent, being differenced to distinguish the work of several moneyers? Variation within a number of varieties might then be construed as reflecting a single change in alloy standard, made by several moneyers at the same time. Is there anything in the evidence that would help us to choose between these options, which put quite a different historical complexion on the coinage? We have to tread carefully between accepting the option that strikes us as making better historical sense, and sticking to the letter of the evidence.

Most of Eadberht's coins that have been analysed by EPMA have also been analysed at the British Museum using similar techniques (SEM).[31] A comparison of the two sets of data may undermine the general historian's sense of well-being, for the results are not impressively similar, and there are a few serious discrepancies, for which no explanation can be offered. It is well understood that surface enrichment (i.e. depletion of the copper phase through corrosion and leaching) is a severe difficulty in the way of discovering the original alloy of the Northumbrian sceattas. The XRF analyses published in 1968, of several of the same coins that have since been re-analysed more thoroughly, usually quoted a wide range of observed silver values, and it now seems that the lower value was to be preferred, and was often reasonably accurate. Sometimes, however, the surface layers had evidently not been sufficiently removed. The XRF analyses serve as a warning of how pronounced surface enrichment often was.

The 'silver' values as measured in the two projects are as set out below. (The starred figures are repeat analyses made after the SEM results revealed the seriousness of the problem. Surface enrichment proved highly misleading even on polished sections using EPMA. Repeat analyses brought figures of 68 down to 60, 69 to 45, 90 to 49, 85 to 63, 96 to 50, and 78 to 58.)

		EPMA	SEM			EPMA	SEM
Ecgberht		47	47	Eadberht	E6	45★	51
"		65	64	"	G2	49★	52
Eadberht	A9	64	72	Alchred/Ecgberht		52	55
"	B2	62	65	Alchred		63★	62
"	B18	60★	62	Æthelred		50★	59

[31] M. M. Archibald and M. R. Cowell, 'The fineness of Northumbrian sceattas', *Metallurgy in Numismatics* 2 (1988), 55-64.

| " | C2 | 60 | 57 | Æelfwald | 47 | 67 |
| " | C8 | 52 | 49 | Æthelred (shrine) | 58★ | 60 |

The simple practical response is to prefer the lower of two conflicting results, but obviously this is a less than rigorously scientific approach. The moral is, perhaps, that we should be looking for the sort of conclusions that are not likely to be vitiated by possible remaining inaccuracies. Thus, a secondary peak in the histogram (if it is clear) is relatively unlikely to have arisen from an accidental conjunction of inaccurate data.

The British Museum's own holdings were also analysed by SEM; and a number of coins in the Yorkshire Museum have been analysed at Bradford, by neutron activation [we understand].[32] If the available results by all methods for Eadberht's seven groups are summarized, and the lowest of any conflicting values are preferred, the picture is as follows (Fig. 6). (The 1968 results are identified as (XRF), and the recent British Museum analyses as (L). The Bradford analyses, which should in principle reflect the composition of the whole flan, and therefore give a weighted average of the corroded and of any uncorroded layers, are marked (B). They should be assumed to escape the extremes of error.)

Ecgberht 70-87(XRF)/47/47, 65/64, 66, 49, 67-72(XRF), 54(L), 59(L), 50(L), 62(L).

A 64/72, 66(L), 87/73(B), 60(B), 60(B), 97(B), 67(B).

B 58-82(XRF)/62/65, 60/62, 63(L), 78(L), 62(L), 71(L) 63(L), 53(L), 81(B), 46-64(XRF).

C 60/57, 52-49.

D 69(EPMA), 82-85(XRF), 92-93(XRF).

D/E 62-66(XRF)/63(B).

E 45/51, 40(L), 46(L), 48(B).

F 94?(EPMA), 65(L).

G 49/52, 44(L), 52(L).

If we attempt to sift through this information of rather mixed quality, the first thing to be said is that there is quite good evidence that Class E is different from most of the others, and is apparently on a standard of half-silver, even falling away a little from 50 per cent. It has been argued above that Classes C and E are different from the rest, being small issues which have had a distinctly higher survival-rate, and which show a technical difference that is likely to be chronological, namely that the obverse die seems (unusually) to have been the more productive die, perhaps therefore the lower die. Classes C and E are thus arguably early.[33] Class C, too, on the above evidence may be on a 50 per cent standard — as may Class G, of which the survival rate has however been normal.

Because the measured silver contents are very unlikely to be too *low*, the

[32] The results are included in the catalogue in Booth, loc.cit.

[33] Metcalf, loc.cit. (note 29 above).

combined evidence of analyses, survival-rates, and obverse/reverse die-ratios encourages us to accept that there was an intended standard of half-silver. This makes it more plausible that some at least of Archbishop Ecgberht's coins, for example, are likewise on a half-silver standard, and sharpens the question whether others of them were two-thirds silver or are merely surface-enriched. If there was an early half-silver standard, superseded by a two-thirds standard, one would expect the analyses to make sense in terms of the classification of Ecgberht's coins into their minor varieties, in particular varieties i-ii and iii-vi

i-ii   47/47, 54(L), 59(L).
iii-vi   65/64, 66(EPMA), 67-72(XRF), 50(L), 62(L).

It has been argued elsewhere that Ecgberht's varieties i-ii are earlier on grounds of their survival-rate and die-ratio. This fits in with what has been said about Classes C and E; but there are low values in variety v. Nevertheless, Ecgberht's coins offer some encouragement to postulate two standards, and it may be that the sequence of varieties iii-v could be rearranged so as to bring v closer in date to i-ii. What we are doing, in effect, is looking for patterns or correlations within the evidence which are clear enough to encourage us to discount the significance of data that do not fit — principally by appealing either to the concept that the alloys sometimes fell below the standard aimed at, or to the possible misleading effects of surface enrichment.

Archibald and Cowell have noticed a correlation between flan size and fineness in Classes A and B of Eadberht's coins. The smallest coins analysed, namely one specimen in each class, A3 and B17, were found to contain 73% (Bradford) and 64% (London). Assuming that these results are reliable, we might be looking at a similar pattern to that of Wærferth's coins for Beonna — almost an experimental opening to the series, or a standard that was quickly abandoned. It has to be said that A3 is not convincingly smaller than the run of Class A. B17, like other examples of variety Bii (not analysed) is from smaller dies and also is on a slightly smaller flan.

Attempts to correlate the weight and fineness of varieties taken as a whole are inconclusive, although there is a slight tendency for coins with lower silver contents to be heavier. The pattern is almost certainly confused through the various effects of leaching.

Class B of Eadberht's coins, with a left-facing beast, gives an unusually compact cluster of values around 62 per cent. This could represent a particular effort to conform to a standard, perhaps when it was first introduced. B23 (53%) is stylistically irregular; and B11 (46-54%) is problematic.

Classes D and F, on limited evidence, could well conform to a two-thirds standard.

For the reign of Alchred (765-74), and especially for his early joint issues with Archbishop Ecgberht, there is adequate evidence of a half-silver standard. One could very reasonably ask, therefore, whether the survival-rates might not be misleading, and whether the history of Eadberht's reign was not of a two-thirds alloy standard later replaced by a half-silver standard, rather than the other way round, as has been argued. On this basis, Class A, the only class in which the coins read EADBERHTVS rather than EOTBERHTVS, would stand at the head of the sequence, and some other explanation would have to be found for the high survival-rate of Classes C and E. A large hoard concealed part-way through Eadberht's reign would resolve the uncertainty.

It might indicate that several of the varieties were concurrent (e.g. each the work of an individual moneyer). Archibald and Cowell have argued that small flans correlate with high silver contents, and are early and, in particular, that Class Bii may have been intended to be three-quarters silver, Bi and Biii two-thirds silver, and Biv perhaps half-silver.[34] We consider it is implausible that flan size alternated, being small at the beginning of Class A, then larger, then small again at the beginning of Class B, then larger again. If the facts about flan size, and about correlation between flan size and fineness, are clear, we think that they constitute a strong argument for placing Classes A and B in parallel, as the concurrent work of two moneyers or two workshops. Moreover, we find the arrangement of varietes within Class B difficult. The main varieties Bi and Bii are typologically distinct. Biii belongs with Bii, and Biv is a single specimen mentioned above (B23) as being stylistically irregular.

Bi	62/65, 63(L), 81(B).
Bii	60/62, 78(L), 62(L).
Biii	71(L), 63(L).
Biv	53(L).

From these figures, Bi and Bii are indistinguishable in silver contents, and Archibald and Cowell's conclusions that Class B declined through three successive alloy-standards seems to go somewhat beyond the prudent handling of the evidence. We would prefer to suspect that the high values of 81 and (perhaps) 78 per cent are affected by leaching. We would likewise be hesitant to generalize the significance of a relationship between small flans and high silver contents, in a situation when the observed silver contents are so erratic, and demonstrably difficult to measure. The weights of all Eadberht's coins, omitting visibly worn specimens, yield a roughly normal distribution, with no significant differences between the varieties, except that Ecgberht's coins are slightly heavier and probably more accurately adjusted (as was true of the stycas of later archbishops — perhaps a morally inspired difference[35]). Thus there is no evidence of the sort of complexity encountered in Beonna's coinage, where silver contents could vary with both weight and fineness.

The tin and zinc contents of Eadberht's coins are discussed below (sections 25 and 26). The one thing that is clear is that both are seriously affected by leaching, etc. The evidence suggests, but is barely enough to prove, higher zinc contents associated with Classes C, E, and G.

[34] Archibald and Cowell, loc.cit., p.59.
[35] D. M. Metcalf, 'Hexham and Cuerdale: two notes on metrology', in *Coinage in Ninth-Century Northumbria*, edited by D. M. Metcalf, Oxford, 1987, at pp.389-90.

To sum up, the analytical evidence for Series Y requires to be handled very cautiously, and the numismatic classification of Eadberht's coins remains a topic for stimulating debate. We are inclined to believe that the intended silver standard was actually adjusted upwards at some point in Eadberht's reign, from half to two-thirds, and went down to half again under Alchred.

Even if the chronology of the varieties needs to be reversed, it would be common ground that the Northumbrian coinage did not fall below half-fine during the secondary phase. In relation to the likely dating of the secondary phase in southern England, Series Y can fortunately be dated securely enough. The issues of Eadberht and Alchred cover the years *c*.740-74, or possibly *c*.745-74, which in any case takes them beyond the most likely dates for Beonna's issues (757 x *c*.765)[36] and *a fortiori* beyond the precipitous decline in silver contents of Series R. The monetary history of Northumbria, in a word, followed a quite different course during the secondary phase from that of East Anglia.

5. *Kent and the Thames valley in the secondary phase*

We have looked at East Anglia, Wessex, and Northumbria, but not yet at the south-east, where the sceatta coinages originated, and which remained an important region of minting and monetary circulation in the secondary phase. The problems are to identify the relevant coin series and to find evidence from which to place them in their relative chronological order, if we are to be able to chart the course of debasement. We have already noticed that the different types with Series K vary widely in fineness, and that Series L is severely debased.

Canterbury is assumed to have been a major mint, but it is sometimes difficult to distinguish between types or varieties minted in Kent and at London, since the coins circulated over roughly the same area.[37] What is clear is that several series have an essentially southern, or even south-of-the-Thames, distribution pattern.[38] They will belong mostly to east Kent, but some could perhaps be shared with London. We are obliged, therefore, to look at the debasement of Series K, L, M, N, O, and V as a whole, as belonging certainly to Kent and the Thames valley. The histogram (Fig. 7) is somewhat over-weighted by specimens of Series K and L. Bearing that in mind, one can see that Series L is different from the various south-of-the-Thames series in being much more debased; that there seems to be a standard of about 50-55 per cent 'silver', and apparently another at about 90 per cent silver (including specimens of Series K, N, O, and V); and that there may

[36] Archibald *et al.* (note 18 above), at p.33, discussing Florence of Worcester's statement that at the time of the death of Cuthbert, in 758, rectè 760, Beornus was king of the East Angles. Another source says that in the time of Offa, Beorna was king of the East Angles. Miss Archibald suggests that Beonna's coinage marks the reassertion of East Anglian independence after the death of Æthelbald in 757.

[37] More than one study has attempted to show that Kentish/Thames valley types, occurring in two main styles, should be divided between two mints. The

additional find evidence that has accumulated since they were written has in one case confirmed, and in another thrown doubt on the distributional patterns of the different styles. D. M. Metcalf and D. R. Walker, The "wolf" sceattas', *BNJ* 36 (1967), 11-28; D. M. Metcalf, 'The "bird and branch" sceattas in the light of a find from Abingdon', *Oxoniensia* 37 (1972), 51-65.

[38] D. M. Metcalf, 'Monetary circulation in southern England in the first half of the eighth century', *SEC*, pp.27-69, at p.44.

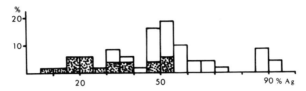

FIG.7   'Silver' contents of secondary-phase sceattas from Kent and the Thames valley (Series K, L, M, N, O, and V). Results for Series L are shaded.

be a standard of 60 per cent, particularly for Series O. If one had ten times as many analyses, the pattern would possibly turn out to be more complex, and it would in any case be possible to describe it more confidently. As it is, the chronological implications for debasement are far from clear. That is because *the minor variations of design in Series K, N, and V do not allow the coins to be arranged into their correct or even into a plausible chronological sequence.* In Series O there is one coin, found at Lewknor, which is arguably the earliest variety of Type 38 and which also is of high weight and has the highest silver contents. It suggests that the series began to be minted before the onset of debasement. The same may be true of Series K, N, and V, but it so happens that there are no convenient numismatic details (except perhaps in V) to provide any proof. To arrange the coins into a chronological sequence that matches a decline in silver contents would therefore risk being nothing more than a circular argument.

We may guess, then, (but it is little more than a guess), that several of the series began, like Beonna's coins, on a reasonably high alloy standard which was quickly abandoned. The concurrent use of several unrelated designs is puzzling, because the normal practice seems to have been for a mint-place to keep to its own distinctive type — for obvious reasons of convenience and public confidence. One hypothesis is that coinage was minted at more than one place on the shores of the Wantsum Channel. (This could only be proved, with great good fortune, from the evidence of numerous finds from sites in east Kent.[39]) Probably one would be looking, as a first hypothesis, at Fordwich as the *wic* for Canterbury and Sandwich as the *wic* for the royal vill of Eastry.[40]

What happened next, we are in no position to say, except that only Series L included plentiful issues on very debased standards. Series L is stylistically complex, and it would be rash to insist that all the coins classified as belonging to it were minted at London, although that may be the case.

Whether or not they were, one needs to know how widely finds of Series L are distributed, in order to judge whether there might have been a late phase of the currency when only 'London' was minting, the east Kentish mint or mints having lapsed into inactivity — or in other words, whether debasement really was

[39] One notes, for example, two die-identical specimens of Series O, Type 38 from Richborough. Unfortunately it is not categorically stated that they were found separately: if they were a miniature hoard (as two die-identical specimens of Series BX from Caistor St. Edmond appear to be) their evidential value would be quite different.

[40] K. P. Witney, *The Kingdom of Kent*, 1982, p.153.

progressive in Kent and the Thames valley. But it is necessary to be careful about the form of the argument: just because Series L includes coins that are very debased, it is not certain that they are later in date. Coins of varying alloy could circulate alongside each other, as we have already seen. For proof of the range of types that were in use concurrently hoard evidence is essential.

The London (Thames) hoard of c.1869 contained a full range of types in Series L, plus Types 32a and 33 in Series K, and 23e, classed with Series L.[41] One imagines that the coins of Series K are the oldest in the hoard, and that they are of better silver than the rest, but no analyses of those particular specimens are available. The Franks parcel (discussed above) may in fact come from the same hoard. There is virtually no other hoard evidence, except for a grave-find from Garton-on-the-Wolds, Yorks (N.Humberside) in which the latest coin was of Series K, Type 32a, buried along with primary or intermediate types.[42]

The puzzle that these two finds together present is to know why Series K should be present in both, when Series N, O, and V are absent, even though the range of their alloys is similar. The numbers of coins in the finds are, of course, minimal, and the absence of the less plentiful types could be merely a matter of statistics. But the prima-facie sense of the evidence is otherwise. Series O, in all probability, began early enough to have been in issue before the date of the Garton-on-the-Wolds grave-find, and the same could be true of Series V. More obviously, Series M, N, O, and V had all presumably been issued before the London (Thames) hoard was concealed.

The recognition of one particular style in Series L as associated especially with finds from Hwiccia has proved deceptive.[43] Four coins in 'Hwiccian' style have been analysed, and found to contain 32, 20, 15, and 8 per cent silver.

6. *Essex in the secondary phase*

Series S, the 'female centaur' type, has a distribution pattern clearly focussed on Essex, and may now be accepted as an East Saxon issue.[44] One would expect monetary trends to be similar to those observed in Kent and the Thames valley.

The great majority of coins of Series S belong to a single variety, which is stylistically compact. Two specimens were analysed, and both were found to contain 47 per cent silver. A scarce variety in another style gave a figure of 42 per cent.[45] Having already found a standard of about half silver in Kent and London, we are perhaps justified in guessing at the same.

[41] See note 24 above.

[42] The Garton-on-the-Wolds coins are all described and illustrated in Rigold, 'The two primary series of sceattas', (note 1 above), p.49 and pl.IV.

[43] D. M. Metcalf, 'Sceattas from the territory of the Hwicce', *NC*[7] 16 (1976), 64-74; M. A. S. Blackburn and M. J. Bonser, 'Single finds of Anglo-Saxon and Norman coins — 3', *BNJ* 56 (1986), 64-101, at p.74.

[44] An updated distribution-map for Series S appears in D. M. Metcalf, 'Some finds of thrymsas and sceattas in England', *BNJ* 56 (1986), 1-15, at p.6. Numerous specimens of Series S have subsequently been recovered as single finds at Tilbury, Essex.

[45] XRF analysis of this 'late' coin had given a result of 49 per cent: D. M. Metcalf, 'Chemical analyses of English sceattas', *BNJ* 48 (1978), 12-19, at p.18.

7. *Series T and Z*

Series T seems to belong north of the Thames, and not in East Anglia: this leaves Essex and the east midlands as possible attributions. Three specimens were found to contain 51, 50, and 41 per cent silver. The same remarks apply as for Series S.

Series Z is equally difficult to locate: one would like to think of Norfolk or the Fen margins but the evidence is slender.[46] The series includes coins of primary quality (96, 95 per cent). A debased specimen (58 per cent silver) may be a nineteenth-century forgery (see section 29 below).

8. *Summary of debasement in the secondary phase*

Debasement proceeded differently in the four main regions of monetary circulation in England, and went furthest in East Anglia. There is substantial evidence of an intended standard of approximately half-silver, everywhere except in Wessex. The duration of the secondary phase is difficult to establish except in Northumbria. The possibility that minting ceased in some regions but that debasement in a sense continued, because coins of lower silver contents entered the region from elsewhere and circulated, can be effectively excluded in Northumbria (except perhaps at Whitby) and in Wessex (where a few debased coins are found, but not many and not necessarily lost after Series H had fallen out of use).

9. *The range of alloys in circulation at the date of deposit of the Aston Rowant hoard*

The Aston Rowant hoard, from the Chilterns, was deposited in the late primary phase, and included Series A-F, R, and Z, with a preponderance of the continental Series D. A sample of 20 specimens was analysed, covering Series C, D, E, R, and Z. It shows a clear correlation between weight and alloy (Fig. 8) with most coins still containing 90-95 per cent silver, but with the introduction of a much lower weight-standard in Series D, where some lighter coins of lower alloy have only two-thirds or less of the intrinsic value of the better coins. (The varieties of Series E found in the Aston Rowant hoard, analysed from specimens with other provenances, fall well into the higher group.)

The diagram makes it sufficiently clear that the first step towards debasement of the English currency was not taken at any of the English mints, but that coins on an abruptly reduced standard were introduced from the continent. Series D is tentatively attributed to Domburg.

[46] For a corpus of Series Z, see Metcalf, 'Some finds' (note 44 above), at pp.12f. and the discussion at p.5. The Aston Rowant variant contains 94, 91, and 88 per cent. Could Series Z (Type 66) be absent from Aston Rowant *because it is too early*? The argument for an attribution of Series Z to its own mint-place, on the 'one kingdom — one type' hypothesis, seems stronger, the earlier the date of the coins. An early date for type 66 entails dismissing the Cimiez coins as forgeries.

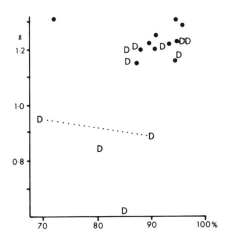

FIG.8   The Aston Rowant hoard: correlation of weight and alloy, from a small sample of specimens. Coins of Series D are shown by the symbol 'D'. The isolated coins in the upper left of the diagram is imitative. The two coins joined by a dotted line are from the same die.

10. 'Porcupines' of post-Aston Rowant varieties

The so-called 'porcupines' (Series E) are the most prolific series of sceattas. There are good arguments for seeing them all as continental rather than English, even though so many have been found in England.[47] It is a plausible guess, given the enormous scale on which they were minted, to associate them with the major emporium of Dorestad. There are two or three associated types (e.g. Types 10, and 53) which might belong to minor mints also in the Rhine mouths area.[48]

Several well-defined varieties of porcupines present in Aston Rowant are of good silver, but the series continues with a profusion of secondary varieties, which are quite widespread among English stray finds, not least in coastal districts. It is reasonable to assume that these were in use in England concurrently during the earlier part of the secondary phase, and perhaps even during the whole of it, although attempts may have been made in Northumbria and in Wessex to remint incoming foreign coin into Series Y and H respectively.

Some twenty secondary porcupines were analysed by XRF in 1968,[49] and seven of these have now been re-analysed by EPMA. The Table, below, shows some discrepancies, the EPMA results sometimes being higher and sometimes

[47] The characteristic 'porcupine' obverse was of course imitated in England, both by the 'Æthiliræd' type and by Series T, and perhaps by a few unofficial insular imitations. But 'one type — one mint' is what we should expect. Metcalf, 'Monetary circulation', at p.32.

[48] There were only two specimens of Type 10 among the Domburg finds. This makes the Escharen find of 1980 all the more interesting: 5 coins of Series D and 4 of Type 10, of which two were die-identical. W. Op den Velde, W. J. de Boone, and A. Pol, 'A survey of sceatta finds from the Low Countries', SEC, pp.117-45, at p.141.

[49] Metcalf and Hamblin, 'The composition of some Frisian sceattas' (note 13 above).

lower. The practical outcome seems to be that one should be cautious of placing reliance on the exact figures, but that the results are at least adequate to demonstrate the approximate degree of debasement.

Comparative analyses of porcupines

XRF	'silver'%	EPMA	'silver'%
0.132	83½ - 85½ = 109		84.5
0.139	72½ - 74½ = 106		82.5
0.140	81½ - 83½ = 280		77.9
0.141	80 - 90 = 285		81.1
0.142	72 - 73 = 286		67.3
M.4	88½ = 115		88.6
M.5	77½ = 116		88.9

Both EPMA, and XRF analyses which were not repeated, are shown in Fig. 9. The diagram suggests a reduced standard somewhere in the range *c*.80-5 per cent. The specimens involved are of a number of minor varieties.

There is no reason to postulate a matching decline in the weight of the secondary porcupines, such as is seen in Series D.

A much better correlation exists between silver and tin contents. The primary porcupines normally contain no measurable amounts of tin, but the secondary varieties nearly all include tin in their alloy — around one per cent when the silver contents are in the eighties, and around 2 per cent with *c*.70 per cent silver, and occasionally even more (Fig. 10). In so far as the porcupines are from a single mint-place, this is likely to reflect changing mint practice, and it should be a useful clue to the chronology of the varieties. Not enough porcupines from Aston Rowant were analysed for us to be sure whether or not small amounts of tin (*c*.0.2 per cent) were already present in the alloy of some coins in circulation at the date of deposit.

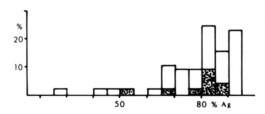

FIG.9 'Silver' contents of post-Aston Rowant porcupines (Series E). Specimens from the Franceschi parcel (possibly part of the Kloster Barte hoard) are shaded.

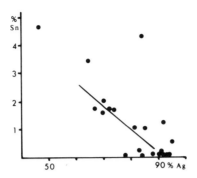

FIG.10   Correlation of silver and tin contents in porcupines.

From the evidence of the composition of the hoard, and from other analyses, it seems clear that there are varieties not represented in it, which are nevertheless of very pure silver. Probably, therefore, such pure coins were still being minted after the beginning of the secondary phase in England. In any case, the debasement of the porcupines proceeded less far than that of the local issues in any of the main regions of England.

Patterns of a sort are visible in the range of alloys among the main secondary varieties, but there is demonstrably quite wide variability between coins from similar dies.

Two specimens were analysed of the broad-flan porcupines of the variety (F) associated with the Franeker hoard. One, probably later than Franeker, and very similar to a find from Marlcliffe, Bidford-on-Avon,[50] proved to be unusually debased (42 per cent).

11. *The Franceschi parcel of porcupines (probably from the 'Hanover' or Kloster Barthe hoard*

Nine of the secondary porcupines just discussed probably derive from the Kloster Barthe hoard.[51] All nine contained less than 90 per cent silver (refer back to Fig. 9). They illustrate a phase of the currency in east Frisian territory when coins of primary quality had dropped out of circulation.

12. *Series G: the coinage of Quentovic?*

Series G, which was once erroneously attributed to a mint in Sussex, appears to be from the opposite coasts of the Channel, somewhere in northern France, possibly from Quentovic.[52] A wide scatter of provenances throughout England has been recorded in recent years. The best specimens are of primary quality, but others are debased: 45 per cent (51.5 - 53.5 per cent for this coin by XRF); and

[50] 'Coin register', *BNJ* 57 (1987), 129, no.56.

[51] D. H. Hill, 'The "Hanover" hoard of porcupine sceattas', *NC*[7] 17 (1977), 173-4.

[52] D. M. Metcalf, 'A new variety of sceat from Repton related to Series J: type 36, with the reverse of type 85', *BNJ* 56 (1986), 19-23.

37 per cent for what seems to be an imitative coin.

An eclectic series of imitations drawing upon both Series J (Types 36/85 and 36 — see below) and G is very debased (35 and 19 per cent silver). Its mint attribution is problematic, and its borrowing of the design of Type 85 (which is usually of reasonably good silver) seems to imply that coins of widely different alloy were being used concurrently.[53]

Many uncertainties will remain until more excavation material from the site of Quentovic is available.

13. Series X: sceattas from Jutland

The Wodan/monster sceattas (Series X), which have been found in such predominance at Ribe in Jutland, and also in hoards from eastern Frisia, have a curious distribution in England. They are much more plentiful in relation to porcupines at Hamwic than they are in east Kent, which must be nearer to their place of origin.[54] Otherwise, there are a few scattered finds from most parts of England.

The Hamwic finds included specimens with 92, 89, and 87+ per cent silver, but also a range of distinctive imitations with 70, 38, 26+, and 20+ per cent silver. The last-mentioned coin came from an early context, and there is other evidence which suggests, unexpectedly, that very debased imitations may be close in date to the good-silver coins.[55]

Unprovenanced specimens of Series X, in regular style, show a considerable range of silver contents, from 96 and 95 per cent, to 87, 84, 63, and even c. 56 per cent. The type is unusual, among the sceattas, in using a range of about a dozen different secret-marks (under the monster's chin), which presumably correspond with the work of individual moneyers or successive phases of output. Given the degree of variation in the alloy indicated above, a Beonna-type project to correlate silver contents with secret marks, on the basis of a large number of analyses of coins from a single hoard, looks promising. Were this work to be done, the by now familiar problem would still remain: the coins cannot be arranged into their chronological sequence on independent evidence, for want of suitable hoards containing different proportions of the varieties, and any proposal to classify the coins according to their declining silver contents would rest to that extent on mere optimism.

In relation to the English currency within which they circulated, it seems likely that the coins of Series X were up to the average standard prevailing, and that they did not contribute to the process of debasement in England.

There are two or three scarce types muling the 'Wodan' design with some other design. One at least appears to be imitated from the Series X coins, rather than merely employing the same motif, drawn from the general stock of Germanic imagery. Type 81, which has been found at Hamwic and near Norwich, is in all

[53] ibid.

[54] D. M. Metcalf, 'Nyt om sceattas af typen Wodan/monster', *Nordisk Numismatisk Unions Medlemsblad* 1986, 110-20; id., in *Southampton Finds*

(note 10 above) pp.19f.

[55] *Southampton Finds*, nos.116 and 121; also 120, 122-3.

probability insular. Analysis showed 91 per cent silver. Types 29 and 30 (perhaps from the same stable) are less certainly derived directly from coins of Series X. One analysis, of a coin of Type 30, showed 96 per cent silver. A relatively early date is indicated.

14. *The 'bird and branch' coinage (Series U, Type 23b/d), an early secondary issue in Kent and the Thames valley*

We saw above (section 5) that Series K, N, O, and V included a few specimens that were of good silver, and that, at least in the case of Series O, such coins were arguably early. This is very thin evidence, however, for progressive debasement in the early secondary phase. The 'bird and branch' coins, Type 23b/d, seem all to be around 80 per cent silver (Fig. 11), thus perhaps a relatively short-lived type (unlike K, N, O, and V). Needless to say there is no useful hoard evidence, and one should hesitate over the argument that the date of an issue can be deduced from its alloy. The early date which has been proposed for Type 23b/d was based partly on a similarity of fabric between Series J (which is certainly early) and U, and partly on a simple expectation that debasement was progressive. Series J and U, however, are from different mints.

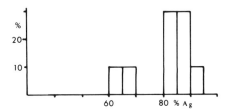

FIG.11   'Silver' contents of Series U, Type 23b/d.

There are two main styles in Type 23b, of which one has a distinct western focus, in the upper Thames valley and at Hamwic.[56] It was the similarity of fabric between Series J and Type 23b, and the similarity of distribution on the western and northern fringes of the areas where sceattas were in use, which were the basis of the argument that they formed a continuous series attributable to Æthelbald at an inland mint.[57] The Hamwic finds considerably strengthen the distributional evidence for Type 23b.

Type 23e, which was once classified with 23b as part of Series U, is very debased (31 and 24 per cent). It was present in the Thames hoard, (and apparently also in Cimiez) and is better seen in that context; its association with Type 23b/d on grounds of typology may be artificial.

[56] ibid., nos.107-11.

[57] D. M. Metcalf, 'The "bird and branch" sceattas in the light of a find from Abingdon', *Oxoniensia* 37 (1972), 51-65; updated in *Southampton Finds* p.49 (introductory note on Type 23b.) Note that the workshop of Type 23c was, on the evidence of no.110, producing coins of a similar standard; and that this link into Series O (Type 21) probably strengthens the two-mint hypothesis for Type 23b.

15. *The portrait types in Series Q and their relationship to Type 23b. The Hallum hoard.*

There are rare types in Series Q (with a distribution focussed on western Norfolk or northern Middle Anglia) which are basically identical with the designs of Type 23b (standing figure/bird) and which show silver contents of 86 and 68 per cent, much higher than the run of Series Q. The more plentiful varieties with beast/bird are either of good silver (Brandon, 87 per cent) or are severely debased, like much of Series R (32, 31, and 27 per cent; Q/R mule, belonging with Q, 34 per cent). Numismatically it seems obvious that the portrait types in Series Q should stand at the beginning of the series.

The dating of the coin types is crucial. If a typological parallel rests on a false belief that the types in question are close in date, the interpretation will fall. And hoard-evidence is in principle sovereign for dating. We say 'in principle', because foreign hoard evidence, i.e., the evidence of coins hoarded outside the country they belong to, has its own pitfalls. The Hallum hoard of 1866, from Frisia, included one specimen hitherto unrecognized as a portrait coin of Series Q, and allegedly also a continental imitation of the pivotal DE LVNDONIA obverse, muled with a porcupine reverse. This rare variety was seen by Blackburn as a precursor of the London type, but there seems to be no justification (seeing that the only other provenance is Rotterdam) in regarding it as other than a copy which post-dates Type 12. It is an intruder in the Hallum hoard.

The Hallum coin of Series Q, Type 67a, is from the same hand as a coin found at Cambridge, imitating Type 41. We analysed the latter by EPMA and measured 83 per cent silver. Type 67b was also analysed, and found to contain 86 per cent silver. We think that it is safe to assume that the Hallum coin is similar.

But the hoard evidence is thorny. The other 'English' types in Hallum are 2 specimens of Series J, Type 85 (=B III B) and 3 of Series G (which is probably continental), — thus distinctly similar to the Garton-on-the-Wolds grave find, and seemingly early. Could one dismiss the coin of Series Q as another early coin, surviving in a 'foreign' hoard of later date? We think that this would be special pleading, and would prefer to suggest that the few 'English' coins in Hallum could have reached Frisia from Northumbria, and that they may illustrate Lebecq's judgement, 'c'est avec ces contrées — actuel Yorkshire — que les marchands/navigateurs frisons du haut moyen âge paraissent avoir entretenu les rapports les plus constants.'

The evidence of the Northumbrian finds (among which Series J, G, and Q are prominent) is discussed in section 23 below.

16. *Series J: the transition from the primary to the secondary phase*

The type which Rigold classified as BIIIB, and later transferred to Series J, where it stands alongside Types 37, 36, 60 and 72, is derivative from the primary series B, and is undoubtedly early, as shown by the evidence of the Garton-on-the-Wolds grave find. It belongs to York.

638

Type 85 (BIIIB) and 37 were both struck mostly on a well-controlled standard of *c.*90 per cent silver, falling in Type 37 to *c.*80 per cent or even *c.*60 per cent (Caister-by-Yarmouth find). There are also specimens of both types which are plated on base metal cores, but which from their style would have passed as official issues.

For Type 36, silver contents of 67 and 58 per cent have been measured. The North Elmham find[58] is a clad coin, with no more than 20 and 40 per cent silver measurable on the obverse and reverse.

A specimen of Type 72 is again plated on a base-metal core, with a surface reading of 66 per cent silver.

All four types regularly contain significant additions of tin to the alloy. (1-2 per cent, rising to 3-4 per cent in the more debased specimens). The cores of plated coins also contain tin (up to *c.*1 per cent), but in far smaller proportions than in the good silver coins, where tin in relation to copper may be in the ratio 1:10 or even 1:5. Tin is virtually unknown in primary sceattas, whether English or continental, but is a standard addition to the alloy throughout the secondary phase.

17. *Why was debasement tolerated in England?*

We have gone some way towards bringing the facts of debasement in the secondary phase into focus, but that still leaves us a long way from understanding the reasons of those who made the decisions, and the constraints under which they had to decide. It is difficult even to speculate, and extremely difficult to back speculations up by showing that they are cogent or that they have explanatory power. There are parallels to be considered, in the debasement of Merovingian gold after the death of Dagobert, and debasement in southern England in the age of Alfred. In both these phases of debasement, political weakness and military threat are indicated. But the very large scale of Burgred's coins demonstrates that shortage of silver supplies was not on that occasion a reason.[59] Nor was it necessarily the reason for the abandonment of high silver standards in the English sceattas. In order to argue that it was, one would have to produce statistical estimates of the scale of the sceatta coinages, showing that they dwindled away early in the secondary phase. The detailed work remains to be done, but one would be very surprised, to judge only from the proportions of different types among the stray finds, if the secondary sceattas were not large-scale coinages. Series H and Y, we know, were each produced from hundreds of dies. One might have expected Northumbria to feel the pinch more sharply than the wealthy south, out of general considerations of historical geography, but there was no collapse of the currency there until *c.*796;[60] and the dating of the Northumbrian sceattas is, fortunately, secure.

[58] There been some confusion in the past about the identification of this coin's type, but it is of Type 36, not 85. It is illustrated in *BNJ* 1977, pl.2, 20.

[59] D. M. Metcalf and J. P. Northover, 'Debasement in southern England in the age of King Alfred', *NC* 145 (1985), 150-76.

[60] J. Booth, 'Coinage and Northumbrian history *c.*790 - *c.*810', in *Coinage in Ninth-Century Northumbria*, edited by D. M. Metcalf, Oxford, 1987, pp.57-89.

There might have been severe short-term fluctuations in the amounts of foreign silver entering England, such as can be documented in the fourteenth century, when mint records are available. But if a debased and unreliable currency had been seen as an evil, and the fluctuations had been short-term, steps could have been taken to restore the situation.

Of one point we are firmly persuaded: sceattas in England were royal coinages, which flourished under royal license and which were seen by kings as being to their profit. Aldfrith, Eadberht, and Beonna were the first to put their names on their coins, but the lack of a royal name on the earlier sceattas does not prove a lack of royal involvement. It is unlikely that the rulers of the various English kingdoms omitted to take an interest in the debasement of the coinage struck in their realm.[61]

Kent and the Thames valley, forming a natural monetary region, included parts of different kingdoms, and the currency there may have been difficult to control, particularly for the Mercian king if he desired access to the Channel ports. But East Anglia was geographically very self-contained, with its own ports. The East Anglian coinage therefore poses problems of interpretation that are particularly acute, because debasement there went so far (while the design of the coins remained conservative). The long reigns of the last two kings of the dynasty of the Wuffingas, Aldwulf (663/4-713) and Ælfwald (c.713-49) were a time of political stability, so far as we can judge, and the debased coinages of Series R were extremely plentiful. A die-study of them remains to be made, but one may be confident that hundreds of dies were used. The only possible escape that we can see from the dilemma arises again from our ignorance of the absolute chronology of the later sceattas. It seems impossible to prove or disprove a 'late' chronology, for example, which places all the worst coins of Series R — say with less than one-third silver — after the death of Ælfwald, when 'Hun, Beonna and Alberht divided the kingdom' — a laconic record of what may well have been stressful political events. We have no idea of how, geographically, the East Anglian kingdom might have been divided into three, and there is no clear evidence in the coin-finds of three zones of circulation, or of sceattas of different types.[62] We have no reason to assume that Beonna's named coinage began immediately when he assumed power; indeed, its distribution might suggest that it was produced in more than one place. In a word, the chronology of the coins might allow us to favour a 'political' explanation for the worst of the debasement. There is, at least, some evidence (from the *œuvres* of the various moneyers, and from the contents of the Middle Harling hoard) that the most debased specimens reflect a very late phase. But independent evidence for dating is quite imprecise. We do not know the end-date of Beonna's reign; we do not know when Offa began to mint good silver pennies in East Anglia, and we cannot even make a better guess than *c.*770 x *c.*785. We do not know for certain when Pepin's reformed deniers became

---

[61] Metcalf, 'Monetary circulation' (note 38 above), at pp.45-7.

[62] D. M. Metcalf, 'The currency of the East Anglian kingdom in the first half of the eighth century', in *Commentationes Numismaticae 1988. Festgabe für Gert und Vera Hatz*, ed. P. Berghaus, Hamburg, 1988, pp.19-27.

available in Domburg and Dorestad — although if the received date of 754/5 is correct, it strongly suggests that debased coins in East Anglia coexisted with a good silver currency in the lower Rhinelands — in spite of evidence that Beonna's coins were carried across the North Sea, and that the 'interlace' design from (?)Maastricht was known in East Anglia.

Bede's description of London as a busy international wic makes the debasement of Series L difficult to understand. All one can say is that under Burgred, severe debasement at the London mint was accompanied by intense activity, based so far as one can judge on international trade. Perhaps, therefore, the debasement of Series L was less damaging than we might have expected it to be. Again, the absolute chronology is a matter of guesswork. Rigold's suggestion, that the coins inscribed DE LVNDONIA advertized Æthelbald's taking absolute lordship of London (from the East Saxons) in 731 x 732, was buttressed by a comparison with the LONDVNIV thrymsas — which cannot, however, be as late as the 660s, as he then thought.[63] Blackburn has pointed out that the date 731 is merely *ex silentio* (i.e. Bede in 731 could still refer to Ingwald as bishop of the East Saxons), and has suggested that Æthelbald's power in London may have grown some years earlier, following the death of Wihtred in 725.

If Series K, M, N, O, and V have to be fitted into a single sequence of debasement, the DE LVNDONIA type, containing *c.*50 per cent silver and sometimes only *c.*25 per cent, would then imply a very tight chronology in the 720s (assuming that it was struck forthwith in *c.*732, and not later: Æthelbald's taking control of London is after all only a *terminus post quem*), — followed by a virtual blank in the 740s and 750s. The Middle Harling hoard, in which there were a few late sceattas among a mass of Beonna's coins, encourages us towards a 'late' chronology for the end of the secondary phase. Our grasp of the chronology of sceattas in the Thames valley remains speculative, however, and really quite tenuous in default of some more hoard evidence, and our ability to interpret the context of debasement is thus greatly curtailed.

We are reduced to pointing out that the intrinsic value of the sceattas did not closely determine their value. Such little hoard evidence as we have from the secondary phase indicates that in spite of significant variations in silver contents (and in weight) coins of different varieties were accepted together, and we must assume at par. In the short term, therefore, the minting authorities could benefit from devaluation, and the only immediate sufferers were those who took English money abroad, — and producers whose markets lay abroad.

18. *The primary phase*

We come at last to the primary phase. The silver contents of Series A, B, C, and of the primary porcupines (the Aston Rowant varieties,[64] notably VICO, 'plumed bird', and variety G) are uniformly very high (Fig. 12 where the *step interval is 1*

---

[63] Rigold, 'The two primary series of sceattas' (note 1 above), at p.24 and n.1.

[64] J. P. C. Kent in *Oxoniensia* 37 (1972), 243-4; Grierson and Blackburn, *MEC* nos.646-55. The range is further indicated by specimens illustrated in auction sale catalogues, e.g. Glendining 3 March 1975, lots 211-42, and Sotheby 18 July 1985, lots 493-506.

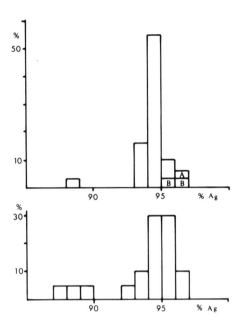

FIG.12 'Silver' contents of English primary sceattas of Series A, B, and C. The coin A2, 2 is marked A, and two of Type BX are marked B. Each step in the histogram represents 1 per cent, not 5 per cent.

FIG.13 'Silver' contents of continental sceattas of early date (porcupines of Aston Rowant varieties). The horizontal scale is the same as in Fig.12.

per cent instead of 5 per cent as in other diagrams). If Beonna's coinage provides evidence of fantastic quality, the English primary sceattas — to shift the wording a little — provide evidence of fantastic quality control. This level of accuracy would be exemplary in the thirteenth century, indeed at any time up to the nineteenth century, if one accepts the premiss that traces of gold and lead were perceived as 'silver'.

Within the pattern, Type BX (the earliest variety of Series B) is even better than the average (see Fig.12) and die A2, 2, which was also used to strike base gold, matches it. Probably the mint-workers made a particular effort when the new silver coinage was introduced. Among the porcupines, the 'plumed bird' variety included some specimens with exceptionally high silver contents (Fig.13).

The status of Type BII, characterized by ΛVΛV legends, and the addition of a small cross in the reverse field, is problematic. It seems that a rather higher proportion of the continental provenances are of BII. No specimens were analysed by EPMA. Two specimens of BII, 3 from the Southend hoard were analysed spectrographically by Forbes and Dalladay, and were found to be 2-3 per cent below the usual primary standards. Of two others analysed by XRF, a specimen of BII, 4 was normal, but a BII, 11 was again sub-standard.[65] This variability reinforces the suspicion that BII might be an imitative coinage from another mint-place, although it may on the other hand just be a later phase of the main series.

The boundary between Series C and R is difficult to determine, but there are two styles in the Aston Rowant hoard, one of which is certainly continuous with C, while the other may represent the earliest issues of R. If C is, as has been suggested, Kentish, these coins of Series R will be the earliest sceattas of the East Anglian kings.[66] The alloy standard is not quite so accurately maintained as in Series C (95, 93, and 91 per cent).

Series W, tentatively attributed to a mint in the Southampton area,[67] begins with primary-phase coins of high quality (96 and 94 per cent).

There are other scarce types which were struck with $c.95$ per cent silver contents, and which include no tin. They are therefore presumably early in date, and they tend to complicate the simple picture drawn by Rigold of a primary phase consisting essentially of only Series A, B, and C, mainly in east Kent. These other types (such as the *Ver* group,[68] Series F, and perhaps the earlier part of Series Z) are absent from the Kentish and East Saxon grave-finds and from the Hougham hoard — as indeed are the primary porcupines. There is a presumption that each mint had its own distinctive design, and it may be that the coins of an outlying small mint would not have circulated very far afield in the first decades of the sceatta currency. Even if there were any hoard evidence to guide us on the chronology of these scarce primary types, it would need to be handled delicately.

19. *Pada and 'Vanimundus', and the transition from gold to silver*

Rigold argued, in his classic article on the primary sceattas, that the successive issues of Pada and 'Vanimundus' both span the transition from gold to silver. PI and PII are low gold, while PIII is silver with no intentional gold content; Va A and Va B 1 and Va B 9 are low gold, whereas Va B 5 and 8 are silver. Rigold saw Series A as an eclectic design which sought to gain the users' confidence by reproducing elements from the types of several of the base gold coinages that it swept away.[69] For Rigold, therefore, the transition from gold to silver in south-eastern England had been accomplished some years at least before the attempt (by King Wihtred) to win public confidence with a new silver coinage, produced on a substantial scale.

[65] J. S. Forbes and D. B. Dalladay, 'Composition of English silver coins (870-1300)', *BNJ* 30 (1960-1), 82-7, at p.84, n.1. and see ibid., pp.48 and 52f.; Metcalf 'Chemical analyses of English sceattas (note 13 above), at p.14.

[66] M. A. S. Blackburn and M. J. Bonser, 'Single finds of Anglo-Saxon and Norman coins — 2', *BNJ* 55 (1985), 55-78. at pp.61f. See the more detailed discussion below (Section 22).

[67] Metcalf, 'Monetary circulation' (note 38 above), at pp.44 and 50-1, emphasizing its absence among the finds from east Kent, and its distinctive design,

which — repeated in a very base alloy — suggests intermittent minting. See now vol.1, pp.152-7. Since those pages were written two new specimens have appeared *dans le commerce*, from the Southampton area (= Warnford) and from the Bournemouth area.

[68] M. Blackburn and M. Bonser, 'A derivative of the *Ver* group of intermediate sceattas found at Springfield, Essex', *SEC* pp.229-31. Plate 14, 2 has 95 per cent 'silver', and a coin very similar to pl.14, 4 has 94 per cent.

[69] Rigold, 'The two primary series of sceattas', p.10, fig.1.

Two coins have come to light which complicate this picture. The first is a coin of Type A2 containing over 12 per cent gold.[70] Type A1 was known to Rigold from only one specimen (the whereabouts of which is at present unknown).[71] His arguments for placing it at the head of his classification were convincing; but little progress can be made until some more specimens turn up — and, one would hope, are analysed. The gold contents of the A2 coin can hardly be fortuitous, and the same die was used (as mentioned above) to strike an exceptionally pure silver coin.

Series F also spans the transition from gold to silver, with one coin (*MEC* 687) containing an estimated 9-11% gold, and others of silver.[72] The mint-place of Series F remains problematic, but the later (silver) varieties have TT/II added into their design, evidently a borrowing from Series A, and therefore within the English orbit.

To avoid postulating an alternation between gold and silver, it seems to be necessary to suggest either that Series A was created during the currency of Series Pa and Va, or that neither of these was east Kentish.

The quality of the silver minted by Pada and 'Vanimundus' was high, but perhaps not quite as uniform as that of Series A, B, and C. The only silver Pada we were able to analyse contained 93 per cent 'silver'; three Vanimunds gave 96, 95, and 92 per cent. Of two Padas excavated at a cemetery at Dover, PIII, 7c is seriously debased; PIIB, 1 may be imitative.[73]

20. *When did the primary phase in Kent end?*

There is a numismatic problem in understanding what happened to minting in Kent when Series C (arguably Kentish: see section 18 above) came to an end — and, indeed, what happened in London or Essex when Series B came to an end. The secondary series such as K, M, N, O, and V look so different that it would be natural to imagine a complete break in minting, and perhaps a different organization. Series A and BI were produced intensively, two or more reverse dies being used with each obverse.[74] We now also have evidence of the very exactly maintained alloy standard, in comparison with which the secondary phase looks haphazard.

When did the break occur? Rigold sketched the political background, pointing out that after the reign of Hlothere (673-85), Kent suffered interference and invasion from Mercia and then Wessex. A succession of client kings ruled for very

---

[70] Metcalf, 'Chemical analyses of English sceattas' (note 13 above), at p.14 (gold value too low). The analysis has now been repeated by EPMA.

[71] In the collection of A. H. F. Baldwin in 1960. Baldwins in 1987 offered various sceattas from old stock to the Ashmolean, including some others published by Hill in 1953 as being in the A. H. F. Baldwin collection, but this coin of type A1 was not among them.

[72] Metcalf, 'Chemical analyses of English sceattas' (note 13 above), at p.15. The underestimation of the

gold contents of A2, 2a (note 72 above) suggests that the figure for Series F might also need upward revision.

[73] Forbes and Dalladay (note 65 above), at p.53, and ibid., pl.2.

[74] Note that Rigold ('The two primary series of sceattas', p.34) did not check the *reverse* dies of Series A for die-identity. There are sufficient examples of more than one reverse die being used with the same obverse, to imply a die-ratio higher than parity.

short periods, until Wihtred expelled the invaders in 691, and, in 694, paid a heavy wergild to the West Saxon royal house for the death of Mul. Rigold's suggestion was that the effort to pay the wergild exhausted the then current coinages of Pada and Vanimundus, and that Series A, in particular, was introduced shortly after 694.[75] Various students have since been inclined to suggest an earlier chronology. The arguments have been ably set out by Blackburn, and need not be repeated here.[76] What is new in the debate is the secure redating of the Cimiez hoard, and the consequent dating of the Aston Rowant hoard to not later than *c.*710. Series A is only residually present in Aston Rowant, and it now looks virtually impossible to propose a chronological framework for the issue of all the types present in that hoard, within the period 694-*c.*710. The Kentish grave-finds illustrate the chronological stages of the issue of Series A, B, and C; and there are two stages of Series R to be fitted in.

Series A looks such an intensive, closely-regulated issue that it is not fanciful to see a strong political will behind it. We would be reluctant to attribute it to the troubled years 685-91, and can see no consequential difficulties (in the dating of the debased gold thrymsas and the sceattas of Pada and Vanimundus) to deter us from an attribution to the later years of Hlothere's reign. This would accord with Hlothere's record of administrative innovation, and his partnership with Archbishop Theodore.[77] From a numismatic point of view, its main merit is that it allows us to make an interruption in the coinage (after Series A and C) coincide with the years *c.*685-*c.*691 (or later). This scheme might also explain why Series B continues longer than A, and it might even provide a context for the curiously short-lived phenomenon of grave-finds of sceattas, of Series A, B, and C, mainly in east Kent, but also in west Kent and Essex.

Series A is not, as Rigold thought, the coinage of Wihtred, '*gloriosus rex Cantiae*' (691-725): the find-evidence now rules that out.

21. *Porcupines with runic Æthiliræd*

Keary assumed that the 'porcupine' imitations with the name Æthiliræd could belong to the Mercian king Æthelred (674-704).[78] Rigold's scheme precluded that, but the 'early' chronology proposed above for Series A, etc. reopens the question at least to the extent that it ought to be considered.

There is the negative evidence that none came to light in the Aston Rowant hoard. More positively, the Æthiliræd coins are on a reduced weight-standard, and two that have now been re-analysed by EPMA are distinctly debased (88 and 86 per cent silver), with small additions of tin. They are thus inferior to Series J, Types 85 and 37.

[75] Rigold, 'The two primary series of sceattas', at pp.27-9.

[76] M. Blackburn, 'A chronology for the sceattas', in *SEC*, pp.165-74, at p.169.

[77] For the history of Hlothere's reign and the years 685-91, see K. P. Witney, *The Kingdom of Kent*, 1982, pp.145-54.

[78] Above, vol.1, pp.120-3.

22. *The beginnings of debasement in East Anglia*

There is a gap still to be filled in our account of the onset of debasement in East Anglia. We saw above (section 18) that the earliest variety of Series R attributable to East Anglia (if Series C, of the same basic design, is given to Kent) was a scarce variety reading Ⱳ ᚻ ᚳ , i.e. *epa* upside-down and retrograde, which was present in the Aston Rowant hoard alongside coins of Series C (reading *æpa*). *BMC* 39 (Rigold 1x, illus.[79]) demonstrates the continuity of these coins with others which add ITΛT or similar. They were also represented in Aston Rowant.[80]

Three specimens with Ⱳ ᚻ ᚳ from Aston Rowant are rather less regular in their alloy than Series A, B, and C, with 95, 93, and 91 per cent silver. Two of the ITΛT variety (not from the hoard) were found to be 96 and 88 per cent fine. *None of these five contains any measurable amounts of tin.*

Later in the secondary phase, as we see from the evidence of the Cambridge hoard (section 2 above), Series R fell to below half-silver. Into the gap we may insert the varieties which Rigold labelled R1z and early R2. They form a stylistically continuous series, which could well be by a single hand, and they read Ⲭ Ⲙ ᚻ ᚱ . They are on a reduced weight-standard of 1.0 - 1.1g (*cf*. 1.2 - 1.25g for the earliest variety, and some at least of the Ⱳ ᚻ ᚳ / ITΛT coins). Four specimens were analysed, and showed 93, 80, 74, and 61 per cent silver. All four contain significant amounts of tin, and are thus distinguishable from Series C and from the earliest coins here attributed to Series R. We recognize that, in default of sufficient provenances to map the circulation area of the Ⱳ ᚻ ᚳ and ITΛT sub-series, its attribution to East Anglia must remain debateable. There is one find from 'North Essex' and one, surprisingly, from Sussex.[81]

A die-study of a larger number of specimens might elucidate the chronological order of the coins: the specimens with 80 and 61 per cent have very similar reverses, perhaps implying that the alloy was variable at any particular moment.

The Ⲭ Ⲙ ᚻ ᚱ coins were apparently absent from Aston Rowant.[82] and it seems safe to conclude, therefore, that serious debasement at the East Anglian mint began at about the date of deposit of the hoard ('not later than *c*.710') or within a few years.

23. *Composition of the currency in Northumbria*

The suggestion that Eadberht might have instituted his own coinage in response to the incipient unreliability of alloy of the sceattas reaching his kingdom from southern England can be critically examined by considering the range of types reported as finds from the East Riding (North Humberside) and from York itself. They include the Garton-on-the-Wolds grave-find and the new material from Fishergate,[83] as well as a body of finds from various other sites in York.

[79] Rigold, 'The two primary series of sceattas' (note 1 above), pl.4.

[80] J. P. C. Kent, in *Oxoniensia* 37 (1972), pl.26, 4.

[81] *BNJ* 56 (1986), 15, pl.2, 20 and 30.

[82] Full publication of the hoard is awaited, but several samples have been illustrated.

[83] We are grateful to Miss E. J. E. Pirie for a preliminary view of the Fishergate finds.

There is an obvious concentration on Series K, and the better-silver part of Q[84] which encourages us to proceed on the hypothesis that finds of southern types mostly antedate the introduction of Eadberht's own issues. As the coins have not been analysed, we need to make the further assumption that their metal contents are similar to specimens that have been analysed. On that rather speculative basis, it now seems probable that the currency had not fallen below about 80 per cent fineness when Eadberht's issues began; and in the light of the new analyses of Eadberht's coins (section 4 above), we doubt whether any of his varieties aimed as high as 80 per cent, except perhaps very briefly.

On the same set of assumptions, the Northumbrian evidence may have something to contribute to the chronology of the secondary phase: Eadberht's coins begin not earlier than 737, yet the southern finds cut off with Series K, Type 32a, and rare, good-silver types belonging to Series Q. Taken at face value, this implies a very late chronology for the later part of the secondary series. It is not immediately obvious how it could be reconciled with the evidence of the Cimiez hoard. The northern finds are, obviously, far from being a balanced selection of all the types in issue in different regions of England in the period to which they belong, and indeed they are themselves an important part of the evidence for northerly or 'peripheral' attributions for Series Q and J.

The contrast between the assemblage of finds from Whitby, and that from York and the East Riding can perhaps be understood in terms of the survival at Whitby of later southern types which would have been compulsorily reminted at York. Several of the coins in question are imitative or of dubious quality.

24. *Summary of the evidence of silver contents for the chronology of the sceattas*

Rigold's classic work established for the first time a scholarly chronology for the sceattas, based upon a wide range of considerations, particularly the hoard evidence, and taking account of the idea of progressive debasement, in order to work out the relative dating of the main types. Absolute dating depends on connecting either the burial of hoards with particular events, or the minting of types with particular rulers or events. Rigold's framework rested on the dates 694 (the wergild for Mul), Wihtred's successful reign (691-725), the unusually explicit DE LVNDONIA legend and Æthelbald's lordship over London, 731 x 732, the Frankish attack on Frisia in 734, and the sack of Cimiez in 737.[85] This chronology appeared to leave a hiatus between the end of the secondary phase of sceattas, and the earliest appearance of the silver pennies associated with Offa.

Grierson and Blackburn have more recently given convincing reasons for redating the Cimiez hoard to not later than *c.*720.[86] Various students have sought to push the beginnings of the sceattas back to an earlier date than that implied by 694 for Series A. And Miss Archibald has argued that they continued later than

---

[84] Of the scarce portrait varieties of Series Q, of reasonably good silver, note *BNJ* 47 (1977), pl.2, 35 and pl.3, 37, both from York and also Type 59, P. V. Hill, *NC*⁶ 13 (1953), pl.7, 6 from near Carlisle. Die-linked or very similar specimens to all three of these have been found in East Anglia.

[85] Rigold, 'The two primary series of sceattas' (note 1 above), esp. at pp.26-9.

[86] Blackburn, 'A chronology for the sceattas' (note 2 above).

had been thought, on the grounds that the Middle Harling hoard contained a few specimens of the last of the sceattas alongside the coins of Beonna.[87] Metcalf has suggested that a few late sceatta types may even have been concurrent with Offa's earlier coins, i.e. that there were reformed coinages in the sceat fabric, — a tertiary phase,[88] but the evidence for that has not stood the test of scrutiny.

Metal analyses do not enter much into the debate in the form of detailed arguments. The main criticism which they support, against Rigold's original chronology, is that the DE LVNDONIA coinage is much too debased to stand at the watershed of the secondary phase. If the beginning of that phase is moved decisively earlier by the redating of the Cimiez hoard, it may be that the historical connexion with Æthelbald's taking lordship over London can stand, although a dating to c.732 would leave very few types to fill the 730s and 740s — and, more positively, would not fit convincingly with the Northumbrian evidence (section 23).

We have tried to expose the logical weaknesses of the case for progressive debasement, by showing that it rests on unproved assumptions about the fine dating of particular varieties of sceattas; and we hope that we have demonstrated (from the hoard evidence) that coins of different intrinsic value were able to circulate together to some extent, at par, and that *debasement proceeded differently in four main regions of England*. Assumptions involving Gresham's Law or anything like it are unwarranted.

A specimen of Series O, Type 38 provides interesting evidence that the secondary phase in Kent began with coins of very good silver.

We restate the arguments for attributing Series A to King Hlothere rather than to Wihtred; but these are essentially historical arguments arising out of the redating of the Cimiez hoard, and out of the history of Kent in the 780s, and do not rely on metal analysis except to establish the very high and uniform quality of the alloy of Series A.

It is difficult to find any conclusive arguments to show how long the secondary phase lasted. We have explored the implications of assuming that Eadberht's coins swept away from the currency of central Northumbria any southern sceattas that were carried north. The latest southern types regularly found in Northumbria, such as Series K, Type 32, and Series Q, Types 67b and 59, *may* therefore antedate Eadberht's reform — the date of which is itself uncertain but may be as early as c.740.

That would apparently imply that the secondary phase in southern England went on through the 740s and 750s. Again, one must be aware of assumptions in any hypothesis of progressive debasement during this late phase.

The division of the East Anglian kingdom in 749 gives the earliest possible date at which Beonna's coinage could have begun; but c.757 is a more plausible guess. There is no obvious argument to say that Beonna did not strike sceattas in the earlier part of his reign, just because he struck signed coins later. The same holds for Offa.

[87] Pers.comm.

[88] D. M. Metcalf, 'Twelve notes on sceatta finds', *BNJ* 46 (1976), 1-18, at pp.17-18.

It has to be admitted that both at the beginning and the end of the sceatta series, its chronology rests on arguments that are still debateable, and to which metal analyses can make only a general contribution. In the middle, the redating of the Cimiez hoard is crucial, and serves to draw attention to the first quarter of the eighth century as the period when debasement began in southern England.

25. *The gold contents of the sceattas*

Virtually all sceattas contain traces of gold, which almost certainly entered the alloy along with the silver. The moneyers were either unaware of it, or else judged that it was not worth the trouble of recovery. Gold may be expected to survive the recycling of silver coinage (i.e. the purification of the silver by cupellation) without any significant change in the gold : silver ratio. It should therefore be a useful marker, to help identify the sources of the silver stocks invested in a regional currency.

As a particularly clear example, Offa's new coinage of pennies has much lower gold trace levels than the sceattas.[89] The implication is that the pennies were not made by re-minting sceattas (which had presumably dwindled away and been lost) but drew on a new source of supply for silver, which had very different characteristics. The changing gold trace patterns of later Anglo-Saxon coinages have been studied, in relation for example to the opening up of the Rammelsberg silver mines.[90] The mingling of different stocks may be expected to lead to intermediate gold trace levels, and to experimental data which are by no means clear cut. But the transition from sceattas to pennies is exceptionally clear cut.

It will be natural to enquire whether there are any significant variations within the sceatta series — for example between the primary and secondary phases, or between English and continental issues. Fig. 14 shows the gold : silver ratios for all the analysed sceattas. They vary very widely, but they approximate to a normal distribution, with three-quarters of the values falling between 1 and 2 parts of gold per hundred. The spread of values raises questions about the metallurgical process, which could usefully be tested experimentally. Our sample of coins may safely be assumed to be random in regard to variable gold traces, and a comparison of the histograms for primary and secondary sceattas ought adequately to reflect any homogenization that occurred through recycling. Any shift in average value ought in principle to be a reflection of changes in the composition of the stock of bullion through wastage, new inputs, etc.

Fig. 15 shows only the primary sceattas. The histogram is again approximately normal, and its spread is no wider than that in Fig. 14. There is the same proportion of the values in the central step, which is however located about 0.2 lower. Fig. 16 shows coins from the lower Rhinelands (Series D and E). The peak is in the same position, but is distinctly taller. (The histograms are on the same vertical percentage scale.) That implies that the bullion being minted was

[89] D. M. Metcalf and J. P. Northover, 'Coinage alloys from the time of Offa and Charlemagne to *c.*864', *NC* 149 (1989), 101-20. The pennies were analysed by exactly the same equipment and procedures as the sceattas.

[90] id., 'Interpreting the alloy of the later Anglo-Saxon coinage', *BNJ* 56 (1986), 35-63.

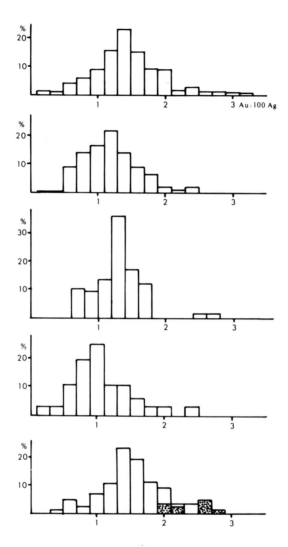

FIG.14   Gold:silver ratios, for all series of sceattas.

FIG.15   Gold:silver ratios, for all primary sceattas.

FIG.16   Gold:silver ratios, for Series D and E.

FIG.17   Gold:silver ratios, for Series Pa, Va, A, B, and C.

FIG.18   Gold:silver ratios, for secondary sceattas with silver contents below 50 per cent. Coins noted as being corroded are shown by the shaded sections of the diagram.

somewhat more homogenous, or was being homogenized more effectively.

The general picture, then, is of a fairly uniform stock of high-gold silver, both in England and on the Continent, with no broad trends, but possibly greater variation in silver stocks within England than on the Continent. Against that background, one should hesitate to recognize smaller-scale differences unless they are statistically convincing. We think the evidence is satisfactory that the earliest English sceattas (Series Pa, Va, A, B, and C) in part reflect a stock of silver with lower gold contents than later became general (Fig. 17). On the other hand, the suggestion which was once put forward that there were differences between A and B, or between A with B, and C,[91] finds no support whatever in the EPMA analyses.

There are tempting hints in several of the secondary series of a narrower range of values than the over-all pattern. Where hypotheses go against general expectation or common sense, one should be doubly careful before giving them credence, and the statistical evidence should be particularly clear. We note for the record, but with the above cautionary remarks, two or three instances. One is Series U, Type 23b/d (Fig. 19), with a very tight distribution which we cannot explain. Another is Series H, where two silver sources are perhaps involved; — there is a peak at about 2.0. A third intriguing instance is the coinage of Archbishop Ecgberht, in Series Y, where three out of four specimens show very low ratios of 0.57, 0.56, and 0.48. The contrast with Eadberht's coinage of the

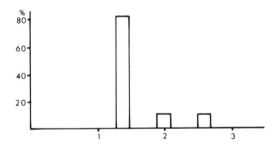

FIG.19   Gold:silver ratios, for Series U, Type 23b/d.

same date might prompt some such hypothesis as the melting down of ecclesiastical treasure. The low gold correlates with unusually low zinc contents (see below, section 29), which is more difficult to explain.

It is evident that corrosion can exaggerate the gold : silver ratio. Many of the specimens that were noted during analysis as being corroded turned out to have a high ratio that is an outlier to the 'normal' distribution. We have wondered whether the small difference in modal value between the primary and secondary sceattas (cf. Figs. 15 and 18) could be an effect of corrosion (i.e. leaching), which

[91] Metcalf, Merrick, and Hamblin, *Studies in the Composition of Early Medieval Coins* (note 12 above), at p.20.

was greater in debased coins, rather than a genuine difference. The histogram of gold : silver ratios for the coins with Ag contents less than 50 per cent (Fig. 18) has a peak of the same percentage height as that for primary sceattas. Recycling of foreign silver (Fig. 16) might perhaps have been expected to raise the peak rather higher.

In relation to the four main circulation areas in England, one would hardly expect to discover any systematic differences, unless silver was being mined locally on a sufficient scale to alter the balance of the regional stock of silver. The sceattas do not lend themselves well to a consideration of that possibility, but the later Saxon pennies, which were struck at many mints and are mint-signed, give no encouragement to the idea that mining was an identifiable source of silver in the coinage.[92]

26. *Bismuth contents*

Bismuth should survive cupellation in recognizable ways, and may in favourable circumstances be a useful indicator of different silver stocks. It is unfortunately difficult to measure the bulk proportion of bismuth in a coin's alloy by surface sampling techniques such as EPMA because of the way that it is segregated. Histograms of bismuth contents show a rather flattened distribution from 0 to 0.05 per cent in the English primary phase (Fig. 20). Lower levels in the secondary phase, with a peak around 0.01 per cent or lower, accord (within the limits of accuracy of the measurements) with the hypothesis that the bismuth entered the coinage metal with the silver (Fig. 21). Variations between series in the secondary phase, *e.g.* higher bismuth : silver ratios in Series Y than the average, are intriguing, but the evidence is too imprecise to support any positive conclusions.

The continental primary sceattas, and in particular the porcupines, show a tighter bismuth distribution than the English primary coins, with a peak at 0.03 per cent (Fig. 22). We would judge that the difference is significant. This is the only within-sample variation to which we think it appropriate to draw attention.

The good-silver coins of Offa and Charlemagne and their successors have slightly higher bismuth traces than the primary sceattas, but are not very obviously different.[93]

27. *Summary of trace elements diagnostic of silver sources*

A type of silver with relatively low gold contents, found among the earliest sceattas (*c.*0.7 - 0.8 parts per hundred, *cf.* a more typical modal value of *c.*1.3 parts), may represent a stock of bullion existing in England before cross-Channel inflows began in the primary phase. There are hints of some similar low-gold silver in Northumbria. Otherwise the evidence of gold and bismuth traces is neutral or tenuous.

[92] Metcalf and Northover (note 90 above).
[93] Metcalf and Northover (note 89 above).

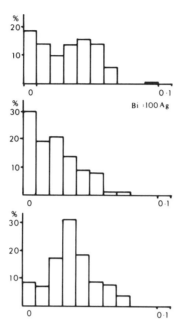

FIG.20   Bismuth contents, for English primary sceattas.

FIG.21   Bismuth contents, for secondary sceattas.

FIG.22   Bismuth contents, for Series D and E.

28. *Additions of tin to the alloy*

Tin is absent or below the level of detection in most primary sceattas, including the ('intermediate') porcupines of the varieties found in the Aston Rowant hoard. There is very little tin in any but the most debased of secondary porcupines. It is regularly present, however, in English secondary sceattas, in increasing amounts as the coinage becomes more debased. The earliest types in which significant amounts occur are the continental Series D and, in England, Series J and Series R ᛉᛗᚢᚠ   (see section 22).

If the ratio of tin to copper is calculated, it is very obvious that coins which were noted during analysis as being corroded have exaggeratedly high tin ratios, — which in many cases would seem to involve the redeposition of tin in the surface layers of the coin. Earlier XRF analyses, reporting high tin contents in some secondary sceatta types, should probably now be discounted.[94] It is difficult to know whether tin enrichment might have affected our EPMA analyses of

[94] e.g. in Series L, analysis O.52 (*BNJ* 1978, p.17), 20% Sn, reduced to 6.6% by EPMA; O.53, 11% reduced to 7.8%; O.54 reduced to 6.2%; O.208, 32% reduced to 9.6%. Series R, O.77, 11.5% reduced to 6.2%.

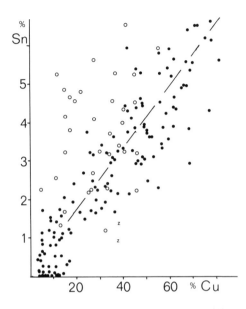

FIG.23   Correlation of tin and copper. Open circles indicate coins from the Southampton excavations, mainly of Series H. The symbol Z indicates two coins of questionable authenticity.

apparently uncorroded coins to a lesser extent. If the results are accepted as a fair approximation, they can be interpreted as showing that tin contents were in a more or less direct proportion to total copper contents. A plot of tin against copper (Fig. 23) yields a straight-line graph, the average ratio of tin to copper being *c.*1:12. This might be classed as a low/medium tin-bronze. Within the pattern there are no very obvious variations from one series to another.

The Hamwic finds nearly all have exaggeratedly high tin contents (shown by open circles in Fig. 23) no doubt reflecting the soil conditions of the site. As this applies both to Series H and to other series, one has to say that there is no clear evidence that the tin : copper ratio was originally any different at the West Saxon mint.

The correlation in replicate measurement of tin by EPMA and SEM for specimens of the Northumbrian Series Y is so poor as to induce severe negative feelings (Fig. 24). This is all the more puzzling, as SEM tin results for coins of Series R from Middle Harling look to be on the high side.

Nevertheless, the evidence of the best quality comes, again, from the coins of Beonna in the Middle Harling hoard. Even though the hoard was ploughed out, and scattered over a distance, all the coins had lain in the soil of the same field, and may have suffered similar leaching. A histogram of their tin : copper ratios (Fig. 25) shows a very pronounced peak between 1 : 10 and 1 : 8. The coins that were noted during analysis as 'slightly corroded' are shown by shaded areas in the histogram. They are not concentrated at the higher end of the range; but the

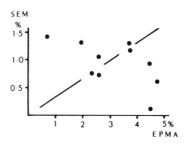

FIG.24   Correlation of tin contents as measured by EPMA and SEM on the same coin.

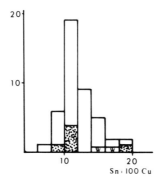

FIG.25   Tin: parts per 100 parts copper in coins of King Beonna from the Middle Harling hoard (44 specimens).

histogram as a whole shows some positive skewness, part of which may be because of unrecognized enrichment.

As with their silver contents, the coins of Beonna reveal complexities of mint-practice that could hardly have been recognized without the benefit of a large sample. Thus, the two coins by the moneyer Wilræd that are on a silver standard of only c.25 per cent have tin : copper ratios of 15.5 and 17.9:100 (identified by W in Fig. 25). Does this imply that, with the decision to reduce the silver contents from c.50 to c.25 per cent, it was also decided to change to a different quality of bronze? — or to add c.10 per cent of pure tin instead of c.5 per cent? Two other of Wilræd's coins (from the Burrow Hill excavation) on the lower side of the half-silver band, have 40-45 per cent 'silver' and 7 per cent tin, which is more than in any other coins except the two with c.25 per cent silver: — an intermediate level of tin? The two Burrow Hill coins are die-linked.

Inspection of all the EPMA analyses of other series does not reveal any instances where changes of silver standard within a type are accompanied by demonstrable changes in the tin : copper ratio, which (as suggested above) seems to conform approximately to a straight-line graph.

655

If we try to assess the historical implications of the tin analyses, what are we to say? So far as one can judge, the practice of adding tin to the coinage metal (perhaps in the form of bronze, but Beonna's coins raise some doubts) was notably uniform in the secondary phase, at a number of mints. There is insufficient analytical evidence for bronze artefacts dateable to the eighth century other than coins, such as might show whether the ratio 1:12/1:15 was a standard alloy at the time.[95] What can be said is that there was a deliberate change in mint practice at the beginning of the secondary phase. The amounts of added tin would not have been enough to change the colour of the coins noticeably, but they might have improved the working properties of the alloy. The tin must, in any case, have been believed to be beneficial.

With Offa's reform, the addition of tin completely ceased. Nor is any found in early Carolingian coins. Its use returns, both in England and France, in the 840s. As the limit of detection for our EPMA analyses is calculated at 0.02 per cent, a coin of Offa containing c.5 per cent copper can be stated to have a tin:copper ratio of less than 0.4:100, or 1:250, or far less than could be sensibly interpreted as a deliberate addition. It seems clear, then, that tin was deliberately and effectively excluded, and that the silver in Offa's pence was alloyed, after cupellation, with essentially tin-free copper.

One sceat which attracts adverse attention because its tin contents are exceptionally low is a specimen of Series Z, which is condemned below after a consideration of its zinc contents and other details.

29. *Zinc contents*

Sceattas, both primary and secondary, almost always contain traces of zinc. Cowell, commenting on the coins of Beonna, suggests that it is likely the zinc entered the alloy as a result of using a bronze containing small amounts of zinc (as well as tin). He notes that Anglo-Saxon copper-based metalwork often contains both tin and zinc, and that a similar source of supply for coinage metal would account for the observed compositions of the coins. In his subsequent discussion of the Northumbrian series, Cowell reiterates this point of view, suggesting that 'scrap bronze and brass, or a copper-based alloy containing both tin and zinc, rather than pure copper, was added to debase the silver. This is substantiated by the high correlation between copper and tin and zinc contents'.[96]

This interpretation of the way the zinc entered the coinage alloy is sensible and should command assent, but it leaves one problem unresolved, namely that zinc is present in primary sceattas *which contain no tin*, showing a normal distribution with a modal value of 0.10 - 0.15 per cent, that is 2-3 per cent zinc in relation to the total copper contents. (The proportions in Offa's pence, which are tin-free, are very similar.) The good-silver porcupines (Series E) contain marginally more

---

[95] Dating the artefacts is the problem. For analytical results, see W. A. Oddy, 'Bronze alloys in Dark-Age Europe, Appendix B', in *The Sutton Hoo Ship Burial*, vol.III, part 2, edited by R. Bruce-Mitford, 1983, pp.945-61.

[96] M. M. Archibald and M. R. Cowell, 'The fineness of Northumbrian sceattas', *Metallurgy in Numismatics* 2 (1988), 55-64, at p.58.

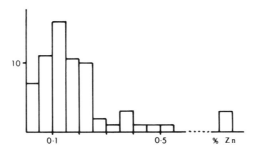

FIG.26   Zinc contents, for primary sceattas.

zinc than the English primary sceattas (Fig. 26).

An inspection of all the analytical results suggests that corrosion and leaching normally result in severe depletion of zinc contents. That tendency adds an element of uncertainty to the interpretation of specimens of Series Y in which a low gold : silver ratio correlates with very low zinc.

The extraordinarily high zinc content and low tin content of a well-known specimen of Series Z, taken together with its abnormally high weight (1.44g), cast doubt on its authenticity. Its silver contents are only 56 per cent, where one would have expected *c.*90 per cent (from other specimens of Series Z). Two other examples, *from the same dies, and also excessively heavy,* were in the Morel-Fatio collection and have been presumed to come from the Cimiez hoard. All three may be nineteenth-century forgeries. But a fourth coin (now in Cardiff) makes matters a little more complicated, because it is from different dies. It, too, contains just 56 per cent silver (!), and has abnormally high zinc and low tin contents (see Fig. 23), but weighs only 0.91g.[97] So far, so good, but here is the rub: the forger's inspiration (if we are correct in condemning these coins) cannot have come from the line-drawing published by Marie de Man in the *Tijdschrift voor Munt- en Penningkunde* in 1895 as something new — because Chabouillet's catalogue of the Morel-Fatio coins was published in 1890. The authenticity of the type is now perfectly well established from recent finds of known provenance.

30. *Lead*

Traces of lead are always left in silver after cupellation. The amount will depend on how thoroughly the cupellation was carried out. If lead entered the coinage metal only in association with refined silver in this way, it would be natural to expect that lead:silver ratios would be more or less independent of silver contents. If on the other hand lead also entered the alloy along with bronze, or copper, or both one might expect to be able to construct a model of total lead contents, e.g. if lead:silver and lead:copper/bronze ratios were the same, the interaction would yield a straight-line graph with uniform lead contents whatever the silver contents

[97] For a corpus, see *BNJ* 56 (1986), 12. The coins in question are nos.1-4.

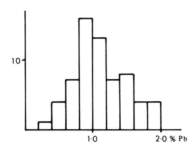

FIG.27   Lead contents, for primary sceattas.

of the coins. Lead contents in fact increase from *c.*1.0 per cent in the primary sceattas (Fig. 27), towards 1.5-2 per cent in the more debased secondary sceattas. If all the lead were regarded as being in association with the copper, the ratios plotted against declining silver contents would rise more or less in a straight line from *c.*1.0 to *c.*2.5 at 67% silver, *c.*3.5 at 50% silver, *c.*5 at 33% silver, to *c.*7 at 10% silver and eventually even higher. Such a pattern cannot sensibly be interpreted as arising merely from careless cupellation, and points us towards a two-source theory, the bronze containing a rather higher level of lead than the silver.

31. *Iron, antimony, cobalt, and nickel*

Iron and antimony each show a clear positive correlation with copper. Iron contents are also enhanced in corroded coins. Cobalt and nickel show no such correlations.

Electron probe micro analysis performed by Dr. J. P. Northover in the Department of Materials, Oxford. For each coin, the results are the mean averages of readings taken at three points on a polished section of the edge, selected to avoid any obvious corrosion. Where the results appeared to be consistent and satisfactory, they were adjusted to 100%. Where it was apparent that there was some corrosion and leaching, the results were corrected in which case *the silver value is as measured*, but zinc, tin, and copper values have been adjusted by calculation. Tin has been reduced and copper increased in an attempt to compensate for corrosion of the copper-rich phase.

In a few instances of severe corrosion, no attempt was made to adjust the measurements, which may add up to considerably less than 100%.

'Silver' consists of the sum of values for silver, lead, and gold, as an approximation to what is likely to have been perceived as the silver content of the alloy by moneyers and others at the time when the sceattas were made and used.

A further 62 EPMA analyses by Dr. Northover, performed in the same way, are published in P. Andrews, *The Coins and Pottery from Hamwic*, Southampton, 1988, pp.34-5. They are not included below except for a few coins of Series H

Cat.no.	Fe	Co	Ni	Cu	Zn	Bi	Sb
'Witmen' type							
E.001	0.05	0.02	0.02	2.00	0.04	—	—
'Two emperors' type							
80	0.02	—	—	3.78	1.20	—	—
E.002	0.04	0.01	tr.	3.19	0.04	—	—
Series Pa							
IA,2	0.03	—	—	3.40	0.17	(—)	—
81	0.02#	0.01#	—	2.94	0.04	(—)	—
E.003	0.36	tr.	tr.	0.81	0.02	—	—
E.004	0.04	—	0.01	2.67	0.03	—	—
82	0.01	—	tr.	5.11	0.34#	—	0.01
Series Va							
84	0.01#	tr.	0.01	3.33	0.08	(—)	—
85	—	—	—	3.52	0.05	0.04	—
86	0.07	0.01	0.01	5.47	2.53	0.05	—
87	0.04	tr.	—	4.06	0.09#	0.03	0.02

ANALYSES

which are in the Oxford collections and in the catalogue. As well as the catalogued coins, the list below includes coins from the National Museum of Wales, Cardiff, and from Caister-by-Yarmouth, and one or two other sites, analysed in Oxford.

—	measured, but not detected.
tr	trace
#, ⋆	corrosion present or inhomogeneity; result probably inaccurate
§	corrected
( )	severe corrosion; uncorrected

Limits of detection. Fe Kα, 0.01. Co Kα, 0.01%. Ni Kα, 0.01%. Cu Kα, 0.01%. Zn Lα, 0.03%. Bi Mα, 0.02%. Sb Lα, 0.02%. Sn Lα, 0.02%. Ag Lα, 0.02%. Pb Mα, 0.04%. Au Mα, 0.04%.

Sn	Ag	Pb	Au	'Silver'	Au:Ag	Pb:Ag	Cat.no.
—	45.04	0.27	52.55	—	—	—	E.001
—	67.53	0.43	21.84	—	—	—	80
—	62.91	0.36	33.47	—	—	—	E.002
—	77.53	0.81	18.05	—	—	—	IA,2
—	77.15	0.07	20.03	—	—	—	81
—	79.06	0.11	19.63	—	—	—	E.003
—	83.24	1.04	12.96	—	—	—	E.004
1.18	89.89	1.74	1.70	93.33	1.89	1.93	82
—	88.52	0.29	8.10	—	—	—	84
—	93.07	1.39	1.93	96.39	2.07	1.49	85
—	90.62	0.95	0.71	92.28	0.78	1.05	86
0.46	94.13	0.64	0.52	§95.29	0.55	0.68	87

Cat.no.	Fe	Co	Ni	Cu	Zn	Bi	Sb
Series A							
88	0.02	0.01	0.01	4.00	—	(—)	tr.
89	tr.	tr.	tr.	4.31	0.04	0.02	—
90	tr.	—	tr.	5.53	0.01	0.04	—
91	tr.	0.01	0.01	5.04	0.18	0.02	—
92	0.02	—	tr.	5.46	0.15	0.05	tr.
95	0.02	tr.	0.01#	6.37	0.45#	tr.	—
Series B							
97	0.03	tr.	tr.	3.52	0.11#	0.05	—
98	0.03	0.02	0.02	4.30	0.09	0.02#	—
100	0.03	—	—	5.43	0.11	0.01	—
101	tr.	—	—	4.97	0.16	0.04	—
102	tr.	—	—	6.84	0.36	0.04	tr.
103	tr.	—	tr.	4.44	0.18#	0.03	tr.
104	0.01	tr.	0.02	5.51	0.14	0.01	—
106	tr.	tr.	0.01	5.16	0.31	(0.08)	—
Caister	0.02	tr.	tr.	5.05	0.39	0.03	tr.
Series C							
117	0.02	—	—	5.69	0.13	0.01	—
118	0.01	—	0.01	4.71	0.39#	0.02#	—
119	0.01	tr.	0.02	5.69	0.26#	0.01	—
120	0.01	0.01	—	5.52	0.46#	0.05	tr.
121	—	tr.	—	6.90	0.25#	0.09	—
122	0.03	—	—	5.45	0.13	0.03	tr.
123	0.04	tr.	tr.	5.03	0.08#	0.04	tr.
124	0.02	0.01	tr.	6.49	0.18	0.06	tr.
125	0.02	—	0.01	6.36	0.08	0.03	—
128	0.02	tr.	tr.	4.80	0.03	0.03	—
130	0.01	tr.	0.01	5.22	0.21	0.06	tr.
131	0.01	0.01	—	7.70	0.15	0.06	tr.
132	0.06#	tr.	—	5.29	0.11	0.05	tr.
Runic porcupines reading Æthiliraêd							
134	0.01	—	0.01	13.19	0.39#	0.01	—
135	0.04	—	tr.	11.04	0.19*	0.07	0.02
Series F							
136	tr.	—	0.02	8.56#	0.16	0.05	tr.
137	0.01	tr.	—	4.71	0.18	0.05	tr.
Series Z, Type 66							
140	—	—	—	4.96	0.03	—	—
141	0.01	—	0.01	4.25	—	0.02	—
—, 'Aston Rowant' type							
143	tr.	tr.	0.02#	10.99	0.11	0.01	—

Sn	Ag	Pb	Au	'Silver'	Au:Ag	Pb:Ag	Cat.no.
—	82.91	0.80	12.25	—	—	—	88
—	93.97	1.00	1.10	96.07	1.17	1.06	89
—	91.36	0.82	2.22	94.40	2.43	0.90	90
—	93.25	0.81	0.67	94.73	0.72	0.87	91
—	93.03	0.61	0.68	94.32	0.73	0.66	92
—	92.04	0.51	0.56	93.11	0.61	0.55	95
—	94.27	1.50	0.67	96.44	0.71	1.59	97
—	93.34	1.57	0.63	95.54	0.67	1.68	98
—	92.64	0.84	0.92	94.40	0.99	0.91	100
—	93.43	0.62	0.77	94.82	0.82	0.66	101
—	90.76	0.72	1.27	92.75	1.40	0.79	102
—	93.51	0.99	0.85	95.35	0.91	1.06	103
—	92.23	0.88	1.15	94.26	1.25	0.95	104
—	89.91	1.35	3.16	94.42	3.51	1.50	106
—	93.37	0.80	0.33	94.50	0.35	0.86	Caister
—	92.83	1.05	0.25	94.13	0.27	1.13	117
—	93.40	0.80#	0.67	94.87	0.72	0.86	118
—	92.15	0.89	0.97	94.01	1.05	0.97	119
—	91.95	1.07	0.91	93.93	0.99	1.16	120
—	90.67	1.33	0.65	92.65	0.72	1.47	121
0.27	91.60	1.00	1.48	94.08	1.62	1.09	122
—	93.32	0.62	0.85	94.79	0.91	0.66	123
—	91.19	0.71	1.33	93.23	1.46	0.78	124
—	91.43	1.01	1.07	93.51	1.17	1.10	125
—	93.42	0.84	0.86	95.12	0.92	0.90	128
—	92.70	0.69	1.13	94.52	1.22	0.74	130
—	90.30	0.85	0.90	92.05	1.00	0.94	131
—	92.29	0.95	1.22#	94.46	1.32	1.03	132
0.59	83.58	1.15	1.08	85.81	1.29	1.38	134
0.86*	84.61	1.59	1.58*	§87.78	1.86	1.88	135
tr.	89.37	0.66	1.08	91.11	1.21	0.74	136
—	93.11	1.29	0.64	95.04	0.69	1.39	137
—	93.22	0.45	1.33	95.00	1.43	0.48	140
—	93.74	0.48	1.49	95.71	1.58	0.51	141
0.08	86.58	0.96	1.15	88.69	1.33	1.11	143

Cat.no.	Fe	Co	Ni	Cu	Zn	Bi	Sb
144	tr.	tr.	—	5.59	tr.	0.04	—
145	0.01	—	tr.	8.93	0.05	tr.	—
The Vernus groups							
147	0.01	tr.	—	5.33	0.43	0.03	0.03
149	0.03	0.01	—	4.62	0.34	0.03	—
The Saroaldo type							
154	0.09	0.01	0.04	49.97	1.41	tr.	0.06
Series W							
155	0.02	tr.	0.01#	3.53	0.07	0.06	—
Type B III A.							
156	0.02	—	0.02	14.13	0.37	0.01#	0.01#
157	0.01	—	tr.	3.95	0.19	0.02#	0.01
Series D							
158	0.03	—	—	4.98	0.07	0.03	tr.
160	0.02	—	0.01	4.79	0.04	0.02	—
163	tr.	tr.	0.02	6.01	0.14	tr.	—
164	0.01	tr.	—	4.15	0.07	0.02	—
165	0.01	0.01	—	4.52	0.23	0.04	0.01
166	0.01	—	tr.	7.30	0.20#	0.04	tr.
167	tr.	0.01	0.01	12.77#	0.19#	0.05	—
168	0.01	tr.	—	13.17#	0.06	0.02	0.01
169	0.02	—	tr.	4.00	0.09	0.03#	—
170	0.08*	—	0.02	4.27	0.03	0.02	0.01
171	0.02	—	—	3.63	0.21	0.02	0.01
172	0.01	tr.	tr.	8.38	0.14	0.02	—
173	0.03	—	0.02	28.06	0.23	0.03	0.01
174	0.03	tr.	tr.	14.80#	3.81#	0.07	0.01
175	0.02	—	—	5.00	0.13	0.03	0.01
176	0.04	0.02	0.01	4.97#	0.09	0.02	tr.
183	0.01	—	—	6.23	0.16	0.01	—
184	tr.	—	0.02	4.89	0.13	0.04	tr.
185	0.04	—	tr.	12.55	0.18	0.05	tr.
186	(0.07	0.01	—	77.54	0.04	tr.	0.04
"	0.01	—	—	15.20	0.13	0.01	0.04
187	tr.	tr.	—	4.38	0.03	(0.06)	—
E.005	tr.	tr.	—	7.23	0.02	tr.	0.01
Caister	0.03	—	0.01	5.36	0.28	0.02	—
Series E: early varieties							
190	(0.02	0.02	—	5.51	0.12	0.04	0.01
192	0.03	0.01	0.01	3.61	0.07	0.03	tr.
193	(0.02	tr.	—	3.69	0.07	0.04	—
E.010	0.05	0.02	—	11.37	0.18	tr.	0.02

Sn	Ag	Pb	Au	'Silver'	Au:Ag	Pb:Ag	Cat.no.
—	92.73	0.63	1.03	94.39	1.11	0.68	144
—	88.71	0.90	1.37	90.98	1.54	1.01	145
0.12	92.31	1.14	0.57	94.02	0.62	1.23	147
—	93.07	1.08	0.81	94.96	0.87	1.16	149
3.80	42.07	1.95	0.61	44.63	1.45	4.63	154
0.16	93.95	0.90	1.30#	96.15	1.38	0.96	155
0.14	83.18	0.97	1.15	85.30	1.38	1.17	156
0.18	93.37	0.81	1.45#	95.63	1.55	0.87	157
—	92.56	0.79	1.53	94.88	1.65	0.85	158
0.06	93.32	0.57	1.17	95.06	1.25	0.61	160
—	91.25	0.90	1.67	93.82	1.83	0.99	163
1.08	91.77	1.21	1.01	93.99	1.10	1.32	164
0.39	93.15	0.81	0.83	94.79	0.89	0.87	165
—	90.45	0.85	1.14	92.44	1.26	0.94	166
0.94	83.89	1.01	1.12	86.02	1.34	1.20	167
1.01	84.32	0.74	0.66	85.72	0.78	0.88	168
—	93.33	0.81	1.70	95.84	1.82	0.87	169
0.04	94.08	0.77	0.67	95.52	0.71	0.82	170
0.45	93.70	0.86	1.11	95.67	1.18	0.92	171
1.22	87.65	1.12	1.43	90.20	1.63	1.28	172
2.39	67.00	1.32	0.90	69.22	1.34	1.97	173
—	79.34	1.35	0.59	81.28	0.74	1.70	174
0.95*	91.13	1.38	1.35	§93.86	1.48	1.51	175
—	92.95	0.77	1.09	§94.81	1.17	0.83	176
—	91.49	0.80	1.30	93.59	1.42	0.87	183
—	92.72	1.06	1.12	94.90	1.21	1.14	184
0.06#	85.76	0.76	0.53	87.05	0.62	0.88	185
0.12	5.22#	0.10	0.10)	—	—	—	core
—	82.72	1.06	0.84	84.62	1.02	1.28	surface
0.02#	92.49	0.71	2.29	95.49	2.48	0.77	187
—	90.55	0.72	1.42	92.69	1.57	0.80	E.005
—	91.00	0.70	2.60	94.30	2.85	0.77	Caister
1.73*	90.51	1.35	1.26)	93.12	1.39	1.49	190
—	93.97	1.06	1.21	§96.24	1.29	1.13	192
0.02	93.14	1.40	1.61#)	96.15	1.72	1.50	193
0.18	84.95	1.82	1.39	88.16	1.64	2.14	E.010

Cat.no.	Fe	Co	Ni	Cu	Zn	Bi	Sb
194	0.02	—	0.02	4.42	0.17	0.04	—
195	0.10*	—	tr.	4.41	0.24	tr.	tr.
196	tr.	—	0.01	4.18	0.25	0.03	—
198	tr.	—	—	5.45	0.24	0.04	—
199	tr.	—	tr.	26.03	0.22	0.06	0.02
200	0.02	—	—	6.66	0.52#	0.03	—
201	0.01	0.01	0.02	4.17	0.15	0.02	—
202	—	0.02	—	4.69	0.23#	0.03	—
204	0.02	0.01	0.01	5.13	0.19	0.02	—
205	—	—	tr.	5.67	0.13	0.03	—
206	tr.	—	0.01#	5.50	0.13	tr.	—
207	0.08	—	—	5.22	0.78	0.02	0.01
209	0.03	—	0.04	5.33	0.08#	0.06	0.02
210	—	0.01	0.01	11.61#	0.28	0.02	0.01
211	0.01	—	—	4.15	0.21	0.03	—
213	tr.	—	—	4.86	0.10	0.05	—

Series E: Kloster Barthe varieties

Cat.no.	Fe	Co	Ni	Cu	Zn	Bi	Sb
214	0.03	—	—	5.61	0.22	0.02	0.01
215	0.01	—	tr.	8.04	0.28	0.02	0.01
216	0.40*	—	0.01#	4.16	0.11	0.05	tr.
218	(0.25	—	tr.	9.12	0.17	tr.	0.03
219	(0.04	—	—	6.31	0.13	0.07	0.02
223	0.01	tr.	0.02	27.66	0.30	0.04	0.02
224	0.07	—	tr.	4.17	0.11	0.04	0.01
225	0.02	0.01	0.01	6.52	0.22#	0.03	—
226	0.02	0.02	0.02	28.40	0.61	0.03	0.03
230	—	0.02	0.01	11.33	0.15	0.04	—
231	0.02#	0.01	0.02	7.34	0.26	0.04	—
234	0.01	—	—	14.01	0.24	0.06	0.01
240	0.02	—	0.01	17.62	0.10	0.01	0.01
241	0.02	—	tr.	30.31	0.50	0.05	0.03
242	0.01	0.01	—	10.48	0.13	0.03	tr.
243	0.05	—	0.02	10.15	0.16	0.03	—
"	0.04	—	0.02	1.70	0.07	—	—
245	0.01#	—	0.01	16.14	0.08	0.03	tr.
246	0.02	tr.	0.03	24.69	0.19	tr.	—
247	0.04	—	0.03	31.54	0.56	0.01	0.02
250	(4.30	tr.	—	3.94	0.11	0.02#	0.03
251	0.06	—	0.02	47.70	1.37	tr.	0.04
252	0.18	0.02	0.04	62.35	3.43	0.01#	0.07
E.009	0.01	tr.	0.01	20.06	0.28	0.03	—

Sn	Ag	Pb	Au	'Silver'	Au:Ag	Pb:Ag	Cat.no.
—	92.47	1.12	1.77#	95.36	1.91	1.21	194
—	93.29	0.49	1.43	§95.21	1.53	0.52	195
—	93.52	0.97	1.03	95.52	1.10	1.04	196
—	92.12	0.90#	1.22	94.24	1.32	0.98	198
1.76	69.78	1.37	0.75	71.90	1.07	1.96	199
—	90.56	1.07	1.12	92.75	1.24	1.18	200
—	93.22	1.19	1.20	95.61	1.29	1.28	201
—	92.97	1.20	0.85	95.02	0.91	1.29	202
—	91.92	1.72	1.03	§94.67	1.12	1.87	204
—	92.27	1.04	0.86	94.17	0.93	1.13	205
—	92.40	0.88	1.06	94.34	1.15	0.95	206
—	92.31	0.45	1.13	§93.89	1.22	0.49	207
tr.	91.87	0.92	1.67#	94.46	1.82	1.00	209
0.29	85.79	1.02	0.96	87.77	1.12	1.19	210
—	93.49	0.92	1.16	95.57	1.24	0.98	211
—	92.65	0.90	1.43	94.98	1.54	0.97	213
—	91.78	0.92	1.41	94.11	1.54	1.00	214
0.16	89.07	1.06	1.32	91.45	1.48	1.19	215
0.63	92.14	1.19	1.31	94.64	1.42	1.29	216
4.40	80.45	2.59	1.33)	84.37	1.65	3.22	218
1.34*	89.63	1.26	1.19)	92.08	1.33	1.41	219
2.08	68.08	0.94	0.87	69.89	1.28	1.38	223
0.70*	91.51	0.78	2.50	94.79	2.73	0.85	224
—	90.71	1.24	1.24	93.19	1.37	1.37	225
1.70	66.90	1.45	0.83	69.18	1.24	2.17	226
0.06	86.48	0.84	1.07	88.39	1.23	0.97	230
—	90.42	0.95	0.92	92.29	1.02	1.05	231
1.15	81.92	1.38	1.21	84.51	1.48	1.68	234
1.18	79.71	0.74	0.60	81.05	0.75	0.93	240
1.83	65.31	1.17	0.79	67.27	1.21	1.79	241
1.15	85.81	1.20	1.17	88.18	1.36	1.40	242
1.01	86.82	0.45	1.31	88.58	1.51	0.52	243
3.11	93.55	0.07	1.45	—	surface enrichment		"
—	81.49	0.75	1.49	83.73	1.83	0.92	245
1.81#	70.95	1.46	0.96	73.37	1.35	2.06	246
3.52	62.33	0.95	1.01	64.29	1.62	1.52	247
4.32	74.23	1.84	1.42)	77.49	corroded		250
4.68	44.57	1.00	0.56	46.13	1.26	2.24	251
4.43	27.37	1.75	0.39	29.51	1.42	6.39	252
0.62	76.72	1.04	1.22	78.98	1.59	1.36	E.009

Cat.no.	Fe	Co	Ni	Cu	Zn	Bi	Sb
Series E: Franeker varieties							
255	0.01	tr.	0.01	17.32	0.20	0.05	0.03
256	tr.	0.01	0.02	9.26	0.19	0.04	tr.
257	0.09	tr.	0.04	52.83	1.70	tr.	0.07
Series E: Type 53							
258	0.01	—	0.02	21.65	0.54	0.02	0.01
259	0.03	tr.	tr.	5.05	1.23	0.03	0.02
260	0.03	—	tr.	6.00	0.38#	0.03	—
261	0.02	tr.	0.02	5.81	0.19	tr.	tr.
262	0.01	tr.	—	9.05	0.37	0.05	tr.
Series E: Type 4 var.							
263	0.01	tr.	0.01	7.94	0.21	0.01	0.02
Series E: Type 12/5							
264	0.17	0.01	0.03	67.08	2.19	0.01	0.06
Type 10							
E.006	tr.	tr.	tr.	3.90	0.02	tr.	—
The 'Maastricht' type							
265	0.06	—	0.01#	53.33#	0.38	0.03	0.07
266	0.06	—	—	23.18	0.25	0.04	0.04
Series G							
267	0.12*	tr.	—	4.61	0.29	0.03	tr.
268	0.04	—	0.01#	5.39	0.22	0.02#	—
Series G: imitative varieties							
271	0.41*	—	0.02	56.37	2.59	0.03	0.09
272	0.20	0.01	0.03	72.74	0.97	0.02	0.08
273	0.20	0.01	0.04	48.25	3.27	0.04	0.05
274	0.11	tr.	0.01	55.09	5.16	0.05	0.05
Series X							
275	tr.	—	tr.	11.65	1.12	0.02#	0.02
276	0.02	tr.	tr.	2.16	0.17	0.02	0.03
277	(0.13	—	—	1.92	0.10	0.04	0.01
278	0.04	—	0.03	38.88	0.63*	—	0.05
280	0.05	—	0.01#	33.69	0.47#	0.02	0.03
281	0.07	0.01	—	1.99	0.14	0.02	tr.
E.024	0.45	—	0.02	2.13	0.51	—	0.01
Secondary sceattas							
Series H							
285	0.83#	tr.	—	17.05	1.07	—	0.07
Series H, Type 48							
289	(0.62	tr.	tr.	18.09	0.64	—	0.06
292	0.09	tr.	0.03	46.83	2.62	—	0.03

Sn	Ag	Pb	Au	'Silver'	Au:Ag	Pb:Ag	Cat.no.
0.38	80.03	1.04	0.98	82.05	1.22	1.30	255
—	88.58	0.76	1.09	90.43	1.23	0.86	256
3.15	39.99	1.56	0.57	42.12	1.42	3.90	257
1.74	73.04	1.85	0.82	error?	—	—	258
tr.	91.59	0.78	1.26	93.63	1.38	0.85	259
—	91.84	1.18	0.86	93.88	0.94	1.28	260
—	91.52	1.15	1.28	93.95	1.40	1.26	261
0.04	88.21	1.62	0.63	90.46	0.71	1.84	262
0.25	88.82	1.11	1.55	91.48	1.75	1.25	263
5.61	23.31	1.11	0.38	24.80	1.63	4.76	264
—	93.47	0.97	1.61	96.05	1.72	1.04	E.006
1.12#	43.67#	1.00	0.32	44.99	0.73	2.29	265
2.77	71.42	1.19	1.06	73.67	1.48	1.67	266
—	93.21	0.59	1.14	94.94	1.22	0.63	267
0.67	91.33	0.95	1.36	93.64	1.49	1.04	268
5.80	32.00	2.18	0.51	34.69	1.59	6.81	271
6.57	18.29	0.92	0.17	19.38	0.93	5.03	272
3.11	42.52	1.86	0.64	45.02	1.51	4.37	273
2.31	35.21	1.46	0.52	37.19	1.48	4.15	274
0.56	84.90	0.50	1.23	86.63	1.45	0.59	275
1.74*	93.20	1.15	1.50	95.85?	1.61	1.23	276
2.80	85.45	1.27	1.15)	87.87	1.35	1.49	277
4.44	53.15	2.15	0.65*	55.95	1.22	4.05	278
3.17	61.50	1.10	0.85	63.45	1.38	1.79	280
2.42	92.87	1.10	1.38	95.35?	1.49	1.18	281
0.89	93.66	0.63	1.65	95.94	1.76	0.67	E.024
4.77	71.99	2.94	1.38	76.31	1.92	4.08	285
9.84	46.15	3.60	1.13)	50.88	2.45	7.80	289
3.28	44.55	1.82	0.73	47.10	1.64	4.08	292

Cat.no.	Fe	Co	Ni	Cu	Zn	Bi	Sb
Series J: Types 85 and 37							
293	0.03	—	tr.	8.66	0.53	0.03	0.02
294	0.01	0.02	0.02	97.17	0.10	0.02	0.17
"	(0.15	—	0.02	23.22	0.27	0.04	0.23
E.030	(0.33	tr.	—	3.73	2.03	—	0.02
296	0.01	—	tr.	18.97	0.55	0.05	tr.
297	0.02	—	—	8.41	0.22	0.03	0.03
298	0.05	—	tr.	5.51	0.51	tr.	0.03
299	0.03	—	—	6.74	0.33	0.02	tr.
E.012	0.19	tr.	0.04	76.58	1.80	—	0.08
Caister	0.10	0.01	0.01	36.76	1.98	—	0.05
Series J: Type 36							
301	0.09	—	—	36.42	0.40	0.02	0.04
N.Elmham	0.01	—	0.02	98.49	0.80	0.01	0.02
"	0.03	0.01	0.03	76.37	1.02	—	0.01
"	0.02	—	0.02	58.18	0.54	tr.	0.08
Type B III C							
304	0.11	—	0.01#	4.47	0.34	0.03	0.04
Series K: Type 33							
306	0.08#	—	—	10.75	0.68	0.06	0.06
Series K: Type 32 (imitations)							
307	0.12	0.01	0.03	56.99	2.26	0.02	0.06
308	(0.22	—	0.03	45.92	0.43	—	0.10
"	(0.19	—	—	7.31	1.96	—	0.05
309	(0.19	0.03	tr.	26.59	0.78	0.05	0.07
Series K: Type 42							
311	0.34*	0.01	—	11.24	0.54	0.02	0.05
312	0.06	—	0.01	35.57	0.74#	0.04	0.03
E.014	(0.10	tr.	tr.	13.67	0.38	—	0.04
Series K: Type 20							
314	0.07	0.01	0.01	42.05	1.90	0.01#	0.03
315	0.07	0.01	0.03	47.12	2.22	0.02#	0.03
316	(0.76	—	0.02	20.43	2.15	—	0.17
"	(0.58	tr.	tr.	5.62	1.30	tr.	0.14
Series K: Type 20/18							
317	0.07	—	0.04	48.01	1.66	0.02	0.04
318	0.15	—	0.03	60.95	1.54	—	0.06
Series L: Type 12							
319	0.08	—	tr.	43.53#	0.83	0.02	0.05
320	(0.28	—	0.03	43.12	3.46	0.01	0.12
321	0.11	—	tr.	46.29	0.46	0.01#	0.08
E.029	(0.35	—	0.01	28.59	1.11	tr.	0.07

Sn	Ag	Pb	Au	'Silver'	Au:Ag	Pb:Ag	Cat.no.
1.59	86.56	1.31	1.27	89.14	1.47	1.51	293
1.09	0.74	0.55	0.02	—	—	—	294
1.98	37.86	4.62	0.90)	43.38	corroded	plating	"
2.46	78.74	1.43	1.05)	81.22	1.33	1.82	E.030
1.96	75.86	1.70	0.95	78.51	1.25	2.24	296
0.88	87.94	1.44	1.03	90.41	1.17	1.64	297
1.93*	88.91	1.69	1.22	91.82	1.37	1.90	298
1.35	88.19	2.14	1.16	91.49	1.32	2.43	299
7.58	10.72	2.85	0.15	13.72	1.40	26.59	E.012
2.16	57.10	1.55	1.27	59.92	2.22	2.71	Caister
3.11	55.18	2.26	1.07	58.51	1.94	4.10	301
0.08	0.39	0.14	0.04	core	—	—	N.Elmham
1.43	20.32	0.44	0.35	surface 1	—	—	"
2.59	36.90	1.19	0.38	surface 2	—	—	"
3.08	88.61	1.69	1.69	91.99	1.91	1.91	304
2.58	82.23	1.96	1.58	85.77	1.92	2.38	306
3.98	34.92	1.20	0.47	36.59	1.35	3.44	307
4.61	32.62	2.00	0.62)	bulk, corroded			308
4.14	70.35	2.92	0.29)	surface, corroded			"
5.63	47.90	1.78	0.94)	50.62	1.96	3.71	309
1.58	82.75	2.00	1.44	86.19	1.74	2.42	311
3.30	55.61	1.60	1.05	58.26	1.89	2.88	312
3.97	69.20	1.86	1.13)	72.19	1.63	2.69	E.014
2.19	51.56	1.43	0.73	53.72	1.42	2.77	314
2.95	45.61	1.39	0.55	47.55	1.21	3.05	315
11.59	35.39	2.88	1.36)	39.63	3.84	8.14	316
9.23	56.32	2.42	1.35)	60.09	2.40	4.30	"
3.14	44.80	1.54	0.66	47.00	1.47	3.44	317
5.19	30.10	1.53	0.46	32.09	1.53	5.08	318
4.24	48.96	1.55	0.75	51.26	1.53	3.16	319
7.75	25.99	1.50	0.57)	28.06	2.19	5.78	320
5.37	44.71	2.17	0.78	47.66	1.74	4.85	321
5.91	45.43	2.35	1.14	48.92	2.51	5.17	E.029

Cat.no.	Fe	Co	Ni	Cu	Zn	Bi	Sb
Series L: Types 15-19							
324	0.18	0.01	0.05	75.73	2.04	0.03	0.08
325	0.26	0.01	0.08	81.39	0.92	0.02	0.07
329	0.14	—	0.03	78.22#	0.26	0.01	0.05
330	0.21	0.01	0.02	69.61	2.53	0.03	0.08
332	0.29	tr.	0.03	71.84	0.91	—	0.08
E.016	0.19	tr.	0.03	70.63	3.80	—	0.07
E.017	(0.67	—	0.01	12.31	1.06	—	0.11
Eclectic groups related to Series K and L							
336	0.15	0.01	0.03	62.17	2.82	tr.	0.05
338	0.16	—	0.03	59.32	2.18	tr.	0.05
340	0.09	—	0.04	83.33	1.19	—	0.05
342	0.15	—	tr.	38.35	0.58	tr.	0.06
343	0.10	0.01	0.03	48.21	0.90	0.01	0.06
344	0.08	—	0.01	41.26#	0.73#	0.03	0.05
345	0.18	—	0.02	54.15	0.45	0.03	0.09
346	0.20	—	0.04	68.10	9.68	—	0.06
350	0.17	—	—	41.03	0.27	0.02	0.06
351	0.09	—	0.05	56.23	1.27	0.02	0.07
353	0.24	0.02	0.04	68.18	3.21	tr.	0.09
355	0.12*	0.01	0.05	65.27	1.78	tr.	0.04
357	0.05	—	0.02	35.69	1.50	0.04	0.03
359	0.10	0.03	0.05	61.51	2.63	—	0.07
362	0.19	0.01	0.02	67.75	4.24	0.02	0.07
Series M							
364	0.06	—	0.02	42.41	0.43	0.04	0.01
365	0.12*	—	tr.	27.52#	0.50	0.01	0.02
366	0.04	—	0.01#	41.41	1.04	0.01	0.05
367	(0.18	0.01	—	1.69	0.34	0.04	0.07
Series N							
368	0.04	—	tr.	45.76	0.68	—	0.03
369	0.06	0.02	0.04	96.27	0.13	0.02	0.06
"	(0.15	—	0.01	45.12	0.09	0.02	0.11
371	0.01	—	—	98.12	0.10	0.02	0.04
"	(—	—	0.01	55.14	0.10	0.05	0.02
372	0.10*	0.01	0.03	47.58	0.52	—	0.03
Series O							
373	0.02	0.01	tr.	5.86	0.06	0.03	—
375	0.11	0.01	—	35.41	0.70	0.03	0.07
377	0.02	—	—	39.55	0.37	0.05	0.04

Sn	Ag	Pb	Au	'Silver'	Au:Ag	Pb:Ag	Cat.no.
6.22	14.41	1.01	0.26	15.68	1.80	7.01	324
9.63	6.72	0.80	0.12	7.64	1.79	11.90	325
6.74	13.32#	0.90#	0.34	14.56	2.55	6.76	329
5.62	20.19	1.43	0.29	21.91	1.44	7.08	330
6.60	17.16	2.84	0.26	20.26	1.52	16.55	332
4.33	19.68	0.98	0.27	20.93	1.37	4.98	E.016
9.18	28.28	1.26	0.74)	30.28	2.62	4.46	E.017
3.90	29.06	1.42	0.38	30.86	1.31	4.89	336
3.57	32.81	1.35	0.54	34.70	1.65	4.11	338
8.75	5.32	1.11	0.13	6.56	2.44	20.86	340
5.97*	51.78	1.93	1.08	54.79	2.09	3.73	342
3.94	44.58	1.78	0.71	47.07	1.59	3.89	343
3.97#*	51.44#	1.57	0.88#	§53.89	1.71	3.05	344
7.72*	33.72	3.02	0.60	§37.34	1.78	8.96	345
2.99	17.89	0.73	0.32	18.94	1.79	4.08	346
4.54	51.03	1.91	0.96	§53.90	1.80	3.74	350
5.27	34.72	1.57	0.70	36.99	2.02	4.52	351
6.55	20.42	0.96	0.28	21.66	1.37	4.70	353
4.95	26.21	1.19	0.34	27.74	1.30	4.54	355
2.70	56.86	1.62	0.86	59.34	1.51	2.85	357
4.32	29.75	1.17	0.39	31.31	1.31	3.93	359
3.76	22.48	1.06	0.39	23.93	1.73	4.72	362
5.98	48.67	1.71	0.66	51.04	1.36	3.51	364
3.20	65.94	1.66	1.01	68.61	1.53	2.52	365
4.18*	50.90	1.59	0.78	53.27	1.53	3.12	366
4.66	70.43	2.39	1.08)	73.90	1.53	3.39	367
4.39	46.80	1.72	0.58	§49.10	1.24	3.68	368
2.33	0.11	0.99	—	core	—	—	369
7.63	0.70	1.34	0.09)	surface	—	—	"
1.04	0.35	0.32	—	core	—	—	371
1.39	26.03	0.68	0.25)	surface	—	—	"
3.96	46.08	1.07	0.59	47.74	1.28	2.32	372
—	92.65	0.24	1.12	94.01	1.21	0.26	373
3.13	58.08	1.55	0.89	§60.52	1.53	2.66	375
3.34	54.11	1.79	0.73	56.63	1.35	3.31	377

Cat.no.	Fe	Co	Ni	Cu	Zn	Bi	Sb
Series O, Type 40							
378	0.02	—	0.02	36.01	1.55	tr.	0.03
379	0.03	0.02	0.02	38.48	1.55	0.01	tr.
380	0.08	tr.	0.02	46.75	0.90	0.01#	0.06
381	0.36*#	tr.	0.02	27.35	0.66	tr.	0.03
Series Q							
382	0.06*	—	—	14.97	0.13	0.01	0.03
383	0.02	—	0.01	12.29	0.06	0.05	—
384	0.12	—	0.02	26.87#	0.49	0.03	0.05
385	0.11*	—	0.01	23.69	0.11	0.02	0.03
L.Sutton	0.06	0.01	tr.	20.95	0.10	0.03	0.03
Brandon							
386	0.17	tr.	0.04	66.68	1.35	0.04	0.07
387	0.13	—	0.02	61.95	1.73	0.02	0.04
Brandon							
Brandon							
Brandon							
Series R: R1 and R2							
391	—	tr.	—	4.45	0.09	0.03	—
392	—	—	0.01	7.44	0.01	0.01	0.01
393	—	—	—	9.12	0.02	0.02#	tr.
394	0.02	0.01	0.02	11.61	0.24	0.03	tr.
395	0.28*	tr.	tr.	3.75	0.22	0.05	0.01
E.031	0.03	—	—	6.15	0.09	—	tr.
Series R: R3 to R7							
396	0.08*	—	tr.	5.24	0.24	0.03#	—
397	tr.	—	0.01#	23.49#	0.92	0.02	0.01
398	0.02	—	0.01#	17.65	1.33#	0.01	0.02
399	0.04	0.01#	0.02	34.93	1.29	0.02	0.02
401	0.06	—	—	7.62	0.25*	0.01	0.01
402	0.13	0.01	0.03	66.51	1.76	—	0.07
403	(0.11	tr.	tr.	12.33	0.68	0.03	0.08
407	0.15	—	—	49.75	1.58	—	0.07
409	0.09	—	0.03	46.69	1.61	0.02	0.06
Series R: R8 and R9							
410	0.11	—	0.03	56.05	1.41	tr.	0.09
413	0.15	—	0.03	57.64	1.82	—	0.04
414	0.16*	—	—	54.61	1.39	—	0.09
417	0.16	0.02	0.03	69.19	1.57	—	0.08
418	0.13	tr.	0.03	62.28	1.81	tr.	0.07
419	0.13	tr.	0.04	60.36	0.75	—	0.05
420	0.01	—	0.03	99.17	0.08	0.02	0.11
"	(0.06	0.01	0.02	50.94	0.57	0.01	0.26

Sn	Ag	Pb	Au	'Silver'	Au:Ag	Pb:Ag	Cat.no.
1.74	58.61	1.25	0.74	60.60	1.26	2.13	378
2.19	55.39	1.54	0.78	57.71	1.41	2.78	379
5.31	44.53	1.68	0.70	46.91	1.57	3.77	380
2.54	66.30	1.68	1.06	§69.04	1.60	2.53	381
2.11	80.13	1.36	1.17	82.66	1.46	1.70	382
1.44	84.25	1.09	0.78	86.12	0.93	1.29	383
4.31*	65.41	1.66	1.04	68.11	1.59	2.54	384
3.86	69.73	1.55	0.67	§71.95	0.96	2.22	385
3.60	72.70	1.16	1.34	75.20	1.84	1.60	L.Sutton
4.5	86.9						5103
5.02	25.05	1.22	0.33	26.60	1.32	4.87	386
4.76	29.56	1.50	0.29	31.35	0.98	5.07	387
7.8*	32.3						4318
10.2*	33.8						4876
25.0*	19.5						4320
—	93.56	0.72	1.13	95.41	1.21	0.77	391
—	91.75	0.52	1.04	93.31	1.13	0.57	392
—	89.32	0.72	0.80	90.84	0.90	0.81	393
—	84.91	1.54	1.62	88.07	1.91	1.81	394
—	94.37	0.75	0.57	95.69	0.60	0.78	395
—	91.83	0.72	1.12	93.67	1.22	0.78	E.031
0.86	91.39	0.98	1.17	93.54	1.28	1.07	396
1.52	71.83#	1.32	0.86#	74.01	1.20	1.83	397
1.24	77.21	1.48	1.00	79.69	1.30	1.92	398
2.28	59.22	1.33	0.84	61.39	1.42	2.25	399
2.06	87.11	1.98	0.90	§89.99	1.03	2.27	401
5.03	24.92	1.16	0.39	26.47	1.57	4.78	402
6.59	63.58	2.28	1.10)	66.96	1.73	3.59	403
3.86	42.38	1.59	0.69	§44.66	1.63	3.75	407
3.05	46.11	1.70	0.63	48.44	1.37	3.69	409
4.57	35.62	1.74	0.38	37.74	1.07	4.88	410
4.28	34.42	1.60	0.46	36.48	1.34	4.65	413
4.47	23.02	2.86	0.53	§26.41	2.30	12.42	414
5.32	21.65	1.64	0.35	23.64	1.62	7.58	417
5.70	27.50	2.17	0.29	29.96	1.05	7.89	418
5.90	31.09	1.43	0.34	32.86	1.09	4.60	419
0.06	0.15	0.38	—	core	—	—	420
2.54	36.37	0.96	0.43)	corroded surface		—	"

Cat.no.	Fe	Co	Ni	Cu	Zn	Bi	Sb
421	0.05	—	0.04	58.86	0.73	0.02	0.05
Series R: Wigraed and Tilbeorht (R10 and R11)							
423	0.17	0.02*	0.06	78.49	2.01	tr.	0.07
E.020	(0.29	—	0.02	28.41	1.52	tr.	0.10
E.027	0.07	0.01	0.04	55.36	1.18	tr.	0.05
426	0.17*	—	0.03	79.70	0.91	0.01#	0.10
427	0.37	tr.	0.04	81.52	2.90	—	0.07
428	0.25	tr.	0.06	82.10	2.10	tr.	0.10
Types 30, 51, etc. and Type 70, etc.							
430	0.05	0.01	—	8.06	0.08	0.01	tr.
432	0.02	—	0.02	3.56	0.48	tr.	0.02
433	(0.07	—	0.01	5.83	0.45	0.04	0.02
434	(0.64	0.01	—	0.08	tr.	—	—
436	0.06	tr.	—	9.77	0.63	tr.	0.02
Series S							
438	0.13	—	0.03	47.43	1.47	—	0.04
439	(0.34	—	—	22.60	1.08	0.04	0.06
"	(0.10	—	—	4.87	0.09	—	0.06
441	0.10	0.02	0.03	51.51	2.21	tr.	0.05
Series T							
442	0.08	tr.	0.03	45.19#	2.04	tr.	0.02
443	0.09	tr.	0.05	49.40	1.96	0.03	0.03
444	0.06	0.01	0.02	43.52	1.70	tr.	0.05
Series U							
445	0.03	tr.	tr.	18.04	0.23	tr.	0.03
446	0.07	—	—	13.06	0.23	—	0.04
448	0.03	—	—	9.78	0.14	0.03	0.01
449	(0.28	0.01	—	14.70	0.39	0.01	0.09
450	0.03	tr.	—	20.42	0.22	0.02	0.02
452	0.04	—	0.02#	32.42	0.75	0.04#	0.04
Series V							
453	0.08	0.01	0.04	50.75	1.63	tr.	0.04
E.022	0.04	tr.	0.02	8.27	0.31	0.04	0.02
E.023	(0.04	0.01	0.01	3.27	0.83	tr.	0.01
E.021	0.10	tr.	0.01	36.19	0.10	tr.	0.05
Series Y: Eadberht							
454	0.04	0.01	0.03	32.55	1.34	0.02	0.02
455	0.07	tr.	—	34.48	0.34*	0.01	0.04
456	0.05	—	0.02	28.18	0.97#	0.06	0.05
458	0.07	tr.	—	35.72	0.93#	0.03	0.04
459	0.11	0.01	0.02	41.69	2.08	0.03	0.05

Sn	Ag	Pb	Au	'Silver'	Au:Ag	Pb:Ag	Cat.no.
5.42	32.25	1.92	0.66	34.83	2.05	5.95	421
6.18	12.28	0.51	0.21	13.00	1.71	4.15	423
8.58	39.22	1.68	0.76)	41.66	1.94	4.28	E.020
3.13	38.28	1.38	0.62	40.28	1.62	3.61	E.027
8.03	9.18	1.74	0.13	11.05	1.42	18.95	426
7.86	4.36	2.79	0.08	7.23	1.83	63.99	427
5.56	9.28	0.47	0.08	9.83	0.86	5.06	428
tr.	89.29	0.86	1.22	91.37	1.37	0.96	430
1.76	91.87	1.10	1.17	94.20	1.27	1.20	432
1.79	79.60	1.36	1.07)	82.03	1.34	1.71	433
—	69.77	0.03	—)	69.80	—	0.04	434
2.82*#	83.57	1.82	1.29	§86.68	1.54	2.18	436
3.53	44.89	1.72	0.74	47.35	1.65	3.83	438
6.32	44.05	1.85	1.35)	47.25	core		439
4.80	83.59	2.92	0.94)	87.45	surface		"
3.58	40.43	1.45	0.61	42.49	1.51	3.59	441
2.92	47.60#	1.56	0.56	49.72	1.18	3.28	442
7.15	39.24	1.43	0.64	41.31	1.63	3.64	443
3.36	49.20	1.39	0.68	§51.27	1.38	2.83	444
2.45	77.00	1.36	1.03	79.39	1.34	1.77	445
1.73	82.31	1.40	1.16	§84.87	1.41	1.70	446
1.48	86.22	1.16	1.15	§88.53	1.33	1.35	448
7.46	53.06	1.95	1.12)	56.93	2.11	3.68	449
2.43	75.21	1.22	1.07	§77.50	1.42	1.62	450
2.35	62.25	1.20	0.88	64.33	1.41	1.93	452
3.74	41.76	1.38	0.56	43.70	1.34	3.30	453
1.72	86.70	1.54	1.21	89.45	1.39	1.78	E.022
3.01	77.90	1.82	1.32)	81.04	1.69	2.34	E.023
5.35	54.79	1.77	0.79	57.35	1.44	3.23	E.021
1.99	61.80	1.49	0.76	64.05	1.23	2.41	454
3.01#*	59.28	1.54	0.93	61.75	1.57	2.60	455
2.31	65.84	1.61	0.91	68.36	1.38	2.45	456
3.57	56.76	1.88	0.98	§59.62	1.73	3.31	458
3.65	49.91	1.70	0.75	52.36	1.50	3.41	459

Cat.no.	Fe	Co	Ni	Cu	Zn	Bi	Sb
460	0.09	0.01	0.01	26.55	0.62*	0.04	0.03
461	(0.03	0.01	—	37.52	tr.	tr.	tr.
462	0.08	tr.	—	2.79	0.13	0.03	0.02
463	—	tr.	0.02	6.91	2.26	0.04	tr.
464	0.06	tr.	—	47.85	0.07	0.01	—
465	0.20#*	0.02	0.02	33.03	0.55#	0.03	0.05
466	(0.10	—	—	10.11	0.03	—	—
Series Y: Alchred to Ælfwald							
467	(0.02	—	0.01	1.88	0.08	0.03	0.03
468	0.03	—	0.03	42.33#	0.66	0.04	0.05
469	0.04	0.01	—	2.19*	0.16	0.03	0.02
470	0.06	0.01	0.01	48.25	0.07	—	tr.
Northumbria							
473	0.04	0.01	0.01	18.64#	0.47	0.05	0.03

Sn	Ag	Pb	Au	'Silver'	Au:Ag	Pb:Ag	Cat.no.
3.22	66.68	1.80	0.89	69.37	1.33	2.70	460
8.17	51.31	0.58	0.20)	52.09	0.39	1.13	461
2.46	92.07	0.95	1.47	(94.49)	1.60	1.03	462
0.67	88.19	0.64	1.23	90.06	1.39	0.72	463
4.64	46.19	0.84	0.26	47.29	0.56	1.82	464
2.48	62.22	1.68	0.98	§64.88	1.58	2.70	465
12.55	64.42	0.98	0.31)	65.71	0.48	1.52	466
2.87	82.76	1.28	1.21)	85.25	1.46	1.55	467
4.41	50.05#	1.81	0.59	52.45	1.18	3.62	468
1.85*	92.91	1.28	1.50	95.69	1.61	1.38	469
4.54	46.02	0.83	0.23	47.08	0.50	1.80	470
2.79	74.99	2.04	0.92	77.95	1.23	2.62	473

AN ANNOTATED
CONCORDANCE
OF TYPES AND SERIES

(*BMC* Types 1-54; Hill Types 55-76; Stewart Types 77-109. Hill's 'mules' and 'variants' are inserted into the sequence.

Type 1. The 'two emperors' thrymsa type, in silver. The style appears to be absolutely regular. The coin, *BMC* 9, is the only known specimen in silver, against upwards of twenty in gold. Illustrated in L. Webster and J. Backhouse (eds.), *The Making of England*, pp.44-6, its patina and pedigree guarantee its authenticity, and the quality of its dies indicate its official character; but when there is only one specimen in silver, against so many in gold, its significance for chronology and/or attribution is problematic.

Type 2a. Series A. Subdivided by Rigold into A1 (unique), A2 and A3, pp.67f., 77-9, 85-93.

Type 2b. A miscellaneous group, belonging mostly either to Series R (*BMC* 25 and 27) or to the VERNVS group (*BMC* 24 is apparently from the same dies as no.148. See p.144. For *BMC* 26 see p.143f.). Add Hill, pl.6, 2 and 3.

Type 2c. Series D, pp.184-90. See also Type 50, and the Hill addendum, pl.6,1, which deserves separate status.

Type 2c/8 'mule' (imitative), p.189 and cat.no.187.

Coins with runic legends. *BMC* amalgamates coins reading *ipa, epa, apa,* and *lepa.* The runic varieties should be divided between Series C, Q, and R. See the general discussion at pp.106-8, and pp.108-16 (for Series C) and pp.498 (Series Q) and 502-23 (Series R). Hill adds some variants, pl.6, 23-6, some of which are better grouped with Types 30 and 51 — see p.532. *A propos* pl.6, 24 (below, Type 78) cf. the specimen in the Garton-on-the-Wolds find (below, Type 79), illustrated at p.510, and see also p.478 and p.303. For substantive runic coins reading *spi,* see Series R, sections V and IX, pp.511-13, and 517-8.

Runic/type 51 (Hill, pl.6, 11). Types 30, 51, etc., at p.532.

Type 3a. Series G, pp.266-74.

Type 3b. Two coins, of which *BMC* 52 belongs to the VERNVS groups, and *BMC* 53 is of the SAROALDO type (see under Type 11).

Types 4-6. Series E, pp.196-242. A very large series, which falls into three chronological sections. The first and third are relatively straightforward, while the second is impenetrably variable.

Type 4 var ('SEDE'), Hill, pl.6, 27. See p.246. Renumbered as Type 89. A second specimen, with a related

obverse but a different reverse type, was very recently found in England.

Type 5/41b, Hill, pl.6, 12. This coin from the Hallum hoard, which remains unique, ties in with a relatively early date of origin for Series N, and tends to support the idea of its emanating from a commercial centre with wide trading links. See the illustration on p.462. Renumbered as Type 88.

Type 7. Series V, pp. 570-5.

Type 8. Series D, pp.191-4.

Type 8Z. See p.195.

Type 9. Series T, pp.545-51. See also the index entry for Type 12/5.

Type 9 var. Hill, pl.6, 28. MONITA-SCORVM. Treated as an eclectic group, pp.435-6, but the suspicion is expressed that coins with this legend could have been minted in more than one place (cf. the Victory types). Hill's Type 9 var. perhaps has affinities with Series Q rather than T.

Type 10. A continental double-obverse type (the so-called 'TILV' type) based on Series D and E, pp.248-50.

Type 11. The SAROALDO type (which includes part of BMC Type 3b), pp.147-51.

Type 12. Series L, pp.406-15, at pp.409-11.

Type 12 var. Hill, pl.6, 29. For a comparable coin in Series L, see p.411 (=Type 15a var.)

Type 12/5. Hill, pl.6, 13 and a second specimen (now in the Ashmolean) were described by Hill as mules in order to distinguish them from Series T. His third specimen, however, (pl.6, 14) may be judged to belong with Series T. A third example of pl.6, 13 has recently been found in England. See pp.246-7 and p.304.

Type 12/34. Hill, pl.6, 15. A 'celtic cross with rosettes' type, re-numbered by Stewart as Type 106. Pp.426-32, section VII.

Type 13. Series L, pp.406-15, at p.409.

Type 14. A 'celtic cross with rosettes' type, copying Series L, pp.426-32, section II.

Type 15a, Series L, pp.406-15.

Type 15a var. Hill, pl.6, 30. Series L, section IV, p.411.

Type 15b (branch left). Series L, 'Hwiccian' style, pp.406-15.

Type 15b var (i). Hill, pl.6, 31. This is part of the C ARIP eclectic group, pp.416-21.

Type 15b var (ii). Hill, pl,6, 32. Series L, section VI, p.413.

Type 16. Series L, pp.406-15, 'Hwiccian' style.

Type 17. Series L, pp.406-15, section I. BMC 99 is in good 'Hwiccian' style.

Type 18. Series L, pp.406-15, section V.

Type 19. Series L, pp.406-15, section IV.

Type 20. Series K, pp. 402-4.

Type 20 var./18. Hill, pl.6, 16. Under this rubric Hill amalgamates specimens with 'hair plain' and with 'hair in plaits' — which we should be disposed to attribute to Series L and K respectively. See p.375, where the variety is (loosely) described as Type 18/20. Most specimens belong to Series K: see pp.402-5. It is not altogether clear that the wreath-ties are plain on Hill, pl.6, 16.

Type 21. Series O, related to Type 23c, pp. 472-4.

Type 22. The 'Victory' types, pp. 440-3.

Type 23a. Placed among the K/N related varieties because of its inner wire border, pp.444-5, and see also p. 421

Type 23a var. Hill, pl.6, 33, said to be from Dorchester, Oxon., and in the Ashmolean. The Dorchester find is reliably illustrated in *NC* 4 (1841-2), p.32 and un-numbered pl., 4. The Ashmolean coin is another specimen of the same variety, which sits on an old ticket, on which the type is described (inaccurately?) as 'man holding cross and sword?', ex Thames hoard. There is no obvious reason to doubt that the Ashmolean coin is ex Thames hoard. See p.445, where the Dorchester coin is omitted by oversight, and the type is listed as 16/41.

Type 23a/51. Hill, pl.6, 17. Listed, with some hesitation, as belonging with Types 30, 51, etc., and illustrated at p.531. Renumbered as Type 87.

Type 23b. Series U, westerly style, pp.552-62, 564-6.

Type 23c. Imitative of Series U, and apparently with a south-westerly or southerly distribution, cf. Type 21, pp.568-9.

Type 23c/34. Hill, pl.6, 18. Renumbered as Type 93. A 'celtic cross with rosettes' type, pp.426-32, section I, and an example of the wide influence of the pecking bird, see p.314.

Type 23d. Series U, south-easterly (Kentish) style, pp.552-64.

Type 23e. Pp.451-2. The affinity with Series L is not particularly close.

Type 23e var. Hill, pl.6, 34. The addition of a flower (= vine with berries?) left probably marks the coin as imitative. There is a photograph in *RN* 5th Ser., 2 (1938), pl.4, 75.

Type 24a. Series F, pp.125-32.

Type 24b. Series F, with TT/II added (= variety b at p.129).

Type 25. Merovingian coin?

Type 26. Type BX, p.96.

Type 27a, *BMC* 124 = BIG, 1. *BMC* 125 = BIIIA, 3.

Type 27b. Series B, pp.94-105.

Type 28. Merovingian coin.

Type 29a, b. Series BZ, pp.133-7.

Type 30a, b. Part of an east-coast series for which Rigold did not provide a separate identity. See also Type 51 and 70, pp. 524-36.

Type 30b/8. Hill, pl.6, 19. Renumbered as Type 82. Discussed and illustrated at p.538.

Type 31. Series X, pp.275-93.

Type 32a. Series K, pp. 385-8 and 395-402.

Type 32b. An eclectic group with rosettes added in the obverse field, pp. 433-4.

Type 33. Series K, pp. 388-91 (and copied in Series L? — pp. 387-8 and 405).

Type 34. A 'celtic cross with rosettes' type, better divided into three varieties, 34a (section VI, p.429) and 34b (section X, p.431), with fleur-de-lis sceptre or cross-on-stand.

Type 35. Series Q, probably imitative of QIH, p.492.

Type 36. Series G imitating Series J, pp.272-4.

Type 37. Series J, pp. 351-3.

Type 37/32a. Discussed under Series J, section VIII, at pp.356-7. Renumbered as Type 84. Possibly a misread specimen of Type 72.

Type 38. The substantive type in Series O. Pp.468-76.

Type 39. Series H, pp. 324-5.

Type 40. Included by Rigold with Series O, but associated more probably with Series N, pp.477-81.

Type 41a and b. Series N and copies, pp.459-67.

Type 41b/23e. Hill, pl.6, 20, renumbered as Type 108. This Whitby find could equally well be seen as a 23e/41, or a 15/41 copy. There are traces of an inner wire border on Hill's coin, cf. p.445, no.5 (from Bradwell-on-Sea).

Type 41b/41a. Hill, pl.6, 21. Discussed with Series N, at p.463.

Type 42, Series K, pp.391-5, where the type is subdivided into three — a, b, and c.

Type 42 var. Hill, pl.6, 35. This mutilated piece is catalogued as no.367, 'imitation of Series M?' One might mention another possible affinity, in a coin from the Barking Abbey excavations, p.395.

Type 43. Probably English, p.482.

Type 44. Series Q, 'modelled' style, section IV, pp.499-501.

Type 44 var. Hill,. pl.6, 36. Variants of Type 44, q.v.

Type 45. Series M, pp.453-8.

Type 46. A unique MONITASCORVM variety, pp.436 and 535 (die-link).

Type 47. Series S, pp.537-44.

Type 48. Included by Rigold with Series H, but it has a more easterly distribution, pp. 333-40.

Type 49. Series H, pp.321-32.

Type 49/48. Hill, pl.6, 22. Unique and presumably imitative. See p.332.

Type 50. An imitation of Type 2c (Series D), pp.189-90.

Type 51. See Type 30, pp. 530-1.

Type 52. A 'triquetras' type, with affinities with Series K, p.425, no.9.

Type 53. The 'porcupine/stepped cross' type, pp.243-5.

Type 54. Series W, pp.152-7. Two finds have appeared *dans le commerce* since vol.1 was finalized, from Warnford, near Winchester (Spink's list) and from the Bournemouth area (Glendining 11 October, 1993, lot 223). They strongly reinforce the proposed attribution to Wessex.

Type 55. Hill, pl.7, 1. Series Va, pp.80-4.

Type 56. Hill, pl.7, 2. The 'L.Sutton' find. Type QIX, p.490.

Type 57. Hill, pl.7, 3-4. Series O, pp.474-5.

Type 58. Hill, pl.7, 5. A 'celtic cross with rosettes' type, section V, pp.428-9.

Type 59, Hill, pl.7, 6. Type QIG, pp.491-2.

Type 60. Hill, pl.7, 7. Series J, pp.354-5.

Type 61. Hill, pl.7, 8. The C ARIP eclectic group, p.418 (top of page).

Type 62. Hill, pl.7, 9. The 'animal mask' eclectic group. Found near Oxford. Pp.446-8.

Type 63. Hill, pl.7, 10. The C ARIP eclectic group, p.416 (first coin).

Type 64. Hill, pl.7, 11. Type QIIIA, pp.495-6.

Type 65. Hill, pl.7, 12. Types QII, A-D, pp.493-5.

Type 66. Hill, pl.7, 13. Series Z, pp.137-8. There are problems of authenticity of specimens known in the nineteenth century.

Type 67a. Hill, pl.7, 14. Type QID, pp.490-1.

Type 67b. Hill, pl.7, 15. Type QIE, pp.490-1.

Type 68. Hill, pl.7, 16. Coins with rosettes in the obverse field, pp.433-4.

Type 69. Hill, pl.7, 17. The 'link' between the two VERNVS groups, p.144.

Type 70. Hill, pl.7, 18-23. See pp.532-4.

Type 71. Hill, pl.7, 24. Type QIF, p.491.

Type 72, Hill, pl.7, 25. Series J, section VII, pp.355-6.

Type 73. Hill, pl.7, 26. Type Q (R), pp.496-8, and 518.

Type 74. Hill, pl.7, 27. An imitation of Series A or C? — VERNVS-related?

Type 75. Hill, pl.7, 28. An imitation of Type 42. Described as base.

Type 76. Hill, pl.7, 29. 'Animal mask' eclectic group, p.448.

Mercia: Peada. Hill, pl.7, 30. Type PaIIA, pp.73-9.

Frisian? Hill, pl.7, 31. 'Maastricht' type, pp.258-60.

Merovingian? Hill, pl.7, 32. Uncertain.

Type 77a. Series C and Series R1-5 (wedge serifs).

Type 77b. Series R (knob serifs).

Type 78. Hill, pl.6, 24. See above, 'coins with runic legends'. P.478.

Type 79. Rigold, pl.4, Type R2Z = the Garton-on-the-Wolds find. Illustrated at p.510.

Type 80. SAROALDO type, imitation, p.150 (at bottom of page). Also *BNJ* 46 (1976), pl.1, 17.

Type 81. Series X, ?insular copy. Hamwic 124, pp.292-3.

Type 82 = Type 30b/8, p.528.

Type 83. Series Z/N imitation .

Type 84 = Type 37/32a, q.v. Pp.356-7.

Type 85 = Rigold BIIIB, now Series J, pp. 345-9.

Type 86a, K/R 'mule'. The Lakenheath find, p. 449.

Type 86b. K/R mule. The Winchester find, pp. 449 and 535.

Type 87 = Type 23a/51, q.v. P.531.

Type 88 = Type 5/41b, q.v. P.462.

Type 89 = Type 4 var., q.v. P.246.

Type 90. Unpublished porcupine variant.

Type 91. The second VERNVS group, pp.144-6.

Type 92. Series D derivative. See under Type 2c.

Type 93 = Type 23c/34. q.v. Pp.426-32.

Type 94. The Archer type, pp. 437-9.

Type 95. Type PaIIA, pp.73-9. See following Type 76.

Type 96. Type PaIIB, pp.73-9.

Type 97. Type PaIII, pp.73-9.

Type 98. Type QIH, p.492.

Type 99. Type QIVE, pp.499-501.

Type 100. Triquetras group, no.1, p.424.

Type 101. Triquetras/Victory type, no.3, p.424.

Type 102. Triquetras group with pecking bird, no.4, p.424.

Type 103 = Type 49/48. q.v., p.332.

Type 104 = Type 42 var, q.v.

Type 105. Æthiliræd porcupines, pp.120-4.

Type 106 = Type 12/34, q.v.

Type 107. Series G, subsidiary series, pp.272-4.

Type 108 = Type 41b/23e, q.v.

Type 109. Triquetras group, no.10, p.425.

PLATE 17

SECONDARY SCEATTAS

SERIES H

References are to the corpus published in P. Andrews (editor), *The Coins and Pottery from Hamwic* (Southampton Finds, vol.1).

TYPE 39

283   0.84g. ↑↙ 69% 'silver' (XRF). Metcalf 24.3. Evans bequest, 1941.

IMITATION OF TYPE 39

284   1.06g. ↑↓ Bt. from finder, 1991. Found Winterbourne Bassett, Wi.

TYPE 49

285   0.82g. ↑↓ *c.*76% 'silver'. Variety 2a. M.58.5. H. de S. Shortt bequest, 1975, ex Miss P. J. Gordon, Wyke Regis. Found in south Hampshire.

286   0.90g (worn). ↑↓ 64% 'silver'. Variety 2a. M.63.3. Bt. 1974, ex G. E. L. Carter colln.

287   1.01g. ↑→ Variety 2a. M.–. Bt. 1986. Said to have been found on the Essex-Herts borders.

288   0.82g. ↑↓ Variety 5a. M.–. Given by D. M. M., 1 November 1988; at second hand from finder. Found Kingston Deverill, Wi, at a ford across the R. Wylie, 1985.

SERIES H, TYPE 48

Although they are not from Hamwic, the coins of Type 48 are included in the corpus in Southampton Finds, vol.1. Chemical analyses are published there.

289   0.96g. ↑→ 51% 'silver'. M.34.7. Given by D. M. M., 1 November 1988. Found Ostia, near Rome.

290   1.20g. ↑↗ *c.*68% 'silver' (XRF). M:31.3. Bt. 1992, ex *NCirc.*1973, p.482 (item 9869).

291   0.97g. ↑↘ Bt. from finder, 1986. Found at St. Nicholas-at-Wade, K.

292   0.78g. ↑↙ 47% 'silver'. M.31.9. H. de S. Shortt bequest, 1975, ex Miss P. J. Gordon, Wyke Regis. Found in south Hampshire.

SERIES J

TYPE 85 (BIIIB)

293   0.99g. ↑→ 89% 'silver'. Rigold BIIIB, 1 (this coin). Magdalen College.

IMITATIONS OF TYPE 85

294   1.00g. ↑→ Plated on base metal core. Plating: 43% 'silver'. Bt. 1974, ex G. E. L. Carter colln.

295   0.79g (worn). ↑↙ Base metal. Bt. 1974, ex G. E. L. Carter colln.

See also BIIIc, below.

TYPE 37 (INCLUDING IMI-TATIONS?)

296   1.05g. ↑↑ 79% 'silver'. Evans bequest, 1941.

297   1.07g. ↑↖ 90% 'silver'. Bt. 1974, ex G. E. L. Carter colln.

298   0.68g. ↑↖ 92% 'silver'. With ears. Evans bequest, 1941.

299   1.01g. ↑↑ 91% 'silver'. With ears. Evans bequest, 1941.

PLATE 17

283

284

285 286 287 288 289

290 291 292 293 294

295 296 297 298 299

PLATE 18

IMITATION OF TYPE 37

300   0.74g. ↑ ↖ Plated on base metal core. Bt. from finder, 1974. Found Banbury, O.

TYPE 36

301   0.86g. ↑↙ 59% 'silver'. Bt. from finder, 1988. Found Sleaford, Li.

302   0.98g. ↑↘ Bt. from finder, 1991. Found near Scunthorpe, Li.

TYPE 72

303   0.80g. ↑↗ Bt. from finder, 1992. Found Plumpton, near Ringmer, Lewes, Sx.

TYPE BIIIc

Rigold lists the two specimens known to him, in his corpus in *BNJ* 1960-1.

304   0.81g. ↑↖ 92% 'silver' (surface enrichment?). BIIIc, 2 (this coin). Evans bequest, 1941.

305   0.95g. ↑↖ Cf. BIIIc, 1. Bt. 1990. Found near Leicester.

SERIES K

A corpus of Types 33, 32a, and 42 was published by Metcalf and Walker in *BNJ* 36 (1967), 11-28. Types 20 and 20/18 have not been fully studied. Type 52 is catalogued elsewhere below as part of the 'triquetras' eclectic group.

TYPE 33

306   1.14g. ↑↑ 86% 'silver'. 'Benediction' variant. Bt. 1987. From spoil from the London area; believed to be from the Thames Barrier (*not* from Billingsgate).

COPIES OF TYPE 32A

307   1.04g. ↑← 37% 'silver'. M. and W. 27. Evans bequest, 1941.

308   0.98g. ↑→ 35% 'silver' (with surface enrichment to 74%). M. and W. 29. Found Shakenoak Farm, Wilcote, O.

309   1.03g. ↑↓ *c.*51% 'silver'. The plated appearance of the coin was not confirmed by EPMA analysis, and is evidently deceptive. M. and W. 33. Ex Bodleian Library, old colln.

310   1.00g. ↑→ M. and W. –. Bt. from finder, 1989. Found Tilbury, Ess.

TYPE 42

There are three varieties, with (a) a plant with berries or buds, (b), a hawk, (c) a cross-sceptre.

311   1.02g. ↑↙ 86% 'silver'. Variety a. M. and W. –. Bt. 1986. Found at Tilbury, Ess.

312   1.04g. ↑← 58% 'silver'. Variety a. M. and W. 21. Ex Bodleian Library, old colln.

313   0.98g. ↑↑ Variety b. M. and W. –. Bt. from finder, 1975. Found at Walbury Camp iron-age hill fort, near Inkpen, Brk.

TYPE 20

314   1.21g. ↑↑ 54% 'silver'. Bt. 1986. Found Tilbury, Ess.

315   1.12g. ↑↓ 48% 'silver'. Given by the Executors of R. C. Lockett, 1955.

316   0.64g. ↑↓ *c.*40% 'silver' (minimum measured), *c.*60% (twice). Wholly corroded. Wire border. Bt. 1992, ex *Seaby Bulletin* 1977, item E.1131. Found Isle of Grain, K.

PLATE 18

300   301   302   303   304

305   306

307   308   309   310   311

312   313   314   315   316

PLATE 19

TYPE 20/18

317   1.02g. ↑↓ 47% 'silver'. Given by the Executors of R. C. Lockett, 1955.

318   1.03g. 32% 'silver'. Ex Lockett colln.

SERIES L

Parts of Series L are catalogued by Metcalf in *NC* 1976, 64-74.

TYPE 12

319   0.85g. ↑↙ 51% 'silver'. Bt.1984.

320   1.11g. ↑↑ 28% 'silver'. Evans bequest, 1941, ex A. W. Franks, ex Thames hoard.

321   1.00g. ↑↓ 48% 'silver'. Given by D. M. M., 1 November 1988; bt. from finder. Found South Weston, O.

322   1.07g. ↑↓ 'Hwiccian' style. Bt. 1992. Found in the Newbury area.

TYPE 15 AND VARIANTS

323   0.91g. ↑← *Obv.* V-shaped element at base of cross. *Rev.* In-curving base, with pellets and tapering ends, possibly representing heads. Bt. 1989.

324   0.97g. ↑↑ 16% 'silver'. *Obv.* Long cross with pellet at base. Evans bequest, 1941, ex A. W. Franks, ex Thames hoard.

325   0.70g (reduced). ↑→ 8% 'silver'. Types as no.324. Bt. 1970 from land-owner. Found Shakenoak Farm, Wilcote, O.

326   0.96g. ↑↓ Very low silver. Bt. from finder, 1991. Found Tilbury, Ess.

327   1.03g. ↑↓ Very low silver. *Obv.* Flower-stalk with two drooping buds. *Rev.* Facing head, with long moustaches. Bt. from finder, 1989. Found Tilbury, Ess.

328   1.01g. ↑↑ Low silver. *Obv.* Branching stem, with annulets at nodes. Bt. 1992.

TYPE 16 AND VARIANTS

329   1.08g. ↑← 15% 'silver'. *Obv.* Vine-scroll in front of face. *Rev.* Branch to left, cross to right. Evans bequest, 1941, ex A. W. Franks, ex Thames hoard.

330   1.11g. ↑→ 22% 'silver'. *Obv.* Cross, ? on rectangular base. *Rev.* Branches to left and right. Evans bequest, 1941, ex A. W. Franks, ex Thames hoard.

TYPE 18 IN VARIOUS STYLES

331   1.05g. ↑↑ *Obv.* Cross on pyramidal base of three pellets. *Rev.* Hawk with head turned back. Bt. 1989. Found near Rochester, K.

332   0.96g. ↑↘ 20% 'silver'. Bt. 1945 from Dr. G. R. Malkin. Found Sedgeberrow, Wo., *c.*1938.

333   0.79g. ↑→ Bt. from finder, 1989. Found Tilbury, Ess.

PLATE 19

317

318

319 320 321 322 323

324 325 326 327 328

329 330 331 332 333

PLATE 20

IMITATION OF TYPE 18

334 0.73g. ↑← Very low silver. *Obv.* Pyramidal neck. *Rev.* 'T' beneath hawk. Bt. from finder, 1989. Found Tilbury, Ess.

TYPE 19

335 0.76g. ↑↓ Very low silver. Given by D. M. M., 1 November 1988; bt. from finder. Found on Thames foreshore at Putney, Sr.

ECLECTIC GROUPS RELATED TO SERIES K AND L

THE C ARIP GROUP

This group, with straight wreath-ties, seems to be L-related. It also copies Series U, Type 23.

336 1.10g. ↑↗ 31% 'silver'. *Rev.* Pecking bird. Given by D. M. M., 1 November 1988, ex Firth, ex Lockett, ex Grantley, ex Montagu, ex Marsham.

337 1.01g. ↑↑ *Rev.* Wolf-worm with porcupine's quills. Cf. Type 61. Bt. 1989. Found near Chichester, Sx.

338 1.07g. ↑↓ 35% 'silver'. *Rev.* Standing figure with two crosses, on straight base-line. Bt. 1986.

339 0.98g. ↑↑ *Rev.* Standing figure, with facing head. Vine to left, both hands hold cross to right. Bt. from finder, 1991. Found Tilbury, Ess.

IMITATION OF THE C ARIP GROUP

340 1.00g. ↑→ 7% 'silver'. *Rev.* There seems to be a row of 3 or 4 small pellets to indicate the tongue. Bt. 1992. Found in the St. Albans area, Hrt.

THE 'TRIQUETRAS' ECLECTIC GROUP

This group, with knotted wreath-ties, includes Type 52, and seems to be K-related. It also copies Series U, Type 23.

341 0.96g. ↑↓ *Obv.* Head and both feet face right. Bt. from finder, 1991. Found Tilbury, Ess.

342 0.96g. ↑← 55% 'silver'. *Obv.* Head and both feet face left. Given by D. M. M., 1 November 1988; bt. from finder, 1988. Found Lewknor, O.

343 1.02g. ↑→ 47% 'silver'. Given by D. M. M., 1 November 1988; ex Mack.

344 0.96g. ↑↑ 54% 'silver'. *Obv.* Cf. Type 52. *Rev.* Pecking bird, laterally reversed. Bt. 1977. Found in the car park of Walbury Camp iron-age hill fort, near Inkpen, Brk.

THE 'CELTIC CROSS WITH ROSETTES' TYPES

The two coins in the collection are in the second category (see text above), with a linear cross superimposed on the 'celtic cross'.

345 0.89g. ↑↗ 37% 'silver'. *Obv.* Helmeted bust. Cross on rectangular base, Given by D. M. M., 1 November 1988. Found Tilbury, Ess.

346 1.10g. ↑↑ 19% 'silver', 10% zinc, 3% tin. Same dies as *BMC* 162. Given by J. G. Milne. Acquired in Brighton, 1940, as part of a small, undistinguished, and ? mainly local collection. The authenticity of this coin, which is of a brass-based alloy, is open to some doubt.

COINS WITH ROSETTES IN THE OBVERSE FIELD

347 1.08g. ↑↓ *Obv.* Quincunx before face. Rosettes to left and right. Bt. 1990.

SCEATTAS READING MONITA-SCORVM OR SCORVM

348 0.87g. ↑→ Bt. 1991.

THE 'ARCHER GROUP'

349 1.13g. ↑← Bt. Glendinings, 9 February 1977. Found near Walbury camp iron-age hill fort, nr. Inkpen, Brk.

PLATE 20

334   335

336   337   338   339   340

341   342   343   344

345   346   347   348   349

PLATE 21

'VICTORY' SCEATTAS

See also no.343 above.

350   1.14g. ↑↑ c. 54% 'silver'. Bt. from finder, 1987. Found near Hinton Parva, Wi.
351   0.91g. ↑→ 37% 'silver'. Bt. 1988. Believed to be the specimen found near Hitchin, Herts.

K/N-RELATED ECLECTIC GROUP (TYPE 23A)

A coin which may be connected with this group has been catalogued with Series K above, as no.316.

352   1.10g. ↑← Bt. from finder, 1989. Found Tilbury, Ess.
353   0.80g. ↑↘ 22% 'silver'. Evans bequest, 1941, ex A. W. Franks, ex Thames hoard.

THE 'ANIMAL MASK' ECLECTIC GROUP

This group, which has affinities with the previous, K/N related, group may have a more northerly origin. It includes a copy of the 'pecking bird' intermediate between Type 23 and the 'archer' group, and also copies of Series Q.

354   0.67g. ↑↘ Bt. from finder, 1991. Found Caldecote, near Oxborough, Nf.
355   0.88g. ↑↓ 28% 'silver'. Given by A. D. Passmore; ex Grantley, ex Montagu. Cf. C. Roach Smith, *Coll. Antiq.* vol.2, p.66. Found near Oxford.
356   0.88g. ↑↓ Bt. from finder, 1991. Found between Croxton and Abbotsley, Ca.

K/R 'MULES'

357   0.96g. ↑↓ 59% 'silver'. Given by D. M. M., 1 November 1988. Found Lakenheath, Sf. Cf. *BNJ* 1977, 41, s.v. (incorrect weight).
358   0.69g. ↑↙ Bt. 1991

SERIES L, TYPE 23E, AND IMITATIONS

359   1.07g. ↑← 31% 'silver'. Bodleian Library.
360   1.05g. ↑↑ Bt. from finder, 1991. Found near Scunthorpe, Li.
361   0.91g. ↑↖ Bt. from finder, 1989. Found Tilbury, Ess.
362   0.78g. ↑↓ 24% 'silver'. Evans bequest, 1941. Found Malton, Ca., 1867.

SERIES M

VARIETIES A – E (SEGMENTED BRANCH)

363   0.90g. ↑↙ Variety a. Bt. 1989.
364   0.91g. ↑↗ 51% 'silver'. Variety b. Bt. 1977. Found in the car park at Walbury Camp iron-age hill fort, nr. Inkpen, Brk.
365   0.98g. ↑← 69% 'silver'. Variety e. Given by D. M. M., 1 November 1988. Found in the Thames at London.

VARIETIES F – G (BRANCH AS CONTINUOUS COIL)

366   1.03g. ↑↗ 53% 'silver'. Variety f. Ex Bodleian Library, old colln.

IMITATION OF SERIES M? (TYPE 42 VAR)

367   0.55 (damaged). 74% 'silver'. *Obv.* Horse? Ex Bodleian Library, old colln.

PLATE 21

350   351   352   353   354

355   356   357   358   359

360   361   362   363   364

365   366   367

PLATE 22

SERIES N

A corpus of Series N was published by Metcalf in *BNJ* 44 (1974), 1-12. The coins listed below have all come to light since then. They all seem to be imitative.

368   1.02g. ↑← *c.* 49% 'silver'. Bt. 1986.

369   0.77g. ↑↙ Plated on base metal core. (EPMA analyses). From the same dies as no.370. Bt. Christies, 4 Nov. 1986, lot 361. Found Caistor-by-Norwich, Nf.

370   0.80g. ↑↖ Plated on base metal core. From the same dies as no.369. Bt. 1991. Found in the Swindon area, near the Ridgeway.

371   1.12g. ↑↙ Plated on base metal core. Surface: 27% 'silver'. Bt. 1987.

372   0.87g. ↑← 48% 'silver'. Bt. 1987. Found Barton, Ca.

SERIES O

TYPE 38

373   1.26g. ↑↘ 94% 'silver'. Given by D. M. M., 1 November 1988. Bt. from finder. Found Lewknor, O.

374   1.12g. ↑← Bt. from finder, 1989. Found Tilbury, Ess.

375   1.14g. ↑↑ 61% 'silver'. Bt. 1986. Found Tilbury, Ess.

TYPE 21

376   0.86g. ↑↓ Bt. from finder. Found Tilbury, Ess.

TYPE 57

377   1.02g. ↑→ 57% 'silver'. Evans bequest, 1941.

SERIES O, TYPE 40

An unpublished type in very similar style has been included here. It seems to be the model for an imitative 'mule' in the Garton-on-the-Wolds grave-find, and is therefore presumably earlier than Type 40.

378   1.16g. ↑↙ 61% 'silver'. Given by D. M. M., 1 November 1988. Bt. 1977.

TYPE 40

379   1.09g. ↑← 58% 'silver'. Inner wire border on rev. Bt. 1986.

380   1.07g. ↑↓ 47% 'silver'. Bt. 1986. Found Tilbury, Ess.

381   1.06g. ↑↗ *c.* 69% 'silver'. Evans bequest, 1941. Found near Hemel Hempstead, Hrt.

PLATE 22

368   369   370   371   372

373   374   375   376   377

378   379   380   381

PLATE 23

SERIES Q

Series Q falls into two stylistic groups, which have been labelled 'linear' (QI-III) and 'modelled' (QIV). Only the former is represented in the collection.

TYPES GROUPED AS QI

382 1.09g. ↑↓ 83% 'silver'. 'Mule' of Types 41 and 40. QIв, 1. Bt.1987. Found Barton, Ca.

383 1.09g. ↑↘ 86% 'silver'. QIе, 2b. Bt. 1977. Found Lakenheath, Sf.

384 1.05g. ↑← 68% 'silver'. QIf. Bt. 1987, ex Montagu 165.

385 0.94g. ↑← c. 72% 'silver'. QIн. Bt. from finder, 1987. Found Saham Toney, nr. Watton, Nf.

TYPES GROUPED AS QIII

386 1.09g. ↑↖ 27% 'silver'. QIIIв. Evans bequest, 1941, ex Cambridge hoard.

387 0.98g. ↑↓ 31% 'silver'. QIIIc.

TYPE Q (R), WITH RUNES *ER*

388 0.62g. ↑↑ Bt. from finder, 1992. Found Bawsey, Nf.

TYPE R, WITH RUNES *ER*

This variety appears to be localized in north-western East Anglia, and is very probably from the same mint-place as Type Q(R).

389 0.98g. ↑← Bt. from finder, 1991. Found Bawsey, Nf.

390 0.74g. ↑← Bt. from finder, 1992. Found Bawsey, Nf.

SERIES R

Types 1-6 have a bust, while Types 7-12, which are later in date, have a head. For an R1/E 'mule', see no.213.

TYPE R1 (WITH *EPA* OUT-WARDS, RETROGRADE)

391 1.23g. ↑↑ 95% 'silver'. Same dies as no.392. Bt. Sotheby, 17 July 1986, lot 181, ex Aston Rowant hoard.

392 1.22g. ↑→ 93% 'silver'. Same dies as no.391. Same source as no.391.

393 1.25g. ↑↑ 91% 'silver'. Same source as no.391.

TYPE R2 (AS R1, with ITAT ADD-ED)

394 1.22g. ↑↗ 88% 'silver'. Bt. 1974, ex G. E. L. Carter colln.

395 1.03g. ↑↑ 95% 'silver'. Bt. 1974, ex G. E. L. Carter colln.

PLATE 23

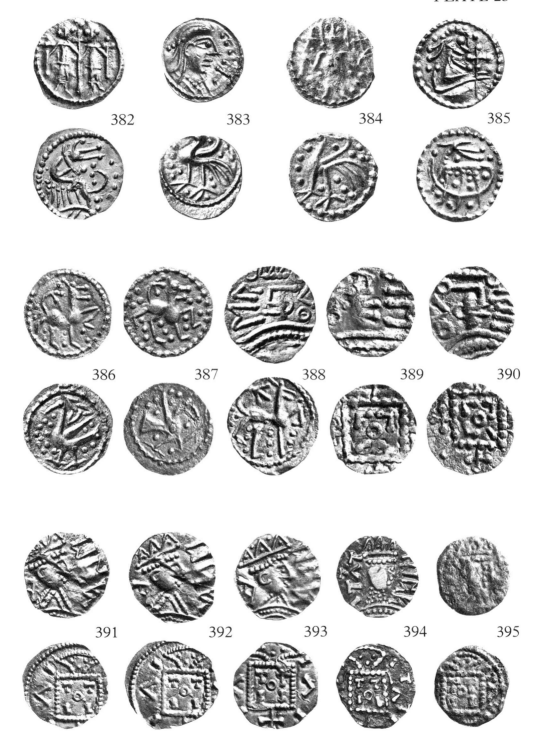

382   383   384   385

386   387   388   389   390

391   392   393   394   395

PLATE 24

TYPE R3 (READING X *EPA*)

There seem to be two varieties, a) with linear pyramidal neck, and added pellets in the field of the standard, and b) with dotted pyramidal neck and no added pellets, but with a pellet in the central annulet.

396   1.10g. ↑↗ 94% 'silver'. Variety a. Bt. Christies, 4 Nov.1986, lot 366. Found Caistor-by-Norwich.
397   1.13g. ↑← 74% 'silver'. Variety a. Bt. 1986.
398   1.03g. ↑↑80% 'silver'. Variety b. C. L. Stainer gift 1934.
399   1.03g. ↑↗ c.61% 'silver'. Variety b. Bt. 1974, ex G. E. L. Carter colln.

IMITATION 'MULING' TYPE R3 WITH SERIES E

400   1.02g. ↑↓ Plated on base metal core. Variety R3, b. Bt. Christies, 4 Nov.1986, lot 367. Found Caistor-by-Norwich.

TYPE R4 (*EPA*)

401   0.67g. ↑→ 90% 'silver'. Bt.1989.

IMITATION OF TYPE R4?

402   0.91g. ↑← 26% 'silver'. Douce bequest, 1834.

TYPE R5 (*EPI* OR *SPI*)

403   0.81g. ↑↓ c.67% 'silver'. *Epi.* C. L. Stainer gift, 1934.
404   0.43g. ↑← *Epa.* Bt. from finder, 1991. Found Bawsey, Nf.
405   0.89g. ↑↑ *Epw.* Bt. 1988. Found Weeting, Nf.
406   1.10g. ↑→ *Spi.* Bt. 1991. Found Binham, Nf.

TYPE R6 (*NM*). IMITATIVE

407   0.90g. ↑← 45% 'silver'. Bt. Christies 4 Nov.1986, lot 368. Found Caistor-by-Norwich.

TYPE R7 (*RHY* OR SIMILAR)

408   1.05g. ↑← Bt. 1989 (from East Anglia).
409   0.83g. ↑↑ 48% 'silver'. Saltire in standard. Bt. G. E. L. Carter, 1974, ex Lockett 231e, ex Carlyon-Britton 142.

TYPE R8 (*PA* LIGATE)

410   1.03g. ↑← 38% 'silver'. Evans bequest, 1941, ex Cambridge hoard.
411   1.03g. ↑↑ 50% 'silver' (XRF, *BNJ* 1978). Bt. 1989, ex Glendining, 20 July 1976, lot 510. Found Normanby, Li.
412   0.73g. ↑↓ Disjointed runes. Bt. from finder, 1991. Found Bawsey, Nf.

PLATE 24

396   397   398   399   400

401   402   403   404   405

406   407   408   409   410

411   412

PLATE 25

413   0.87g. ↑← 36% 'silver'. Diagonally symmetrical standard. Evans bequest, 1941, ex Cambridge hoard.

414   0.78g. ↑← c.26% 'silver'. Irregular pattern in standard. Bt. G. E. L. Carter, 1974.

IMITATIONS OF TYPE R8

415   1.13g. ↑← Blundered runes. Bt. from finder, 1991. Found near Keelby, Li. Cf. no.229.

416   0.70g. ↑? Bt. from finder, 1991. Found Bawsey, Nf.

TYPE R8R (LEFT-FACING HEAD)

417   0.77g. ↑↓ 24% 'silver'. Polygonal flan. Bt. 1987.

418   0.93g. ↑→ 30% 'silver'. Bt. 1987.

419   0.70g. ↑← 33% 'silver'. Bt. 1987. Found in the Norwich area.

IMITATION OF R8R

420   1.03g. ↑↖ Plated on base metal core. Surface: 38% 'silver'. Same dies as *BMC* 27. Bt. from British Museum, 1937, ex Barnett bequest duplicates.

TYPE R9 (*SPI*)

421   0.70g. ↑↑ 35% 'silver'. Bt. 1987. Found in the Norwich area.

IMITATION

422   0.69g. ↑↑ *Obv. epp*? imitation of Type R1? *Rev.* Imitation of Type R8 or similar type? Bt. from finder, 1991. Found Bawsey, Nf.

TYPE R10 (WIGRÆD)

423   0.94g. ↑↑ 13% 'silver'. Evans bequest, 1941, ex Cambridge hoard, no.8.

424   0.75g. ↑↑ Bt. from finder, 1991. Found Bawsey, Nf.

425   0.84g. ↑↓ Bt. 1991.

TYPE R11 (TILBEORHT)

426   0.91g. (broken). ↑← 11% 'silver'. C. L. Stainer gift, 1934, ex P. Carlyon-Britton colln.

427   0.75g. ↑↓ 7% 'silver'. Bt. 1987.

428   0.82g. ↑← 10% 'silver'. Given by D. M. M., 1 November 1988. Said to have been found at Deptford, K. (in error for Thetford, Nf?)

PLATE 25

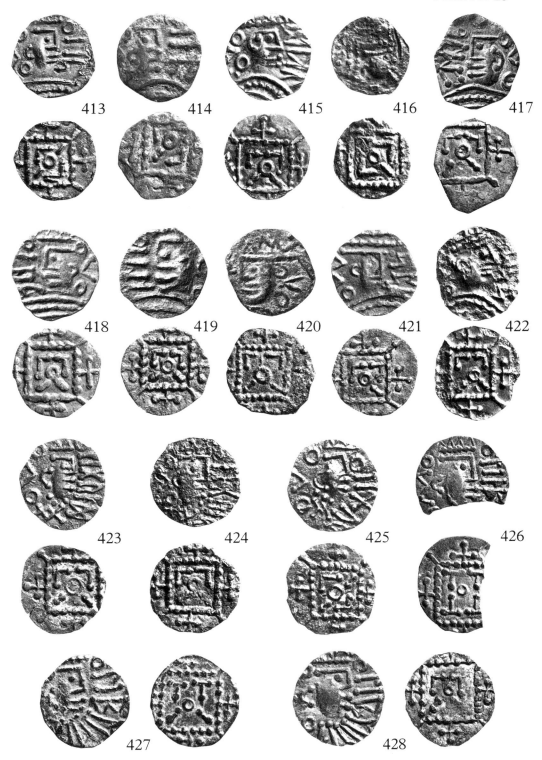

413   414   415   416   417

418   419   420   421   422

423   424   425   426

427   428

PLATE 26

TYPE 30, 51, ETC.
THE SALTIRE-STANDARD TYPES

TYPE 30B/8 'MULE'

429   1.05g. ↑← Bt. from finder, 1992. Found between East Ilsley and West Ilsley, Brk.

TYPE 30B

430   1.22g. ↑↓ 91% 'silver'. Ashmolean Museum, old colln. (Oman 18, Ingram 67)

TYPE 30A

431   1.14g. ↑↙ Bt. from finder, 1989. Found Tilbury, Ess.

TYPE 51

432   1.07g. ↑↘ 94% 'silver'. Bt. 1987. Found in the Thetford area.
433   1.08g. ↑↙ *c.*82% 'silver'. Bt. from finder, 1986. Found Lewknor, O.

CF. TYPE 51

434   1.32g. ↑↓ *c.*70% 'silver'. Exchanged, 1988. Found Tilbury, Ess.

R3/TYPE 51 'MULE'

435   0.90g. ↑↓ Bt. from finder, 1991. Found Alkborough, Li.

TYPE 70, ETC.

436   0.94g. ↑↓ *c.*87% 'silver'. Bt. 1974, ex G. E. L. Carter colln.
437   0.91g. ↑← Evans bequest, 1941.

SERIES S

TYPE S1

438   0.92g. ↑↙ 47% 'silver'. Bt. 1986. Found Tilbury, Ess.
439   0.69g. ↑↘ Corroded. 47% 'silver' in core (= original composition?), 87% 'silver', at surface. Given by D. M. M., 1 November 1988. Found Houghton Regis, Bd.

IMITATION OF TYPE S1

440   1.00g. ↑↓ Obv. laterally reversed. Bt. from finder, 1989. Found Tilbury, Ess.

TYPE S2

441   1.12g. ↑↓ 42% 'silver'. Given by D. M. M., 1 November 1988. Ex C. Hersch colln.

SERIES T

TYPE T1

442   1.04g. ↑↖ 50 % 'silver'. Variety 1b, i. Ashmolean Museum, old colln.
443   1.06g. ↑← 41% 'silver'. Bt. 1986. Found Tilbury, Ess.

TYPE T2

444   1.17g. ↑↓ *c.*51% 'silver'. Bt. 1986. Found Tilbury, Ess.

PLATE 26

429 430 431 432 433

434 435 436 437

438 439 440 441 442

443 444

PLATE 27

SERIES U

Types other than Type 23 b-d have been catalogued above as parts of other series, e.g. nos.352-3 and 359-62.

TYPE 23B

445   1.07g. ↑→ 79% 'silver'. Bt. from finder, 1971. Found Abingdon, O.
446   1.15g. ↑↑ 85% 'silver'. Bt. Grantley sale ii, 27 Jan.1944, lot 692, ex Rashleigh sale, lot 29. Found Dorchester, O.
447   1.15g. ↑↗ Same dies as *BMC* 113. Bt. from finder, 1991. Found near Scunthorpe, Li.
448   1.02g. ↑↑ 89% 'silver'. Bt. from finder, 1978. Found Moulsford, O.

TYPE 23D

449   0.93g. ↑← *c*.57% 'silver'. Given by D. M. M., 1 November 1988. Found Houghton Regis, Bd.

450   1.09g. ↑← *c*.78% 'silver'. Ex Bodleian Library, old colln.

IMITATION OF TYPE 23B/D

451   0.89g. (chipped). ↑↓ Given by the finder, Mr. M. Bennett, 1991. Found South Weston, O.

TYPE 23C

452   1.12g. ↑↗ 64% 'silver'. Given by D. M. M., 1 November 1988. Found Walbury Camp iron-age hill fort, nr. Inkpen, Brk.

SERIES V

453   1.14g. ↑↓ 44% 'silver'. Evans bequest, 1941.

SERIES Y

A corpus of Series Y has been published by J. Booth, in *Sceattas in England and on the Continent*, pp.71-111.

EADBERHT, 738-757
CLASS A

454   0.98g. ↑↘ 64% 'silver'. Booth A9. Bt. 1971, ex Lingford colln., bt.1933.

CLASS B

455   0.98g. ↑↓ 62% 'silver'. Variety i. Booth B2. Evans bequest, 1941, ex Brockett, ex Boyne.
456   1.05g.↑↑ 68% 'silver'. Variety ii. Booth B18. Bt. 1971, ex Lingford colln., ex C. C. Browne, 1935.

IMITATION OR FORGERY MULING CLASSES B AND A

457   0.91g. ↑↖ 76% silver plus 10% gold. Bt. 1979.

CLASS C

458   0.77g. ↑↑ *c*.60% 'silver'. Variety i. Booth C2. Bt. 1971, ex Lingford colln., ex Grantley, ex Carlyon-Britton (1913), 178.
459   0.86g. ↑↗ 52% 'silver'. Variety ii. Booth C8. Bt. 1971, ex Lingford colln., ex Grantley 762, ex Rashleigh 128, ex Pembroke (1848).

CLASS D

460   1.00g. ↑↘ 69% 'silver'. Booth D6. Bt. 1971, ex Lingford colln,. ex Grantley 764.

CLASS E

461   1.02g. ↑↓ 52% 'silver'. Booth E6. Bt. 1971, ex Lingford colln., ex Grantley 761.

PLATE 27

445 446 447 448

449 450 451 452 453

454 455 456 458 459

460 461

PLATE 28

CLASS F

462   0.97g. ↑← 94% 'silver'. Variety vii. Booth F12. Bt. from finder, 1983. Found Epworth, Li.

CLASS G

463   1.03g. ↑→ 90% 'silver'. Variety i. Booth G2. Bt. 1971, ex Lingford colln., bt. Sotheby 14 Dec.1936, lot 85.

EADBERHT AND ARCH-BISHOP ECGBERHT

464   1.11g. ↑↙ 47% 'silver'. Variety i. Booth 2. Browne Willis gift, c.1746 or earlier.

465   0.88g. ↑↗ 65% 'silver'. Pierced and plugged. Variety iii. Bt. 1971, ex Lingford, ex C. C. Browne, (Mar.1935, lot 343), ex Parsons, ex Haywood.

466   1.07g. ↑↓ c.66% 'silver'. Variety vi. Booth 27. Given by D. M. M., 1 November 1988. Found Newbald ('Sancton'), Y.

ALCHRED, 765-774

467   1.15g. ↑← c.85% 'silver'. Booth 1. Bt. 1979, ex C. Firth, ex Grantley 765.

ALCHRED AND ARCHBISHOP ECGBERHT, 734-766

468   0.87g. ↑↖ 52% 'silver'. Booth 2. Bt. 1979, ex C. Firth, ex Grantley 799 or 800 (see note by Booth, p.95).

ÆTHELRED I, FIRST REIGN, 774-779

469   1.24g. ↑→ 96% 'silver'. Booth 1. Bt. 1979, ex C. Firth, ex Grantley 766, ex Robinson 1891. Found at Hornsea, Y., 1875.

ÆLFWALD, 779-788

470   0.99g. ↑↑ 47% 'silver'. Booth 2. Bt. 1979, ex C. Firth, ex Lockett 288, ex Cuff, Rashleigh, and Barcom.

NORTHUMBRIA, c.790-c.810

A corpus of coins by named moneyers is published in J. Booth, 'Coinage and Northumbrian history: *c*.790-*c*.810', in *Coinage in Ninth-Century Northumbria*, pp.57-89.

ÆTHELRED I, SECOND REIGN, c.790-796

Ceolbeald

471   0.90g. ↑→ Variety iii. Booth 12. Bt. 1951, ex Lingford colln.
472   0.73g. (broken). ↑→ Variety viii. Booth 28. Bt. 1951, ex Lingford colln.

Cuthgils

473   0.88g. ↑↓ 78% 'silver' with surface enrichment (EPMA); 60% silver (SEM). Booth 34. Bt. 1979, ex C. Firth, ex Grantley.

Cuthheard

474   0.99g. ↑↙ Booth 45. Bt. 1951, ex Lingford colln.

Tidwulf

475   0.81g. ↑↓ Booth 68. Bt. 1951, ex Lingford colln.

Uncertain

476   0.67g. Ælfwald or Æthelred? Bt. 1971, ex Lingford colln.

ÆTHELRED AND ARCHBISHOP EANBALD I, 778-796

477   0.82g. ↑↘ Booth 54. Given by D. M. M., 1992. Found Newbald ('Sancton'), Y.

EAST ANGLIA: KING BEONNA

A corpus of coins of King Beonna was published in M. M. Archibald, 'The coinage of Beonna in the light of the Middle Harling hoard', *BNJ* 55 (1985), 10-54.

478   1.03g. ↑↓ Efe. Bt. 1955, ex Lockett 408, ex Montagu and Maynard. *SCBI* 57.

PLATE 28

462 463 464 465 466

467 468 469 470 471

472 473 474 475 476

477 478